Rasmus Björn Anderson

# Norse Mythology

Fourth Edition

Rasmus Björn Anderson

**Norse Mythology**
*Fourth Edition*

ISBN/EAN: 9783337182243

Printed in Europe, USA, Canada, Australia, Japan

Cover: Foto ©Thomas Meinert / pixelio.de

More available books at **www.hansebooks.com**

# NORSE MYTHOLOGY;

OR,

# THE RELIGION OF OUR FOREFATHERS,

CONTAINING ALL THE

# MYTHS OF THE EDDAS,

SYSTEMATIZED AND INTERPRETED.

WITH

## AN INTRODUCTION, VOCABULARY AND INDEX.

By R. B. ANDERSON, A.M.,

PROFESSOR OF THE SCANDINAVIAN LANGUAGES IN THE UNIVERSITY OF
WISCONSIN, AUTHOR OF "AMERICA NOT DISCOVERED BY
COLUMBUS," "DEN NORSKE MAALSAG," ETC.

FOURTH EDITION.

CHICAGO:
S. C. GRIGGS AND COMPANY.
LONDON: TRÜBNER & CO.
1884.

TO

# HENRY WADSWORTH LONGFELLOW,

### THE AMERICAN POET,

WHO HAS NOT ONLY REFRESHED HIMSELF AT THE CASTALIAN FOUNTAIN, BUT
ALSO COMMUNED WITH BRAGE, AND TAKEN DEEP DRAUGHTS
FROM THE WELLS OF URD AND MIMER,

## THIS VOLUME IS DEDICATED,

WITH THE GRATEFUL REVERENCE OF

## THE AUTHOR.

I think Scandinavian Paganism, to us here, is more interesting than any other. It is, for one thing, the latest: it continued in these regions of Europe till the eleventh century: eight hundred years ago the Norwegians were still worshipers of Odin. It is interesting also as the creed of our fathers; the men whose blood still runs in our veins, whom doubtless we still resemble in so many ways. Strange: they did believe that, while we believe so differently. Let us look a little at this poor Norse creed, for many reasons. We have tolerable means to do it: for there is another point of interest in these Scandinavian mythologies: that they have been preserved so well.

Neither is there no use in *knowing* something about this old Paganism of our fathers. Unconsciously, and combined with higher things, it is in *us* yet, that old faith withal. To know it consciously brings us into closer and clearer relations with the past,— with our own possessions in the past. For the whole past, as I keep repeating, is the possession of the present. The past had always something *true*, and is a precious possession. In a different time, in a different place, it is always some other *side* of our common human nature that has been developing itself.

— *Thomas Carlyle.*

# PREFACE.

AMERICA NOT DISCOVERED BY COLUMBUS having been so favorably received by the press generally, as well as by many distinguished scholars, who have expressed themselves in very flattering terms of our recent *début* in English, we venture to appear again; and, although the subject is somewhat different, it still (as did the first) has its fountain head in the literature of the North.

We come, this time, encouraged by all your kind words, with higher aspirations, and perhaps, too, with less timidity and modesty. We come to ask your opinion of Norse mythology. We come to ask whether Norse mythology is not equally as worthy of your attention as the Greek. Nay, we come to ask whether you will not give the Norse the *preference*. We propose to call your attention earnestly, in this volume, to the merits of our common Gothic or Teutonic inheritance, and to chat a few hours with you about the imaginative, poetic and prophetic period of our Gothic history.

We are well aware that we are here giving you a book full of imperfections so far as style, originality, arrangement and external adornment of the

subject is concerned, and we shall not take it much
to heart, even if we are severely criticised in these
respects; we shall rather take it as an earnest admo-
nition to study and improve in language and composition for the future.

But, if the spirit of the book, that is, the cause
which we have undertaken to plead therein,— if that
be frowned down, or rejected, or laughed at, we shall
be the recipient of a most bitter disappointment, and
yet we shall not wholly despair. The time must
come, when our common Gothic inheritance will be
loved and respected. There will come men — ay,
there are already men in our midst who will advo-
cate and defend its rights on American soil with
sharper steel than ours. And, though we may find
but few roses and many thorns on our pathway, we
shall not suffer our ardor in our chosen field of
labor to be diminished. We are determined not to
be discouraged.

What we claim for this work is, that it is
the *first complete and systematic presentation of the
Norse mythology in the English language;* and this
we think is a sufficient reason for our asking a
humble place upon your book-shelves. And, while we
make this claim, we fully appreciate the value of the
many excellent treatises and translations that have
appeared on this subject in England. We do not
undervalue the labors of Dasent, Thorpe, Pigott, Carlyle, etc., but none of these give a comprehensive

account of all the deities and the myths in full. There is, indeed, no work outside of Scandinavia that covers the whole ground. So far as America is concerned, the only work on Norse mythology that has hitherto been published in this country is BAR-CLAY PENNOCK's translation of the Norse Professor Rudolph Keyser's *Religion of the Northmen.* This is indeed an excellent and scholarly work, and a valuable contribution to knowledge; but, instead of *presenting* the mythology of the Norsemen, it *interprets* it; and Professor Keyser is yet one of the most eminent authorities in the exposition of the Asa doctrine. Pennock's translation of Keyser is a book of three hundred and forty-six pages, and of these only *sixteen* are devoted to a synopsis of the mythology; and it is, as the reader may judge, nothing but a very brief synopsis. The remaining three hundred and thirty pages contain a history of Old Norse literature, an interpretation of the Odinic religion, and an exhibition of the manner of *worship* among the heathen Norsemen. In a word, Pennock's book *presupposes* a knowledge of the subject; and for one who has this, we would recommend *Pennock's* KEY-SER as the best work *extant* in English. We are indebted to it for many valuable paragraphs in this volume.

This subject has, then, been investigated by many able writers; and, in preparing this volume, we have borrowed from their works all the light they could shed upon our pathway. The authors we have chiefly consulted are named in the accompanying list. While we have used their very phrase whenever it was convenient, we have not followed them in a slavish manner. We have made such changes as in our judgment seemed necessary to give our work harmony and symmetry throughout. We at first felt disposed to give the reader a mere translation either of N. M. Petersen, or of Grundtvig, or of P. A. Munch; but upon further reflection we came to the conclusion that we could treat the subject more satisfactorily to ourselves, and fully as acceptably to our readers, by sketching out a plan of our own, and making free use of all the best writers upon this subject. And as we now review our pages, we find that N. M. Petersen has served us the most. Much of his work has been appropriated in an almost unchanged form.

Although many of the ideas set forth in this work may seem new to American readers, yet they are by no means wholly original. Many of them have for many years been successfully advocated in Scandinavian countries, and to some extent, also, in Germany and England. Our aim has not at present been so much to make original investigations, as — that which is far more needed and to the purpose — to give the fruits of the labors performed in the North, and call the attention of the American public earnestly to the wealth stored up in the Eddas and Sagas of Iceland. No one can doubt the correctness of our position in this matter, when he reflects that we are now drawing near the close of the *nineteenth* century, and have not yet had a complete Norse mythology in the English language, while the number of Greek and Roman mythologies is legion. Bayard Taylor said to us, recently, that the Scandinavian languages, in view of their rich literature, in view of the light which this literature throws upon early English history, and in view of the importance of Icelandic in a successful study of English and Anglo-Saxon, ought to be taught in every college in Vinland; and that is the very pith of what we have to say in this preface.

We have had excellent aid from Dr. S. H. Carpenter, who combines broad general culture with a thorough knowledge of Old English and Anglo-Saxon. He has read every page of this work. and we hereby thank him for the generous sympathy and advice which he has invariably given us. To President John Bascom we are under obligations for kind words and valuable suggestions. We hereby extend heartfelt thanks to Professor Willard Fiske, of Cornell University, for aid and encouragement; to Mrs. Ole Bull, for free use of her excellent library; and to the poet, H. W. Longfellow, for permitting us to make extracts from his works, and to inscribe this volume to him as the Nestor among American writers on Scandinavian themes. May the persons here named find that this our work, in spite of its faults, advances, somewhat, the interest in the studies of Northern literature in this country.

While Mallet's *Northern Antiquities* is a very valuable work, we cannot but make known our regrets that Blackwell's edition of it ever was published. Mr. Blackwell has in many ways injured the cause which he evidently intended to promote. While we, therefore, urge caution in the use of Mallet's *Northern Antiquities* by Blackwell, we can with all our heart recommend such writers upon the North as Dasent, Laing, Thorpe, Gosse, Pennock, Boyesen, Marsh, Fiske, the Howitts, Pigott, Lord Dufferin, Maurer, Möbius, Morris, Magnússon, Vigfusson, Hjaltalin, and several others.

It is sincerely hoped that by this our effort we may, at least for the present, fill a gap in English literature, and accomplish something in awakening among students some interest in Norse mythology, history, literature and institutions. Let it be remembered, that Carlyle, and many others of our best scholars, claim that it is from the Norsemen we have derived our vital energy, our freedom of thought, and, in a measure that we do not yet suspect, our strength of speech.

We are conscious that our work contains many imperfections, and that others might have performed the task better; and thus we commend this volume to the kind indulgence of the critic and the reader.

R. B. ANDERSON.

*University of Wisconsin, May 15, 1875.*

# LIST OF WORKS CONSULTED.

The following authors have been consulted in preparing this work, and to them the reader is referred, if he wishes to make special study of the subject of Norse mythology.

Of the Elder Edda we have used Benjamin Thorpe's translation and Sophus Bugge's edition of the original. It has been found necessary to make a few alterations in Thorpe's translation. Of the Younger Edda we have used Dasent's translation and Sveinbjorn Egilsson's edition of the original. Of modern Scandinavian writers we have confined ourselves mainly to N. M. Petersen, N. F. S. Grundtvig, P. A. Munch, Rudolph Keyser, Finn Magnússon, and Christian Winther. Other authors borrowed from more or less are: H. W. Longfellow, H. G. Möller, R. Nyerup, E. G. Geier, M. Hammerich, F. J. Mone, Jacob Grimm, Thomas Keightly, Thomas Carlyle, Max Müller, and Geo. W. Cox.

The recent excellent work of Alexander Murray has been referred to on the subject of Greek mythology. It claims on its title-page to give an account of Norse mythology; but we were surprised to find that the author dismisses the subject with fifteen pages and a few wood-cuts of questionable value.

The philological notes are chiefly based upon the Icelandic Dictionary recently published by Macmillan & Co., and edited by Gudbrand Vigfusson, of Oxford University, England. It is indeed a scholarly work, and marks a new epoch in the study of the Icelandic language.

To all who are interested in northern literature, we take great pleasure in recommending the following recent publications:

1. *The Myths of the Rhine*, translated from the French of X. B. Saintine by Prof. M. Schele De Vere. This work gives an admirable sketch of primitive Teutonic times, of the Druids and their creed, of the Odinic religion and worship, and of a great variety of old customs and traditions. The translation is excellent, and it contains, moreover, a large number of very fine illustrations by Gustave Doré.

2. On pp. 375–382 of this work is given a brief synopsis of the Niblung story, showing its mythical connection with the gods of the North, giving the origin and history of the cursed ring (the Niblung hoard), etc. The Niblung story has been handed down to us in four versions, three Norse and one German. The Norse are: (a) *Fragmentary Lays in the Elder Edda;* (b) *The Volsunga Saga;* (c) *The Vilkina Saga.* The German is *The Nibelungen-Lied.* In addition to these are numerous fragmentary accounts of the story, among which may be mentioned *The Faroe Sigurd's Saga*, some

old Danish popular ballads, several Norse and German
folk-lore stories, parts of *The Book of the Heroes* (Helden-
buch), etc. There are also, both in Icelandic and in
German, various additions and variations, conspicuous
among which are *The Lay of Hildebrand*, and the so-
called *Klage* (Lament), the latter containing the lamentations of Etzel, Hildebrand and Ditrich over the
dead, and the former treating of the return of Hildebrand with Ditrich of Bern after the fall of the Niblungs. During the last hundred years a whole army of
writers have been busy, especially in Germany and Scandinavia, in publishing in the original languages, in
translating, in criticizing, in dramatizing, in lecturing
and commenting on the Niblung literature. If all the
editions of the four prominent versions, the additions,
variations, the fragmentary poems and sagas, and the
folk-lore stories belonging to the Niblung cycle, were
collected, they would make a large library; and if we add
to this all the translations and all the essays and commentaries, the result would be a most formidable collection of books and pamphlets. The following are the
names of some of the more prominent Scandinavian and
German writers on this subject: P. E. Müller, Unger,
Bugge, Munch, Keyser, Petersen, Grundtvig, Bodmer,
Von der Hagen, Schlegel, the brothers Grimm, Simrock,
Lachmann, Mone, Jordan, Braunsfeld, Fischer, Holtz-
mann, Volmer, Menzel, Bartsch, Geibel, Wagner, Mass-
mann, Raszmann and Rehorn. In English, we have
essays and criticism by Max Müller, Thomas Carlyle and
H. W. Longfellow (*Poets and Poetry of Europe*). There

are in all three English translations of the German Nibelungen-Lied. The first is by Birch (London, 1848);
the second by Lettsom (London, 1850), and the third is
a most excellent transprosing, or retelling in prose, by
Auber Forestier (Chicago, 1877 *). This is the first
American edition of the Niblung epic, and it is to be
recommended to all who wish to make a beginning in
searching this wonderful mist-land, both for the easy,
graphic and dramatic prose in which it is told, and for
the scholarly and exhaustive introduction, which en-
larges upon the various versions and traces their origin
back to the gods of Asgard.

During the present decade we have had what may
be termed a pan-Teutonic epoch of the Niblung literature. The various versions found in different countries
have been combined and fashioned into one grand epic
for the whole Teutonic race. Of such versions we have
three, namely: (a) W. Jordan's *Nibelunge* (erster Theil,
*Sigfridsage ;* Zweiter Theil, *Hildebrants Heimkehr*); (b)
W. R. Wagner's great musical and dramatic tetralogy
called the *Nibelungen Ring,* performed under royal pat-
ronage and imperial countenance at Baireuth in 1876;
(c) *The Story of Sigurd the Volsung and the Fall of the
Niblungs,* by William Morris (London, 1877).

The intimate relation between the Niblung epic and
Norse mythology is evident, and the reader is requested
to regard this paragraph as supplementary to our note
on page 382.

---

* *Echoes from Mist-Land,* or the Nibelungen Lay revealed to Lovers of Romance and Chivalry, by Auber Forestier. Chicago: S. C. Griggs & Co.

# TABLE OF CONTENTS.

2 (17)

## CHAPTER IV.
### ROMAN MYTHOLOGY.

## CHAPTER V.
### INTERPRETATION OF NORSE MYTHOLOGY.

## CHAPTER VI.
### THE NORSE MYTHOLOGY FURNISHES ABUNDANT AND EXCELLENT MATERIAL FOR THE USE OF POETS, SCULPTORS AND PAINTERS.

## CHAPTER VII.
### THE SOURCES OF NORSE MYTHOLOGY AND INFLUENCE OF THE ASA-FAITH.

# NORSE MYTHOLOGY.

## PART I.

### THE CREATION AND PRESERVATION OF THE WORLD.

#### CHAPTER I.

##### THE CREATION.

#### CHAPTER II.

##### THE PRESERVATION.

#### CHAPTER III.

##### EXEGETICAL REMARKS UPON THE CREATION AND PRESERVATION OF THE WORLD.

# PART II.

## THE LIFE AND EXPLOITS OF THE GODS.

### CHAPTER I.

#### ODIN.

### CHAPTER II.

#### HERMOD, TYR, HEIMDAL, BRAGE AND IDUN.

### CHAPTER III.

#### BALDER AND NANNA, HODER, VALE AND FORSETE.

### CHAPTER IV.

#### THOR, HIS WIFE SIF AND SON ULLER.

### CHAPTER V.

## CHAPTER VI.

### THE VANS.

## CHAPTER VII.

### THE DEVELOPMENT OF EVIL, LOKE AND HIS OFFSPRING.

# PART III.

### RAGNAROK AND REGENERATION.

## CHAPTER I.

## CHAPTER II.

# INTRODUCTION.

## CHAPTER I.

### WHAT IS MYTHOLOGY AND WHAT IS NORSE MYTHOLOGY?

The word mythology (μυθολογία, from μύθος, word, tale, fable, and λόγος, speech, discourse,) is of Greek origin, and our vernacular tongue has become so adulterated with Latin and Greek words; we have studied Latin and Greek in place of English, Anglo-Saxon, Norse and Gothic so long that we are always in a quandary (qu'en dirai-je?), always tongue-tied when we attempt to speak of something outside or above the daily returning cares of life. Our own good old English words have been crowded out by foreign ones; this is our besetting sin. But, as the venerable Professor George Stephens remarks in his elaborate work on Runic Monuments, we have watered our mother tongue long enough with bastard Latin; let us now brace and steel it with the life-water of our own sweet and soft and rich and shining and clear-ringing and manly and world-ranging, ever-dearest ENGLISH.

Mythology is a system of myths; a collection of popular legends, fables, tales, or stories, relating to the gods, heroes, demons or other beings whose names have been preserved in popular belief. Such tales are not found in the traditions of the ancient Greeks. Hindoos and Egyptians, only, but every nation has had its system of mythology; and that of the ancient Norsemen is more simple, earnest, miraculous, stupendous and divine than any other mythological system of which we have record.

The myth is the oldest form of truth; and mythology is the knowledge which the ancients had of the Divine.   The object of mythology is to find God and come to him.   Without a written revelation this may be done in two ways: either by studying the intellectual, moral and physical nature of man, for evidence of the existence of God may be found in the proper study of man; or by studying nature in the outward world in its general structure, adaptations and dependencies; and truthfully it may be said that God manifests himself in nature.

Our Norse forefathers (for it is their religion we are to present in this volume) had no clearly-defined knowledge of any god outside of themselves and nature. Like the ancient Greeks, they had only a somewhat vague idea about a supreme God, whom the rhapsodist or skald in the Elder Edda (Hyndluljóð 43, 44) dare not name, and whom few, it is said, ever look far enough to see.  In the language of the Elder Edda:

Then one is born
Greater than all;
He becomes strong
With the strengths of earth;
The mightiest king
Men call him,
Fast knit in peace
With all powers.

Then comes another
Yet more mighty;

*But him dare I not*
*Venture to name.*
Few further may look
Than to where Odin
To meet the wolf goes.

Odin goes to meet the Fenriswolf in Ragnarok (the twilight of the gods; that is, the final conflict between all good and evil powers); but now let the reader compare the above passage from the Elder Edda with the following passage from the seventeenth chapter of the Acts of the Apostles:

Then Paul stood in the midst of Mars' Hill and said: Ye men of Athens, I perceive that in all things ye are too superstitious; for as I passed by and beheld your devotions, I found an altar with this inscription: TO THE UNKNOWN GOD. Whom therefore ye ignorantly worship, him declare I unto you.

It was of this same *unknown God* that one of the ancient Greek poets had said, that in him we live and move and have our being. Thus did the Greeks find Jehovah in the labyrinth of their heathen deities; and when we claim that the Norse mythology is more *divine* than any other system of mythology known. we mean by this assertion, that the supreme God is mentioned and referred to oftener, and stands out in bolder relief in the Norseman's heathen belief, than in any other.

It is a noticeable fact that long before Christianity was introduced or had even been heard of in Iceland, it is recorded that Ingemund the Old, a heathen Norseman, bleeding and dying, prayed God to forgive Rolleif, his murderer.

Another man of the heathen times, Thorkel Maane, a supreme judge of Iceland, a man of unblemished life and distinguished among the wisest magistrates of that island during the time of the republic, avowed that he would worship no other God but him who had created the sun; and in his dying hour he prayed the Father of Light to illuminate his soul in the darkness of death. Arngrim Jonsson tells us that when Thorkel Maane had arrived at the age of maturity and reflection, he disdained a blind obedience to traditionary custom, and employed much of his time in weighing the established tenets of his countrymen by the standard of reason. He divested his mind of all prejudice; he pondered on the sublimity of nature, and guided himself by maxims founded on truth and reason. By these means he soon discovered not only the fallacy of that faith which governed his countrymen, but became a convert to the existence of a supreme power more mighty than Thor or Odin. In his maker he acknowledged his God, and to him alone directed his homage from a conviction that none other was worthy to be honored and worshiped. On perceiving the approach of death, this pious and sensible man requested to be conveyed into the open air, in order that, as he said, he might in his last moments contemplate the glories of Almighty God, who has created the heavens and the earth and all that in them is.

Harald Fairfax (Haarfager), the first sovereign of Norway, the king that united Norway under his scepter in the year 872, is another remarkable example in this respect. He was accustomed to assist at the public offerings made by his people in honor of their gods. As no better or more pure religion was known in those days, he acted with prudence in not betraying either contempt or disregard for the prevailing worship of the country, lest his subjects, stimulated by such example, might become indifferent, not only to their sacred, but also to their political, duties. Yet he rejected from his heart these profane ceremonies, and believed in the existence of a more powerful god, whom he secretly adored. I swear, he once said, never to make my offerings to an idol, but to that God alone whose omnipotence has formed the world and stamped man with his own image. It would be an act of folly in me to expect help from him whose power and empire arises from the accidental hollow of a tree or the peculiar form of a stone.

Such examples illustrate how near the educated and reflecting Norse heathen was in sympathy with Christianity, and also go far toward proving that the object of mythology is to find God and come to him.

Still we must admit that of this supreme God our forefathers had only a somewhat vague conception; and to many of them he was almost wholly unknown. Their god was a natural human god, a person. There can be no genuine poetry without impersonation, and a perfect system of mythology is a finished poem. Mythology is, in fact, religious truth expressed in poetical language. It ascribes all events and phenomena in the outward world to a personal cause. Each cause is some divinity or other — some god or demon. In this manner, when the ancients heard the echo from the woods or mountains, they did not think, as we now do, that the waves of sound were reflected, but that there stood a dwarf, a personal being, who repeated the words spoken by themselves. This dwarf had to have a history, a biography, and this gave rise to a myth. To our poetic ancestors the forces of nature were not veiled under scientific names. As Carlyle truthfully remarks, they had not yet learned to reduce to their fundamental elements and lecture learnedly about this beautiful,

green, rock-built, flowery earth, with its trees, mountains and many-sounding waters; about the great deep
sea of azure that swims over our heads, and about the
various winds that sweep through it. When they saw
the black clouds gathering and shutting out the king
of day, and witnessed them pouring out rain and ice
and fire, and heard the thunder roll, they did not think,
as we now do, of accumulated electricity discharged from
the clouds to the earth, and show in the lecture room
how something like these powerful shafts of lightning
could be ground out of glass or silk, but they ascribed
the phenomenon to a mighty divinity — Thor — who in
his thunder-chariot rides through the clouds and strikes
with his huge hammer, Mjolner. The theory of our
forefathers furnishes food for the imagination, for our
poetical nature, while the reflection of the waves of
sound and the discharge of electricity is merely dry
reasoning — mathematics and physics. To our ancestors Nature presented herself in her naked, beautiful
and awful majesty; while to us in this age of New-
tons, Millers, Oersteds, Berzeliuses and Tyndalls, she is
enwrapped in a multitude of profound scientific phrases.
These phrases make us flatter ourselves that we have
fathomed her mysteries and revealed her secret workings, while in point of fact we are as far from the real
bottom as our ancestors were. But we have robbed
ourselves to a sad extent of the poetry of nature. Well
might Barry Cornwall complain:

> O ye delicious fables! where the wave
> And the woods were peopled, and the air, with things
> So lovely! Why, ah! why has science grave
> Scattered afar your sweet imaginings?

The old Norsemen said: The mischief-maker Loke
cuts for mere sport the hair of the goddess Sif, but

the gods compel him to furnish her new hair. Loke gets dwarfs to forge for her golden hair, which grows almost spontaneously. We, their prosaic descendants, say: The heat (Loke) scorches the grass (Sif's hair), but the same physical agent (heat) sets the forces of nature to work again, and new grass with golden (that is to say bright) color springs up again.

Thus our ancestors spoke of all the workings of nature as though they were caused by personal agents; and instead of saying, as we now do, that winter follows summer, and explaining how the annual revolutions of the earth produce the changes that are called seasons of the year, they took a more poetical view of the phenomenon, and said that the blind god Hoder (winter) was instigated by Loke (heat) to slay Balder (the summer god).

This idea of personifying the visible workings of nature was so completely developed that prominent faculties or attributes of the gods also were subject to impersonation. Odin, it was said, had two ravens, Hugin and Munin; that is, reflection and memory. They sit upon his shoulders, and whisper into his ears. Thor's strength was redoubled whenever he girded himself with Megingjarder, his belt of strength; his steel gloves, with which he wielded his hammer, produced the same effect. Nay, strength was so eminent a characteristic with Thor that it even stands out apart from him as an independent person, and is represented by his son Magne (strength), who accompanies him on his journeys against the frost-giants.

In this manner a series of myths were formed and combined into a system which we now call mythology; a system which gave to our fathers gods whom they worshiped, and in whom they trusted, and which gives to us a mirror in which is reflected the popular life, the intellectual and moral characteristics of our ancestors. And these gods were indeed worthy of reverence; they were the embodiments of the noblest thoughts and purest feelings, but these thoughts and feelings could not be awakened without a personified image. As soon as the divine idea was born, it assumed a bodily form, and, in order to give the mind a more definite comprehension of it, it was frequently drawn down from heaven and sculptured in wood or stone. The object was by images to make manifest unto the senses the attributes of the gods, and thus the more easily secure the devotion of the people. The heathen had to see the image of God, the image of the infinite thought embodied in the god, or he would not kneel down and worship. This idea of wanting something concrete, something within the reach of the senses, we find deeply rooted in human nature. Man does not want an abstract god, but a *personal*, visible god, at least a visible sign of his presence. And we who live in the broad daylight of revealed religion and science ought not to be so prone to blame our forefathers for paying divine honors to images, statues and other representations or symbols of their gods, for the images were, as the words imply, not the gods themselves to whom the heathen addressed his prayers and supplications, but merely the symbols of these gods; and every religion, Christianity included, is mythical in its development. The tendency is to draw the divine down to earth, in order to rise with it again to heaven. When God suffers with us, it becomes easier for us to suffer; when he redeems us, our salvation becomes certain. God is in all systems of religion seen, as it were, through a glass — never face to face. No one can see Jehovah and live.

Even as in our present condition our immortal soul cannot do without the visible body, and cannot without this reveal itself to its fellow-beings, so our faith requires a visible church, our religion must assume some form in which it can be apprehended by the senses. Our faith is made stronger by the visible church in the same manner as the mind gains knowledge of the things about us by means of the bodily organs. The outward rite or external form and ceremonial ornament, which are so conspicuous in the Roman and Greek Catholic churches, for instance, serve to awaken, edify and strengthen the soul and assist the memory in recalling the religious truths and the events in the life of Christ and of the saints more vividly and forcibly to the mind; besides, pictures and images are to the unlettered what books are to those educated in the art of reading. Did not Christ himself combine things supersensual with things within the reach of the senses? The purification and sanctification of the soul he combined with the idea of cleansing the body in the sacrament of baptism. The remembrance of him and of his love, how he gave his body and blood for the redemption of fallen man, he combined with the eating of bread and drinking of wine in the sacrament of the Lord's Supper. He gave his religion an outward, visible form; and, just as the soul is mirrored in the eyes, in the expression of the countenance, in the gestures and manners of the body, so our faith is reflected in the church. This is what is meant by mythical development; and when we discover this tendency to cling to visible signs and ceremonies manifesting itself so extensively even in the Christian church of our own time, it should teach us to be less severe in judging and blaming the heathen for their idol-worship.

As long as the nations have inhabited the earth,
there have been different religions among men; and
how could this be otherwise? The countries which
they have inhabited; the skies which they have looked
upon; their laws, customs and social institutions; their
habits, language and knowledge; have differed so widely
that it would be absurd to look for uniformity in the
manner in which they have found, comprehended and
worshiped God.   Nay, this is not all.   Even among
Christians, and, if we give the subject a careful examination, even among those who confess one and the same
faith and are members of one and the same church, we
find that the religion of one man is never perfectly
like that of another.   They may use the same prayers,
learn and subscribe to the same confession, hear the
same preacher and take part in the same ceremonies,
but still the prayer, faith and worship of the one will
differ from the prayer, faith and worship of the other.
Two persons are never precisely alike, and every one
will interpret the words which he hears and the ceremonies in which he takes part according to the depth
and breadth of his mind and heart — according to the
extent and kind of his knowledge and experience, and
according to other personal peculiarities and characteristics.   Even this is not all.   Every person changes his
religious views as he grows older, as his knowledge and
experience increase, so that the faith of the youth is
not that of the child, nor does the man with silvery
locks approach the altar with precisely the same faith
as when he knelt there a youth.   For it is not the
words and ceremonies, but the thoughts and feelings,
that we combine with these symbols, that constitute
our religion; it is not the confession which we learned
at school, but the ideas that are suggested by it in our

minds, and the emotions awakened by it in our hearts, that constitute our faith.

If the preachers of the Christian religion realized these truths more than they generally seem to do, they would perhaps speak with more charity and less scorn and contempt of people who differ from them in their religious views. They would recognize in the faith of others the same connecting link between God and man for them, as their own faith is for themselves. They would not hate the Jew because he, in accordance with the Mosaic commandment, offers his prayers in the synagogue to the God of his fathers; nor despise the heathen because *he,* in want of better knowledge, in childlike simplicity lifts his hands in prayer to an image of wood or stone; for, although this be perishable dust, he still addresses the prayer of his inmost soul to the supreme God, even as the child, that kisses the picture of his absent mother, actually thinks of her.

The old mythological stories of the Norsemen abound in poetry of the truest and most touching character. These stories tell us in sublime and wonderful speech of the workings of external nature, and may make us cheerful or sad, happy or mournful, gay or grave, just as we might feel, if from the pinnacle of Gausta Fjeld we were to watch the passing glories of morning and evening tide. There is nothing in these stories that can tend to make us less upright and simple, while they contain many thoughts and suggestions that we may be the better and happier for knowing. All the so-called disagreeable features of mythology are nothing but distortions, brought out either by ill-will or by a superficial knowledge of the subject; and, when these distortions are removed, we shall find only things beautiful, lovely and of good report. We shall find the

3

simple thoughts of our childlike, imaginative, poetic and prophetic forefathers upon the wonderful works of their maker, and nothing that we may laugh at, or despise, or *pity*. These words of our fathers, if read in the right spirit, will make us feel as we ought to feel when we contemplate the glory and beauty of the heavens and the earth, and observe how wonderfully all things are adapted to each other and to the wants of man, that the thoughts of him who stands at the helm of this ship of the universe (Skidbladner) must be very deep, and that we are sensible to the same joys and sufferings, are actuated by the same fears and hopes and passions, that were felt by the men and women who lived in the dawn of our Gothic history. We will begin to realize how the great and wise Creator has led our race on — slowly, perhaps, but nevertheless surely — to the consciousness that he is a loving and righteous Father, and that he has made the sun and moon and stars, the earth, and all that in them is, in their season.

The Norse mythology reflects, then, the religious, moral, intellectual and social development of our ancestors in the earliest period of their existence. We say *our* ancestors, for we must bear in mind that in its most original form this mythology was common to all the Teutonic nations, to the ancestors of the Americans and the English, as well as to those of the Norsemen, Swedes and Danes. Geographically it extended not only over the whole of Scandinavia, including Iceland, but also over England and a considerable portion of France and Germany. But it is only in Iceland, that weird island of the icy sea, with the snow-clad volcano Mt. Hecla for its hearth, encircled by a wall of glaciers, and with the roaring North Sea for its grave,—it is

only in Iceland that anything like a complete record
of this ancient Teutonic mythology was put in writing and preserved; and this fact alone ought to be
quite sufficient to lead us to cultivate a better acquaintance with the literature of Scandinavia. To use the
words of that excellent Icelandic scholar, the Englishman George Webbe Dasent: It is well known, says
he, that the Icelandic language, which has been preserved almost incorrupt in that remarkable island, has
remained for many centuries the depository of literary
treasures, the common property of all the Scandinavian
and Teutonic races, which would otherwise have perished, as they have perished in Norway, Denmark,
Sweden, Germany and England. There was a time
when all these countries had a common mythology,
when the royal race in each of them traced its descent
in varying genealogies up to Odin and the gods of
Asgard. Of that mythology, *which may hold its own
against any other that the world has seen,* all memory,
as a systematic whole, has vanished from the mediæval
literature of Teutonic Europe. With the introduction
of Christianity, the ancient gods had been deposed
and their places assigned to devils and witches. Here
and there a tradition, a popular tale or a superstition
bore testimony to what had been lost; and, though
in this century the skill and wisdom of the Grimms
and their school have shown the world what power
of restoration and reconstruction abides in intelli-
gent scholarship and laborious research, *even the
genius of the great master of that school of criticism
would have lost nine-tenths of its power had not faithful Iceland preserved through the dark ages the two
Eddas, which present to us, in features that cannot be
mistaken, and in words which cannot die, the very form*

*and fashion of that wondrous edifice of mythology which
our forefathers in the dawn of time imagined to themselves as the temple at once of their gods and of the
worship due to them from all mankind on this middle
earth.* For man, according to their system of belief,
could have no existence but for those gods and stalwart
divinities, who, from their abode in Asgard, were ever
watchful to protect him and crush the common foes of
both, the earthly race of giants, or, in other words, the
chaotic natural powers. Any one, therefore, that desires
to see what manner of men his forefathers were in their
relation to the gods, how they conceived their theogony,
how they imagined and constructed their cosmogony,
must betake himself to the Eddas, as illustrated by the
Sagas, and he will there find ample details on all these
points; while the Anglo-Saxon and Teutonic literatures
only throw out vague hints and allusions. As we read
Beowulf and the Traveler's Song, for instance, we meet
at every step references to mythological stories and mythical events, which would be utterly unintelligible were
it not for the full light thrown upon them by the Icelandic literature. Thus far Dasent's opinion.

The Norse mythology, we say, then, shows what the
religion of our ancestors was; and their religion is the
main fact that we care to know about them. Knowing
this well, we can easily account for the rest. Their religion is the soul of their history. Their religion tells
us what they felt; their feelings produced their thoughts,
and their thoughts were the parents of their acts. When
we study their religion, we discover the unseen and
spiritual fountain from which all their outward acts
welled forth, and by which the character of these was
determined.

The mythology is neither the history nor the poetry

nor the natural philosophy of our ancestors; but it is the germ and nucleus of them all. It *is* history, for it treats of events; but it is *not* history in the ordinary acceptance of that word, for the persons figuring therein have never existed. It *is* natural philosophy, for it investigates the origin of nature; but it is *not* natural philosophy according to modern ideas, for it personifies and deifies nature. It *is* metaphysics, for it studies the science and the laws of being; but it is *not* metaphysics in our sense of the word, for it rapidly overleaps all categories. It is poetry in its very essence; but its pictures are streams that flow together. Thus the Norse mythology is history, but limited to neither time nor place; poetry, but independent of arses or theses; philosophy, but without abstractions or syllogisms.

We close this chapter with the following extract from Thomas Carlyle's essays on Heroes and Hero-worship; an extract that undoubtedly will be read with interest and pleasure:

In that strange island — Iceland — burst up, the geologists say, by fire, from the bottom of the sea; a wild land of barrenness and lava; swallowed, many months of the year, in black tempests, yet with a wild, gleaming beauty in summer-time; towering up there, stern and grim, in the North Ocean; with its snow-jökuls, roaring geysers, sulphur pools and horrid volcanic chasms, like the waste, chaotic battle-field of frost and fire — where of all places we least looked for literature or written memorials; the record of these things was written down. On the seaboard of this wild land is a rim of grassy country, where cattle can subsist, and men, by means of them and of what the sea yields; and it seems they were poetic men, these — men who had deep thoughts in them, and uttered musically their thoughts. Much would be lost had Iceland not been burst up from the sea — not been discovered by the Northmen! The old Norse poets were many of them natives of Iceland.

Sæmund, one of the early Christian priests there, who perhaps had a lingering fondness for paganism, collected certain of

their old pagan songs, just about becoming obsolete then —
poems or chants, of a mythic, prophetic, mostly all of a religious, character: this is what Norse critics call the *Elder* or
Poetic *Edda*. *Edda*, a word of uncertain etymology, is thought
to signify *Ancestress*. Snorre Sturleson, an Iceland gentleman,
an extremely notable personage, educated by this Sæmund's
grandson, took in hand next, near a century afterwards, to put
together, among several other books he wrote, a kind of prose
synopsis of the whole mythology, elucidated by new fragments
of traditionary verse; a work constructed really with great
ingenuity, native talent, what one might call unconscious art;
altogether a perspicuous, clear work — pleasant reading still.
This is the *Younger* or Prose *Edda*. By these and the numerous other *Sagas*, mostly Icelandic, with the commentaries, Icelandic
or not, which go on zealously in the North to this day, it is
possible to gain some direct insight even yet, and see that old
system of belief, as it were, face to face. Let us forget that it
is erroneous religion: let us look at it as old thought, and try
if we cannot sympathize with it somewhat.

The primary characteristic of this old Northland mythology
I find to be impersonation of the visible workings of nature —
earnest, simple recognition of the workings of physical nature,
as a thing wholly miraculous, stupendous and divine. What we
now lecture of as science, they wondered at, and fell down in
awe before, as religion. The dark, hostile powers of nature
they figured to themselves as *Jötuns* (giants), huge, shaggy
beings, of a demoniac character. Frost, Fire, Sea, Tempest, these
are *Jötuns*. The friendly powers, again, as Summer-heat, the
Sun, are gods. The Empire of this Universe is divided between
these two; they dwell apart in perennial internecine feud. The
gods dwell above in *Asgard*, the Garden of the *Asas*, or Divinities; *Jötunheim*, a distant, dark, chaotic land, is the home of
the Jötuns.

Curious, all this; and not idle or inane if we will look at
the foundation of it. The power of *Fire* or *Flame*, for instance,
which we designate by some trivial chemical name, thereby hid-
ing from ourselves the essential character of wonder that dwells
in it, as in all things, is, with these old Northmen, *Loge*, a most
swift, subtle demon, of the brood of the Jötuns. The savages
of the Ladrones Islands, too (say some Spanish voyagers), thought
Fire, which they had never seen before, was a devil, or god,

that bit you sharply when you touched it, and lived there upon dry wood. From us, too, no chemistry, if it had not stupidity to help it, would hide that flame is a wonder. What is flame? Frost the old Norse seer discerns to be a monstrous, hoary Jötun, the giant *Thrym, Hrym,* or *Rime,* the old word, now nearly obsolete here, but still used in Scotland to signify hoar-frost. *Rime* was not then, as now, a dead chemical thing, but a living Jötun, or Devil; the monstrous Jötun *Rime* drove home his horses at night, sat combing their manes;—which horses were *Hail-clouds,* or fleet *Frost-winds.* His cows—no, not his, but a kinsman's, the giant Hymer's cows—are *Icebergs.* This Hymer looks at the rocks with his devil-eye, and they *split* in the glance of it.

Thunder was then not mere electricity, vitreous or resinous; it was the god Donner (Thunder), or Thor,—god, also, of the beneficent Summer-heat. The thunder was his wrath; the gathering of the black clouds is the drawing down of Thor's angry brows; the fire-bolt bursting out of heaven is the all-rending hammer flung from the hand of Thor. He urges his loud chariot over the mountain tops—that is the peal; wrathful he blows in his red beard—that is the rustling storm-blast before the thunder begins. Balder, again, the White God, the beautiful, the just and benignant, (whom the early Christian missionaries found to resemble Christ,) is the sun—beautifulest of visible things: wondrous, too, and divine still, after all our astronomies and almanacs! But perhaps the notablest god we hear tell of is one of whom Grimm, the German etymologist, finds trace: the god Wünsch, or Wish. The god *Wish,* who could give us all that we *wished!* Is not this the sincerest and yet the rudest voice of the spirit of man? The *rudest* ideal that man ever formed, which still shows itself in the latest forms of our spiritual culture. Higher considerations have to teach us that the god *Wish* is not the true God.

Of the other gods or Jötuns, I will mention, only for etymology's sake, that Sea-tempest is the Jötun *Ægir,* a very dangerous Jötun; and now to this day, on our river Trent, as I learn, the Nottingham bargemen, when the river is in a certain flooded state (a kind of back-water or eddying swirl it has, very dangerous to them), call it *Eager.* They cry out, Have a care! there is the *Eager* coming! Curious, that word surviving, like the peak of a submerged world! The *oldest* Nottingham barge-

men had believed in the god Ægir. Indeed, our English blood,
too, in good part, is Danish, Norse,— or rather, at the bottom,
Danish and Norse and Saxon have no distinction, except a
superficial one — as of Heathen and Christian, or the like. But
all over our island we are mingled largely with Danes proper
— from the incessant invasions there were; and this, of course,
in a greater proportion along the east coast; and greatest of all,
as I find, in the north country. From the Humber upward, all
over Scotland, the speech of the common people is still in a
singular degree Icelandic; its Germanism has still a peculiar
Norse tinge. They, too, are Normans, Northmen — if that be
any great beauty!

Of the chief god, Odin, we shall speak by-and-by. Mark,
at present, so much: what the essence of Scandinavian, and,
indeed, of all paganism, is: a recognition of the forces of nature
as godlike, stupendous, personal agencies — as gods and demons.
Not inconceivable to us. It is the infant thought of man opening itself with awe and wonder on this ever stupendous universe. It is strange, after our beautiful Apollo statues and
clear smiling mythuses, to come down upon the Norse gods
brewing ale to hold their feast with Aegir, the Sea-Jötun;
sending out Thor to get the caldron for them in the Jötun
country; Thor, after many adventures, clapping the pot on his
head, like a huge hat, and walking off with it — quite lost in it,
the ears of the pot reaching down to his heels! A kind of
vacant hugeness, large, awkward gianthood, characterizes that
Norse system; enormous force, as yet altogether untutored,
stalking helpless, with large, uncertain strides. Consider only
their primary mythus of the Creation. The gods having got the
giant Ymer slain — a giant made by warm winds and much
confused work out of the conflict of Frost and Fire — determined
on constructing a world with him. His blood made the sea;
his flesh was the Land; the Rocks, his bones; of his eyebrows
they formed Asgard, their gods' dwelling; his skull was the
great blue vault of Immensity, and the brains of it became the
Clouds. What a Hyper-Brobdignagian business! Untamed
thought; great, giantlike, enormous; to be tamed, in due time,
into the compact greatness, not giantlike, but godlike, and
stronger than gianthood of the Shakespeares, the Goethes!
Spiritually, as well as bodily, these men are our progenitors.

# CHAPTER II.

WHY CALL THIS MYTHOLOGY NORSE? OUGHT IT NOT
RATHER TO BE CALLED GOTHIC OR TEUTONIC?

IN its original form, the mythology, which is to be presented in this volume, was common to all the Teutonic nations; and it spread itself geographically over England, the most of France and Germany, as well as over Denmark, Sweden, Norway, and Iceland. But when the Teutonic nations parted, took possession of their respective countries, and began to differ one nation from the other, in language, customs and social and political institutions, and were influenced by the peculiar features of the countries which they respectively inhabited, then the germ of mythology which each nation brought with it into its changed conditions of life, would also be subject to changes and developments in harmony and keeping with the various conditions of climate, language, customs, social and political institutions, and other influences that nourished it, while the fundamental myths remained common to all the Teutonic nations. Hence we might in one sense speak of a Teutonic mythology. That would then be the mythology of the Teutonic peoples, as it was known to them while they all lived together, some four or five hundred years before the birth of Christ, in the southeastern part of Russia, without any of the peculiar features that have been added later by any of the several

(41)

branches of that race. But from this time we have no Teutonic literature. In another sense, we must recognize a distinct German mythology, a distinct English mythology, and even make distinction between the mythologies of Denmark, Sweden, and Norway.

That it is only of the Norse mythology we have anything like a complete record, was alluded to in the first chapter; but we will now make a more thorough examination of this fact.

The different branches of the Teutonic mythology died out and disappeared as Christianity gradually became introduced, first in France, about five hundred years after the birth of Christ; then in England, one or two hundred years later; still later, in Germany, where the Saxons, Christianized by Charlemagne about A. D. 800, were the last heathen people.

But in Norway, Sweden, Denmark and Iceland, the original Gothic heathenism lived longer and more independently than elsewhere, and had more favorable opportunities to grow and mature. The ancient mythological or pagan religion flourished here until about the middle of the eleventh century; or, to speak more accurately, Christianity was not completely introduced in Iceland before the beginning of the eleventh century; in Denmark and Norway, some twenty to thirty years later; while in Sweden, paganism was not wholly eradicated before 1150.

Yet neither Norway, Sweden nor Denmark give us any mythological literature. This is furnished us only by the Norsemen, who had settled in Iceland. Shortly after the introduction of Christianity, which gave the Norsemen the so-called Roman alphabetical system instead of their famous Runic *futhorc*, there was put in writing in Iceland a colossal mythological and his-

torical literature, which is the full-blown flower of
Gothic paganism. In the other countries inhabited
by Gothic (Scandinavian, Low Dutch and English) and
Germanic (High German) races, scarcely any mythological literature was produced. The German *Niebelungen-Lied* and the Anglo-Saxon *Beowulf's Drapa* are
at best only semi-mythological. The overthrow of heathendom was too abrupt and violent. Its eradication
was so complete that the heathen religion was almost
wholly obliterated from the memory of the people.
Occasionally there are found authors who refer to it,
but their allusions are very vague and defective, besides
giving unmistakable evidence of being written with prejudice and contempt. Nor do we find among the early
Germans that spirit of veneration for the memories of
the past, and desire to perpetuate them in a vernacular
literature; or if they did exist, they were smothered by
the Catholic priesthood. When the Catholic priests
gained the ascendancy, they adopted the Latin language
and used that exclusively for recording events, and they
pronounced it a sin even to mention by name the old pagan gods oftener than necessity compelled them to do so.

Among the Norsemen, on the other hand, and to a
considerable extent among the English, too, the old
religion flourished longer; the people cherished their
traditions; they loved to recite the songs and Sagas,
in which were recorded the religious faith and brave
deeds of their ancestors, and cultivated their native
speech in spite of the priests. In Iceland at least, the
priests did not succeed in rooting out paganism, if you
please, before it had developed sufficiently to produce
those beautiful blossoms, the Elder and Younger Eddas.
The chief reason of this was, that the people continued
to use their mother-tongue, in writing as well as in speak-

ing, so that Latin, the language of the church, never got a foothold. It was useless for the monks to try to tell Sagas in Latin, for they found but few readers in that tongue. An important result of this was, that the Saga became the property of the people, and not of the favored few. In the next place, our Norse Icelandic ancestors took a profound delight in poetry and song. The skald sung in the mother-speech, and taking the most of the material for his songs and poems from the old mythological tales, it was necessary to study and become familiar with these, in order that he might be able, on the one hand, to understand the productions of others, and, on the other, to compose songs himself. Among the numerous examples which illustrate how tenaciously the Norsemen clung to their ancient divinities, we may mention the skald Hallfred, who, when he was baptized by the king Olaf Tryggvesson, declared bravely to the king, that he would neither speak ill of the old gods, nor refrain from mentioning them in his songs.

The reason, then, why we cannot present a complete and thoroughly systematic Teutonic or German or English or Danish or Swedish Mythology, is not that these did not at some time exist, but because their records are so defective. Outside of Norway and Iceland, Christianity, together with disregard of past memories, has swept most of the resources, with which to construct them, away from the surface, and there remain only deeply buried ruins, which it is difficult to dig up and still more difficult to polish and adjust into their original symmetrical and comprehensive form after they have been brought to the surface. It is difficult to gather all the scattered and partially decayed bones of the mythological system, and with the breath of human intellect reproduce a living vocal organism. Few have attempted to do this with greater success than the brothers Grimm.

For the elucidation of our mythology in its Germanic form, for instance, the materials, although they are not wholly wanting, are yet difficult to make use of, since they are widely scattered, and must be sought partly in quite corrupted popular legends, partly in writings of the middle ages, where they are sometimes found interpolated, and where we often least should expect to find them. But in its Norse form we have ample material for studying the Asa-mythology. Here we have as our guide not only a large number of skaldic lays, composed while the mythology still flourished, but even a complete religious system, written down, it is true, after Christianity had been introduced in Iceland, still, according to all evidence, without the Christian ideas having had any special influence upon its delineation, or having materially corrupted it. These lays, manuscripts, etc., which form the source of Norse mythology, will be more fully discussed in another chapter of this Introduction.

We may add further, that if we had, in a complete system, the mythology of the Germans, the English, etc., we should find, in comparing them with the Norse, the same correspondence and identity as we find existing between the different branches of the Teutonic family of languages. We should find in its essence the same mythology in all the Teutonic countries, we should find this again dividing itself into two groups, the Germanic and the Gothic, and the latter group, that is, the Gothic, would include the ancient religion of the Scandinavians, English, and Low Dutch. If we had sufficient means for making a comparison, we should find that any single myth may have become more prominent, may have become more perfectly developed by one branch of the race than by another; one branch of the great Teutonic family may have become more attached to a certain myth than another, while the myth itself would remain identical everywhere. Local myths, that is, myths produced by the contemplation of the visible workings of external nature, are colored by the atmosphere of the people and country where they are fostered. The god Frey received especial attention by the Asa-worshipers in Sweden, but the Norse and Danish Frey are still in reality the same god. Thunder produces not the same effect upon the people among the towering and precipitous mountains of Norway and the level plains of Denmark, but the Thor of Norway and of Denmark are still the same god; although in Norway he is tall as a mountain, his beard is briers, and he rushes upon his heroic deeds with the strength and frenzy of a berserk, while in Denmark he wanders along the sea-shore, a youth, with golden locks and downy beard.

It is the Asa-mythology, as it was conceived and cherished by the Norsemen of Norway and Iceland, which the Old Norse literature properly presents to us, and hence the myths will in this volume be presented in their Norse dress, and hence its name, *Norse Mythology*. From what has already been said, there is no reason to doubt that the Swedes and Danes professed. in the main the same faith, followed the same religious customs, and had the same religious institutions; and upon this supposition other English writers upon this subject, as for instance Benjamin Thorpe, have entitled their books *Scandinavian Mythology*. But we do not know the details of the religious faith, customs and

institutions of Sweden and Denmark, for all reliable
inland sources of information are wanting, and all the
highest authorities on this subject of investigation, such
as Rudolph Keyser, P. A. Munch, Ernst Sars, N. M.
Petersen and others, unanimously declare, that although
the ancient Norse-Icelandic writings not unfrequently
treat of heathen religious affairs in Sweden and Denmark, yet, when they do, it is always in such a manner
that the conception is clearly *Norse,* and the delineation
is throughout adapted to institutions as they existed in
Norway. We are aware that there are those who will
feel inclined to criticise us for not calling this mythology Scandinavian or Northern (a more elastic term),
but we would earnestly recommend them to examine
carefully the writings of the above named writers before
waxing too zealous on the subject.

As we closed the previous chapter with an extract
from Thomas Carlyle, so we will close this chapter with
a brief quotation from an equally eminent scholar, the
author of *Chips from a German Workshop.* In the
second volume of that work Max Müller says:*

There is, after Anglo-Saxon, no language, no literature, no
mythology so full of interest for the elucidation of the earliest
history of the race which now inhabits these British isles as the
Icelandic. Nay, in one respect Icelandic beats every other dialect of the great Teutonic family of speech, not excepting Anglo-
Saxon and Old High German and Gothic. It is in Icelandic alone
that we find complete remains of genuine Teutonic heathendom.
Gothic, as *a language,* is more ancient than Icelandic; but the
only literary work which we possess in Gothic is a translation
of the Bible. The Anglo-Saxon literature, with the exception of
the Beowulf, is Christian. The old heroes of the Niebelunge,
such as we find them represented in the Suabian epic, have been
converted into church-going knights; whereas, in the ballads of

* Max Müller's Review of Dr. Dasent's *The Norseman in Iceland.*

the Elder Edda, Sigurd and Brynhild appear before us in their full pagan grandeur, holding nothing sacred but their love, and defying all laws, human and divine, in the name of that one almighty passion. The Icelandic contains the key to many a riddle in the English language and to many a mystery in the English character. Though the Old Norse is but a dialect of the same language which the Angles and Saxons brought to Britain, though the Norman blood is the same blood that floods and ebbs in every German heart, yet there is an accent of defiance in that rugged northern speech, and a spring of daring madness in that throbbing northern heart, which marks the Northman wherever he appears, whether in Iceland or in Sicily, whether on the Seine or on the Thames. At the beginning of the ninth century, when the great northern exodus began, Europe, as Dr. Dasent remarks, was in danger of becoming too comfortable. The two nations destined to run neck-and-neck in the great race of civilization, Frank and Anglo-Saxon, had a tendency to become dull and lazy, and neither could arrive at perfection till it had been chastised by the Norsemen, and finally forced to admit an infusion of northern blood into its sluggish veins. The vigor of the various branches of the Teutonic stock may be measured by the proportion of Norman blood which they received; and the national character of England owes more to the descendants of Hrolf Ganger * than to the followers of Hengist and Horsa.

But what is known of the early history of the Norsemen? Theirs was the life of reckless freebooters, and they had no time to dream and ponder on the past, which they had left behind in Norway. Where they settled as colonists or as rulers, their own traditions, their very language, were soon forgotten. Their language has nowhere struck root on foreign ground, even where, as in Normandy, they became earls of Rouen, or, as in these isles, kings of England. There is but one exception — Iceland. Iceland was discovered, peopled and civilized by Norsemen in the ninth century; and in the nineteenth century the language spoken there is still the dialect of Harald Fairhair, and the stories told there are still the stories of the Edda, or the Venerable Grandmother. Dr. Dasent gives us a rapid sketch of the first landings of the Norse refugees on the fells and forths of Iceland. He describes how love of freedom drove the subjects

--------

* The founder of Normandy in France.

of Harald Fairhair forth from their home; how the Teutonic tribes, though they loved their kings, the sons of Odin, and sovereigns by the grace of God, detested the dictatorship of Harald. He was a mighty warrior, so says the ancient Saga, and laid Norway under him, and put out of the way some of those who held districts, and some of them he drove out of the land; and besides, many men escaped out of Norway because of the overbearing of Harald Fairhair, for they would not stay to be subjects to him. These early emigrants were pagans, and it was not till the end of the tenth century that Christianity reached the Ultima Thule of Europe. The missionaries, however, who converted the freemen of Iceland, were freemen themselves. They did not come with the pomp and the pretensions of the church of Rome. They preached Christ rather than the Pope; they taught religion rather than theology. Nor were they afraid of the old heathen gods, or angry with every custom that was not of Christian growth. Sometimes this tolerance may have been carried too far, for we read of kings, like Helge, who mixed in their faith, who trusted in Christ, but at the same time invoked Thor's aid whenever they went to sea or got into any difficulty. But on the whole, the kindly feeling of the Icelandic priesthood toward the national traditions and customs and prejudices of their converts must have been beneficial. Sons and daughters were not forced to call the gods whom their fathers and mothers had worshiped, devils; and they were allowed to use the name of Allfadir, whom they had invoked in the prayers of their childhood, when praying to Him who is our Father in Heaven.

The Icelandic missionaries had peculiar advantages in their relation to the system of paganism which they came to combat. Nowhere else, perhaps, in the whole history of Christianity, has the missionary been brought face to face with a race of gods who were believed by their own worshipers to be doomed to death. The missionaries had only to proclaim that Balder was dead, that the mighty Odin and Thor were dead. The people knew that these gods were to die, and the message of the One Everliving God must have touched their ears and their hearts with comfort and joy. Thus, while in Germany the priests were occupied for a long time in destroying every trace of heathenism, in condemning every ancient lay as the work of the

4

devil, in felling sacred trees and abolishing national customs, the missionaries of Iceland were able to take a more charitable view of the past, and they became the keepers of those very poems and laws and proverbs and Runic inscriptions which on the continent had to be put down with inquisitorial cruelty. The men to whom the collection of the ancient pagan poetry of Iceland is commonly ascribed were men of Christian learning : the one,* the founder of a public school ; the other,† famous as the author of a history of the North, the Heimskringla (the Home-Circle — the World). It is owing to their labors that we know anything of the ancient religion, the traditions, the maxims, the habits of the Norsemen. Dr. Dasent dwells most fully on the religious system of Iceland, which is the same, at least in its general outline, as that believed in by all the members of the Teutonic family, and may truly be called one of the various dialects of the primitive religious and mythological language of the Aryan race. There is nothing more interesting than religion in the whole history of man. By its side, poetry and art, science and law, sink into comparative insignificance.

*Sæmund the Wise.     †Snorre Sturleson.

# CHAPTER III.

DR. DASENT says the Norse mythology may hold its own against any other in the world. The fact that it is the religion of our forefathers ought to be enough to commend it to our attention; but it may be pardonable in us to harbor even a sense of pride, if we find, for instance, that the mythology of our Gothic ancestors suffers nothing, but rather is the gainer in many respects by a comparison with that world-famed paganism of the ancient Greeks. We would therefore invite the attention of the reader to a brief comparison between the Norse and Greek systems of mythology.

A comparison between the two systems is both interesting and important. They are the two grandest systems of cosmogony and theogony of which we have record, but the reader will generously pardon the writer if he ventures the statement already at the outset, that of the two the Norse system is the grander. These two, the Greek and the Norse, have, to a greater extent than all other systems of mythology combined, influenced the civilization, determined the destinies, socially and politically, of the European nations, and shaped their polite literature. In literature it might indeed seem that the Greek mythology has played a more important part. We admit that it has acted a more *conspicuous* part, but we imagine that there exists a wonderful blindness, among many writers, to the transcendent influence of the blood and spirit of ancient Norseland on North European, including English and American, character, which character has in turn stamped itself upon our literature (as, for instance, in the case of Shakespeare, the Thor among all Teutonic writers); and, furthermore, we rejoice in the absolute certainty to which we have arrived by studying the signs of the times, that the comparative ignorance, which has prevailed in this country and in England, of the history, literature, ancient religion and institutions of a people so closely allied to us by race, national characteristics, and tone of mind as the Norsemen, will sooner or later be removed; that a school of Norse philology and antiquities will ere long flourish on the soil of the Vinland of our ancestors, and that there is a grand future, not far hence, when Norse mythology will be copiously reflected in our elegant literature, and in our fine arts, painting, sculpturing and music.

The Norse mythology differs widely from the Greek. They are the same in essence; that is to say, both are a recognition of the forces and phenomena of nature as gods and demons; but all mythologies are the same in this respect, and the differences, between the various mythological systems, consist in the different ways in which nature has impressed different peoples, and in the different manner in which they have comprehended the universe, and personified or deified the various forces and phenomena of nature. In other words, it is in the ethical clothing and elaboration of the myths, that the different systems of mythology differ one from the other. In the Vedic and Homeric poets the germs of mythology are the same as in the Eddas of Norseland, but this common stock of materials, that is, the forces and phenomena of nature, has been moulded into an infinite variety of shapes by the story-tellers of the Hindoos, Greeks and Norsemen.

Memory among the Greeks is *Mnemosyne*, the mother of the muses, while among the Norsemen it is represented by Munin, one of the ravens perched upon Odin's shoulders. The masculine Heimdal, god of the rainbow among the Norsemen, we find in Greece as the feminine Iris, who charged the clouds with water from the lakes and rivers, in order that it might fall again upon the earth in gentle fertilizing showers. She was daughter of Thaumas and Elektra, granddaughter of Okeanos, and the swift-footed gold-winged messenger of the gods. The Norse Balder is the Greek Adonis. Frigg, the mother of Balder, mourns the death of her son, while Aphrodite sorrows for her special favorite, the young rosy shepherd, Adonis. Her grief at his death, which was caused by a wild boar, was so great that she would not allow the lifeless body to be taken from her arms until the gods consoled her by decreeing that her lover might continue to live half the year, during the spring and summer, on the earth, while she might spend the other half with him in the lower world. Thus Balder and Adonis are both summer gods, and Frigg and Aphrodite are goddesses of gardens and flowers. The Norse god of Thunder, Thor (Thursday), who, among the Norsemen, is only the protector of heaven and earth, is the Greek Zeus, the father of gods and men. The gods of the Greeks are essentially free from decay and death. They live forever on Olympos, eating ambrosial food and drinking the nectar of immortality, while in their veins flows not immortal blood, but the imperishable ichor. In the Norse mythology, on the other hand, Odin himself dies, and is swallowed by the Fenriswolf; Thor conquers the Midgard-serpent, but retreats only nine paces and falls poisoned by the serpent's breath; and the body of the good and beautiful Balder is consumed in the flames of his funeral pile. The Greek dwelt in bright and sunny lands, where the change from summer to winter brought with it no feelings of overpowering gloom. The outward nature exercised a cheering influence upon him, making him happy, and this happiness he exhibited in his mythology. The Greek cared less to commune with the silent mountains, moaning winds, and heaving sea; he spent his life to a great extent in the cities, where his mind would become more interested in human affairs, and where he could share his joys and sorrows with his kinsmen. While the Greek thus was brought up to the artificial society of the town, the hardy Norseman was inured to the rugged independence of the country. While the life and the nature surrounding it, in the South, would naturally have a tendency to make the Greek more human, or rather to deify that which is human, the popular life and nature in the North would have a tendency to form in the minds of the Norsemen a sublimer and profounder conception of the universe. The Greek clings with tenacity to the beautiful earth; the earth is his mother. Zeus, surrounded by his gods and goddesses, sits on his golden throne, on Olympos, on the top of the mountain, in the cloud. But that is not lofty enough for the spirit of the Norsemen. Odin's Valhal is in heaven; nay, Odin himself is not the highest god; Muspelheim is situated above Asaheim, and in Muspelheim is Gimle, where reigns a god, who is mightier than Odin, the god whom Hyndla ventures not to name.

In *Heroes and Hero Worship*, Thomas Carlyle makes the following striking comparison between Norse and Greek mythology: To me, he says, there is in the

Norse system something very genuine, very great and manlike. A broad simplicity, rusticity, so very different from the light gracefulness of the old Greek paganism, distinguishes this Norse system. It is *thought*, the genuine thought of deep, rude, earnest minds, fairly opened to the things about them, a face-to-face and heart-to-heart inspection of things — the first characteristic of all good thought in all times. Not graceful lightness, half sport, as in the Greek paganism; a certain homely truthfulness and rustic strength, a great rude sincerity, discloses itself here. Thus Carlyle.

As the visible workings of nature are in the great and main features the same everywhere; in all climes we find the vaulted sky with its sun, moon, myriad stars and flitting clouds; the sea with its surging billows; the land with its manifold species of plants and animals, its elevations and depressions; we find cold, heat, rain, winds, etc., although all these may vary widely in color, brilliancy, depth, height, degree, and other qualities; and as the minds and hearts of men cherish hope, fear, anxiety, passion, etc., although they may be influenced and actuated by them in various ways and to various extents; and as mythology is the impersonation of nature's forces and phenomena as contemplated by the human mind and *heart*, so all mythologies, no matter in what clime they originated and were fostered, must of necessity have their stock of materials, their groundwork or foundation and frame in common, while they may differ widely from each other in respect to peculiar characteristics, both in the ethical elaboration of the myth and in the architectural effect of the *tout ensemble*. Thus we have a tradition about a deluge, for instance, in nearly every country on the globe, but no two nations tell it alike. In Genesis we read of Noah and his ark,

and how the waters increased greatly upon the earth,
destroying all flesh that moved upon the earth excepting those who were with him in the ark. In Greece,
Deukalion and his wife Pyrrha become the founders of
a new race of men. According to the Greek story, a great
flood had swept away the whole human race, except
one pair, Deukalion and Pyrrha, who, as the flood
abated, landed on Mt. Parnassos, and thence descending, picked up stones and cast them round about, as
Zeus had commanded. From these stones sprung a new
race — men from those cast by Deukalion, and women
from those cast by his wife. In Norseland, Odin and
his two brothers, Vile and Ve, slew the giant Ymer, and
when he fell, so much blood flowed from his wounds,
that the whole race of frost-giants was drowned, except
a single giant, who saved himself with his household
in a skiff (ark), and from him descended a new race of
frost-giants. Now this is not a tradition carried from
one place to the other; it is a natural expression of the
same thought; it is a similar effort to account for the
origin of the land and the race of man. A people develops its mythology in the same manner as it develops its
language. The Norse mythology is related to the Greek
mythology to the same extent that the Norse language
is related to the Greek language, and no more; and
comparative mythology, when the scholar wields the
pen, is as interesting as comparative philology.

The Greeks have their chaos, the all-embracing space,
the Norsemen have Ginungagap, the yawning abyss
between Niflheim (the nebulous world) and Muspelheim
(the world of fire). The Greeks have their titans, corresponding in many respects to the Norse giants. The
Greeks tell of the Melian nymphs; the Norsemen of
the elves, etc.; but these comparisons are chiefly inter-

esting for the purpose of studying the differences between the Norse and Greek *mind*, which reflects itself in the expression of the thought.

The hard stone weeps tears, both in Greece and in Norseland; but let us notice how differently it is expressed. In Greece, Niobe, robbed of her children, was transformed into a rugged rock, down which tears trickled silently. She becomes a stone and still continues her weeping —

Et lacrymas etiamnum marmora manant,

as the poet somewhere has it. In Norseland all nature laments the sad death of Balder, even the stones weep for him (gráta Baldr).

Let us take another idea, and notice how differently the words symbolize the same truth or thought in the Bible, in Greece, and in Norseland. In the Bible:

And Jesus sat over against the treasury, and beheld how people cast money into the treasury: and many that were rich cast in much. And there came a certain poor widow, and she threw in two mites, which make a farthing. And he called unto him his disciples and said unto them, Verily I say unto you, that this poor widow hath cast more in, than all they which have cast into the treasury: for all they did cast in of their abundance; but she of her want did cast in all that she had, even all her living.

In Greece:

A rich Thessalian offered to the temple at Delphi one hundred oxen with golden horns. A poor citizen from Hermion took as much meal from his sack as he could hold between two fingers, and he threw it into the fire that burned on the altar. Pythia said, that the gift of the poor man was more pleasing to the gods than that of the rich Thessalian.

In Norseland the Elder Edda has it:

> Knowest thou how to pray?
> Knowest thou how to offer?
> Better not pray at all
> Than to offer too much,
> Better is nothing sent
> Than too much consumed.

In these few and simple words are couched the same thought as in the Jewish and Greek accounts just given. It is this identity in thought, with diversity of depth, breadth, beauty, simplicity, etc., in the expression or symbol that characterizes the differences between all mythological systems. Each has its own peculiarities stamped upon it, and in these peculiarities the spirit of the people, their tendency to thorough investigation or superficiality, their strength or weakness, their profoundness or frivolity, are reflected as in a mirror.

The beauty of the Greek mythology consists not so much in the system, considered as a whole, as in the separate single groups of myths. Each group has its own center around which it revolves, each group moves in its own sphere, and there develops its own charming perfection, without regard to the effect upon the system of mythology considered as a whole. Each group is exquisite, and furnishes an inexhaustible fountain of legendary narrative, but the central thought that should bind all these beautiful groups into one grand whole is weak. Nay, the complex multiplicity into which it constantly kept developing, as long as the Greek mind was in vigorous activity, was the cause that finally shattered it. Is not this same spirit, which we find so distinctly developed in the Greek mythology, this want of a centralizing thought, most wonderfully and perfectly reflected in the social and political characteristics of the Greek states, and in all the more recent Romance nations? Each Greek state developed a peculiar beauty and perfection of its own; but between the different states (Sparta, Athens, etc.,) there was no strong bond of union which could keep them together, and hence all the feuds and civil wars and final dissolution. In the Norse mythology, on the other hand, the centralizing idea or thought is its peculiar feature; in it lies its strength and beauty. In the Norse mythology, the one myth and the one divinity is inextricably in communion with the other; and thus, also, the idea of unity, centralization, is a prominent feature, and one of the chief characteristics of the Teutonic nations. While the Greek mythology foreshadowed all the petty states of Greece, as well as those of South Europe and South America, the Norse mythology foreshadowed the political and social destinies of *united* Scandinavia, *united* Great Britain, *united* Germany, and the *United* States of North America. When the Greeks unite, they *fall.* We Northerners live only to be *united.*

As we would be led to suppose, from a study of the physical and climatical peculiarities of Greece and Norseland, we find that the Greek mythology forms an epic poem, and that the Norse is a tragedy. Not only the mythology, considered as a whole, but even the character of its speech, and of its very words and phrases, must necessarily be suggested and modified by the external features of the country. Thus in Greece, where the sun's rays never scorch, and where the northern winds never pierce, we naturally find in the speech of the people, brilliancy rather than gloom, life rather than decay, and constant renovation rather than prolonged lethargy. But in the frozen-bound regions of the North, where the long arms of the glaciers clutch the valleys in their cold embrace, and the death-portending avalanches cut their way down the mountain-sides.

the tongue of the people would, with a peculiar intensity of feeling, dwell upon the tragedy of nature.

The Danish poet Grundtvig expressed a similar idea more than sixty years ago, when he said that the Asa-Faith unfolds in five acts the most glorious drama of victory that ever has been composed, or ever could be composed, by any mortal poet. And Hauch defines these five acts as follows:

Act I. The Creation.
Act II. The time preceding the death of Balder.
Act III. The death of Balder.
Act IV. The time immediately succeeding the death of Balder.
Act V. Ragnarok, the Twilight of the gods, that is, the decline and fall immediately followed by the regeneration of the world.

It is an inestimable peculiarity of the Norse mythology, that it, in addition to beginning with a theogony (birth of the gods), also ends with a theoktony (death of the gods). In the Greek mythology, the drama lacks the fifth or final act, and we have only a prosaic account of how the people at length grew tired of their gods, and left them when they became old and feeble. But the Eddas have a theoktonic myth, in which the heroic death of the gods is sung with the same poetic spirit as their youthful exploits and victories. As the shades of night flee before the morning dawn, thus Valhal's gods had to sink into the earth, when the idea, that an idol is of no consequence in this world, first burst upon the minds of the idol-worshipers. This idea spontaneously created the myth of Ragnarok. All the elements of its mythical form were foreshadowed in the older group of Norse conceptions. The idea of Ragnarok was suggested already in the Creation; for the gods are there represented as proceeding from giants, that is, from an evil, chaotic source, and, moreover, that

which can be born must die.    The Greeks did not
release the titans from their prisons in Tartaros and
bring them up to enter the last struggle with the gods.
Signs of such a contest flitted about like clouds in the
deep-blue southern sky, but they did not gather into a
deluging thunder-storm.    The ideas were too broken
and scattered to be united into one grand picture.
The Greek was so much allured by the pleasures of
life, that he could find no time to fathom its depths
or rise above it.    And hence, when the glories of this
life had vanished, there remained nothing but a vain
shadow, a lower world, where the pale ghosts of the
dead knew no greater happiness than to receive tidings
from this busy world.

The Norseman willingly yields the prize to the Greek
when the question is of precision in details and external
adornment of the figures; but when we speak of deep
significance and intrinsic power, the Norseman points
quietly at Ragnarok, the Twilight of the gods, and
the Greek is silent.

The Goth, as has before been indicated, concentrated
life; the Greek divided it into parcels.    Thus the
Greek mythology is frivolous, the Norse is profound.
The frivolous mind lives but to enjoy the passing moment; the profound mind reflects, considers the past
and the future.    The Greek abandoned himself wholly
to the pleasures of this life, regardless of the past
or future.    The Norseman accepted life as a good
gift, but he knew that he was merely its transient possessor.    Over every moment of life hangs a threatening
sword, which may in the next moment prove fatal.
Life possesses no hour of the future.    And this is the
peculiar characteristic of the heroic life in the North,
that our ancestors were powerfully impressed with the

uncertainty of life.    They constantly witnessed the
interchange of life and death, and this nourished in
them the thought that life is not worth keeping, for
no one knows how soon it may end.    Life itself has
no value, but the object constantly to be held in view
is to die an honorable death.    While we are permitted
to live, let us strive to die with honor, it is said in
Bjarkemaal; and in the lay of Hamder of the Elder
Edda we read:

> Well have we fought;
> On slaughtered Goths we stand,
> On those fallen by the sword,
> Like eagles on a branch.
> Great glory we have gained;
> Though now or to-morrow we shall die,—
> No one lives till eve
> Against the norns' decree.

It is this same conception of the problem of life
that in the Christian religion has assumed a diviner
form.    Though his ideas were clothed in a ruder form,
the Norseman still reached the same depth of thought
as when the Christian says: I am ready to lay down
my life, if I may but die happy, die a child of God;
for what is a man profited if he shall gain the whole
world, and lose his own soul?

The Norseman always concentrated his ideas as much
as possible.    For this reason he knew but three sins —
perjury, murder, and adultery; that is, sin against God,
sin against the state, and sin against fellow-man; and
all these are in fact but one sin — deceitfulness.    In
the same manner the Norseman concentrated his ideas
in regard to the punishment of sin.    When the Eddas
tell us about the punishment of the wicked, they sum
it all up in Naastrand (the strand of corpses), that place

far from the sun, that large and terrible cave, the doors
of which open to the north. This cave is built of
serpents wattled together, and the heads of all the serpents turn into the cave, filling it with streams of
poison, in which perjurers, murderers and adulterers
have to wade. The suffering is terrible; gory hearts
hang outside of their breasts; their faces are dyed in
blood; strong venom-dragons fiercely run through their
hearts; their hands are riveted together with ever-
burning stones; their clothes are wrapped in flames;
remorseless ravens tear their eyes from their heads:

> But all the horrors
> You cannot know,
> That Hel's condemned endure;
> Sweet sins there
> Bitterly are punished,
> False pleasures
> Reap true pain.

The point to be observed is, that all the punishment here described is the same for all the wicked.

But with this, the versatile Greek is not content.
He multiplies the sins and the punishments. Tartaros
is full of despair and tears, and the wicked there suffer
a variety of tortures. Enormous vultures continually
gnaw the liver of Tityos, but it always grows again.
Ixion is lashed with serpents to a wheel, which a
strong wind drives continually round and round. Tan-
talos suffers from an unceasing dread of being crushed
by a great rock that hangs over his head; he stands in
a stream of water that flows up to his throat, and he
almost perishes from thirst; whenever he bends his
head to drink the water recedes; delicious fruits hang
over his head, whenever he stretches out his hand they
evade his grasp. Thus it is to be *tantalized*. The

Danaïdes must fill a cistern that has holes in the bottom; all the water they pour in runs out equally fast. Sisyphos, sweating and all out of breath, rolls his huge stone up the mountain side; when he reaches the summit, the stone rolls down again.

The fundamental idea is always the same. It is always punishment for sin; but it is expressed and illustrated in so many different ways. The variety enhances the beauty. The Greek mythology is rich, for profuseness of illustration is wealth. The Norse mythology is poor, because it is so strong; it consumes all its strength in the profoundness of its thought. The Norse mythology excels in the concentratedness and strength of the whole system; the Greek excels in the beauty of the separate groups of myths. The one is a religion of *strength,* the other of *beauty.*

The influence that the outward features of a country exercise upon the thoughts and feelings of men, especially during the vigorous, imaginative, poetic and prophetic childhood of a nation, can hardly be overestimated. Necessarily, therefore, do we find this influence affecting and modifying a nation's mythology, which is a child-like people's thoughts and feelings, contemplating nature reflected in a system of religion. Hence, it is eminently fitting, in comparing the Norse mythology with the Greek, to take a look at the home of the Norsemen. We, therefore, cordially invite the traveler from the smooth-beaten tracks of southern Europe to the mountains, lakes, valleys and fjords of Norseland. You may come in midsummer, when Balder (the summer sunlight) rules supreme, when the radiant dawn and glowing sunset kiss each other and go hand in hand on the mountain tops; but we would also invite you to tarry until Balder is slain, when the wintry gloom, with its long nights, sits brooding over the country, and Loke (Thok, fire) weeps his arid tears (sparks) over the desolation he has wrought.

Norway is dark, cloudy, severe, grand, and majestic. Greece is light, variegated, mild, and beautiful. No one can long more deeply for the light of summer, with its mild and gentle breezes from the south, than the Norseman. When he has pondered on his own thoughts during the long winter, when the sun entirely or nearly disappeared from above the horizon, and nothing but northern lights flickered and painted the colors of the rainbow over his head, he welcomes the spring sun with enthusiastic delight. It was this deep longing for Balder that drove swarms of Norsemen on viking expeditions to France, Spain, and England; through the pillars of Hercules to Italy, Greece, Constantinople and Palestine, and over the surging main to Iceland, Greenland and Vinland. It is this deep longing for Balder that every year brings thousands of Norsemen to alight upon our shores and scatter themselves to their numberless settlements in these United States. Still every Norse emigrant, if he has aught in him worthy of his race, thinks he shall once more see those weird, gigantic, snow-capped mountains, that stretched their tall heads far above the clouds and seemed to look half anxiously, half angrily after him as his bark was floating across the deep sea.

There is something in the natural scenery of Norway — a peculiar blending of the grand, the picturesque, the gigantic, bewildering and majestic. There is something that leaves you in bewildering amazement, when you have seen it, and makes you ask yourself, Was it real or was it only a dream? Norway is in fact one huge imposing rock, and its valleys are but great clefts

5

in it. Through these clefts the rivers, fed by vast glaciers upon the mountains, find their way to the sea.
They come from the distance, now musically and chat-
tingly meandering their way beneath the willows, now
tumbling down the slopes, reeking and distorted by the
rocks that oppose them, until they reach some awful
precipice and tumble down some eight hundred to a
thousand feet in a single leap into the depths below,
where no human being ever yet set his foot. . We are
not overdrawing the picture. You cannot get to the
foot of such falls as the Voring Force or Rjukan Force,
but you may look over the precipice from above and see
the waters pouring like fine and fleecy wool into the
seething caldron, where you can discern through the
vapory mists shoots of foam at the bottom, like rockets
of water, radiating in every direction. You hear a low
rumbling sound around you, and the very rock vibrates
beneath your feet; and as you hang half giddy over
the cliff, clasping your arms around some young birch-
tree that tremblingly leans over the brink of the steep,
and turn your eyes to the huge mountain mass that
breasts you,— its black, melancholy sides seemingly
within a stone's throw, and its snow-white head far in
the clouds above,— your thoughts involuntarily turn to
*him*, the God, whom the skald dare not name, to *him*
at whose bidding Gausta Fjeld and Reeking Force
sprang from Ginungagap, from the body of the giant
Ymer, from chaos. You look longer upon this wonderful scene, and you begin to think of Ragnarok, of
the Twilight of the gods. Once seen, and the grand
picture, which defies the brush of the painter, will forever afterwards float before your mind like a dream.

Make a journey by steamer on some of those noble
and magnificent fjords on the west coast of Norseland.

The whole scenery looks like a moving panorama of the finest description. The dark mountains rise almost perpendicularly from the water's edge to an enormous height; their summits, crowned with ice and snow, stand out sharp and clear against the bright blue sky; and the ravines on the mountain tops are filled with huge glaciers, that clasp their frosty arms around the valley, and send down, like streams of tears along the weather-beaten cheeks of the mountains, numerous waterfalls and cascades, falling in an endless variety of graceful shapes from various altitudes into the fjord below. Sometimes a solitary peak lifts its lordly head a thousand feet clear above the surrounding mountains, and towering like a monarch over all, it defiantly refuses to hold communion with any living thing save the eagle. Here and there a force appears, like a strip of silvery fleecy cloud, suspended from the brow of the mountain, and dashing down more than two thousand feet in one leap; and all this marvelously grand scenery, from base to peak, stands reflected, as deep as it is lofty, in the calm, clear, sea-green water of the fjord, perfect as in a mirror.

There is no storm; the deep water of the fjord is silent and at rest. Not even the flight of a single bird ruffles its glassy surface. As the steamer glides gently along between the rocky walls, you hear no sound save the monotonous throbbing of the screw and the consequent splashing of the water. All else is still as death. The forces hang in silence all around, occasionally overarched by rainbows suspended in the rising mist. The naked mountains have a sombre look, that would make you melancholy were it not for the overpowering grandeur. Sunshine reaches the water only when the sun's rays fall nearly vertically, in consequence of the immense height of the mountains' sides, whose enormous shadows almost perpetually overshade the narrow fjord. The noonday sun paints a streak of delicate palish green on one side, forming a striking contrast to the other dark overshadowed side of the profound fjord. It is awe-inspiring. It is stupendous. It is solemnly grand. You can but fancy yourself in a fairy land, with elves and sprites and neckens and trolls dancing in sportive glee all around you.

Words can paint no adequate picture of the stupendousness, majesty and grandeur of Norse scenery; but can the reader wonder any longer that this country has given to the world such marvelous productions in poetry, music and the fine arts? Nay, what is more to our purpose at present, would you not look for a grand and marvelous mythological system from the poetic and imaginative childhood of the nation that inhabits this land? Knock, and it shall be opened unto you! and entering the solemn halls and palaces of the gods, where all is cordiality and purity, you will find there perfectly reflected the wild and tumultuous conflict of the elements, strong rustic pictures, full of earnest and deep thought, awe-inspiring and wonderful. You will find that simple and martial religion which inspired the early Norsemen and developed them like a tree full of vigor extending long branches over all Europe. You will find that simple and martial religion which gave the Norsemen that restless unconquerable spirit, apt to take fire at the very mention of subjection and constraint; that religion which forged the instruments that broke the fetters manufactured by the Roman emperors, destroyed tyrants and slaves, and taught men that nature having made all free and equal, no other reason but their mutual happiness could be assigned for making them dependent. You will find that simple and martial religion which was cherished by those vast multitudes which, as Milton says, the populous North

———— poured from her frozen loins to pass
Rhene or the Danaw, when her barbarous sons
Came like a deluge on the South and spread
Beneath Gibraltar and the Libyan sands.

But it may be necessary for the reader to refresh himself with a few draughts of that excellent beverage kept in Mimer's gushing fountain, and drink with *his* glittering horn, before he will be willing to accept these and many more such statements that we will make in the course of this introduction.

To return to our theme. The gods of Norseland are stern and awe-inspiring; those of Greece are gentle and lovely. In the Norse mythology we find deep devotion, but seldom tears. In the Greek, there are violent emotions and the tears flow copiously. In Norseland, there is plenty of imagination; but it is not of that light, variegated, butterfly, soap-bubble nature as in Greece. In the Norse mythology there is plenty of cordiality and sincerity, and the gods treat you hospitably to flesh of the boar, Sæhrimner; and the valkyries will give you deep draughts from bowls flowing with ale. In Greece there is gracefulness, a perfect etiquette, and you dine on ambrosia and nectar; there Eros and Psyche, the graces and muses, hover about you like heavenly cherubs. Graces and muses are wanting in Norseland, The Norse mythology is characterized throughout by a deep and genuine sincerity; the Greek, on the other hand, by a sublime gracefulness; but, with Carlyle, we, think that sincerity is better than grace.

But the comparison between Norse and Greek mythology is too vast a field for us to attempt to do justice to it in this volume. It would be an interesting work to show how Norse and Greek mythologies respectively have colored the religious, social, political and literary character of Greek and Romance peoples on the one hand, and Norsemen and Teutons on the other. Somebody will undoubtedly in due time be inspired to undertake such a task. We must study both, and when they are harmoniously blended in our nature, we must let them together shape our political, social and literary destinies, and, tempered by the Mosaic-Christian religion, they may be entitled to some consideration even in our religious life.

# CHAPTER IV.

IN all that has been said up to this time Roman mythology has not once been mentioned. Why not? Properly speaking, there is no such thing. It is an historical fact, that nearly the whole Roman literature, especially that part of it which may be called *belles-lettres*, is scarcely anything but imitation. It did not, like the Greek and Old Norse, spring from the popular mind, by which it was cherished through centuries; but at least a large portion of it was produced for pay and for ornament, mostly in the time of the tyrant Augustus, to tickle his ear and gild those chains that were artfully forged to fetter the peoples of southern Europe. This is a dry but stubborn truth, and it is wonderful with what tenacity the schools in all civilized lands have clung to the Roman or Latin language, after it had become nothing but a mere corpse; as though it could be expected that any genuine culture could be derived from this dead monster.

It is, however, an encouraging fact that the Teutonic races are indicating a tendency to emancipate themselves from the fetters of Roman bondage, and happy should we be if our English words were emancipated therefrom. We should then use neither *emancipate*, nor *tendency*, nor *indicate*, but would have enough of Gothic words to use in place of them. Ay, the signs

(71)

of the times are encouraging.    Look at what is being done at Oxford and Cambridge, in London and in Edinburgh.    Behold what has been done during these later years by Dasent, Samuel Laing, Thorpe, Carlyle, Max Müller, Cleasby, Vigfusson, Magnússon, Morris, Hjaltalin, and others.    And look at the publications of the Clarendon press, which is now publishing Icelandic Sagas in the original text.    This is right.    Every scrap of Icelandic and Anglo-Saxon literature must be published, for we must see what those old heroes, who crushed Rome and instituted a new order of things, thought in every direction.    We must find out what their aspirations were.    To the credit of the Scandinavians it must here be said, that they began to appreciate their old Icelandic literature much sooner than the rich Englishman realized the value of the Anglo-Saxon, and that the English are indebted to Rasmus Rask, the Danish scholar, for the most valuable contribution to Anglo-Saxon studies; but it must also be admitted, in the first place, that the Scandinavians have done far too little for Icelandic, and, in the next place, that without a preparation in Icelandic, but little progress could be made in the study of Anglo-Saxon. But England, with its usual liberality in literary matters, is now rapidly making amends for the past. And well she might.    In the publication of the Icelandic and Anglo-Saxon literature she is the greatest gainer, for it is nothing less than a bridge, that will unite her present and past history.    Maurer and Möbius are watching with Argos eyes the interests of Teutonic studies in Germany.

Greek should be studied, for that is no imitation. It is indigenous.    It is a crystal clear stream flowing unadulterated from the Castalian fountain of Parnassos.

Our warfare, therefore, is not against Greek, but against
Latin. We have suffered long enough with our necks
under the ponderous Roman yoke in all its various
forms; take it as fetters forged by the Roman emperors,
as crosiers in the hands of the Roman popes, or as
rods in the hands of the Roman school-masters. The
Goths severed the fetters of the Roman emperors,
Luther and the Germans broke the crosiers of the
Roman popes, but all the Teutons have submissively
kissed the rod of the Roman school-master, although
this was the most dangerous of the three: it was the
deadly weapon concealed in the hand of the assassin.

The Romans were a people of robbers both in a
political and in a literary sense. Nay, the Roman writers themselves tell us that the divine founder of the
city, Romulus, was a captain of *robbers ;* that *Mars,*
the god of *war,* was his father; and that a *wolf (rapa-
city ),* descending from the mountains to drink, ran at
the cry of the child and fed him under a fig-tree,
caressing and licking him as if he had been her own
son, the infant hanging on to her as if she had been
his mother. This Romulus began his great exploits by
*killing his own brother.* When the new city seemed
to want women, to insure its duration, he proclaimed
a magnificent feast throughout all the neighboring vil-
lages, at which feast were presented, among other things,
the terrible shows of *gladiators.* While the strangers
were most intent upon the spectacle, a number of Roman youths rushed in among the Sabines, *seized* the
youngest and fairest of their wives and daughters, and
carried them off by *violence.* In vain the parents and
husbands protested against this *breach of hospitality.*
This same Romulus ended his heroic career by being
*assassinated* by his friends, or, as others say, *torn in*

*pieces* in the senate-house. Certain it is that the Romans *murdered* him, and then declared him the guardian spirit of the city; thus worshiping as a god, by name Quirinus, him whom they could not bear as a king. Such falsehoods as the one the senate invented, when they said that Romulus, whom they had murdered, had been taken up into heaven, the Roman writers tell us were constantly taught to the Romans by Numa Pompilius, and by other Sabine and Etrurian priests; and such instruction laid the foundation of their myths. The history of Romulus is, in fact, in miniature, the history of Rome.

But in spite of this, and much else that can in justice be said against Rome and Latin, we cannot afford to throw the language and literature of the Romans entirely overboard. Their history was too remarkable for that; besides, many scribbled in Latin down through the middle ages, and the Latin language has played so conspicuous a part in English literature, and in the sciences, that no educated man can very well do without it. What we respectfully object to is making it the foundation of all education, this *bringing the scholar up,* so to speak, on Latin language, history and literature; this nourishing and moulding the tender heart and mind on *Roman thought,*— thus making the man, intellectually and morally, a slave bound in Roman chains, while we free-born Goths, the descendants of Odin and Thor, ought to begin our education and receive our first impressions from our own ancestors. The tree should draw its nourishment from its own roots; and we Americans are the youngest and most vigorous branch of that glorious Gothic tree, the beautiful and noble Ygdrasil in the Norse cosmogony, whose three grand roots strike down among the Anglo-Saxons,

Scandinavians, and Germans.    In order fully to comprehend the man, we must study the life of the child;
and in order to comprehend ourselves as a people, we
must study our own ancient history and literature and
make ourselves thoroughly acquainted with the imaginative and prophetic childhood of the Teutonic race.
We must give far more attention than we do, first, to
English and Anglo-Saxon, and we must, as we have
heard Dr. S. H. Carpenter, of the University of Wisconsin, most truthfully remark, begin with the most
modern English, and then follow it step by step, century by century, back to the most ancient Anglo-Saxon.
A *living* language can be learned ten times as fast as a
dead one, and we would apply Dr. Carpenter's* principle still further.    We would make one of the living
Romanic languages (French, Italian, or Spanish,) a key
to the Latin; and above all, we would make modern
Greek a preparation for old classic Greek.    It cannot
be controverted that children learn to read and write a
language much sooner and easier if they first learn to
speak it, even though the book-speech may differ con-
siderably from the dialect which the child learned from
his mother; ample evidence of which fact may be found
in the different counties of England and Scotland and
throughout the European countries.

In the next place, that is, next after English and
Anglo-Saxon, we must study German, Mæso-Gothic and
the Scandinavian languages, and especially Icelandic,
which is the only *living* key to the history of the middle ages, and to the Old Norse literature.    It is the only
language now in use in an almost unchanged form,
through a knowledge of which we can read the litera-

* Author of *English of the Fourteenth Century* and of *An Introduction to
the Study of the Anglo-Saxon Language.*

ture of the middle ages.  We must by no means forget
that we have Teutonic antiquities to which we stand
in an entirely different and far closer relation than we
do to Greece or Rome.  And the Norsemen have an old
literature, which the scholar must of necessity be familiar with in order to comprehend the history of the
middle ages.

When we have thus done justice to our own Teutonic race we may turn our attention to the ancient
peoples around the Mediterranean Sea, the most important of which in literary and historical respects are the
Hebrews, Greeks and Romans.  The antiquities of these
peoples will always form important departments in our
colleges and universities, and it is our duty to study
them; but they should not, as they still to a great
extent do, constitute the all-absorbing subject of our
attention, the *summa summarum,* the foundation and
superstructure of our education and culture.

It has been argued by some that the Latin is
more terse than English; but did the reader ever reflect
that it takes about *sixty syllables* in Latin to express
all that we can say in English with *forty syllables?*
The large number of inflectional endings have also been
lauded as a point of superior excellence in the Latin;
but as a language *grows* and makes *progress,* it gradually emancipates itself from the thraldom of inflection
and contents itself with the abstract, spiritual chain
that links the words together into sentences; and
did the reader ever run across this significant truth,
expressed by George P. Marsh, who says that in
Latin you have to be able to analyse and parse a
sentence before you can comprehend it, while in English you must comprehend the sentence before you
can analyse or parse?  *Forward* has been and will

forever be the watchword of languages. They must either progress or die.

When the question is asked, whether Hebrew, Greek or Latin should be preferred by the student, we answer that the choice is not a difficult one to make, and our opinion has in fact already been given. Latin is the language of a race of robbers; most of it is nothing but imitation, and besides it is a mere corpse, while Greek is the only one of the three that is still living, and modern Greek — for that is what we must begin with — is the key to the old Greek literature with its rich, beautiful and original store of mythology, poetry, history, oratory, and philosophy. As Icelandic in the extreme north of Europe is the *living* key to the middle ages and to the celebrated Old Norse Eddas and Sagas, so modern Greek in the far south is the *living* language, that introduces us to the spirit of Homer, Herodotus, Demosthenes, and Plato; and thus the norns or fates, who preside over the destinies of men and nations, have in a most wonderful manner knit, or rather woven, us together with the Greeks, and the more we investigate the development and progress of nations and civilization, the more vividly the truth will flash upon our minds, that the Greek and the Icelandic are two silver-haired veterans, who hold in their hands two golden keys,— the one to unlock the treasures of ancient times, the other those of the middle ages; the one the treasures of the south and the other those of the north of Europe. But we must free ourselves from the bondage of Rome!

When we get away from Rome, where slaves were employed as teachers, and pay more attention to the antiquities of Greece, where it was the highest honor that the greatest, noblest and most eloquent men could attain to, to be listened to by youths eager to learn and to be taught, then the present slavery both of the teacher and of the student will cease, but scarcely before then.

The case of Shakespeare is an eminent example to us of what the Goth is able to accomplish, when he breaks the Roman chains. His works are not an imitation of Seneca or Æschylus, nor are they the fruit of a careful study of the *Ars Poetica* or *Gradus ad Parnassum*. No, he knew but little Latin and less Greek, but what made him the undisputed Hercules in English literature was the heroic spirit of Gothdom which flowed in his veins, and which drove him away from the Latin school before his emotional nature had been flogged and tortured out of him. Shakespeare, and not Roman literature and scholasticism, is the lever that has raised English literature and given it the first rank among all the Teutons. It is not, we repeat, the deluge of Latin words that flood it, that has given this preëminence to English, but it is the genuine Gothic strength that everywhere has tried to break down the Roman walls. The slaves of Latin will find it difficult enough to explain how Shakespeare, who was not for an age, but for all time,— he whose Latin was small and whose Greek was less,— how he, the star of poets, the sweet swan of Avon, was *made* as well as born. Ay, he was made. *He* was also one of those who, to cast a living line had to sweat, and strike the second heat upon the Muses' anvil. It is true that Shakespeare did not arrive at a full appreciation of the Gothic spirit, for he did not have an opportunity to acquaint himself thoroughly with the Gothic myths; but then they ever haunted him like the ghost of Hamlet, accusing their

murderer, without finding any avenger. We therefore
count Shakespeare on our side of this great question.

May the time speedily come, nay, the time must come,
when Greek and Anglo-Saxon and Old Norse and Gothic
and German will shake hands over the bloody chasm of
Roman vandalism!

We fancy we see more than one who reads this chapter, and does not remember that he is a son of Thor,
stretch out his hand for Mjolner, that huge and mighty
hammer of Thor, to swing it at us for what we have said
and have not said about Rome, Roman mythology, and
the Latin language and literature; but, alas! for him,
and fortunately for us, the Roman school-master took
Thor's hammer away from him and whipped the strength
wherewith to wield it out of him. We only repeat that
we know nothing of Roman mythology, but the Greek
and Norse are twin sisters, and with the assistance of the
Mosaic-Christian religion they have a grand mission in
the Gothic-Greek development of the world.

Note.—Fearing lest some of our readers may consider these emphatic
assertions wild, unfounded, and not sustained by the highest authority, we
take the liberty of making the following quotations from H. A. Taine, who is
himself a disciple of Guizot, the historian of civilization. On page 17 of
Taine's *English Literature*, Vol. I (Van Laun's translation), we read: If man,
reduced to narrow conceptions and deprived of all speculative refinement, is at
the same time altogether absorbed and straightened by practical occupations,
you will find, *as in Rome*, rudimentary deities, mere hollow names, serving to
designate the trivial details of agriculture, generation, household concerns, eti-
quettes,— in fact, of marriage, of the farm,— producing a mythology, a philosophy, a poetry, either worth nothing or borrowed.

On page 20 of that same work Taine says: Among the ancients, the Latin
literature is worth *nothing* at the outset, then borrowed and imitative.

Thus it will be seen that we are not alone in our opposition to Romanism,
and with Taine we might even be willing to be wrong for the present.

# CHAPTER V.

## INTERPRETATION OF NORSE MYTHOLOGY.

CONSIDERABLE has been said on this subject in the preceding pages, and the interpretation which will be adhered to in this volume has been clearly indicated. We propose now to give a general synopsis of the more prominent methods of interpreting Norse mythology.

In one thing all undoubtedly agree, namely, that all mythologies embody religious faith. As we, even to this day, each in his own way, seek to find God by philosophical speculation (natural theology), by our emotions, by good deeds, or by all these at one time; and as we, when we have found him, rest upon his breast, although we do not fully agree as to our conception of him, each one of us having his own God as each has his own rainbow; thus our forefathers sought God everywhere — in the rocks, in the babbling stream, in the heavy ear of grain, in the star-strewn sky of night, and in the splendor of the sun. It was revelations of divinity that they looked for. The fundamental element in their mythology was a religious one, and this fact must never be lost sight of. To interpret a myth, then, is not only to give its source, but also its aim and object, together with the thoughts and feelings that it awakens in the human breast.

Some writers (William and Mary Howitt and others) maintain that the Norse mythology is a degradation of,

or aberration from, the *true religion*, which was revealed
to man in the earliest period of the history of the human
race and is found pure and undefiled in the Bible;
that it presents sparkling waters from the original fountain of tradition. They point with seriousness to it as
something that bears us on toward the primal period
of one tongue and one religion. In reference to the
Elder Edda, they say that it descended through vast
ages, growing, like all traditions, continually darker,
and accumulating lower matter and more divergent and
more pagan doctrines, as the walls of old castles become
covered with mosses and lichens, till it finally assumed
the form in which it was collected from the mouths
of the people, and put in a permanent written form.
These interpreters claim that through all mythologies
there run certain great lines, which converge toward
one common center and point to an original source of
a religious faith, which has grown dimmer and more
disfigured, the further it has gone. The geographical
center, they say, from which all these systems of heathen
belief have proceeded is the same — Central Asia; they
point to the eastern origin of the Norseman; they assert,
with full confidence, that the religious creed of the Norseman is the faith of Persia, India, Greece, and every other
country, transferred to the snow-capped mountains of
Norway and jokuls of Iceland, having only been modified
there, so as to give it an air of originality without destroying its primeval features. They argue that Loke
of the Norsemen, Pluto of the Greeks, Ahriman of the
Persians, Siva of the Hindoos, etc., are all originally the
devil of the Bible, who has changed his name and more
or less his personal form and characteristics. The
biblical Trinity is degenerated into the threefold trinity
of Odin, Vile, and Ve; Odin, Hœner, and Loder; and

6

Odin, Thor, and Balder.   They find in the Norse cosmogony, in a somewhat mutilated and interpolated condition, the Scripture theory of the creation, preservation,
destruction and regeneration of the world.   Ygdrasil
is the tree of life in the garden of Eden; Ask and
Embla, the first human pair, are Adam and Eve; the
blood of the slain giant Ymer, in which the whole race
of frost-giants was drowned, (excepting one pair, who
were saved, and from whom a new giant race descended,)
is the flood of Noah, the deluge; the citadel called Midgard is the tower of Babel; in the death of Balder, by
Hoder, who was instigated by Loke, they find the cruci-
fixion of Christ by Judas, instigated by the devil, etc.;
displaying a vast amount of erudition, profoundness and
ingenuity, that might have been applied to some good
purpose.   We refrain from giving more of the results
of their learned and erudite investigations, from fear
of seducing ourselves or our readers into the adoption
of their absurdities.

Other scholars (Snorre Sturleson, Saxo Grammaticus,
Suhm, Rask, and others,) give us what is called an *historical* interpretation, asserting that Odin, Thor, Balder,
and the other deities that figure in the Norse mythology,
are veritable ancestors of the Norsemen,— men and
women who have lived in the remote past; and as distance lends enchantment to the view, so the ordinary
kings and priests of pre-historic times have been magnified
into gods.   Odin and the other divinities are in Snorre
Sturleson's Heimskringla represented as having come to
Norseland from the great Svithiod, a country lying between the Black Sea and the Caspian Sea.   According to
the historical interpretation the mythical worlds are real
countries that can be pointed out on the map.   This was
the prevailing view taken during the last two centuries,

and even that sagacious scholar of the earlier part of this century, Professor Rasmus Rask, adheres almost exclusively to the historical interpretation.

It is curious to read these old authors and observe how sincerely they have looked upon Odin as an extraordinary and enterprising person who formerly ruled in the North and inaugurated great changes in the government, customs and religion of Norway, Sweden, and Denmark. They speak of the great authority which he enjoyed, and how he even had divine honors paid to him. They ingeniously connect Odin with the Roman Commonwealth, with Mithridates and Pompey (see p. 232). This historical sketch of Odin will be given in connection with the Odinic myth; suffice it here to say that the king of Pontus and all his barbarian allies were obliged to yield to the genius of Pompey. And here it is said that Odin was one of the number defeated by Pompey. He was obliged to withdraw himself by flight from the vengeance of the Romans! Odin came to Norway by way of Holstein and Jutland. On his way through Denmark he founded the city Odinse, and placed his son Skjold upon the Danish throne. How profound! What erudition! How much like the enthusiastic work of the Swede Rudbeck, who makes out the Atlantis of Plato to be Sweden, and shows that Japhet, son of Noah, came there and settled with his family! What profound learning (*gelahrtheit*) these men must have possessed! We are amazed and confounded at the vast amount of mental force that has been brought into activity, at the untiring zeal and the marvelous ingenuity, with which these theories have been set up; but we cannot witness all this without a feeling of deep regret that so much erudition and ingenuity. so much mental strength, was so fruitlessly thrown away. They were generally profound *Latin* scholars, and wrote the most of their books in Latin; but those ponderous tomes make their authors fools in folios in. the light of modern historical knowledge. They studied by that kind of lamp that illuminates a small spot on the table, but leaves the whole room dark. A more careful and enlightened study of our early literature has of course given the death-blow to so prosaic an interpretation of the Norse mythology as the purely historical one is.

Then we are met by the so-called *ethical* interpretation of mythology, seeking its origin in man's peculiar nature, especially in a moral point of view. The advocates of this theory claim that mythology is a mere fiction created to satisfy man's spiritual, moral, and emotional nature. The gods according to this interpretation represent man's virtues and vices, emotions, faculties of mind and muscle, etc., personified. Odin, they say, is wisdom; Balder is goodness; Thor is strength; Heimdal is grace, etc. Again: Thor is the impersonation of strength and courage; the giants represent impotent sloth and arrogance; the conflicts between Thor and the giants are a struggle going on in the human breast. And again: the mischief-maker Loke instigated the blind Hoder to kill the good Balder; Nanna, Balder's wife, took her husband's death so much to heart, that she died of grief; Hoder is afterwards slain by Odin's son Vale; all nature weeps for Balder, but still he is not released from Hel (hell). That is, physical strength with its blind earthly desires (Hoder), guided by sin (Loke), unconsciously kills innocence, (Balder). Love (Nanna) dies broken-hearted; reflection (Vale) is aroused and subdues physical strength (Hoder); but innocence (Balder) has vanished from the world to remain in Hel's regions until the earth is regenerated, after Ragnarok. The ethical interpretation makes the gods the faculties of the spirit, and the giants the faculties of the body, in man; and between the two, soul and body, there is a constant struggle for supremacy. This interpretation is very good, because it is very *poetic*, but it has more to do with the application of the myths than with their primary source.

Finally, an interpretation, that has frequently been alluded to in the preceding pages of this introduction, is the *physical*, or interpretation from nature,— impersonation of the visible workings of nature. The divinities are the forces and phenomena of nature personified; and evidence of the correctness of this view can be abundantly presented by defining etymologically the names of the several divinities, their attributes, dwellings and achievements, and by showing how faithfully the works of the gods correspond with the events and scenes of the outward world. There is no doubt that this is the true interpretation of all mythologies; and that it is, so to speak, the key to the Norse mythology, it is hoped will be sufficiently demonstrated in the second part of this book in connection with the myths themselves; but the ethical, or perhaps better the spiritual, interpretation must by all means be added. The spiritual or ethical and the physical interpretation must be combined. In other words, we can scarcely make the interpretation too *anthropomorphic*. The phenomena and forces of nature have been personified by our forefathers into deities, but the myths have been elaborated to suit and correspond with the moral, intellectual and emotional nature,— the inner life of man. The deities have been conceived in a human form, with human attributes and affections. The ancient Norsemen have made their mythology reflect human nature, and have clothed the gods with their own faculties of mind and body in respect to good and evil, virtue and vice, right and wrong. As Rudolf Keyser beautifully expresses himself:

The gods are the ordaining powers of nature clothed in personality. They direct the world, which they created; but beside them stand the mighty goddesses of fate and time, the great norns, who sustain the world-structure, the all-embracing tree of the world (Ygdrasil). The life of the world is a struggle between the good and light gods on the one side, and the offspring of chaotic matter, the giants, nature's disturbing forces, on the other. This struggle extends also into man's being: the spirit proceeds from the gods, the body belongs to the world of the giants; they struggle with each other for the supremacy. If the spirit conquers by virtue and bravery, man goes to heaven after death, to fight in concert with the gods against the evil powers; but if the body conquers and links the spirit to itself by weakness and low desires, then man sinks after death to the world of the giants in the lower regions, and joins himself with the evil powers in the warfare against the gods.

Nature is the mother at whose breast we all are nourished. In ancient times she was the object of childlike contemplation, nay, adoration. Nature and men were in close communion with each other, much closer than we now are. They had a more delicate perception of, and more sympathy for, suffering nature; and it were well if some of the purity of this thought could be breathed down to us, their prosaic descendants, who have abandoned the offerings to give place to avarice (die Habsucht nahm zu, als die Opfer aufhörten.— Grimm).

It was a beautiful custom, which is still preserved in some parts of Norway, to fasten a bundle of grain to a long pole, which on Christmas eve was erected somewhere in the yard, or on the top of the house or barn, for the wild birds to feed upon early on Christmas-day morning,— (our heathen ancestors also had the Christmas or Yule-tide festival). In our degenerate times we think of chickens and geese and turkeys, but who thinks of the innocent and suffering little birds ? Nay, our ancestors lay nearer to nature's breast. Have we had our hearts hardened by the iron yoke of civilized government ? We certainly need to ask ourselves that question.

The contemplation of the heavens produced the myth about Odin, and the thunder-storm suggested Thor, as in the Greek mythology Argos with his hundred eyes represents the starry heavens, and the wandering Io, whom Hera had set him to watch, is the wandering moon. But stopping here would be too prosaic; it would be leaving out the better half; it would be giving the empty shell and throwing away the kernel; it would be giving the skull of the slain warrior without any ale in it; it would be doing great injustice to our forefathers and robbing ourselves of more than half of the intellectual pleasure that a proper study of their myths afford. The old Frisians contemplated the world as a huge ship, by name Mannigfual (a counterpart of our ash-tree Ygdrasil); the mountains were its masts; the captain must go from one place to another of the ship, giving his orders, on horseback; the sailors go aloft as young men to make sail, and when they come down again their hair and beard are white. Ay, we are all sailors on board this great ship, and we all have enough to do, each in his own way, to climb its rope ladders and make and reef its sails, and ere we are aware of it our hairs are gray; but take the anthropomorphic element out of this myth, and what is there left of it ?

Our ancestors were not prosaic. They were poetic in the truest sense of that word. Our life is divided

between the child, the vigorous man, and old age,—
the imaginative and prophetic child, the emotional and
active man, and the reflecting elder. So a nation,
which like the ancient Greek and Norse, for instance,
has had a natural growth and development, has first
its childhood of imagination and prophecy, producing
poetry (Homer and the Eddas); then its manhood
of emotion and activity, producing history (Herodotus
and the Sagas); and then its old age of mature reflection, producing philosophy (Socrates). Dividing the
three periods in Greek history more definitely, we will
find that imagination and poetry predominated during
the whole time before Solon; emotion, activity and
history during the time between Solon and Alexander
the Great; and then reflection and philosophy, such as
they were, from Alexander to the collapse of the Greek
states.

Even among the Romans, the most prosaic of all
peoples, that nation of subduers, enslavers and robbers,
traces of this growth from poetic childhood through
historic manhood to philosophic old age can be found,
which proves moreover that this is a law of human
development that cannot be eradicated, although it may
be perverted. That of the Romans is a most distorted
growth, showing that as the twig is bent the tree is
inclined. *Ut sementem feceris, ita metes* — as you sow,
so will you reap,— to quote the Romans' own words
against them. The Romans had their poetic and prophetic age during the reign of the seven kings; their
emotional and historical age during the most prosperous
and glorious epoch of the republic; and finally, their
age of reflection and philosophy began with the time
of the elder Cato. Rome took a distorted, misan-
thropic course from the beginning, so that her pro-

foundest and most poetic myth is that of the *warlike* Mars and the *rapacious wolf*, the father and nurse of the *fratricide* Romulus. This myth is prophetic, and in it the whole history of Rome is reflected as in a mirror. The Romans themselves claim that their Sibylline books (prophecy) belong to the time of their kings. When, during the transition period from the emotional to the philosophic age, Rome was to have dramatic writers, she produced in comedy the clumsy Plautus, whom the Romans employed in turning a hand-mill; and in tragedy the flat Ennius, whose works were lost; so that her only really poetical tragedy is the fate of her dramatic poets. Her other poetical works, of which the world has boasted so much, came later, after the death of Cicero, their most famous orator, during the life of the crowned Augustus; they came like an Iliad after Homer, and the most of them was a poor imitation of Greek literature, just as this book is a poor imitation of Scandinavian literature. *Ex ipso fonte dulcius bibuntur aquæ* — go to the fountain itself if you want to drink the pure and sparkling water. The Roman literature is eminently worthy of the consideration of the historical philosopher, but it ought not to be canonized and used to torture the life out of students with.

The Hebrews have their imaginative, poetic and prophetic age from Genesis to Moses; their emotional and historical age from Moses to Solomon, and then begins their age of reflection and philosophy.

Taking a grand, colossal, general view of the history of the world, we would say that the ancients belong chiefly to the poetic age, the middle ages to the emotional age, and modern times to the reflecting age, of the human race. Thus the life of the individual is, in miniature, the life of a people or of the whole human family.

This was a digression, and we confess that it is not the first one we have made; but in the world of thought, as in the world of music, monotony is tedious; and the reader having perhaps refreshed his mind by the interlude, we will proceed to discuss further the union of the ethical with the physical interpretation of mythology. Physical interpretation alone is the shell without the kernel. Nature gives us only the source of the myth; but we want its value in the minds and hearts of a people in their childhood. The touching gracefulness of Nanna, and of Idun reclining on Brage's breast, was not suggested by nature alone, but the pictures of these reflect corresponding natures in our ancestors. To explain a myth simply by the phenomenon in external nature (be it remembered, however, that man also constitutes a part of nature) that suggested it to the ancients, would be reducing mythology to a natural science; and it is sad to witness how the beautiful and poetical Eddas, in the hands of some, have dwindled down into the dry chemistry, chronology, electro-magnetism, mathematics, astronomy, or, if you please, the almanacs, of our forefathers, instead of being presented as the grand, prophetic drama which foreshadowed the heroic and enterprising destiny of the Teutonic nations. The twelve dwellings of the gods, they say, represent the twelve signs of the zodiac; Balder they make the constellation of the lion; Odin's twelve names, they say, are the twelve months of the year; his fifty-two names, which he himself enumerates in Grimnismaal, are the fifty-two weeks in the year; the thirteen valkyries are the thirteen new moons in the year. How profound! How perfectly everything adapts itself to the theory! This invaluable discovery was made on the seventh of December, 1827. It ought to be a legal holiday! The one ox, three measures of mead and eight salmon which Thor, according to the Elder Edda, consumed, when he had come to Jotunheim to fetch his hammer, they claim also represent the year's twelve months, for $1+3+8=12$. Furthermore, the three gods, Haar, Jafnhaar, and Thride, are the three fundamental elements, sulphur, mercury, and salt; Odin, Vile, and Ve, are the three laws of the universe, gravity, motion, and affinity. Thor is electricity; his belt is an electric condenser, his gloves an electric conductor. Hrungner, with whom he contends, is petrifaction; the Mokkerkalfe, whom Thjalfe slew, is the magnetic needle. Gunlad is oxygen, Kvaser is sugar, etc. But this will do. Are not these golden keys, with which to unlock the secret chambers of the Eddas!

All the deities do not represent phenomena and forces of nature, and this fact gives if possible still more importance to the anthropomorphic interpretation. Some myths are mere creations of the imagination, to give symmetry and poetical finish to the system, or we might say to the drama — to complete the delineations of the characters that appear on the stage of action. Hermod, for instance, is no phenomenon in physical nature: he is the servant of Odin in the character of the latter as the god of war. Odin is the god of the heavens, but it is not in this capacity he sends out the valkyries to pick up the fallen heroes on the field of battle.

In rejecting the historical interpretation, we do by no means mean to deny the influence of the mythology upon the social, religious, political and literary life of the Norsemen. But this is not an explanation of the mythology itself, but of its influence upon the minds of the people. If we mean it in a prophetic sense, the Norse mythology has also an historical interpretation. In it was mirrored the grand future of the Norse spirit; by it the Norsemen were taught to make those daring expeditions to every part of the civilized world, making conquests and planting colonies; to cross the briny deep and open the way to Iceland, Greenland and America; to take possession of Normandy in France, subdue England and make inroads into Spain and Italy; to pass between the pillars of Hercules, devastate the classic fields of Greece, and carve their mysterious runes on the marble lion in Athens; to lay the foundations of the Russian Empire, penetrate the walls of Constantinople and swing their two-edged battle-axes in its streets; to sail up the rivers Rhine, the Scheldt, the Seine, and the Loire, conquering Cologne and Aachen and besieging Paris; to lead the van of the chivalry of Europe in rescuing the holy sepulchre and rule over Antioch and Tiberias under Harald; to sever the fetters forged by the Roman emperors, break the crosiers in the hands of the Roman popes and infuse a nobler and freer spirit into the nations of the earth; and by their mythology they were taught to give to the world that germ of liberty that struck root in the earliest literature of France, budded in the Magna Charta of England, and developed its full-blown flowers in the American Declaration of Independence.

The principal object of the second part of this volume is to give a faithful, accurate and *complete* presentation of the myths; but interpretations and reflections will be freely indulged in. The basis of the interpretation will be the physical and ethical combined, the two taken as a unit. The reflections will consist in

pointing out occasionally the fulfilment of the prophecies historically, or rather the application of the myths
to historical philosophy. When only the physical source
of the myth is given, its anthropomorphic element must
be supplied in the mind of the reader. When Thor is
given as the impersonation of thunder, and Heimdal as
the rainbow, clothed with personality, then the reader
must consider what sensations would be awakened in his
own breast by these phenomena if he had been taught
to regard them as persons. And when he has given
them stature, gait, clothing, bearing, expression of the
eye and countenance, and personal character corresponding with their lofty positions in the management of the
affairs of the world, then he can form some idea of these
deities as contemplated by the ancient Norsemen.

# CHAPTER VI.

## THE NORSE MYTHOLOGY FURNISHES ABUNDANT AND EXCELLENT MATERIAL FOR THE USE OF POETS, SCULPTORS AND PAINTERS.

IN a previous chapter it was claimed that the time must come when Norse mythology will be copiously reflected in our elegant literature and in our fine arts; and we insist that we who are Goths, and branches of the noble ash Ygdrasil, ought to develop some fibre, leaves, buds and flowers with nourishment drawn from the roots of our own tree of existence, and not be constantly borrowing from our neighbors. If our poets would but study Norse mythology, they would find in it ample material for the most sublime poetry. The Norse mythology is itself a finished poem, and has been most beautifully presented in the Elder Edda, but it furnishes at the same time a variety of themes that can be combined and elaborated into new poems with all the advantages of modern art, modern civilization and enlightenment. With the spirit of Christianity, a touch of beauty and grandeur can be unconsciously thrown over the loftiness of stature, the growth of muscle, the bold masses of intellectual masonry, the tempestuous strength of passions, those gods and heroes of impetuous natures and gigantic proportions, those overwhelming tragedies of primitive vigor, which are to be found in the Eddas. If our American poet would but pay

a visit to Urd's fountain, to Time's morning in our
Gothic history, and tarry there until the dawn tinges
the horizon with crimson and scarlet and the sun breaks
through the clouds and sends its inspiring rays into his
soul,— then his poetry and compositions would reflect
those auroral rays with intensified effulgence; it would
shine upon and enlighten and gladden a whole nation.
We need poets who can tell us, in words that burn,
about our Gothic ancestors, in order that we may be
better able to comprehend ourselves. It has heretofore
been explained how the history of nations divides itself
into three periods — the imaginative, the emotional, and
reflective; poetry, history, and philosophy; and how
these have their miniature counterparts in the life of
any single person — childhood, manhood, and old age;
and now we are prepared to present this claim, that the
poetic, imaginative and prophetic period of our race
should be compressed into the soul of the child. The
poetic period of *his own* race should be melted and
moulded into poetry, touched by a spark of Christian
refinement and love, and then poured, so to speak, into
the soul of the child. The child's mind should feed
upon the mythological stories and the primitive folk-
lore of his race. It should be nourished with milk
from its own mother's breast. Does any one doubt this?
Let him ask the Scandinavian poets: ask what kindled
the imaginative fancy of Welhaven; ask what inspired
the force and simplicity of phrase in Oelenschlæger's
poetry; ask what produced the unadorned loveliness
with which Björnstjerne Björnson expresses himself, and
the mountain torrent that rushes onward with impetuous speed in Wergeland; ask what produced the refinement of phrase of Tegner, and the wild melodious
abandon of Ibsen;— and they will tell him that in the

deep defiles of that sea-girt and rock-bound land called
Norseland, where the snow-crowned mountains tower like
castle-walls, they found in a leafy summer bower a Saga-
book full of magic words and beautiful pictures, and,
like Alexander of old, they made this wonderful book
their pillow.   They may tell you that the Scandinavian
schools, like the American, are pretty thoroughly Latin-
ized, but that they stole out of the school-room, studied
this Saga-book, and from it they drew their inspiration.

The writer once asked the famous Norse violinist, Ole
Bull, what had inspired his musical talent and given his
music that weird, original, inexplicable expression and
style.   He said, that from childhood he had taken a profound delight in the picturesque and harmonious combination of grandeur, majesty, and gracefulness of the
flower-clad valleys, the silver-crested mountains, the singing brooks, babbling streams, thundering rivers, sylvan
shores and smiling lakes of his native land.   He had
eagerly devoured all the folk-lore, all the stories about
trolls, elves and sprites that came within his reach; he
had especially reveled in all the mythological tales about
Odin, Thor, Balder, Ymer, the Midgard-serpent, Ragnarok,
etc.; and these things, he said, have made my music.
Truthfully has our own poet Longfellow, who has himself taken more than one draft from Mimer's fountain,
and communed more than once with Brage — said of
Ole Bull:

> He lived in that ideal world
> Whose language is not speech, but song;
> Around him evermore the throng
> Of elves and sprites their dances whirled;
> The Strömkarl sang, the cataract hurled
> Its headlong waters from the height,
> And mingled in the wild delight
> The scream of sea-birds in their flight,

The rumor of the forest trees,
The plunge of the implacable seas,
The tumult of the wind at night,
Voices of eld, like trumpets blowing
Old ballads and wild melodies
Through mist and darkness pouring forth
Like Elivagar's rivers flowing
Out of the glaciers of the North.

These are the things that make poets, and musicians are poets. Then continues the same author:

And when he played, the atmosphere
Was filled with music, and the ear
Caught echo of that harp of gold
Whose music had so weird a sound,
The hunted stag forgot to bound,
The leaping rivulet backward rolled,
The bird came down from bush and tree,
The dead came from beneath the sea,
The maiden to the harper's knee.

Only these few lines make it clear that Longfellow has not only communed with Brage, but has also refreshed himself at the Castalian fountain; that he has not only penetrated the mysteries of the Greek mythology, but has also visited the deities of the North.

If you do not believe that the Norse mythology furnishes suitable themes for poetry, then do not echo the voice of the multitude and cry the idea down because it seems new. Men frequently act like ants. When a red ant appears among the black ones, they all attack it, for they have once for all made up their minds that all ants must necessarily be black; they have themselves been black all their lives, and all their ancestors were black, so far as they know anything about them. Thus it has become a fixed opinion with many, that mythology necessarily means Greek or Roman. We said to one of our friends:

7

We are writing a book on Norse mythology. Says our
learned friend: Are not those old stories about Jupiter
and Mars pretty well written up by this time? We
said we thought they were, too much so; but we are
writing about Odin and Thor. Then our learned friend
shook his head in surprise and said that he never heard
of those gentlemen before. If our reader's case is the
same as that of our learned friend, then let him examine
the subject for himself. Let him read the Norse mythology through carefully. Let him then tell us what themes
suggestive of sublime poetry he found in the upper, the
middle and the lower worlds of the Odinic mythology;
how he was impressed with the regions of the gods, of the
giants, and of the dwarfs; what he thought of the various
exploits of the gods; how he was impressed with the great
and wise Odin, the good and shining Balder, the mighty
Thor, the subtle and malicious Loke, the queenly Frigg,
the genial Frey, the lovely Idun reclining on the eloquent
Brage's breast, and the gentle Nanna. Let him read and
see whether or not he will be delighted with all the magnificent scenery of Gladsheim, Valhal, Midgard, Niflheim,
Muspelheim, and Ginungagap; with the norns Urd,
Verdande, and Skuld; with the glorious ash Ygdrasil;
with the fountain of Mimer (let him take a deep drink,
while he is there); with the heavenly bridge Bifrost (the
rainbow), upon which the gods daily descend to the Urdar-
fountain; and with the wild tempest-traversed regions of
Ran (the goddess of the sea, wife of Æger). The celebrated poet Oelenschlæger found in all these things inexhaustible scope for poetic embellishments, and he availed
himself of it in his work, entitled *Gods of the North*, with
the zeal and power of a genuine poet. He revived the
memories of the past. He bade the gods come forward
out of the mists of the centuries, and he accomplished in

less than fifty years what *Latin* versions of the Eddas had not been able to accomplish in three centuries. Two of Oelenschlæger's poems are given translated in *Poets and Poetry of Europe,* and Mr. Longfellow has given us permission to present them here. We will now avail ourselves of his kindness and not discuss this portion of the subject of this chapter any further, knowing that the reader will find the poems *Thor's Fishing* and *The Dwarfs* far more pleasing and convincing than any additional arguments we might be able to produce. Here they are:

## THOR'S FISHING.

On the dark bottom of the great salt lake
Imprisoned lay the giant snake,
With naught his sullen sleep to break.

Huge whales disported amorous o'er his neck;
Little their sports the worm did reck,
Nor his dark, vengeful thoughts would check.

To move his iron fins he has no power,
Nor yet to harm the trembling shore,
With scaly rings he is covered o'er.

His head he seeks 'mid coral rocks to hide,
Nor e'er hath man his eye espied,
Nor could its deadly glare abide.

His eye-lids half in drowsy stupor close,
But short and troubled his repose,
As his quick heavy breathing shows.

Muscles and crabs, and all the shelly race,
In spacious banks still crowd for place
A grisly beard, around his face.

When Midgard's worm his fetters strives to break,
Riseth the sea, the mountains quake;
The fiends in Naastrand merry make

Rejoicing flames from Hecla's caldron flash,
Huge molten stones with deafening crash
Fly out,—its scathed sides fire-streams wash.

The affrighted sons of Ask do feel the shock,
As the worm doth lie and rock,
And sullen waiteth Ragnarok.

To his foul craving maw naught e'er came ill;
It never he doth cease to fill;
Nath' more his hungry pain can still.

Upward by chance he turns his sleepy eye,
And, over him suspended nigh,
The gory head he doth espy.

The serpent taken with his own deceit,
Suspecting naught the daring cheat,
Ravenous gulps down the bait.

His leathern jaws the barbed steel compress,
His ponderous head must leave the abyss;
Dire was Jormungander's hiss.

In giant coils he writhes his length about,
Poisonous streams he speweth out,
But his struggles help him naught.

The mighty Thor knoweth no peer in fight,
The loathsome worm, his strength despite,
Now o'ermatched must yield the fight.

His grisly head Thor heaveth o'er the tide,
No mortal eye the sight may bide,
The scared waves haste i' th' sands to hide.

As when accursed Naastrand yawns and burns,
His impious throat 'gainst heaven he turns
And with his tail the ocean spurns.

The parched sky droops, darkness enwraps the sun;
Now the matchless strength is shown
Of the god whom warriors own.

Around his loins he draws his girdle tight,
His eye with triumph flashes bright,
The frail boat splits aneath his weight;

The frail boat splits,—but on the ocean's ground
Thor again hath footing found;
Within his arms the worm is bound.

Hymer, who in the strife no part had took,
But like a trembling aspen shook,
Rouseth him to avert the stroke.

In the last night, the vala hath decreed
Thor, in Odin's utmost need,
To the worm shall bow the head.

Thus, in sunk voice, the craven giant spoke,
Whilst from his belt a knife he took,
Forged by dwarfs aneath the rock.

Upon the magic belt straight 'gan to file;
Thor in bitter scorn to smile;
Mjolner swang in air the while.

In the worm's front full two-score leagues it fell;
From Gimle to the realms of hell
Echoed Jormungander's yell.

The ocean yawned; Thor's lightnings rent the sky;
Through the storm, the great sun's eye
Looked out on the fight from high.

Bifrost i' th' east shone forth in brightest green;
On its top, in snow-white sheen,
Heimdal at his post was seen.

On the charmed belt the dagger hath no power;
The star of Jotunheim 'gan to lour;
But now, in Asgard's evil hour,

When all his efforts foiled tall Hymer saw,
Wading to the serpent's maw,
On the kedge he 'gan to saw.

The Sun, dismayed, hastened in clouds to hide,
Heimdal turned his head aside;
Thor was humbled in his pride.

The knife prevails, far down beneath the main,
The serpent, spent with toil and pain,
To the bottom sank again.

The giant fled, his head 'mid rocks to save,
Fearfully the god did rave,
With his lightnings tore the wave.

To madness stung, to think his conquest vain,
His ire no longer could contain,
Dared the worm to rise again.

His radiant form to its full height he drew,
And Mjolner through the billows blue
Swifter than the fire-bolt flew.

Hoped, yet, the worm had fallen beneath the stroke;
But the wily child of Loke
Waits her turn at Ragnarok.

His hammer lost, back wends the giant-bane,
Wasted his strength, his prowess vain;
And Mjolner must with Ran remain.

## THE DWARFS.

Loke sat and thought, till his dark eyes gleam
    With joy at the deed he'd done;
When Sif looked into the crystal stream,
    Her courage was well-nigh gone.

For never again her soft amber hair
    Shall she braid with her hands of snow;
From the hateful image she turned in despair,
    And hot tears began to flow.

In a cavern's mouth, like a crafty fox,
    Loke sat 'neath the tall pine's shade,
When sudden a thundering was heard in the rocks,
    And fearfully trembled the glade.

Then he knew that the noise good boded him naught,
 He knew that 't was Thor who was coming;
He changed himself straight to a salmon-trout,
 And leaped in a fright in the Glommen.*

But Thor changed, too, to a huge sea-gull,
 And the salmon-trout seized in his beak;
He cried: Thor, traitor, I know thee well,
 And dear shalt thou pay thy freak!

Thy caitiff's bones to a meal I'll pound,
 As a mill-stone crusheth the grain.
When Loke that naught booted his magic found,
 He took straight his own form again.

And what if thou scatter'st my limbs in air?
 He spake, will it mend thy case?
Will it gain back for Sif a single hair?
 Thou'lt still a bald spouse embrace.

But if now thou'lt pardon my heedless joke,—
 For malice sure meant I none,—
I swear to thee here, by root, billow and rock,
 By the moss on the Bauta-stone,†

By Mimer's well, and by Odin's eye,
 And by Mjolner, greatest of all,
That straight to the secret caves I'll hie,
 To the dwarfs, my kinsmen small;

And thence for Sif new tresses I'll bring
 Of gold ere the daylight's gone,
So that she will liken a field in spring,
 With its yellow-flowered garment on.

Him answered Thor: Why, thou brazen knave,
 To my face to mock me dost dare?
Thou know'st well that Mjolner is now 'neath the wave
 With Ran, and wilt still by it swear?

---

 * A river in Norway.    † A stone raised over a grave.

O a better hammer for thee I'll obtain;
    And he shook like an aspen-tree,
For whose stroke shield, buckler and greave shall be vain,
    And the giants with terror shall flee!

Not so! cried Thor, and his eyes flashed fire;
    Thy base treason calls loud for blood,
And hither I'm come with my sworn brother Frey,
    To make thee of ravens the food.

I'll take hold of thy arms and thy coal-black hair, .
    And Frey of thy heels behind,
And thy lustful body to atoms we'll tear,
    And scatter thy limbs to the wind.

O spare me, Frey, thou great-souled king!
    And, weeping, he kissed his feet;
O mercy, and thee I'll a courser bring,
    No match in the wide world shall meet.

Without whip or spur round the earth you shall ride;
    He'll ne'er weary by day nor by night;
He shall carry you safe o'er the raging tide,
    And his golden hair furnish you light.

Loke promised as well with his glozing tongue
    That the asas at length let him go,
And he sank in the earth, the dark rocks among,
    Near the cold-fountain, far below.

He crept on his belly, as supple as eel,
    The cracks in the hard granite through,
Till he came where the dwarfs stood hammering steel,
    By the light of a furnace blue.

I trow 't was a goodly sight to see
    The dwarfs, with their aprons on,
A-hammering and smelting so busily
    Pure gold from the rough brown stone.

Rock crystals from sand and hard flint they made,
    Which, tinged with the rosebud's dye,
They cast into rubies and carbuncles red,
    And hid them in cracks hard by.

They took them fresh violets all dripping with dew,
    Dwarf-women had plucked them, the morn,—
And stained with their juice the clear sapphires blue,
    King Dan in his crown since hath worn.

Then for emeralds they searched out the brightest green
    Which the young spring meadow wears,
And dropped round pearls, without flaw or stain,
    From widows' and maidens' tears.

And all around the cavern might plainly be shown
    Where giants had once been at play;
For the ground was with heaps of huge muscle-shells strewn,
    And strange fish were marked in the clay.

Here an ichthyosaurus stood out from the wall,
    There monsters ne'er told of in story,
Whilst hard by the Nix in the waterfall
    Sang wildly the days of their glory.

Here bones of the mammoth and mastodon,
    And serpents with wings and with claws;
The elephant's tusks from the burning zone
    Are small to the teeth in their jaws.

When Loke to the dwarfs had his errand made known,
    In a trice for the work they were ready;
Quoth Dvalin: O Lopter, it now shall be shown
    That dwarfs in their friendship are steady.

We both trace our line from the selfsame stock;
    What you ask shall be furnished with speed,
For it ne'er shall be said that the sons of the rock
    Turned their backs on a kinsman in need.

They took them the skin of a large wild-boar,
    The largest that they could find,
And the bellows they blew till the furnace 'gan roar,
    And the fire flamed on high for the wind.

And they struck with their sledge-hammers stroke on stroke,
    That the sparks from the skin flew on high,
But never a word good or bad spake Loke,
    Though foul malice lurked in his eye.

The thunderer far distant, with sorrow he thought
  On all he'd engaged to obtain,
And, as summer-breeze fickle, now anxiously sought
  To render the dwarfs' labor vain.

Whilst the bellows plied Brok, and Sindre the hammer,
  And Thor, that the sparks flew on high,
And the sides of the vaulted cave rang with the clamor,
  Loke changed to a huge forest-fly.

And he sat him all swelling with venom and spite, ·
  On Brok, the wrist just below;
But the dwarf's skin was thick, and he recked not the bite,
  Nor once ceased the bellows to blow.

And now, strange to say, from the roaring fire
  Came the golden-haired Gullinburste,
To serve as a charger the sun-god Frey,
  Sure, of all wild-boars this the first.

They took them pure gold from their secret store,
  The piece 't was but small in size,
But ere 't had been long in the furnace roar,
  'T was a jewel beyond all prize.

A broad red ring all of wroughten gold,
  As a snake with its tail in its head,
And a garland of gems did the rim enfold,
  Together with rare art laid.

'T was solid and heavy, and wrought with care,
  Thrice it passed through the white flames' glow;
A ring to produce, fit for Odin to wear,
  No labor they spared, I trow.

They worked it and turned it with wondrous skill,
  Till they gave it the virtue rare,
That each thrice third night from its rim there fell
  Eight rings, as their parent fair.

'T was the same with which Odin sanctified
  God Balder's and Nanna's faith;
On his gentle bosom was Draupner laid,
  When their eyes were closed in death.

Next they laid on the anvil a steel-bar cold,
  They needed nor fire nor file ;
But their sledge-hammers, following, like thunder rolled,
  And Sindre sang runes the while.

When Loke now marked how the steel gat power,
  And how warily out 't was beat
('T was to make a new hammer for Ake-Thor),
  He'd recourse once more to deceit.

In a trice, of a hornet the semblance he took,
  Whilst in cadence fell blow on blow,
In the leading dwarf's forehead his barbed sting he stuck,
  That the blood in a stream down did flow.

Then the dwarf raised his hand to his brow for the smart,
  Ere the iron well out was beat,
And they found that the haft by an inch was too short,
  But to alter it then 't was too late.

Now a small elf came running with gold on his head,
  Which he gave a dwarf woman to spin,
Who the metal like flax on her spinning wheel laid,
  Nor tarried her task to begin.

So she span and span, and the gold thread ran
  Into hair, though Loke thought it a pity ;
She span and sang to the sledge-hammer's clang
  This strange, wild spinning-wheel ditty :

Henceforward her hair shall the tall Sif wear,
  Hanging loose down her white neck behind ;
By no envious braid shall it captive be made,
  But in native grace float in the wind.

No swain shall it view in the clear heaven's blue,
  But his heart in its toils shall be lost ;
No goddess, not e'en beauty's faultless queen,
  Such long glossy ringlets shall boast.

Though they now seem dead, let them touch but her head,
  Each hair shall the life-moisture fill ;
Nor shall malice nor spell henceforward prevail
  Sif's tresses to work aught of ill.

His object attained, Loke no longer remained
  'Neath the earth, but straight hied him to Thor,
Who owned than the hair ne'er, sure, aught more fair
  His eyes had e'er looked on before.

The boar Frey bestrode, and away proudly rode,
  And Thor took the ringlets and hammer;
To Valhal they hied, where the asas reside,
  'Mid of tilting and wassal the clamor.

At a full solemn ting, Thor gave Odin the ring,
  And Loke his foul treachery pardoned;
But the pardon was vain, for his crimes soon again
  Must do penance the arch-sinner hardened.

For the benefit of those who can read Danish, we
will give in the original the last ten stanzas of the
latter poem of Oehlenschlæger, beginning with the spinning of Sif's hair:

Nu kom med Guldet en Dværgeflok
  Og gave det til Dværginden;
Hun satte, som Hör, det paa sin Rok,
  Hvis Hjul hensused for Vinden.

Og spandt og spandt, mens Guldtraaden randt
  Til Haar for den deilige Dise;
Hun snurred og sang, ved Kildernes Klang,
  En underlig Spindevise:

Gudinden i Vaar skal bære sit Haar
  Hel frit for Vinden herefter,
Ei flette det mer, at yndig sig ter
  Dets Glands med straalende Kræfter.

Hver Svend, som det saa, fra Himmelens Blaa,
  Hans Hjerte skal Haarene fange.
Selv Lokker vist ei paa veneste Frey
  Nedbölge saa blöde, saa lange.

Skjönt Guldet er dödt, saasnart det har mödt
  Gudindens Tinding, den höie,
Det levende blier og efter sig gier,
  Og lader, som Hörren, sig böie.

Beholder sin Glands, i Vindenes Dands,
  Og lader sig aldrig udrykke;
Som Middagens Skin, det svöber sig ind
  Bag Hjelmens ludende Skygge!—

Saa sang hun og gik med ydmyge Blik
  For Thor, og rakte ham Haaret;
Paa Lokken han saa og maatte tilstaa:
  Saa fager var ingen baaret.

Fra Bjerget valt nu Frey paa sin Galt
  Og Thor med Haaret og Hammer,
Til Valhal de for, hvor Hærfader bor
  I Lysets salige Flammer.

Da satte paa Sif lig Tang paa et Rif,
  Sig fast Guldhaaret paa stande,
Og monne sig slaa i Lokker saa smaa,
  ˙ Trindt om den hvælvede Pande.

Paa straalende Thing fik Odin sin Ring,
  Man tilgav Loke sin Bröde.
Men snart dog igjen Bjergtroldenes Ven
  Maa for sin Trolöshed böde.

There remains now to discuss briefly whether the
Norse mythology furnishes subjects for painting and
sculpture. If the reader has become convinced that there
is material in it worthy of the greatest poet, then it is
not necessary to say much about painting and sculpture, for we know that most things that can be said in
verse can be made visible on the canvas, or be chiseled
in marble. We shall therefore be brief on this particular
point, but after the presentation of a few subjects for
the painter or sculptor, we shall have something to say
about nude art.

Can the brush or the chisel ask for more suggestive
subjects than Odin, Balder,• Thor, Frey, Idun, Nanna,
Loke, etc.? or groups like the norns at the Urdar-

fountain? or Urd (the past) and Verdande (the present), who stretch from east to west a web, which is torn to pieces by Skuld (the future); the valkyries in the heat of the battle picking up the slain; or when they carry the fallen Hakon Adelsten to Valhal? Cannot a beautiful picture be made of Æger and Ran and their daughters, the waves? of the gods holding their feast with Æger and sending out Thor to fetch a caldron for them from Jotunheim? or of Thor clapping the pot on his head like a huge hat and walking off with it? What more touching scene can be perceived than the death of Balder? Only in that short poem Hamarsheimt (fetching the hammer) there are no less than three beautiful subjects: (1) Thor wakes up and misses his hammer; he feels around him for it; he is surprised and hesitates; he wrinkles his brows and his head trembles. Loke looks down upon him from above; the rogue is in his eye; he would like to break out in a roar of laughter, but dare not. (2) All the gods are engaged in dressing Thor in Freyja's clothes; he is a tall straight youth with golden hair and a fine brown beard; lightning flashes from his eyes; while Fulla puts on him Freyja's jewels there is a terrible conflict going on in his breast with this humiliation of his dignity, which he cannot overcome. Loke stands half-ready near by as maid-servant; he dresses Thor's hair and is himself half-covered by the bridal-veil which Thor is to wear. All take an intense interest in the work, for they are so anxious to have the stratagem succeed. (3) The giants have laid the hammer in the lap of the bride; Thor seizes it, and as he pushes aside the veil he literally grows into his majestic divinity, for whenever he wields his mighty Mjolner his strength is redoubled. The disappointed desire of Thrym, the astounded giants, the amused Loke; all furnish an endless variety of excellent material for the brush of the painter. The plastic art can find no more exquisite group than Loke bound upon three stones, and his loving wife, Sigyn, leaning over him with a dish, wherein she catches the drops of venom that would otherwise fall into his face and intensify his agonies. A volume of themes might be presented, but it is not necessary. Suffice it then to say that for poetry, painting and the plastic arts, there is in the Norse mythology a fountain of delight whose waters but few have tasted, but which no man can drain dry.

We promised to say something about nude art. It is this: We Goths are, and have forever been, a *chaste* race. We abhor the loathsome nudity of Greek art. We do not want nude figures, at least not unless they embody some very sublime thought. The people of southern Europe differ widely from us Northerners in this respect; and this difference reaches far back into our respective mythologies, adding additional proof to the fact that the myths foreshadow the social life of a nation or race of people. The Greek gods were generally conceived as nude, and hence Greek art would naturally be nude also. Whether the licentiousness and lasciviousness of the Greek communities were the primary causes of the unæsthetical features of their mythology or their Bacchanalian revels sprang from the mythology, it is difficult to determine. We undoubtedly come nearest the truth when we say that the same primeval causes produced both the social life and mythology of the Greeks; that there thenceforward was an active reciprocating influence between the religion on the one side and the popular life on the other, an influence that

we may liken unto that which operates between the
soul and the body; and thus it may be said that the mythology and the popular life combined produced their
nude art. To say that the popular character of the
Greeks, taken individually or collectively, was stimulated into life by their mythology; that the virtues
and the vices of the people originated in it *alone;*
would certainly be an incorrect and one-sided view of
the subject. The Greeks brought with them, from their
original home into Greece, the germs of that faith which
afterwards became developed in a certain direction under
the influence of the popular life and the action of
external circumstances upon that life, but which in turn
reacted upon the popular life with a power which
increased in proportion as the system of mythology
acquired by development a more decided character.
The same is true of the Norsemen and of the Goths
in general. When it is found, for instance, that the
mythological representation of Odin as father of the
slain (Val-father), and that Valhal (the hall of the slain),
the valkyries and einherjes, contain a strong incentive
to warlike deeds, then it must not be imagined that this
martial spirit, that displayed itself so powerfully among
the Goths generally, and among the Norsemen particularly, was the offspring of the mythology of our ancestors; but we may rather conceive that the Norsemen
were from the beginning a race of remarkable physical
power, that accidental external causes, such as severe
climate, mountainous country, conflicts with neighboring peoples, etc., brought this inherent physical force
into activity and thus awakened the warlike spirit; and
then it may be said that this martial spirit stamped
itself upon their religious ideas, upon their mythology,
and finally that the mythology, when it had received

this characteristic impress from the people, again reacted to preserve and even further inflame that martial spirit. And there is no inconsistency between this view of the subject and that which was presented in the third chapter.

It was said at the outset that we Goths are a chaste race, and abhor the loathsome nudity of Greek art. We were a chaste people before our fathers came under the influence of Christianity. The Elder Edda, which is the grand depository of the Norse mythology, may be searched through and through, and there will not be found a single nude myth, not an impersonation of any kind that can be considered an outrage upon virtue or a violation of the laws of propriety; and this feature of the Odinic religion deserves to be urged as an important reason why our painters and sculptors should look at home for something wherewith to employ their talent, before they go abroad; look in our own ancient Gothic history, before going to ancient Greece.

But the artist who is going to chisel out an Odin, a Thor, a Balder, a Nanna, or a Loke, must not be a mere imitator. He must possess a creative mind. He must not go to work at a piece of Norse art with his imagination full of Greek myths, much less must he attempt to apply Greek principles to a piece of Gothic art. He will find the Norse chisel a somewhat more ponderous weapon to swing; and you cannot turn as rapidly with a railroad car as you can with a French *fiacre* or American gig. To try to chisel out the gods of *our* forefathers after South European patterns would be like attempting to write English with the mind full of Latin syntax. Hence we repeat, that we do not want an imitator, but an original genius. Greek mythology has been presented so many times, and so well,

8

that the imitation, the repetition, is comparatively easy. He who would bring out Gothic art (and but little of it has hitherto been brought out) must himself be a poet, and what a mine of wealth there is open to him! Would that genuine art fever would attack our artists and that some of the treasures that lie hid in the granite quarries of the Norse mythology might speedily be exhumed!

In his work, entitled *Science of Beauty*, Dr. John Bascom has taken decided grounds against nude figures in art. We would recommend the eighth chapter of that work to the careful consideration of the reader. We are not able for want of space to give his opinion in full, but make the following brief extract:

There is one direction in which art has indulged itself in a most marked violation of propriety, and that too on the side of vice. I refer to the frequent nudity of its figures. This is a point upon which artists have been pretty unanimous, and disposed to treat the opinions of others with *hauteur* and disdain, as arising at best from a virtue more itching and sensitive than wise, from instincts more physical than æsthetical. This practice has been more abused in painting than in sculpture, both as less needed, and hence less justifiable, and as ever tending to become more loose and lustful in the double symbols of color and form, than when confined to the pure, stern use of the latter in stone or metal. Despite alleged necessities,—despite the high-toned claims and undisguised contempt of artists,—our convictions are strongly against the practice, as alike injurious to taste and morals. Indeed, if injurious to morals, it cannot be otherwise than injurious to taste, since art has no more dangerous enemy than a lascivious perverted fancy.

Nay, in the radiant dawn of our Gothic history our poets and artists may, if they would but look for them, find chaste themes to which they may consecrate the whole ardor of their souls for the æsthetical elevation and ennoblement of our race. As a people we are growing too prosaic and, therefore, too ungodly; we nourish the tender minds of our children too early and too extensively on dry reasoning, mathematics and philosophy, instead of strengthening, stimulating and beautifying their souls with some of the poetic thoughts, some of the mythology and folk-lore of our forefathers. These mythological stories, these fairy tales and all this folklore, illuminated by the genial rays of the Christian religion shining upon them, should be made available in our families and schools, by our poets, painters and sculptors, and then our children would in turn get their æsthetical natures developed so as to be able to beautify their own life and that of their posterity with still finer productions in poetry, painting, and sculpture.

# CHAPTER VII.

## THE SOURCES OF NORSE MYTHOLOGY AND INFLUENCE OF THE ASA-FAITH.

IN order to thoroughly comprehend the Odinic mythology it is necessary to make a careful study of the history, literature, languages and dialects of the Teutonic races and of their popular life in all its various manifestations.

The chief depositories of the Norse mythology are the Elder or Sæmund's Edda (poetry) and the Younger or Snorre's Edda (prose). In Icelandic *Edda* means *great-grandmother*, and some think this appellation refers to the ancient origin of the myths it contains. Others connect it with the Indian *Veda* and the Norse *vide* (Swedish *veta*, to know).

### I. *The Elder Edda.*

This work was evidently collected from the mouths of the people in the same manner as Homer's *Iliad*, and there is a similar uncertainty in regard to who put it in writing. It has generally been supposed that the songs of the Elder Edda were collected by Sæmund the Wise (born 1056, died 1133), but Sophus Bugge and N. M. Petersen, both eminent Icelandic scholars, have made it seem quite probable that it was not put in writing before the year 1240. This is not the place for a discussion of this difficult question, and the reader is referred to Sophus Bugge's Introduction to *Sæmundar Edda* and

to Petersen's *History of Northern Literature*, if he wishes
to investigate this subject. There are thirty-nine poems
in the Elder Edda, and we have here to look at their
contents. Like the most of the Icelandic poetry, these
poems do not distinguish themselves, as does the poetry of
Greece and Rome, by a metrical system based on quantity, but have an arrangement of their own in common
with the poetry of the other old Gothic nations, the Anglo-
Saxons, etc. This system consists chiefly in the number of *long syllables* and in *alliteration*. The songs are
divided into strophes commonly containing eight verses
or lines. These strophes are usually divided into two
halves, and each of these halves again into two parts,
which form a fourth part of the whole strophe, and
contain two verses belonging together and united by
alliteration.

The alliteration (letter rhyme) is the most essential
element in Icelandic versification. It is found in all
kinds of verse and in every age, the Icelanders still
using it; and its nature is this, that in the two lines
belonging together, three words occur beginning with
the same letter, two of which must be in the first
line and the third in the beginning of the second.
The third and last of these is called the chief letter
(*höfuðstafr*, head-stave), because it is regarded as ruling
over the two others which depend on it and have the
name sub-letters (*studlar*, supporters). All rhyme-letters must be found in accented syllables, and no more
words in the two lines should begin with the same
letter — at least no chief word, which takes the accent
on the first syllable. This principle is illustrated by
the following first half of the seventh strophe of Völuspá, the oldest song in the Elder Edda:

> *T*efldu í *t*úni,
> *T*eitir váru;
> *V*ar þeim *v*ettugis
> *V*ant ór gulli.

Free version in English:

> With *g*olden tablets in the *g*arden
> *G*lad they played,
> Nor *w*as there to the *v*aliant gods
> *W*ant of gold.

The rhyme-letters here are those in *italics*.

The poems of the Elder Edda are in no special connection one with the other, and they may be divided into three classes: purely mythological, mythological-didactic, and mythological-historical poems.

The Elder Edda presents the Norse cosmogony, the doctrines of the Odinic mythology, and the lives and doings of the gods. It contains also a cycle of poems on the demi-gods and mythic heroes and heroines of the same period. It gives us as complete a view of the mythological world of the North as Homer and Hesiod do of that of Greece. But (to use in part the language of the Howitts) it presents this to us not as Homer does, worked up into one great poem, but as the rhapsodists of Greece presented to Homer's hands the materials for that great poem in the various hymns and ballads of the fall of Troy, which they sung all over Greece. No Homer ever arose in Norseland to mould all these sublime lyrics of the Elder Edda into one lordly epic. The story of Sigurd and Brynhild, which occupies the latter portion of the Elder Edda, was, in later times in Germany moulded into the great and beautiful *Niebelungen-Lied;* although it was much altered by the German poet or by German tradition. The poems of the Elder Edda show us what the myths of Greece would have been without a Homer. They remain huge, wild and fragmentary; full of strange gaps rent into their very vitals by the strokes of rude centuries; yet like the ruin of the Colosseum or the temples of Pæstum, standing aloft amid the daylight of the present time, magnificent testimonials of the stupendous genius of the race which reared them. There is nothing besides the Bible, which sits in a divine tranquillity of unapproachable nobility like a king of kings amongst all other books, and the poem of Homer itself, which can compare in all the elements of greatness with the Edda. There is a loftiness of stature, and a firmness of muscle about it which no poets of the same race have ever since reached. The only production since, that can be compared with the Elder Edda in profoundness of thought, is that of Shakespeare, the Hercules or Thor in English literature, that heroic mind of divine lineage which passed through the hell-gates of the Roman school-system unscathed. The obscurity which still hangs over some parts of the Elder Edda, like the deep shadows crouching amid the ruins of the past, is the result of neglect, and will in due time be removed; but amid this stand forth the boldest masses of intellectual masonry. We are astonished at the wisdom which is shaped into maxims, and at the tempestuous strength of passions to which all modern emotions seem puny and constrained. Amid the bright sun-light of a far-off time, surrounded by the densest shadows of forgotten ages, we come at once into the midst of gods and heroes, goddesses and fair women, giants and dwarfs, moving about in a world of wonderful construction, unlike any other world or creation which God has founded or man has imagined, but still beautiful beyond conception.

The Elder Edda opens with Völuspá (the vala's prophecy), and this song may be regarded as one of the oldest, if not the oldest, poetic monument of the North. In it the mysterious vala, or prophetess, seated somewhere unseen in the marvelous heaven, sings an awful song of the birth of gods and men; of the great Ygdrasil, or Tree of Existence, whose roots and branches extend through all regions of space, and concludes her thrilling hymn with the terrible Ragnarok, or Twilight of the gods, when Odin and the other gods perish in the flames that devour all creation, and the new heavens and new earth rise beautifully green to receive the reign of Balder and of milder natures.

The second song in the Elder Edda is Hávamál (the high-song of Odin). Odin himself is represented as its author. It contains a pretty complete code of Odinic morality and precepts of wisdom. The moral and social axioms that are brought together in Hávamál will surprise the reader, who has been accustomed to regard the Norsemen as a rude and half wild race, hunting in the savage forests of the North, or scouring the coasts of Europe in quest of plunder. They contain a profound knowledge, not merely of human nature, but of human nature in its various social and domestic relations. They are more like the proverbs of Solomon than anything in human literature.

The third poem in the Elder Edda is Vafthrudnismál (that is, Vafthrudner's speech or song). Vafthrudner is derived from *vaf*, a web or weaving, and *thrúð*, strong; hence Vafthrudner is the *powerful weaver*, the one powerful in riddles, and it is the name of a giant, who in the first part of the poem propounds a series of intricate

questions or riddles. Odin tells his wife Frigg that he
desires to visit the all-wise giant Vafthrudner, to find
out from him the secrets of the past and measure strength
with him. Frigg advises him not to undertake this
journey, saying that she considers Vafthrudner the
strongest of all giants. Odin reminds her of his many
perilous adventures and experiences, arguing that these
are sufficient to secure him in his curiosity to see Vafthrudner's halls. Frigg wishes him a prosperous journey and safe return, and also the necessary presence of
mind at his meeting with the giant. Odin then proceeds on his journey and enters the halls of Vafthrudner
in the guise of a mortal wayfarer, by name Gangraad.
He greets the lord of the house, and says he is come to
learn whether he was a wise or omniscient giant. Such
an address vexes Vafthrudner, coming as it did from a
stranger, and he soon informs Gangraad that if he is
not wiser than himself he shall not leave the hall alive.
But the giant, finding, after he had asked the stranger
a few questions, that he really had a worthy antagonist
in his presence, invites him to take a seat, and challenges
him to enter into a disputation, that they might measure
their intellectual strength, on the condition that the van-
quished party — the one unable to answer a question put
to him by the other — should forfeit his head. Odin
accepts this dangerous challenge. They accordingly discuss, by question and answer, the principal topics of
Norse mythology. The pretended Gangraad asks the
giant many questions, which the latter answers correctly;
but when the former at length asks his adversary what
Odin whispered in the ear of his son Balder before he
had been placed on the funeral pile — a question by
which the astonished giant becomes aware that his antagonist is Odin himself, who was alone capable of

answering it,— the giant acknowledges himself van-
quished, and sees with terror that he cannot avoid the
death which he in his cruel pride had intended to inflict
upon an innocent wanderer.

The fourth song is Grimnismál (the song of Grimner). It begins with a preface in prose, in which it is
related that Odin, under the name of Grimner, visited
his foster-son Geirrod, and the latter, deceived by a false
representation by Frigg, takes him for a sorcerer, makes
him sit between two fires and pine there without nourishment for eight days, until Agnar, the king's son,
reaches him a drinking-horn. Hereupon Grimner sings
the song which bears his name. Lamenting his con-
finement and blessing Agnar, he goes on to picture the
twelve abodes of the gods and the splendors of Valhal,
which he describes at length, and then speaks of the
mythological world-tree Ygdrasil, of the valkyries, of
the giant Ymer, of the ship Skidbladner, and adds
various other cosmological explanations.

The fifth song is Skírnismál, or För Skirnis (the
journey of Skirner). This gives in the form of a dialogue the story of Frey and Gerd, of his love to her,
and his wooing her through the agency of his faithful
servant Skirner, after whom the song is named.

The sixth is the Lay of Harbard. It is a dialogue
between Thor and the ferryman Harbard, who refuses
to carry him over the stream. This furnishes an occasion for each of them to recount his exploits. They
contrast their deeds and exploits. The contest is continued without interruption until near the end of the
poem, where Thor finally offers a compromise, again re-
questing to be taken over the river. Harbard, who is
in fact Odin, again refuses in decided terms. Then
Thor asks him to show him another way. This request

Harbard seems in a manner to comply with, but refers Thor to Fjorgyn, his mother. Thor asks how far it is, but Harbard makes enigmatical answers. Thor ends the conversation with threats and Harbard with evil wishes.

The seventh poem is the Song of Hymer. The gods of Asgard are invited to a banquet with the sea-god Æger. Thor goes to the giant Hymer for a large kettle, in which to brew ale for the occasion. When Thor has arrived at the home of Hymer he persuades the giant to take him along on a fishing expedition, in which Thor fishes up the Midgard-serpent, which he would have killed had it not been for Hymer, who cut off the fish-line. Thor succeeds in carrying off the kettle, but has to slay Hymer and other giants who pursue him.

The eighth is Lokasenna (or Loke's quarrel.) This poem has a preface in prose. This is also a banquet at Æger's. It takes place immediately after Balder's death. Loke was present. He slew one of Æger's servants and had to flee to the woods, but soon returns, enters Æger's hall, and immediately begins to abuse the gods in the most shameful manner: first Brage, then Idun, Gefjun, Odin, Frigg, Freyja, Njord, and the others, until Thor finally appears and drives him away. There is a prose conclusion to this poem, describing Loke's punishment. A profound tragedy characterizes this poem. Although Loke is abusive, he still speaks the truth, and he exposes all the faults of the gods, which foreshadow their final fall. Peace disappeared with the death of Balder, and the gods, conscious that Ragnarok is inevitable, are overpowered by distraction and sorrow.

The ninth poem is the Song of Thrym. This gives an account of the loss of Thor's hammer, and tells how

Loke helped him to get it back from the giant Thrym.

The tenth is the Song of Alvis (the all-wise). Alvis comes for Thor's daughter as his bride. Thor cunningly detains him all night by asking him questions concerning the various worlds he has visited. Alvis answers and teaches him the names by which the most important things in nature are called in the respective languages of different worlds: of men, of the gods, of the vans, of the giants, of the elves, of the dwarfs, and finally of the realms of the dead and of the supreme god. The dwarf, being one of those mythical objects which cannot endure the light of day, was detained till dawn without accomplishing his object.

The eleventh poem is Vegtam's Lay. Odin assumes the name Vegtam. In order to arrive at certainty concerning the portentous future of the gods, he descends to Niflheim, goes into the abodes of Hel, and calls the vala up from her grave-mound, asking her about the fate of Balder. She listens to him indignantly, answers his questions unwillingly, but at last discovers that Vegtam is the king of the gods, and angrily tells him to ride home.

We will omit a synopsis of the remainder, and merely give their titles, as they do not enter so completely into the system of mythology as the first eleven: (12) Rigsmaal (Song of Rig), (13) The Lay of Hyndla, (14) The Song of Volund, (15) The Song of Helge Hjorvardson, (16) Song of Helge Hundingsbane I, (17) Song of Helge Hundingsbane II, (18) Song of Sigurd Fafnisbane I, (19) Song of Sigurd Fafnisbane II, (20) Song of Fafner, (21) Song of Sigdrifa, (22) Song of Sigurd, (23) Song of Gudrun I, (24) Song of Gudrun III, (25) Brynhild's Ride to Hel, (26) Song of Gudrun II, (27) Song of Gudrun III, (28) The Weeping of Odrun, (29)

The Song of Atle, (30) The Speech of Atle, (31) The Challenge of Gudrun, (32) The Song of Hamder, (33) The Song of Grotte, (34) Extracts from the Younger Edda, (35) Extracts from the Volsunga Saga, (36) Song of Svipdag I, (37) Song of Svipdag II, (38) The Lay of the Sun, (39) Odin's Raven-Cry.

The antiquity of these poems cannot be fixed, but they certainly carry us back to the remotest period of the settlement of Norway by the Goths.

It may be added here that many of the poems of the Elder Edda, as well as much of the Old Norse poetry generally, are very difficult to understand, on account of the bold metaphorical language in which they are written. The poet did not call an object by its usual name, but borrowed a figure by which to present it, either from the mythology or from some other source. Thus he would call the sky *the skull of the giant Ymer;* the rainbow he called *the bridge of the gods;* gold was *the tears of Freyja;* poetry, *the present* or *drink of Odin.* The earth was called indifferently *the wife of Odin, the flesh of Ymer, the daughter of night, the vessel that floats on the ages,* or *the foundation of the air;* herbs and plants were called *the hair* or *the fleece of the earth.* A battle was called *a bath of blood, the hail of Odin, the shock of bucklers;* the sea was termed *the field of pirates, the girdle of the earth;* ice, *the greatest of all bridges;* a ship, *the horse of the waves;* the tongue, *the sword of words,* etc.

## II. *The Younger Edda,*

written by Snorre Sturleson, the author of the famous *Heimskringla* (born 1178, died 1241), is mostly prose, and may be regarded as a sort of commentary upon the Elder Edda. The prose Edda consists of two parts:

Gylfaginning (the deluding of Gylfe), and the Bragaræ-
ður or Skáldskaparmál (the conversations of Brage, the
god of poetry, or the treatise on poetry). Gylfaginning
tells how the Swedish king Gylfe makes a journey to
Asgard, the abode of the gods, where Odin instructs
him in the old faith, and gradually relates to him
the myths of the Norsemen. The manner in which
the whole is told reminds us of *A Thousand and One
Nights*, or of poems from a later time, as for instance
Boccaccio's *Decameron*. It is a prose synopsis of the
whole Asa faith, with here and there a quotation
from the Elder Edda by way of elucidation. It shows
a great deal of ingenuity and talent on the part of
its author, and is the most perspicuous and clear
presentation of the mythology that we possess.

But all the material for the correct presentation
of the Norse mythology is not found in the Eddas;
or rather we do not perfectly understand the Eddas,
if we confine our studies to them alone. For a full
comprehension of the myths, it is necessary to study
carefully all the semi-mythological Icelandic Sagas,
which constitute a respectable library by themselves;
and in connection with these we must read the Anglo-
Saxon *Beowulf's Drapa*, and the German *Niebelungen-
Lied*. In the next place, we must examine carefully
all the folk-lore of the Gothic race, and we must, in
short, study the manifestations of the Gothic mind
and spirit everywhere: in the development of the
State and of the Church, in their poetry and history,
in their various languages and numerous dialects, in
their literature, in their customs and manners, and
in their popular belief. If we neglect all these we
shall never understand the Eddas; if we neglect the
Eddas we shall never understand the other sources of

mythology. They mutually explain each other, and
the Gothic race must sooner or later begin to study
its own history.

That the Odinic mythology exercised a mighty influence in forming the national character of the Norsemen, becomes evident when we compare the doctrines
of their faith with the popular life as portrayed in the
Sagas. Still we must bear in mind that this national
spirit was not created by this faith. The harsh climate of the North modified not only the Norse mythology, but also moulded indefinitely the national
character, and then the two, the mythology and the
national character, acted and reacted upon each other.
Thus bred up to fight with nature in a constant
battle for existence, and witnessing the same struggle
in the life of his gods, the Norseman became fearless,
honest and truthful, ready to smite and ready to forgive, shrinking not from pain himself and careless
about inflicting it on others. Beholding in external
nature and in his mythology the struggle of conflict-
ing forces, he naturally looked on life as a field for
warfare. The ice-bound fjords and desolate fells, the
mournful wail of the waving pine-branches, the stern
strife of frost and fire, the annual death of the short-
lived summer, made the Norseman sombre, if not
gloomy, in his thoughts, and inured him to the rugged
independence of the country. The sternness of the land
in which he lived was reflected in his character; the
latter was in turn reflected in the tales which he
told of his gods and heroes, and thus the Norseman
and his mythology mutually influenced each other.

The influence of the Asa faith, says Prof. Keyser,
upon the popular spirit of the Norsemen, must be regarded from quite another point of view than that

of Christianity at a later period. The Asa faith was, so to speak, inborn with the Norsemen, as it had developed itself from certain germs and assumed form with the popular life almost unconsciously to the latter. Christianity, on the other hand, was given to the people as a religious system complete in itself, intended for all the nations of the earth; one which by its own divine power opened for itself a way to conviction, and through that conviction operated on the popular spirit in a direction previously pointed out by the fundamental principles of the religion itself. As the system of the Asa faith arose without any conscious object of affecting the morals, therefore it did not embrace any actual code of morals in the higher sense of this term. The Asa doctrine does not pronounce by positive expression what is virtue and what is vice; it presupposes a consciousness thereof in its votaries. It only represents virtue as reaping its own rewards and vice its own punishment, if not here upon the earth, then with certainty beyond the grave. Thus Keyser.

The Norse system of mythology embodied the doctrine of an imperishable soul in man; it had Valhal and Gimle set apart for and awaiting the brave and virtuous, and Helheim and Naastrand for the wicked.

The moral and social maxims of the Norsemen are represented as being uttered by Odin himself in the Hávamál (high song of Odin), the second song of the Elder Edda, and by the valkyrie Sigdrifa in the Sigrdrífumál (the lay of Sigdrifa), the twenty-first poem of the same work. Read these poems and maxims, and judge whether they will warrant the position repeatedly taken in this work, that the electric spark that has made England and America great and free came not from the aboriginal Britons, not from the Roman enslavers, but must be sought in the prophetic, imaginative and poetic childhood of the Gothic race. Read these poems and judge whether the eminent English writer, Samuel Laing, is right when he says:

All that men hope for of good government and future improvement in their physical and moral condition,—all that civilized men enjoy at this day of civil, religious and political liberty,—the British constitution, representative legislation, the trial by jury, security of property, freedom of mind and person, the influence of public opinion over the conduct of public affairs, the Reformation, the liberty of the press, the spirit of the age, —all that is or has been of value to man in modern times as a member of society, either in Europe or in the New World, may be traced to the spark left burning upon our shores by these northern barbarians.

Read these poems and find truth in the words of Baron Montesquieu, the admirable author of *The Spirit of Laws* (L'Esprit des Lois), when he says: The great prerogative of Scandinavia, and what ought to recommend its inhabitants beyond every people upon earth, is, that they afforded the great resource to the liberty of Europe, that is, to almost all the liberty that is among men; and when he calls the North the forge of those instruments which broke the fetters manufactured in the South.

In the old Gothic religion were embodied principles and elements which had a tendency to make its votaries brave, independent, honest, earnest, just, charitable, prudent, temperate, liberty-loving, etc.; principles and morals that in due course of time and under favorable circumstances evolved the Republic of Iceland, the Magna Charta of England, and the Declaration of Independence.

The rules of life as indicated by the High Song of Odin and in Sigrdrífumál, in which the valkyrie gives

9

counsel to Sigurd Fafnisbane, are briefly summed up
by Professor Keyser as follows:

1. The recognition of the depravity of human nature, which
calls for a struggle against our natural desires and forbearance
toward the weakness of others.
2. Courage and faith both to bear the hard decrees of the
norns and to fight against enemies.
3. The struggle for independence in life with regard to
knowledge as well as to fortune; an independence which should,
therefore, be earned by a love of learning and industry.
4. A strict adherence to oaths and promises.
5. Candor and fidelity as well as foresight in love, devotion
to the tried friend, but dissimulation toward the false and war
to the death against the implacable enemy.
6. Respect for old age.
7. Hospitality, liberality, and charity to the poor.
8. A prudent foresight in word and deed.
9. Temperance, not only in the gratification of the senses, but
also in the exercise of power.
10. Contentment and cheerfulness.
11. Modesty and politeness in intercourse.
12. A desire to win the good will of our fellow men, especially to surround ourselves with a steadfast circle of devoted
kinsmen and faithful friends.
13. A careful treatment of the bodies of the dead.

Listen now to Odin himself, as he gives precepts of
wisdom to mankind in

HÁVAMÁL:

1. All door-ways
   Before going forward,
   Should be looked to;
   For difficult it is to know
   Where foes may sit
   Within a dwelling

2. Givers, hail!
   A guest is come in:

Where shall he sit?
In much haste is he,
Who on his ways has
To try his luck.

3. Fire is needful
   To him who is come in,
   And whose knees are frozen;
   Food and raiment
   A man requires,
   Who o'er the fell has traveled.

4. Water to him is needful,
   Who for refection comes,
   A towel and hospitable invitation,
   A good reception;
   If he can get it,
   Discourse and answer.

5. Wit is needful
   To him who travels far:
   At home all is easy.
   A laughing-stock is he
   Who nothing knows,
   And with the instructed sits.*

6. Of his understanding
   No one should be proud,
   But rather in conduct cautious.
   When the prudent and taciturn
   Come to a dwelling,
   Harm seldom befalls the cautious;
   For a firmer friend
   No man ever gets
   Than great sagacity.

7. A wary guest
   Who to refection comes
   Keeps a cautious silence;
   With his ears listens,
   And with his eyes observes:
   So explores every prudent man.

* Beowulf, 1839.

8. He is happy
   Who for himself obtains
   Fame and kind words:
   Less sure is that
   Which a man must have
   In another's breast.

9. He is happy
   Who in himself possesses
   Fame and wit while living;
   For bad counsels
   Have oft been received
   From another's breast.

10. A better burthen
    No man bears on the way
    Than much good sense;
    That is thought better than riches
    In a strange place;
    Such is the recourse of the indigent.

11. A worse provision
    On the way he cannot carry
    Than too much beer-bibbing;
    So good is not,
    As it is said,
    Beer for the sons of men.

12. A worse provision
    No man can take from table
    Than too much beer-bibbing,
    For the more he drinks
    The less control he has
    Of his own mind.

13. Oblivion's heron 'tis called
    That over potations hovers;
    He steals the minds of men.
    With this bird's pinions
    I was fettered
    In Gunlad's dwelling.

14. Drunk I was,
    I was over-drunk,
    At that cunning Fjalar's.
    It's the best drunkenness
    When every one after it
    Regains his reason.

15. Taciturn and prudent,
    And in war daring
    Should a king's children be;
    Joyous and liberal
    Everyone should be
    Until his hour of death.

16. A cowardly man
    Thinks he will ever live
    If warfare he avoids;
    But old age will
    Give him no peace,
    Though spears may spare him.

17. A fool gapes
    When to a house he comes,
    To himself mutters or is silent;
    But all at once,
    If he gets drink,
    Then is the man's mind displayed.

18. He alone knows,
    Who wanders wide
    And has much experienced,
    By what disposition
    Each man is ruled,
    Who common sense possesses.

19. Let a man hold the cup,
    Yet of the mead drink moderately,
    Speak sensibly or be silent.
    As of a fault
    No man will admonish thee,
    If thou goest betimes to sleep.

20. A greedy man,
    If he be not moderate,
    Eats to his mortal sorrow.
    Oftentimes his belly
    Draws laughter on a silly man
    Who among the prudent comes.

21. Cattle know
    When to go home
    And then from grazing cease;
    But a foolish man
    Never knows
    His stomach's measure.

22. A miserable man,
    And ill-conditioned,
    Sneers at everything:
    One thing he knows not,
    Which he ought to know,
    That he is not free from faults.

23. A foolish man
    Is all night awake,
    Pondering over everything;
    He then grows tired,
    And when morning comes
    All is lament as before.

24. A foolish man
    Thinks all who on him smile
    To be his friends;
    He feels it not,
    Although they speak ill of him,
    When he sits among the clever.

25. A foolish man
    Thinks all who speak him fair
    To be his friends;
    But he will find,
    If into court he comes,
    That he has few advocates.

26. A foolish man
Thinks he knows everything
If placed in unexpected difficulty;
But he knows not
    What to answer
    If to the test he is put.

27. A foolish man,
Who among people comes,
Had best be silent;
For no one knows
That he knows nothing
Unless he talks too much.
He who previously knew nothing
    Will still know nothing,
Talk he ever so much.

28. He thinks himself wise
Who can ask questions
And converse also;.
Conceal his ignorance
No one can,
    Because it circulates among men.

29. He utters too many
Futile words
Who is never silent;
    A garrulous tongue,
If it be not checked,
    Sings often to its own harm.

30. For a gazing-stock
    No man shall have another,
Although he come a stranger to his house.
Many a one thinks himself wise,
If he is not questioned,
And can sit in a dry habit.

31. Clever thinks himself
The guest who jeers a guest,
If he takes to flight.
Knows it not certainly
He who prates at meat,
Whether he babbles among foes.

32.  Many men are mutually
         Well-disposed,
     Yet at table will torment each other.
     That strife will ever be;
     Guest will guest irritate.

33.  Early meals
     A man should often take,
     Unless to a friend's house he goes;
     Else he will sit and mope,
     Will seem half famished,
     And can of few things inquire.

34.  Long is and indirect the way
     To a bad friend's,
     Though by the road he dwell;
     But to a good friend's
     The paths lie direct,
     Though he be far away.

35.  A guest should depart,
     Not always stay
     In one place:
     The welcome becomes unwelcome
     If he too long continues
     In another's house.

36.  One's own house is best,
     Small though it be;
     At home is every one his own master.
     Though he but two goats possess,
     And a straw-thatched cot,
     Even that is better than begging.

37.  One's own house is best,
     Small though it be;
     At home is every one his own master.
     Bleeding at heart is he
     Who has to ask
     For food at every meal-tide.

38. Leaving in the field his arms,
       Let no man go
    A foot's length forward;
    For it is hard to know
       When on his way
    A man may need his weapon.

39. I have never found a man so bountiful
    Or so hospitable
    That he refused a present;
    Or of his property
    So liberal
    That he scorned a recompense.

40. Of the property
    Which he has gained,
    No man should suffer need;
    For the hated oft is spared
    What for the dear was destined:
    Much goes worse than is expected.

41. With arms and vestments
    Friends should each other gladden,
    Those which are in themselves most sightly.
    Givers and requiters
    Are longest friends,
    If all else goes well.

42.   To his friend
    A man should be a friend,
    And gifts with gifts requite;
    Laughter with laughter
    Men should receive,
    But leasing with lying.

43.   To his friend
    A man should be a friend,
    To him and to his friend;
      But of his foe
      No man shall
      His friend's friend be.

44. Know if thou hast a friend
    Whom thou fully trustest,
And from whom thou would'st good derive;
Thou should'st blend thy mind with his,
    And gifts exchange,
    And often go to see him.

45. If thou hast another
    Whom thou little trustest,
    Yet would'st good from him derive,
    Thou should'st speak him fair,
    But think craftily,
    And leasing pay with lying.

46. But of him yet further
    Whom thou little trustest,
    And thou suspectest his affection,
    Before him thou should'st laugh,
    And contrary to thy thoughts speak;
    Requital should the gift resemble.

47. I once was young,
    I was journeying alone
    And lost my way;
    Rich I thought myself
    When I met another:
    Man is the joy of man.

48. Liberal and brave
    Men live best,
    They seldom cherish sorrow;
    But a bare-minded man
    Dreads everything;
    The niggardly is uneasy even at gifts.

49. My garments in a field
    I gave away
    To two wooden men:
    Heroes they seemed to be
    When they got cloaks :*
    Exposed to insult is a naked man.

    * The tailor makes the man.

50. A tree withers
    That on a hill-top stands;
    Protects it neither bark nor leaves:
    Such is the man
    Whom no one favors:
    Why should he live long?

51. Hotter than fire
    Love for five days burns
    Between false friends;
    But is quenched
    When the sixth day comes,
    And friendship is all impaired

52. Something great
    Is not always to be given,
    Praise is often for a trifle bought
    With half a loaf         *
    And a tilted vessel
    I got myself a comrade.

53. Little are the sand grains,
    Little the wits,
    Little the minds of men;
    For all men
    Are not wise alike:
    Men are everywhere by halves

54. Moderately wise
    Should each one be,
    But never over-wise;
    For a wise man's heart
    Is seldom glad,
    If he is all-wise who owns it

55. Moderately wise
    Should each one be,
    But never over-wise:
    Of those men
    The lives are fairest
    Who know much well.

56. Moderately wise
    Should each one be,
    But never over-wise:
    His destiny let know
    No man beforehand;
    His mind will be freest from care.

57. Brand burns from brand
    Until it is burnt out,
    Fire is from fire quickened:
    Man to man
    Becomes known by speech,
    But a fool by his bashful silence.

58. He should rise early
    Who another's property or life
    Desires to have:
    Seldom a sluggish wolf
    Gets prey,
    Or a sleeping man victory.

59. Early should rise
    He who has few workers,
    And go his work to see to;
    Greatly is he retarded
    Who sleeps the morn away.
    Wealth half depends on energy.

60. Of dry planks
    And roof shingles
    A man knows the measure;
    Of the firewood
    That may suffice
    Both measure and time.

61. Washed and refected
    Let a man ride to *Thing*,*
    Although his garments be not too good;
    Of his shoes and breeches
    Let no one be ashamed,
    Nor of his horse,
    Although he have not a good one.

    * The public assembly.

62. Inquire and impart
    Should every man of sense,
    Who will be accounted sage.
    Let one only know,
    A second may not;
    If three, all the world knows.

63. Gasps and gapes,
    When to the sea he comes,
    The eagle over old ocean;
    So is a man
    Who among many comes,
    And has few advocates.

64. His power should
    Every sagacious man
    Use with discretion,
    For he will find,
    When among the bold he comes,
    That no one alone is doughtiest.

65. Circumspect and reserved
    Every man should be,
    And wary in trusting friends;
    Of the words
    That a man says to another
    He often pays the penalty.

66. Much too early
    I came to many places,
    But too late to others;
    The beer was drunk,
    Or not ready:
    The disliked seldom hits the moment.

67. Here and there I should
    Have been invited
    If I a meal had needed;
    Or two hams had hung
    At that true friend's
    Where of one I had eaten.

68. Fire is best
    Among the sons of men,
    And the sight of the sun,
    If his health
    A man can have,
    With a life free from vice.

69. No man lacks everything,
    Although his health be bad:
    One in his sons is happy,
    One in his kin,
    One in abundant wealth,
    One in his good works.

70. It is better to live,
    Even to live miserably;
    A living man can always get a cow.
    I saw fire consume
    The rich man's property,
    And death stood without his door.

71. The halt can ride on horseback,
    The one-handed drive cattle;
    The deaf, fight and be useful:
    To be blind is better
    Than to be burnt:*
    No one gets good from a corpse.

72. A son is better
    Even if born late,
    After his father's departure.
    Gravestones seldom
    Stand by the way-side
    Unless raised by a kinsman to a kinsman.

73. Two are adversaries:
    The tongue is the bane of the head:
    Under every cloak
    I expect a hand.

    * That is, *dead* on the funeral pile.

74. At night is joyful
    He who is sure of traveling entertainment;
    A ship's yards are short;
    Variable is an autumn night.
    Many are the weather's changes
    In five days,
    But more in a month.

75. He knows not,
    Who knows nothing,
    That many a one apes another.
    One man is rich,
    Another poor:
    Let him not be thought blameworthy.

76. Cattle die,
    Kindred die,
    We ourselves also die ;
    But the fair fame
    Never dies
    Of him who has earned it.

77. Cattle die,
    Kindred die,
    We ourselves also die ;
    But I know one thing
    That never dies,—
    Judgment on each one dead.

78. Full storehouses I saw
    At Dives' sons':
    Now bear they the beggar's staff.
    Such are riches,
    As is the twinkling of an eye:
    Of friends they are most fickle.

79. A foolish man,
    If he acquires
    Wealth or woman's love,
    Pride grows within him,
    But wisdom never:
    He goes on more and more arrogant.

80. Thus 't is made manifest,
    If of runes thou questionest him,
    Those to the high ones known,
    Which the great powers invented,
    And the great talker * painted,
    That he had best hold silence.

81. At eve the day is to be praised,
    A woman after she is burnt,†
    A sword after it is proved,
    A maid after she is married,
    Ice after it has been crossed,
    Beer after it is drunk.

82. In the wind one should hew wood,
    In a breeze row out to sea,
    In the dark talk with a lass,
    Many are the eyes of day.
    In a ship voyages are to be made,
    But a shield is for protection,
    A sword for striking,
    But a damsel for a kiss.

83. By the fire one should drink beer,
    On the ice slide;
    Buy a horse that is lean,
    A sword that is rusty;
    Feed a horse at home,
    But a dog at the farm.

84. In a maiden's words
    No one should place faith,
    Nor in what a woman says;
    For on a turning wheel
    Have their hearts been formed,
    And guile in their breasts been laid.

85. In a creaking bow,
    A burning flame,
    A yawning wolf,
    A chattering crow,

* Odin.                    † Dead.

A grunting swine,
A rootless tree,
A waxing wave,
A boiling kettle,

86. A flying dart,
A falling billow,
A one night's ice,
A coiled serpent,
A woman's bed-talk
Or a broken sword,
A bear's play
Or a royal child,

87. A sick calf,
A self-willed thrall,
A flattering prophetess,
A corpse newly slain,
A serene sky,
A laughing lord,
A barking dog
And a harlot's grief,

88. An early-sown field,
Let no one trust,
Nor prematurely in a son:
Weather rules the field,
And wit the son,
Each of which is doubtful.

89. A brother's murderer,
Though on the high-road met,
A half-burnt house,
An over-swift horse
(A horse is useless
If a leg be broken):
No man is so confiding
As to trust any of these.

90. Such is the love of women,
Who falsehood meditate,
As if one drove not rough-shod
On slippery ice,

A spirited two-year-old
And unbroken horse;
Or as in a raging storm
A helmless ship is beaten;
Or as if the halt were set to catch
A reindeer in the thawing fell.*

91. Openly I now speak,
Because I both sexes know:
Unstable are men's minds toward women;
'Tis then we speak most fair,
When we most falsely think:
That deceives even the cautious.

92. Fair shall speak,
And money offer,
Who would obtain a woman's love
Praise the form
Of a fair damsel;
He gets, who courts her.

93. At love should no one
Ever wonder
In another:
A beauteous countenance
Oft captivates the wise,
Which captivates not the foolish.

94. Let no one wonder at
Another's folly,
It is the lot of many.
All-powerful desire
Makes of the sons of men
Fools even of the wise.

95. The mind only knows
What lies near the heart;
That alone is conscious of our affections
No disease is worse
To a sensible man
Than not to be content with himself.

* Such lines as this show the *Norse* origin of the Edda.

96. That I experienced
    When in the reeds I sat
    Awaiting my delight.
    Body and soul to me
    Was that discreet maiden:
    Nevertheless I possess her not.

97. Billing's lass
    On her couch I found,
    Sun-bright, sleeping.
    A prince's joy
    To me seemed naught,
    If not with that form to live.

98. Yet nearer eve
    Must thou, Odin, come, she said,
    If thou wilt talk the maiden over;
    All will be disastrous
    Unless we alone
    Are privy to such misdeed.

99. I returned,
    Thinking to love
    At her wise desire;
    I thought
    I should obtain
    Her whole heart and love.

100. When next I came,
     The bold warriors were
     All awake,
     With lights burning,
     And bearing torches:

101. But at the approach of morn,
     When again I came,
     The household all was sleeping;
     The good damsel's dog
     Alone I found
     Tied to the bed.

102. Many a fair maiden,
When rightly known,
Toward men is fickle:
That I experienced
When that discreet maiden
I decoyed into danger:
Contumely of every kind
That wily girl
Heaped upon me;
Nor of that damsel gained I aught.

103. At home let a man be cheerful,
And toward a guest liberal;
Of wise conduct he should be,
Of good memory and ready speech;
If much knowledge he desires,
He must often talk on what is good.
Fimbulfambi he is called
Who little has to say:
Such is the nature of the simple.

---

104. The old giant I sought;
Now I am come back:
Little got I there by silence;
In many words
I spoke to my advantage
In Suttung's halls.*

105. Gunlad gave me,
On her golden seat,
A draught of the precious mead;
A bad recompense I afterwards made her
For her whole soul,
Her fervent love.

106. Rate's mouth I caused
To make a space,
And to gnaw the rock;
Over and under me

* For the story of Suttung and Gunlad, see second part, pp. 246-253.

Were the giant's ways:
Thus I my head did peril.

107. Of a well assumed form
I made good use:
Few things fail the wise,
For Odrærer is now come up
To men's earthly dwellings.

108. 'T is to me doubtful,
That I could have come
From the giant's courts,
Had not Gunlad aided me,—
That good damsel
Over whom I laid my arm.

109. On the day following
Came the frost-giants
To learn something of the High One
In the High One's hall;
After Bolverk they inquired,
Whether he with the gods were come,
Or Suttung had destroyed him.

110. Odin I believe
A ring-oath* gave.
Who in his faith will trust?
Suttung defrauded,
Of his drink bereft,
And Gunlad made to weep!

111. Time 't is to discourse
From the speaker's chair.
By the well of Urd
I silent sat,
I saw and meditated,
I listened to men's words.

* In the North a holy oath was taken on a ring kept in the temple for
that purpose.

112. Of runes I heard discourse,
And of things divine,
Nor of risting* them were they silent,
Nor of sage counsels,
At the High One's hall.
In the High One's hall
I thus heard say:

113. I counsel thee, Lodfafner,
To take advice;
Thou wilt profit, if thou takest it.
Rise not at night,
Unless to explore,
Or art compelled to go out.

114. I counsel thee, Lodfafner,
To take advice;
Thou wilt profit, if thou takest it.
In an enchantress' embrace
Thou mayest not sleep,
So that in her arms she clasp thee.

115. She will be the cause
That thou carest not
For *Thing* or prince's words;
Food thou wilt shun
And human joys;
Sorrowful wilt thou go to sleep.

116. I counsel thee, Lodfafner,
To take advice;
Thou wilt profit, if thou takest it.
Another's wife
Entice thou never
To secret converse.

117. I counsel thee, Lodfafner,
To take advice;
Thou wilt profit, if thou takest it.
By fell or firth
If thou have to travel,
Provide thee well with food.

* Curving: runes arc risted = runes are carved.

118. I counsel thee, Lodfafner,
     To take advice;
     Thou wilt profit, if thou takest it.
     A bad man
     Let thou never
     Know thy misfortunes;
     For from a bad man
     Thou never wilt obtain
     A return for thy good will.

119. I saw mortally
     Wound a man
     A wicked woman's words;
     A false tongue
     Caused his death,
     And most unrighteously.

120. I counsel thee, Lodfafner,
     To take advice;
     Thou wilt profit, if thou takest it.
     If thou knowest thou hast a friend,
     Whom thou well canst trust,
     Go oft to visit him;
     For with brushwood overgrown
     And with high grass
     Is the way that no one treads.

121. I counsel thee, Lodfafner,
     To take advice;
     Thou wilt profit, if thou takest it.
     A good man attract to thee
     In pleasant converse,
     And salutary speech learn, while thou livest.

122. I counsel thee, Lodfafner,
     To take advice;
     Thou wilt profit, if thou takest it.
     With thy friend
     Be thou never
     First to quarrel.
     Care gnaws the heart,

If thou to no one canst
Thy whole mind disclose.

123. I counsel thee, Lodfafner,
To take advice;
Thou wilt profit, if thou takest it.
Words thou never
Shouldst exchange
With a witless fool.

124. For from an ill-conditioned man
Thou wilt never get
A return for good;
But a good man will
Bring thee favor
By his praise.

125. There is a mingling of affection,
Where one can tell
Another all his mind.
Everything is better
Than being with the deceitful.
He is not another's friend
Who ever says as he says.

126. I counsel thee, Lodfafner,
To take advice;
Thou wilt profit, if thou takest it.
Even in three words
Quarrel not with a worse man:
Often the better yields,
When the worse strikes.

127. I counsel thee, Lodfafner,
To take advice;
Thou wilt profit, if thou takest it.
Be not a shoemaker,
Nor a shaftmaker,
Unless for thyself it be;
For a shoe, if ill made,
Or a shaft if crooked,
Will call down evil on thee.

128. I counsel thee, Lodfafner,
    To take advice;
    Thou wilt profit, if thou takest it.
    Wherever of injury thou knowest,
    Regard that injury as thy own;
    And give to thy foes no peace.

129. I counsel thee, Lodfafner,
    To take advice;
    Thou wilt profit, if thou takest it.
    Rejoiced at evil
    Be thou never,
    But let good give thee pleasure.

130. I counsel thee, Lodfafner,
    To take advice;
    Thou wilt profit, if thou takest it.
    In a battle
    Look not up,*
    (Like swine †
    The sons of men then become),
    That men may not fascinate thee.

131. If thou wilt induce a good woman
    To pleasant converse,
    Thou must promise fair,
    And hold to it:
    No one turns from good, if it can be got.

132. I enjoin thee to be wary,
    But not over-wary;
    At drinking be thou most wary,
    And with another's wife;
    And thirdly,
    That thieves delude thee not.

133. With insult or derision
    Treat thou never
    A guest or wayfarer;
    They often little know,

* In a battle we must not look up, but forward.
† To become panic-stricken, which the Norsemen called to become swine.

Who sit within,
Of what race they are who come.

134. Vices and virtues
The sons of mortals bear
In their breasts mingled;
No one is so good
That no failing attends him,
Nor so bad as to be good for nothing.

135. At a hoary speaker
Laugh thou never,
Often is good that which the aged utter;
Oft from a shriveled hide
Discreet words issue,
From those whose skin is pendent
And decked with scars,
And who go loitering among the vile.

136. I counsel thee, Lodfafner,
To take advice;
Thou wilt profit, if thou takest it.
Rail not at a guest,
Nor from thy gate thrust him;
Treat well the indigent,
They will speak well of thee.

137. Strong is the bar
That must be raised
To admit all.*
Do thou give a penny,
Or they will call down on thee
Every ill on thy limbs.

138. I counsel thee, Lodfafner,
To take advice;
Thou will profit, if thou takest it.
Wherever thou beer drinkest,

* The meaning is, it is difficult to show hospitality to everybody. A door
would have to be strong to stand so much opening and shutting.

Invoke to thee the power of earth;
For earth is good against drink,
Fire for distempers,
The oak for constipation,
A corn-ear for sorcery,
A hall for domestic strife.
In bitter hates invoke the moon;
The bitter for bite-injuries is good,
But runes against calamity;
Fluid let earth absorb.

This is all of the famous Hávamál of the Elder Edda except the so-called Runic Chapter, which will be given in the second part in connection with the myth of Odin. Hear now what the valkyrie has to say to Sigurd Fafnisbane in

SIGRDRÍFUMÁL (*the Lay of Sigdrifa*).

Sigurd rode up the Hindarfiall, and directed his course southward toward Frankland. In the fell he saw a great light, as if a fire were burning, which blazed up to the sky. On approaching it, there stood a *skialdborg*, and over it a banner. Sigurd went into the skialdborg, and saw a warrior lying within it asleep, completely armed. He first took the helmet off the warrior's head, and saw that it was a woman. Her corselet was as fast as if it had grown to her body. With his sword, Gram, he ripped the corselet from the upper opening downwards, and then through both sleeves. He then took the corselet off from her, when she awoke, sat up, and, on seeing Sigurd, said:

1.  What has my corselet cut?
    Why from my sleep have I started?
    Who has cast from me
    The fallow bands?

SIGURD:

Sigmund's son
(Recently did the raven
Feed on carrion)*
And Sigurd's sword.

SHE:

2. Long have I slept,
Long been with sleep oppressed,
Long are mortals' sufferings!
Odin is the cause
That I have been unable
To cast off torpor.

Sigurd sat down and asked her name. She then took a horn filled with mead, and gave him the *minnis-cup* (cup of memory).

SHE:

3. Hail to Day!
Hail to the sons of Day!
To Night and her daughter, hail!
With placid eyes
Behold us here,
And here sitting give us victory.

4. Hail to the gods!
Hail to the goddesses!
Hail to the bounteous earth!
Words and wisdom
Give to us noble twain,
And healing hands while we live.

She was named Sigdrifa, and was a valkyrie. She said that two kings had made war on each other, one of whom was named Hialmgunnar; he was old and a great warrior, and Odin had promised him victory. The other was Agnar, a brother of Aud, whom no divinity would patronize. Sigdrifa overcame Hialmgunnar in battle; in revenge for which Odin pricked her with a

---

* The parenthesis refers to Fafner's death.

sleep-thorn, and declared that thenceforth she should never have victory in battle, and should be given in marriage. But, said she, I said to him that I had bound myself by a vow not to espouse any man who could be made to fear. Sigurd answers, and implores her to teach him wisdom, as she had intelligence from all worlds:

SIGDRIFA:

5. Beer I bear to thee,
   Column of battle!
   With might mingled.
   And with bright glory:
   'Tis full of song,
   And salutary saws,
   Of potent incantations,
   And joyous discourses.

6. Sig-runes thou must know,
   If victory (*sigr*) thou wilt have,
   And on thy sword's hilt rist them;
   Some on the chapes,
   Some on the guard,
   And twice name the name of Tyr.

7. Öl-(ale-)runes thou must know,
   If thou wilt not that another's wife
   Thy trust betray, if thou
   In her confide.
   On the horn must they be risted,
   And on the hand's back,
   And Naud* on the nail be scored.

8. A cup must be blessed,
   And against peril guarded,
   And garlick in the liquor cast;
   Then I know
   Thou wilt never have
   Mead with treachery mingled.

* The name of a rune; our *N*.

9. Biarg-(help-)runes thou must know,
   If thou wilt help
   And loose the child from women;
   In the palm they must be graven,
   And round the joints be clasped,
   And the dises prayed for aid.

10. Brim-(sea-)runes thou must know,
    If thou wilt have secure
    Afloat thy sailing steeds.
    On the prow they must be risted,
    And on the helm-blade,
    And with fire to the oar applied.
    No surge shall be so towering,
    Nor waves so dark,
    But from the ocean thou safe shalt come.

11. Lim-(branch-)runes thou must know,
    If thou a leech would be,
    And wounds know how to heal.
    On the bark they must be risted,
    And on the leaves of trees,
    Of those whose boughs bend eastward.

12. Mál-(speech-)runes thou must know,
    If thou wilt that no one
    For injury with hate requite thee.
    Those thou must wind,
    Those thou must wrap round,
    Those thou must altogether place
    In the assembly,
    Where people have
    Into full court to go.

13. Hug-(thought-)runes thou must know,
    If thou a wiser man wilt be
    Than every other.
    Those interpreted,
    Those risted,
    Those devised Hropt,*
    From the fluid
    Which had leaked

* Odin.

From Heiddraupner's * head,
And from Hoddropner's * horn.

14. On 'a rock he stood,
With edged sword,
A helm on his head he bore.
Then spake Mimer's head
Its first wise word,
And true sayings uttered.

15. They are, it is said,
On the shield risted
Which stands before the shining god,
On Aarvak's † ear,
And on Alsvinn's † hoof,
On the wheel which rolls
Under Rogner's ‡ car,
On Sleipner's teeth,
And on the sledge's bands.

16. On the bear's paw,
And on Brage's tongue,
On the wolf's claws,
And the eagle's beak,
On bloody wings,
And on the bridge's end,
On the releasing hand,
And on healing's track.

17. On glass and on gold,
On amulets of men,
In wine and in ale,
And in the welcome seat,
On Gungner's point,
And on Grane's breast,
On the norn's nail,
And the owl's neb.

18. All were erased
That were inscribed,
And mingled with the sacred mead,
And sent on distant ways ;

---

* Mimer.        † The horses of the sun.        ‡ Odin.

They are with the gods,
They are with the elves;
Some with the wise vans,
Some human beings have.

19. Those are bôk-runes
Those are biarg-runes,
And all öl-(ale-)runes,
And precious megin-(power-)runes
For those who can,
Without confusion or corruption,
Turn them to his welfare.
Use, if thou hast understood them,
Until the powers perish.

20. Now thou shalt choose,
Since a choice is offered thee,
Keen armed warrior!
My speech or silence:
Think over it in thy mind.
All evils have their measure.

SIGURD:

21. I will not flee,
Though thou shouldst know me doomed:
I am not born a craven.
Thy friendly councils all
I will receive,
As long as life is in me.

SIGDRIFA:

22. This I thee counsel first:
That toward thy kin
Thou bear thee blameless.
Take not hasty vengeance,
Although they raise up strife:
That, it is said, benefits the dead.

23. This I thee counsel secondly:
That no oath thou swear,
If it not be true.
Cruel bonds

Follow broken faith:
Accursed is the faith-breaker.

24. This I thee counsel thirdly:
That in the assembly thou
Contend not with a fool;
For an unwise man
Oft utters words
Worse than he knows of.

25. All is vain,
If thou holdest silence;
Then wilt thou seem a craven born,
Or else truly accused.
Doubtful is a servant's testimony,
Unless a good one thou gettest.
On the next day
Let his life go forth,
And so men's lies reward.

26. This I counsel thee fourthly:
If a wicked sorceress
Dwell by the way,
To go on is better
Than there to lodge,
Though night may overtake thee.

27. Of searching eyes
The sons of men have need,
When fiercely they have to fight:
Oft pernicious women
By the wayside sit,
Who swords and valor deaden.

28. This I thee counsel fifthly:
Although thou see fair women
On the benches sitting,
Let not their kindred's silver*
Over thy sleep have power.
To kiss thee entice no woman.

* Which thou mightest get by marriage.

11

29. This I thee counsel sixthly:
    Although among men pass
    Offensive tipsy talk,
    Never, while drunken, quarrel
    With men of war:
    Wine steals the wits of many.

30. Brawls and drink
    To many men have been
    A heart-felt sorrow;
    To some their death,
    To some calamity:
    Many are the griefs of men!

31. This I thee counsel seventhly:
    If thou hast disputes
    With a daring man,
    Better it is for men
    To fight than to be burnt
    Within their dwelling.

32. This I thee counsel eighthly:
    That thou guard thee against evil,
    And eschew deceit.
    Entice no maiden,
    Nor wife of man,
    Nor to wantonness incite.

33. This I thee counsel ninthly:
    That thou corpses bury,
    Wherever on the earth thou findest them;
    Whether from sickness they have died,
    Or from the sea,
    Or are from weapons dead.

34. Let a mound be raised
    For those departed;
    Let their hands and head be washed,
    Combed, and wiped dry,
    Ere in the coffin they are laid;
    And pray for their happy sleep.

35. This I thee counsel tenthly:
That thou never trust
A foe's kinsman's promises,
Whose brother thou hast slain,
Or sire laid low:
There is a wolf
In a young son,
Though he with gold be gladdened.

36. Strifes and fierce enmities
Think not to be lulled,
No more than deadly injury.
Wisdom and fame in arms
A prince not easily acquires,
Who shall of men be foremost.

37. This I counsel thee eleventhly:
That thou at evil look,
What course it may take.
A long life, it seems to me,
The prince may [not] enjoy;
Fierce disputes will arise.

Sigurd said: A wiser mortal exists not, and I swear that I will possess thee, for thou art after my heart. She answered: Thee I will have before all others, though I have to choose among all men. And this they confirmed with oaths to each other.

Here ends the lay of Sigdrifa.

The reader may find some of these rules of *Hávamál* and *Sigrdrífumál* somewhat inconsistent with our ideas of a supreme deity; but are not many of these principles laid down in the Odinic morality worthy of a Christian age and of a Christian people, and do they not all reveal a profound knowledge of human nature in all its various phases?

These rules of life, says Professor Keyser, were variously understood, and as variously carried out into practice. But on the whole we find them reflected in the popular character of the Norsemen, such as history teaches it to us during heathendom. Bravery, prudence, and a love of independence are its brightest features, although bravery often degenerated into warrior fierceness, prudence into dissimulation, and the love of independence into self-will. If on the one hand we find a noble self-command, devoted faithfulness in friendship and love, noble-hearted hospitality and generosity, a love of right and of legal order, we also see, on the other hand, unyielding stubbornness, a fierce spirit of revenge, a repulsive arrogance, a far-reaching self-interest, and an excessive dependence upon the formalities of the law. A cold and unmoved exterior often concealed a soul torn by the bitterest grief, or stirred up by the wildest passions. A passionate outburst of joy or of grief was considered undignified. Few words, but energetic action, was esteemed in conduct, and complaint was silenced in order that vengeance could strike the more surely and heavily. Under a tranquil, indifferent mien were concealed the boldest and most deep-laid plans, and the real intention first came to light in the decisive moment. On the whole, there was certainly an impress of rigidity, insensibility and self-goodness stamped upon the popular character, but this stamp was more upon the outside than in its innermost character, more the result of inordinate prudence than of an evil disposition; and through all its failings there shines forth a dignity of soul which ennobled power and held up glory in this life and in after ages as the highest object of human undertakings.*

The part assigned to the Norsemen in the grand drama of European history was to free the human mind

* _Religion of the Northmen_, chap. xvii.

from the Cæsarian thraldom of Rome, in which it had so long been chained; to show what marvels self-government and free institutions can accomplish, and thus hand down to us, their descendants, a glorious heritage of imperishable principles, which we must study and in a great measure be guided by.

We retain in the days of the week the remembrance of this religion, which was brought to England more than fourteen hundred years ago by the Goths, who came to give that country a new name and a new fate in the world. The Goths taught the people of Britain to divide the week into their *Sun*-day, *Moon*-day, *Tys*-day, *Odin's*-day, *Thor's*-day, and *Frey's* or *Freyja's*-day. The name of Saturday the English owe to the Roman god Saturnus; but the last day of the week was known among the early Norsemen, and is still known among them, as *Laugar*-dag, *Lör*-dag, that is *Washing*-day. It is possible, as E. C. Otté quaintly remarks, that our Anglo-Saxon forefathers may have wished to change this name when, in later times, they had ceased to have only *one* washing-day out of the seven, like their northern ancestors.

We are now prepared to present the Norse mythology, and we shall divide it into three divisions: THE CREATION AND PRESERVATION, THE LIFE AND EXPLOITS OF THE GODS, and RAGNAROK AND REGENERATION. These three divisions we dedicate respectively to URD, VERDANDE, and SKULD, the three norns, WAS, IS, and SHALL BE, which uphold the world's structure and preside over the destinies of gods and men.

# NORSE MYTHOLOGY.

Urðar orði
kveðr engi maðr.
Vafin er Verðandi reyk.
Lítið sjáum aptr,
en ekki fram;
skyggir Skuld fyrir sjón.

MATTHIAS JOCHUMSSON.

# PART I.

## THE CREATION AND PRESERVATION OF THE WORLD.

# URD.

Urðar orði
kveðr engi maðr.

# CHAPTER I.

## THE CREATION.

THE condition of things before the creation of the world is expressed negatively. There was nothing of that which sprang into existence. This transition from empty space into being demands the attention of the whole human race. Therefore the vala, or wandering prophetess, begins her mysterious song, the grand and ancient Völuspá, the first lay in the Elder Edda, as follows:

> Give ear
> All ye divine races,
> Great and small,
> Sons of Heimdal!
> I am about to relate
> The wonderful works of Valfather,
> The oldest sayings of men,
> The first I remember.
>
> It was Time's morning
> When Ymer lived:
> There was no sand, no sea,
> No cooling billows;
> Earth there was none,
> No lofty heaven,
> Only Ginungagap,
> But no grass.

The beginning was this: Many ages, ere the earth was made, there existed two worlds. Far to the north was Niflheim (the nebulous world), and far to the south was Muspelheim (the fire world). Between them was Ginungagap (the yawning gap). In the middle of Niflheim lay the spring called Hvergelmer, and from it flowed twelve ice-cold streams, the rivers Elivagar, of which Gjol was situated nearest Hel-gate. Muspelheim was so bright and hot that it burned and blazed and could not be trodden by those who did not have their home and heritage there. In the midst of this intense light and burning heat sat Surt, guarding its borders with a flaming sword in his hand.

SECTION II. THE ORIGIN OF THE GIANTS (RHIMTHURSAR).

The first beings came into existence in the following manner: When those rivers that are called Elivagar, and which flowed from the spring Hvergelmer, had flowed far from their spring-head the venom which flowed with them hardened, as does dross that runs from a furnace, and became ice. And when the ice stood still, and ran not, the vapor arising from the venom gathered over it and froze to rime, and in this manner were formed in the yawning gap many layers of congealed vapor piled one over the other. That part of Ginungagap that lay toward the north was thus filled with thick and heavy ice and rime, and everywhere within were fogs and gusts; but the south side of Ginungagap was lightened by the sparks and flakes that flew out of Muspelheim. Thus while freezing cold and gathering gloom proceeded from Niflheim, that part of Ginungagap which looked toward Muspelheim was hot and bright; but Ginungagap was as light as windless air; and when the heated blast met the frozen vapor it melted into drops, *and by the might*

*of him who sent the heat,** these drops quickened into
life and were shaped into the likeness of a man. His
name was Ymer, but the frost-giants called him Aurgelmer. Ymer was not a god; he was bad (evil, *illr*),
as were all his kind. When he slept, he fell into a
sweat, and from the pit of his left arm waxed a man
and a woman, and one of his feet begat with the other
a son, from whom descend the frost-giants, and therefore Ymer is called the old frost-giant (Rhimthurs).
Thus the Elder Edda, in the lay of Vafthrudner:

> Countless winters
> Ere earth was formed,
> Was born Bergelmer;
> Thrudgelmer
> Was his sire,
> His grandsire Aurgelmer.

> From Elivagar
> Sprang venom drops,
> Which grew till they became a giant;
> But sparks flew
> From the south-world:
> To the ice the fire gave way.

> Under the armpit grew,
> 'T is said, of Rhimthurs,
> A girl and boy together;
> Foot with foot begat,
> Of that wise giant,
> A six-headed son.

SECTION III. THE ORIGIN OF THE COW AUDHUMBLA
AND THE BIRTH OF THE GODS.

On what did the giant Ymer live, is a pertinent
question. Here is the answer: The next thing, when
the rime had been resolved into drops, was that the

---

* The supreme god.

cow, which is called Audhumbla, was made of it. Four
milk-rivers ran out of her teats, and thus she fed Ymer.
On what did the cow feed? She licked rime-stones,
which were salt; and the first day that she licked the
stones there came at evening out of the stones a man's
hair, the second day a man's head, and the third day
all the man was there. His name was Bure. He was
fair of face, great and mighty. He begat a son by name
Bor. Bor took for his wife a woman whose name was
Bestla, a daughter of the giant Bolthorn, and they had
three sons, Odin, Vile and Ve, the rulers of heaven and
earth; and Odin, adds the Younger Edda, is the greatest
and lordliest of all the gods.

The frost-giants were, then, the first race or the
first dynasty of gods. The Elder Edda makes this dynasty embrace three beings, for Aurgelmer in the passage
quoted is the same as Ymer.

Odin descended from the frost-giants, which is also
proved by a passage in the Younger Edda, where Ganglere asks where Odin kept himself ere heaven and earth
were yet made. Then he was, answered Haar, with the
frost-giants (Rhimthursar).


SECTION IV.  THE NORSE DELUGE AND THE ORIGIN OF
HEAVEN AND EARTH.

Bor's sons, Odin, Vile and Ve, slew the giant Ymer,
but when he fell there ran so much blood out of his
wounds, that with that they drowned all the race of
the frost-giants, save one, who got away with his household; him the giants call Bergelmer. He went on board
his boat, and with him went his wife, and from them
came a new race of frost-giants. Thus the Elder Edda:

Winters past counting,
Ere earth was yet made,
Was born Bergelmer:
Full well I remember
How this crafty giant
Was stowed safe in his skiff.

Odin, Vile and Ve dragged the body of Ymer into the middle of Ginungagap, and of it they formed the earth. From Ymer's blood they made the seas and waters; from his flesh the land; from his bones the mountains; from his hair the forests, and from his teeth and jaws, together with some bits of broken bones, they made the stones and pebbles. From the blood that ran from his wounds they made the vast ocean, in the midst of which they fixed the earth, the ocean encircling it as a ring; and hardy, says the Younger Edda, will he be who attempts to cross those waters. Then they took his skull and formed thereof the vaulted heavens, which they placed over the earth, and set a dwarf at the corner of each of the four quarters. These dwarfs are called East, West, North, and South. The wandering sparks and red-hot flakes that had been cast out from Muspelheim they placed in the heavens, both above and below Ginungagap, to give light unto the world. The earth was round without and encircled by the deep ocean, the outward shores of which were assigned as a dwelling for the race of giants. But within, round about the earth, the sons of Bor raised a bulwark against turbulent giants, employing for this structure Ymer's eye-brows. To this bulwark they gave the name Midgard.* They afterwards threw and scattered the brains of Ymer in the air, and made of them the melancholy clouds. Thus the Elder Edda, in the lay of Vafthrudner:

* The Tower of Babel.

From Ymer's flesh
The earth was formed,
And from his bones the hills,
The heaven from the skull
Of that ice-cold giant,
And from his blood the sea.

And in Grimner's lay:

Of Ymer's flesh
Was earth created,
Of his blood the sea,
Of his bones the hills,
Of his hair trees and plants,
Of his skull the heavens,
And of his brows
The gentle powers
Formed Midgard for the sons of men;
But of his brain
The heavy clouds are
All created.

### SECTION V.   THE HEAVENLY BODIES, TIME, THE WIND, THE RAINBOW.

The heavenly bodies were formed of the sparks from Muspelheim. The gods did not create them, but only placed them in the heavens to give light unto the world, and assigned them a prescribed locality and motion. By them days and nights and seasons were marked. Thus the Elder Edda, in Völuspá:

The sun knew not
His proper sphere;
The stars knew not
Their proper place;
The moon knew not
Where her position was.

There was nowhere grass
Until Bor's sons

The expanse did raise,
By whom the great
Midgard was made.
From the south the sun
Shone on the walls;
Then did the earth
Green herbs produce.
The moon went ahead
The sun followed,
His right hand held
The steeds of heaven.

Mundilfare was the father of the sun and moon. It is stated in the Younger Edda that Mundilfare had two children, a son and a daughter, so lovely and graceful that he called the boy Maane* (moon) and the girl Sol* (sun), and the latter he gave in marriage to Glener (the shining one).

But the gods, being incensed at Mundilfare's presumption, took his children and placed them in the heavens, and let Sol drive the horses that draw the car of the sun. These horses are called Aarvak (the ever-wakeful) and Alsvinn(the rapid one); they are gentle and beautiful, and under their withers the gods placed two skins filled with air to cool and refresh them, or, according to another ancient tradition, an iron refrigerant substance called *isarnkol*. A shield, by name Svalin (cool), stands before the Sun, the shining god. The mountains and the ocean would burn up if this shield should fall away. Maane was set to guide the moon in her course, and regulate her increasing and waning aspect.

A giant, by name Norve, who dwelt in Jotunheim, had a daughter called Night (*nótt*), who, like all her race, was of a dark and swarthy complexion. She was

---

* In the Norse language, as also in the Anglo-Saxon, the sun is of the feminine and the moon of the masculine gender.

first wedded to a man called Naglfare, and had by him
a son named Aud, and afterward to another man called
Annar, by whom she had a daughter called Earth (*jörd*).
She finally espoused Delling (day-break), of asa-race,
and their son was Day (*dagr*), a child light and fair like
his father.   Allfather gave Night and Day two horses
and two cars, and set them up in the heavens that they
might drive successively one after the other, each in
twenty-four hours' time, round the world.   Night rides
first with her steed Hrimfaxe (rime-fax),* that every
morn, as he ends his course, bedews the earth with the
foam from his bit.   The steed driven by Day is called
Skinfaxe (shining-fax), and all the sky and earth glistens
from his mane.   Thus the Elder Edda, in the lay of
Vafthrudner:

> Mundilfare hight he
> Who the moon's father is,
> And also the sun's:
> Round heaven journey
> Each day they must,
> To count years for men.

In the lay of Grimner:

> Aarvak and Alsvinn,
> Theirs it is up hence
> Tired the sun to draw ·
> Under their shoulder
> These gentle powers, the gods,
> Have concealed an iron-coolness.

> Svalin the shield is called
> Which stands before the sun,
> The refulgent deity ;
> Rocks and ocean must, I ween,
> Be burnt,
> Fell it from its place.

* Fax = mane.

In the lay of Vafthrudner:

> Delling called is he
> Who the Day's father is,
> But Night was of Norve born;
> The new and waning moons
> The beneficent powers created
> To count years for men.

> Skinfaxe he is named
> That the bright day draws
> Forth over human kind;
> Of coursers he is best accounted
> Among faring men;
> Ever sheds light that horse's mane.

> Hrimfaxe he is called
> That each night draws forth
> Over the beneficent powers;
> He from his bit lets fall
> Drops every morn
> Whence in the dells comes dew.

The sun speeds at such a rate as if she feared that some one was pursuing her for her destruction. And well she may; for he that seeks her is not far behind, and she has no other way to escape than to run before him. But who is he that causes her this anxiety? There are two wolves: the one, whose name is Skol, pursues the sun, and it is he that she fears, for he shall one day overtake and devour her. The other, whose name is Hate Hrodvitneson, runs before her and as eagerly pursues the moon, that will one day be caught by him. Whence come these wolves? Answer: A giantess dwells in a wood called Jarnved (ironwood). It is situated east of Midgard, and is the abode of a race of witches. This old hag is the mother of many gigantic sons, who are all of them shaped like wolves, two of whom are Skol and Hate. There is one of tha.

race who is the most formidable of all. His name is
Maanagarm (moon-swallower): he is filled with the life-
blood of men who draw near their end, and he will
swallow up the moon, and stain the heavens and the
earth with blood. As it is said in the Völuspá, of the
Elder Edda:

> Eastward in the Ironwood
> The old one sitteth,
> And there bringeth forth
> Fenrer's fell kindred.
> Of these, one, the mightiest,
> The moon's devourer,
> In form most fiend-like,
> And filled with the life-blood
> Of the dead and the dying,
> Reddens with ruddy gore
> The seats of the high gods.
> Then shall the sunshine
> Of summer be darkened,
> And fickle the weather.
> Conceive ye this or not?

The gods set Evening and Midnight, Morning and
Noon, Forenoon and Afternoon, to count out the year.
There were only two seasons, summer and winter; hence
spring and fall must be included in these two. The
father of Summer is called Svasud (the mild), who is
such a gentle and delicate being, that what is mild is
from him called sweet (*sváslegt*). The father of Winter
has two names, Vindlone and Vindsval (the wind-cool);
he is the son of Vasud (sleet-bringing), and, like all his
race, has an icy breath and is of grim and gloomy
aspect.

Whence come the winds, that are so strong that
they move the ocean and fan fire to flame, and still are
so airy that no mortal eye can discern them? Answer:
In the northern extremity of the heavens sits a giant

called Hræsvelger (corpse-swallower), clad with eagles' plumes. When he spreads out his wings for flight, the winds arise from under them.

Which is the path leading from earth to heaven? The gods made a bridge from earth to heaven and called it Bifrost (the vibrating way). We have all seen it and call it the rainbow. It is of three hues and constructed with more art than any other work. But though strong it be, it will be broken to pieces when the sons of Muspel, after having traversed great rivers, shall ride over it. There is nothing in nature that can hope to make resistance when the sons of Muspel sally forth to the great combat. Now listen to the Elder Edda on some of these subjects.

In the lay of Grimner:

> Skol the wolf is named
> That the fair-faced goddess
> To the ocean chases;
> Another Hate is called,
> He is Hrodvitner's son:
> He the bright maid of heaven shall precede.

In the Völuspá:

> Then went the powers all
> To their judgment seats,
> The all-holy gods,
> And thereon held council:
> To night and to the waning moon
> Gave names;
> Morn they named
> And mid-day,
> Afternoon and eve,
> Whereby to reckon years.

In the lay of Vafthrudner:

> Vindsval is his name
> Who winter's father is,

And Svasud summer's father is:
Yearly they both
Shall ever journey,
Until the powers perish.

Hræsvelger is his name
Who at the end of heaven sits,
A giant in an eagle's plumage:
From his wings comes,
It is said, the wind
That over all men passes.

In reference to Maane, it should be added, that the Younger Edda tells us, that he once took children from earth. Their names were Bil and Hjuke. They went from the spring called Byrger, and bore on their shoulders the bucket called Sæger with the pole called Simul. Their father's name was Vidfin. These children follow Maane, as may be seen, from the earth.

SECTION VI. THE GOLDEN AGE. THE ORIGIN OF THE DWARFS. THE CREATION OF THE FIRST MAN AND WOMAN.

In the beginning Allfather (Odin) appointed rulers and bade them judge with him the fate of men and regulate the government of the celestial city. They met for this purpose in a place called Idavold (the plains of Ida), which is the center of the divine abode (Asgard, the abode of the asas). Their first work was to erect a court or hall, where there are twelve seats for themselves, besides the throne which is occupied by Allfather. This hall is the largest and most magnificent in the universe, being resplendent on all sides both within and without with the finest gold. Its name is Gladsheim (home of gladness). They also erected another hall for the sanctuary of the goddesses. It is a fair structure and is called Vingolf (friends'-floor). Thereupon they built a smithy and furnished it with hammers, tongs and anvils, and with these made all other requisite instruments with which they worked in metals, stone and wood, and composed so large a quantity of the metal called gold, that they made all their house-furniture of it. Hence that age was called the Golden Age. This was the age that lasted until the arrival of the women out of Jotunheim, who corrupted it.

Then the gods seating themselves upon their thrones distributed justice, and remembered how the dwarfs had been bred in the mould of the earth, just as worms in a dead body. The dwarfs were quickened as maggots in the flesh of the old giant Ymer, but by the command of the gods they received the form and understanding of men; their abode was, however, in the earth and rocks. Four dwarfs, Austre (east), Vestre (west), Nordre (north), and Sudre (south), were appointed by the gods to bear up the sky. Of the race of dwarfs Modsogner and Durin are the principal ones.

There were not yet any human beings upon the earth, when one day, as the sons of Bor (Odin, Hœner and Loder) were walking along the sea-beach, they found two trees and created from them the first human pair, man and woman. Odin gave them life and spirit, Hœner endowed them with reason and the power of motion, and Loder gave them blood, hearing, vision and a fair complexion. The man they called Ask, and the woman Embla. The newly created pair received from the gods Midgard as their abode; and from Ask and Embla is descended the whole human family. Thus the Elder Edda, in Völuspá.

The asas met
On Ida's plains;
They altars raised
And temples built;
Furnaces they established,
Precious things forged,
Their strength they tried
In many ways
When making tongs
And forming tools.

On the green they played
In joyful mood,
Nor knew at all
The want of gold,
Until there came
Three giant maids
Exceeding strong
From Jotunheim.

Then all the powers
Went to the throne,
The holy gods,
And held consult
Who should of dwarfs
The race then fashion
From the livid bones
And blood of the giant.

Modsogner, chief
Of the dwarfish race,
And Durin, too,
Were then created;
And like to men
Dwarfs in the earth
Were formed in numbers
As Durin ordered.

And then there came
Out of the ranks,
Powerful and fair,
Three asas home,

And found on shore,
In helpless plight,
Ask and Embla,*
Without their fate.

They had not yet
Spirit or mind,
Blood or beauty
Or lovely hue.
Odin gave spirit,
Hœner gave mind,
Loder gave blood
And lovely hue.

### SECTION VII.   THE GODS AND THEIR ABODES.

In the Old Norse language a god is called *áss* (pl.
*æsir*) and a goddess *ásynja*. The gods dwell in Asgard.
In its midst are the plains of Ida (*Idavöllr*, the assembling-place of the gods), and Odin's high-seat Hlidskjalf, from where he looks out upon all the worlds.
But above the heaven of the asas are higher heavens,
and in the highest stands the imperishable gold-roofed
hall Gimle, which is brighter than the sun.

The gods, to whom divine honors must be rendered,
are twelve in number, and their names are Odin, Thor,
Balder, Tyr, Brage, Heimdal, Hoder, Vidar, Vale, Uller,
Forsete, Loke. In this list Njord and Frey are not
mentioned, for they originally belonged to the vans or
sea-gods, and were received among the asas by virtue
of a treaty in which Njord was given as a hostage, and
Frey is his son.

Of goddesses we find the number twenty-six, and
Vingolf is their hall. Odin's hall is the great Valhal.
Spears support its ceiling; it is roofed with shields, and
coats of mail adorn its benches. Thither and to Vin-

* Ash and Elm.

golf Odin invites all men wounded by arms or fallen in battle. Therefore he is called Valfather (father of the slain), and his invited guests are called einherjes. They are waited upon by valkyries.

The dwelling of Thor is Thrudvang or Thrudheim. His hall, the immense Bilskirner. Uller, Thor's son, lives in Ydaler. Balder lives in Breidablik, where nothing impure is found. Njord, one of the vans, dwells in Noatun by the sea. Heimdal inhabits Himinbjorg, which stands where Bifrost's bridge approaches heaven. Forsete has Glitner for his dwelling, whose roof of silver rests on golden columns. The chief goddess Frigg, wife of Odin, has her dwelling-place in Fensal, and Freyja, the goddess of love, dwells in Folkvang; her hall is Sessrymner. Saga dwells in the great Sokvabek under the cool waves; there she drinks with Odin every day from golden vessels.

We have so far mentioned the following classes of deities: giants, gods, goddesses, vans (sea-deities), and dwarfs. In addition to these the Younger Edda mentions two kinds of elves: elves of light and elves of darkness. The elves of light dwell in Alfheim (home of the elves), but the elves of darkness live under the earth, and differ from the others still more in their actions than in their appearance. The elves of light are fairer than the sun, but the elves of darkness blacker than pitch.

Then we have a lot of inferior spirits, such as trolls, hulder, witches (vættr), nisses, necks, etc., all of which figure extensively in the Norse folk-lore, but an extensive description of them will not be attempted in this work.

SECTION VIII. THE DIVISIONS OF THE WORLD.

Nine worlds are mentioned: Muspelheim, Asaheim, Ljosalfaheim, Vanaheim, Mannaheim, Jotunheim, Svartalfaheim, Helheim, Niflheim. The highest is Muspelheim (the fire-world), the realm of Surt, and in its highest regions it appears that Gimle (heaven) was thought to be situated. The lowest is Niflheim (the mist-world), the realm of cold and darkness, and in its midst is the fountain Hvergelmer, where the dragon Nidhug dwells. Between the two is Mannaheim (the world of man) or Midgard, the round disk of the earth, surrounded by the great ocean. The gods gave Ask and Embla, the first human pair, and their descendants, this world to dwell in. Far above Mannaheim is Asaheim (the world of the gods), forming a vault above the earth. In the midst of this world is Idavold, the assembling-place of the gods, and here is also Odin's lofty throne Hlidskjalf. Beyond the ocean is Jotunheim (the world of the giants). This world is separated from Asaheim by the river Ifing, which never freezes over. Nearest above the earth is Vanaheim (the world of the vans), and between it and Asaheim is Ljosalfaheim (the world of the light elves). Proceeding downward, we come first to Svartalfaheim (world of the dark elves), below Mannaheim, and between Svartalfaheim and Niflheim we have Helheim (the world of the dead, hell). Thither the way from the upper worlds led down by the north through Jotunheim over the stream Gjol, the bridge over which, called Gjallar-bridge, was roofed over with shining gold.

# CHAPTER II.

## THE PRESERVATION.

### THE ASH YGDRASIL. MIMER'S FOUNTAIN. URD'S FOUNTAIN. THE NORNS OR FATES.

YGDRASIL is one of the noblest conceptions that ever entered into any scheme of cosmogony or human existence. It is in fact the great tree of life, wonderfully elaborated and extended through the whole system of the universe. It furnishes bodies for mankind from its branches; it strikes its roots through all worlds, and spreads its life-giving arms through the heavens. All life is cherished by it, even that of serpents, which devour its roots and seek to destroy it. It has three grand roots far apart. One of them extends to the asas, another to the giants in that very place where was formerly Ginungagap, and the third stands over Niflheim, and under this root, which is constantly gnawed by the serpent Nidhug and all his reptile brood, is the fountain Hvergelmer. Under the root that stretches out toward the giants is Mimer's fountain, in which wisdom and wit lie hid. The owner of this fountain is called Mimer. He is full of wisdom, because he drinks the waters of the fountain every morning with the Gjallarhorn. Once Odin came and begged a draught of this water, which he received, but he had to leave one of his eyes in pawn for it. Thus it is recorded in the Elder Edda:

Full well I know,
Great Odin, where
Thine eye thou lost;
In Mimer's well,
The fountain pure,
Mead Mimer drinks
Each morning new,
With Odin's pledge.
Conceive ye this?

Under the root of Ygdrasil, which extends to the asas in heaven, is the holy Urdar-fountain. Here the gods sit in judgment. Every day they ride up hither on horseback over Bifrost (the rainbow), which is called the bridge of the gods (*ásbrú*). Odin rides his gray eight-footed Sleipner, Heimdal on Goldtop. The other horses are Glad (bright), Gyller (gilder), Gler (the shining one), Skeidbrimer (fleet-foot), Silfrintop (silver top), Siner (sinews), Gisl (the sunbeam), Falhofner (pale hoof), Letfet (light-foot). It has been stated before that the gods worthy of divine honors were twelve, and here we have ten horses named. Balder's and Thor's are wanting. Balder's horse was burnt with his master's body, and as for Thor, he has to go on foot. He cannot pass the Asabridge, for the thunder, which he is, would destroy it; therefore he daily wades through the rivers Kormt, Ormt, and two others called Kerlaug, to get to the council of the gods.

The giants cannot pass the Asabridge, for the red in it is burning fire and the waters of heaven roar around it. If it were easy for every one to walk over it, the giants would go up to heaven by that bridge, and perhaps succeed in bringing ruin upon the gods.

At the Urdar-fountain dwell also three maidens, named Urd, Verdande and Skuld (Present, Past and Future). These maidens fix the lifetime of all men,

and are called norns. They guard the fountain, which
takes its name from the first and highest of the three,
Urd (Urdar-fount). Besides these there are other norns,
some of which are of heavenly origin, but others belong to the races of elves and dwarfs. The norns
who are of good origin are good themselves, and dis-
pense good destinies. Those men to whom misfortunes happen ought to ascribe them to the evil
norns. Thus it is that some men are fortunate and
wealthy, while others acquire neither riches nor honors;
some live to a good old age, while others are cut off in
their prime.

Furthermore it must be stated of the ash Ygdrasil,
that on its topmost bough sits an eagle who knows
many things, and between the eagle's eyes sits a hawk
by name Vedfolner. A squirrel, whose name is Ratatosk,
runs up and down the tree, and seeks to cause strife
between the eagle and the serpent Nidhug. Four stags
leap about beneath its branches and feed on its buds.
They are called Daain, Dvalin, Duneyr, and Durathror.
But there are so many snakes with Nidhug in the fountain Hvergelmer, that no tongue can count them. Thus
the Elder Edda:

> The tree Ygdrasil
> Bears a sorer burden
> Than men imagine.
> Above the stags bite it,
> On its sides age rots it,
> Nidhug gnaws below.
>
> More serpents lie
> Under Ygdrasil's ash
> Than simpletons think of;
> Goin and Moin,
> The sons of Grafvitner,

> Graabak and Grafvollud,
> Ofner and Svafner,
> Must for aye, methinks,
> Gnaw the roots of that tree.

The norns, who dwell by the Urdar-fount, every day draw water from this spring, and with it, and the clay that lies around the fount, they sprinkle the ash, in order that the boughs may continue green, and not rot and wither away. This water is so holy that everything placed in the spring becomes as white as the film within an egg-shell. Thus the Elder Edda:

> An ash know I standing
> Named Ygdrasil,
> A stately tree sprinkled
> With water, the purest;
> Thence come the dewdrops
> That fall in the dales;
> Ever blooming it stands
> O'er the Urdar-fountain.

The dew that falls from the tree on the earth men call honey-dew, and it is the food of the bees. Finally, two swans swim in the Urdar-fountain, and they are the parents of the race of swans. Thus all the tribes of nature partake of the universal tree.

# CHAPTER III.

---

IN the Norse as in all mythologies, the beginning
of creation is a cosmogony presenting many questions difficult of solution. The natural desire of knowledge asks for the origin of all things; and as the
beginning always remains inexplicable, the mind tries
to satisfy itself by penetrating as far into the primeval
forms of matter and means of sustaining life as possible. We follow the development of the tree back to the
seed and then to the embryo of the seed, but still we
are unable to explain how a miniature oak can exist in
scarcely more than a mere point in the acorn. We even
inspect the first development of the plant with the
microscope, but we acquire knowledge not of the force,
but only of its manifestations or phenomena. Such was
also the experience of our ancestors, when they inquired
into the origin of this world. They had the same desire
to know, but were not so well provided with means of
finding out, as we are with our microscopic, telescopic,
and spectrum analysis instruments.

The first effort of the speculative man is to solve the
mystery of existence. The first question is: How has
this world begun to be? What was in the beginning,
or what was there before there yet was anything? In
the Greek mythology many forms seem to arise out of
night, which seems to shroud them all. Thus in the

Norse mythology the *negative* is the first, a *conditio sine qua non,* space we might say, which we must conceive of as existing, before anything can be conceived as existing in it. Our ancestors imagined in the beginning only a yawning gap in which there was absolutely nothing. Wonderfully enough they said that the one side of this immense gulf extended to the north and the other to the south, as though there could be such things as *north* and *south* before the creation of the world. The north side was cold, the south warm; and thus we find by closer inspection that this nothing still was something, that contained in itself opposite forces, cold and heat, force of contraction and force of expansion, but these forces were in a state of absolute inertia. Thus also the Greek chaos:

> . . . . . . rudis indigestaque moles,
> Nec quidquam nisi pondus iners, congestaque eodem
> Non bene junctarum discordia semina rerum.

We cannot conceive how a body containing two forces can be a *pondus iners,* for every force is infinite and cannot rest unless it is prisoned by its opposite force, and this is then strife. The Norse view is, philosophically speaking, more correct. Here the opposite forces are separated by a gulf, and as they cannot penetrate the empty space, they remain inert.

It has before been stated that the Norsemen believed in a great and almighty god. who was greater than Odin. This god appears in the creation of the world, where he sends the heated blasts from Muspelheim and imparts life to the melted drops of rime. He will appear again as the just and mighty one, who is to reign with Balder in the regenerated earth. He is the true Allfather.

When the thought was directed to inquire into the

13

origin of the world, one question would naturally suggest another, thus:

Question: What produced the world? Answer: The giant Ymer.

Question: But on what did the giant Ymer live? Answer: On the milk of a cow.

Question: What did the cow live on? Answer: On salt.

Question: Where did the salt come from? Answer: From the rime.

Question: Whence came the rime? Answer: From ice-cold streams.

Question: Whence came the cold? Answer: From Niflheim.

Question: But what gave life to the rime? Answer: The heat.

Question: Whence came the heat? Answer: From him who sent it.

Here inquiry could go no further. This process brought the inquirer to the god whom he dared not name, the author and ruler of all things. This unknown god thus appears only before the creation and after the fall of the world. He is not a god of time but of eternity. He is from everlasting to everlasting.

The Elder Edda calls Ymer, Aurgelmer, father of Thrudgelmer and grandfather of Bergelmer (Berggelmer.) The first syllables of these words express the gradual hardening of matter from *aur* (loose clay) to *thrud* (packed, compressed, strong clay), and finally to *berg* (rock). Ymer, that is, the first chaotic world-mass, is produced by the union of frost and fire. The dead cold matter is quickened by the heat into a huge shapeless giant, which has to be slain; that is, the crude matter had to be broken to pieces before it could be remodeled into the various forms which nature since has assumed. This living mass, Ymer, produces many beings like himself, frost-cold, stone-like, shapeless frost-giants and mountain giants (icebergs and mountains). In these forms evil is still predominant. All are allied to the world of cold and darkness. It is only the lower, the physical, world-life which moves in them.

But a better being, although of animal nature,— the cow Audhumbla — came into existence from the frozen vapor, as the nurse of Ymer. This power nourishes the chaotic world, and at the same time calls forth by its refining agency — by licking the rime-clumps — a higher spiritual life, which unfolds itself through several links — through Bure, the bearing (father), and Bor, the born (son) — until it has gained power sufficient to overcome chaotic matter — to kill Ymer and his off-spring. This conquering power is divinity itself, which now in the form of a trinity goes forth as a creative power — as spirit, will and holiness, in the brothers Odin, Vile and Ve. The spirit quickens, the will arranges, and holiness banishes the impure and evil. It is how-ever only in the creation of the world that these three brothers are represented as coöperating. Vile and Ve are not mentioned again in the whole mythology. They are blended together in the all-embracing, all-pervading world-spirit Odin, who is the essence of the world, the almighty god.

This idea of a trinity appears twice more in the Norse mythology. In the Gylfaginning of the Younger Edda, Ganglere sees three thrones, raised one above the other, and a man sitting on each of them. Upon his asking what the names of these lords might be, his guide answered: He who sitteth on the lowest throne is a king. and his name is Haar (the high or lofty one);

the second is Jafnhaar (equally high); but he who
sitteth on the highest throne is called Thride (the
third). Then in the creation of man the divinity appears in the form of a trinity. The three gods, Odin,
Hœner, and Loder, create the first human pair, each
one imparting to them a gift corresponding to his
own nature. Odin (*önd*, spirit) gives them spirit, the
spiritual life; he is himself the spirit of the world,
of which man's is a reflection. Hœner (light) illuminates the soul with understanding (*ódr*). Loder (fire,
Germ. *lodern*, to flame) gives the warm blood and
the blushing color, together with the burning keenness
of the senses. It is evident that Odin's brothers on
these occasions are mere emanations of his being, they
proceed from him, and only represent different phases
of the same divine power. Loder is probably the
same person as afterwards steps forward as an independent divinity by name Loke. When he was united
with Odin in the trinity he sends a quiet, gentle and
invisible flame of light through the veins of Ask and
Embla, that is of mankind. Afterwards, assuming the
name of Loke, he becomes the consuming fire of the
earth. Loder produces and develops life; Loke cor-
rupts and destroys life.

By the creation the elements are separated. Ymer's
body is parceled out; organic life begins. But the
chaotic powers, though conquered, are not destroyed;
a giant escapes in his ark with his family, and from
them comes a new race of giants. Disturbing and
deadly influences are perceptible everywhere in nature,
and these influences are represented by the hostile
dispositions of the giants toward the asas and of
their struggles to destroy the work of the latter. The
giants have been forced to fly to Jotunheim, to Ut-

gard, to the outermost deserts beyond the sea; but still they manage to get within Midgard, the abode of man, and here they dwell in the rugged mountains, in the ice-clad jokuls and in the barren deserts, in short, everywhere where any barrenness prevails. Their agency is perceptible in the devastating storms caused by the wind-strokes of Hræsvelger, the giant eagle in the North; it is felt in winter's cold, snow and ice, and in all the powers of nature which are unfriendly to fruitfulness and life.

> The golden age of the gods, when
> On the green they played
> In joyful mood,
> Nor knew at all
> The want of gold,
> Until there came
> Three giant maids
> From Jotunheim,

represents the golden age of the child and the childhood of the human race. The life of the gods in its different stages of development resembles the life of men. Childhood is innocent and happy, manhood brings with it cares and troubles. The gods were happy and played on the green so long as their development had not yet taken any decided outward direction; but this freedom from care ended when they had to make dwarfs and men, and through them got a whole world full of troubles and anxieties to provide for and protect,—just as the golden age ends for the child when it enters upon the activities of life, and for the race, when it enters into the many complications and cares of organized society. The gods played with pieces of gold. The pure gold symbolizes innocence. These pieces of gold (*gullnar töflur*) were lost, but were found again in the green grass of the regenerated earth. From the above it must be clear that the three giant maids, who came from Jotunheim and put an end to the golden age, must be the norns, the all-pervading necessity that develops the child into manhood. It does not follow, therefore, that these maids were giantesses, for the gods themselves *descended* from the giants. Nor did the norns introduce evil into the world, but they marked out for the gods a career which could not be changed; and immediately after the appearance of the maids from Jotunheim the gods must create man, whose fate those same norns would afterwards determine.

The gods did not create the dwarfs, but only determined that they were to have the form and understanding of men.

Man was made of trees — of the ash and the elm. There is something graceful in this idea. The Norse conception certainly is of a higher order than those which produce man from earth or stones. It is more natural and more noble to regard man as having been made of trees, which as they grow from the earth heavenward show an unconscious attraction to that which is divine, than, as the Greeks do, to make men stand forth out of cold clay and hard stones. We confess that the Norse myth looks Greek and the Greek looks Norse; yet there may be a good reason for it. The plastic Greek regarded man as a statue, which generally was formed of clay or stone, but to which a divine spark of art gave life. The Norsemen knew not the plastic arts, and therefore had to go to nature, and not to art, for their symbols. The manner in which Odin breathes spirit and life into the trees reminds us very forcibly of the Mosaic narrative. It is interesting to study the various mythological theories in regard to the origin of man. The inhabitants of Thibet have a theory that undoubtedly is of interest to the followers of Darwin. In Thibet the three gods held counsel as to how Thibet might be peopled. The first one showed in a speech that the propagation of the human race could not be secured unless one of them changed himself into an ape. The last one of the three gods did this, and the goddess Kadroma was persuaded to change herself into a female ape. The plan succeeded, and they have left a numerous offspring.*

Various classes of beings are mentioned in the mythology. Life is a conflict between these beings, for the spiritual everywhere seeks to penetrate and govern the physical; but it also everywhere meets resistance. The asas rule over heaven and earth, and unite themselves with the vans, the water divinities. The giants war with the asas and vans. The elves most properly belong to the asas, while the dwarfs are more closely allied to the giants, but they serve the asas. The most decided struggle, then, is between the asas and giants.

The spiritual and physical character of the giants is clearly brought out in the myths. They constitute a race by themselves, divided into different groups, but have a common king or ruler. Their bodies are of superhuman size, having several hands and heads. Sterkodder had six arms; Hymer had many heads, and they were hard as stones; Hrungner's forehead was harder than any kettle. The giantesses are either horribly ugly or charmingly beautiful. As the offspring of darkness, the giants prefer to be out at night. The sunlight, and especially lightning, terrifies them. On land and sea they inhabit large caves, rocks and mount-

* Wagner, p. 192.

ains. Their very nature is closely allied to stones and mountains. When Brynhild drove in a chariot on the way to Hel, and passed through a place in which a giantess dwelt, the giantess said:

> Thou shalt not
> Pass through
> My stone-supported
> Dwelling-place.

The weapons of the giants, as the following myths will show, were stones and rocks; they had clubs and shields of stone. Hrungner's weapons were flint-stones. The giants also have domesticated animals. The giant Thrym sat on a mound plaiting gold bands for his greyhounds and smoothing the manes of his horses. He had gold-horned cows and all-black oxen. They possess abundance of wealth and treasures.

The giant is old, strong and powerful, very know-ing and wise, but also severe, proud and boasting. The giantess is violent, passionate and impertinent. In their lazy rest the giants are good-natured; they may be as happy as children; but they must not be teased.

The giants representing the wild, disturbing, chaotic forces in nature, the beneficent gods can subdue or con-trol them in two ways: The one is to kill them and use their remains for promoting the fruitfulness of the earth, the other is to unite with them, in other words, to marry them. This forms the subject of a large number of myths, which, when we have formed a correct general conception of the giants, need no further explanation. Odin kills Sokmimer, the destructive maelstrom of the ocean. Thor crushes Hrungner, the barren mountain. Odin marries Gunlad, Njord marries Skade, Frey marries Gerd, etc.

When the Odinic mythology was superseded by the

Christian religion it left a numerous offspring of elves, trolls (dwarfs), nisses, necks, mermaids, princes, princesses, etc., all of which still live in the memory and traditions of Scandinavia. They may be said to belong to the fairy mythology of these countries. We give a brief sketch of these objects of popular belief, chiefly from the excellent work of Thomas Keightley. A general knowledge of them is necessary in order to appreciate the rich folk-lore literature of Norseland.

The elves still retain their distinction into *white* and *black*. The white or good elves dwell in the air, dance on the grass, or sit in the leaves of trees; the black or evil elves are regarded as an underground people, who frequently inflict sickness or injury on mankind, for which there is a particular kind of doctors and doctresses in most parts of Scandinavia. The elves are believed to have their kings, and to celebrate their weddings and banquets, just the same as the dwellers above ground. There is an interesting intermediate class of them called in popular tradition hill-people (*haugafolk*), who are believed to dwell in caves and small hills. When they show themselves they have a handsome human form. The common people seem to connect with them a deep feeling of melancholy, as if bewailing a half-quenched hope of salvation. Their sweet singing may occasionally be heard on summer nights out of their hills, when one stands still and listens, or, as it is expressed in the ballads, lays his ear to the elf-hill; but no one must be so cruel as by the slightest word to destroy their hopes of salvation, for then the spritely music will be turned into weeping and lamentation. The Norsemen usually call the elves *hulder* or *huldrefolk*, and their music *huldreslaat*. It is in the minor key, and of a dull and mournful sound.

Norse fiddlers sometimes play it, being thought to have
learned it by listening to the underground people among
the hills and rocks.   There is also a tune called the elf-
kings' tune, which several of the good fiddlers know
right well, but never venture to play, for as soon as it
begins both old and young, and even inanimate objects,
are compelled to dance, and the player cannot stop unless
he can play the air backwards, or that some one comes
behind him and cuts the strings of his fiddle.   Ole Bull
and Thorgeir Andunson, the people think, learned to
play the fiddle from the hill-people.   The little underground elves, who are thought to dwell under the houses
of mankind, are described as sportive and mischievous,
and as imitating all the actions of men.   They are said
to love cleanliness about the house and place, and to
reward such servants as are neat and cleanly.

The dwarfs have become trolls.   They are not generally regarded as malignant.   They are thought to live
inside of hills, mounds and mountains; sometimes in
single families, sometimes in societies.   They figure
extensively in the folk-lore.   They are thought to be
extremely rich, for when on great occasions of festivity
they have their hills raised up on red pillars, people
that have chanced to be passing by have seen them
shoving large chests full of money to and fro, and
opening and clapping down the lids of them.   Their
dwellings are very magnificent inside, being decorated
with gold and crystal.   They are obliging and neighborly,
freely lending and borrowing and otherwise keeping up
a friendly intercourse with mankind.   But they have a
sad propensity to stealing, not only provisions, but also
women and children.   Trolls have a great dislike to
noise, probably from the recollection of the time when
Thor used to be flinging his hammer after them, while

this would indicate that the giants are their true ancestors. The hanging of bells in the churches has for this reason driven the most of them out of the country.

The nisse is the German kobold and the Scotch brownie. He seems to be of the dwarf family, as he resembles them in appearance, and like them has plenty of money and a dislike to noise and tumult. He is of the size of a year-old child, but has the face of an old man. His usual dress is gray, with a pointed red cap, but on Michaelmas day he wears a round hat like those of the peasants. No farm-house goes on well unless there is a nisse in it, and well it is for the maids and the men when they are in favor with him. They may go to their beds and give themselves no trouble about their work, and yet in the morning the maids will find the kitchen swept and water brought in, and the men will find the horses in the stable well cleaned and curried, and perhaps a supply of corn cribbed for them from the neighbor's barns. But he punishes them for any irregularity that takes place.

The neck is the river-spirit. Sometimes he is represented as sitting during the summer nights on the surface of the water, like a pretty little boy with golden hair hanging in ringlets, and a red cap on his head; sometimes as above the water, like a handsome young man, but beneath like a horse; at other times as an old man with a long beard, out of which he wrings the water as he sits on the cliffs. The neck is very severe against any haughty maiden who makes an ill return to the love of her wooer; but should he himself fall in love with a maid of human kind. he is the most polite and attentive suitor in the world. The neck is also a great musician: he sits on the water and plays on his gold harp, the harmony of which operates on all nature.

To learn music of him, a person must present him with a black lamb and also promise him resurrection and redemption.

The stromkarl, called in Norway *grim* or *fosse-grim* (force-grim), is a musical genius like the neck. He who has learned from him can play in such a masterly manner that the trees dance and waterfalls stop at his music.

The merman is described as of a handsome form with green or black hair and beard. He dwells either in the bottom of the sea or in cliffs near the sea-shore, and is regarded as rather a good and beneficent kind of being.

The mermaid (*haffrue*) is represented in the popular tradition sometimes as good, at other times as evil and treacherous. Her appearance is beautiful. Fishermen sometimes see her in the bright summer's sun, when a thin mist hangs over the sea, sitting on the surface of the water, and combing her long golden hair with a golden comb, or driving up her snow-white cattle to feed on the strands or small islands. At other times she comes as a beautiful maiden, chilled and shivering with the cold of the night, to the fires the fishermen have kindled, hoping by this means to entice them to her love. Her appearance prognosticates both storm and ill success in their fishing. People that are drowned, and whose bodies are not found, are believed to be taken into the dwellings of the mermaids.

It is the prevalent opinion among the common people of the North that all these various beings were once worsted in a conflict with superior powers, and condemned to remain until doomsday in certain assigned abodes. The rocks were given to the dwarfs; the groves and leafy trees to the elves; the caves and caverns to the hill-people; the sea, lakes and rivers to the merman, mermaids and necks; and the small forces (waterfalls) to the fossegrims. Both the Catholic and Protestant priests have tried to excite an aversion to these beings, but in vain. They still live and fill the fairy-tales and folk-lore with their strange characters, and are capable of furnishing a series of unrivaled subjects for the painter and sculptor. These weird stories are excellently adapted to adorn our epic and dramatic poetry as well as our historic novels. But they must be thoroughly understood first, not only by the poet, but also by his reader. Thomas Keightley, from whom we have given a short abstract, has given us an excellent work in English on Gothic fairy mythology, and we would recommend our readers to read his work in connection with Dr. Dasent's *Tales from the Fjeld*. *We* have to present the original mythology, not its offspring.

Ygdrasil is a most sublime and finished myth. It is a symbol uniting all the elements of mythology into a poetical system. The tree symbolizes, and extends its roots and branches into, the whole universe. Its roots are gnawed by serpents, and stags bite its branches, but the immortal tree still stands firm and flourishes from age to age. The Norsemen's whole experience of life is here presented in a picture that either in regard to beauty or depth of thought finds no equal in all the other systems of mythology. Thomas Carlyle says: I like too that representation they (the Norsemen) have of the tree Ygdrasil: all life is figured by them as a tree. Ygdrasil, the Ash-tree of Existence, has its roots deep down in the kingdom of *Hela*, or Death; its trunk reaches up heaven-high, spreads its boughs over the whole universe. It is the Tree of Existence. At the foot of it, in the Death-kingdom, sit three *Nornas* (fates),— the Past, Present,

Future,— watering its roots from the Sacred Well. Its boughs, with their buddings and disleafings — events, things suffered, things done, catastrophes,— stretch through all lands and times. Is not every leaf of it a biography, every fiber there an act or word? Its boughs are histories of nations; the rustle of it is the noise of human existence, onwards from of old. It grows there, the breath of human passion rustling through it; or storm-tost, the storm-wind howling through it like the voice of all the gods. It is Ygdrasil, the Tree of Existence. It is the past, the present, and the future; what was done, what is doing, what will be done; the infinite conjugation of the verb *to do*. Considering how human things circulate, each inextricably in communion with all,— how the word I speak to you to-day is borrowed, not from Ulfila, the Mæso-Goth only, but from all men since the first man began to speak,— I find no similitude so true as this of a tree. Beautiful altogether, beautiful and great. The machine of the universe! Alas, do but think of that in contrast!

The name Ygdrasil is derived from Odin's name, *Yggr* (the deep thinker), and *drasill* (carrier, horse). Ygdrasil, therefore, means the *Bearer of God*, a phrase which finds a literal explanation when Odin hangs nine nights on this tree before he discovered the runes. Thus the Elder Edda:

> I know that I hung
> Nine whole nights,
> And to Odin offered,
> On that tree,
> From what root it springs.
> On a wind-rocked tree,
> With a spear wounded,
> Myself to myself,
> Of which no one knows.

* *Heroes and Hero-worship.*

All the tribes of nature partake of this universal tree, from the eagle who sits on the topmost bough down through the different stages of animal life; the hawk in the lower strata of air, the squirrel who busily leaps about in the branches, the stags by the fountain, to the serpents beneath the surface of the earth.

The peculiar feature of this myth is its comprehensiveness. How beautiful the sight of a large tree! Its far-extending branches, its moss-covered stem, its high crown and deep roots, remind us of the infinity of time: it has seen ages roll by before we were born. In the evening, when our day's work is done, we lie down in its broad shade and think of the rest that awaits us when all our troubles are ended. Its leaves rustle in the breezes and the sunshine; they speak to us of that which is going on above this sorrow-stricken earth. But the tree is not the whole symbol. It is connected with the great waters, with the clear fountain with its egg-white waves, and with the turbulent streams that flow in the bowels of the earth. While the calm firmness of the tree and the monotonous rustling of the wind through its leaves invites the soul to rest, the ceaseless activity of the various tribes of animals that feed upon its roots and branches remind us of nature never at rest and never tiring. The tree sighs and groans beneath its burden; the animals move about in it and around it; every species of animals has its place and destination; the eagle soars on his broad wings over its top; the serpent winds his slimy coils in the deep; the swan swims in the fountain; and while all the tribes of animated life are busily engaged, the dew-drops fall to refresh and cool the earth and the heart of man. Nay, this is not all. There is one who has planted the tree, and there are many who watch and care for it; higher beings protect it. Gods and men, all that possesses life and consciousness, has its home in this tree and its work to do. The norns constantly refresh it with water from the Urdar-fountain; the elves hover about it; Heimdal suspends his tricolored arch beneath it; the glory of Balder shines upon it; Mimer lifts his head in the distance, and the pale Hel watches the shades of men who have departed this earth and journey through the nine worlds over Gjallarbro to their final rewards. The picture is so grand that nothing but an infinite soul can comprehend it; no brush can paint it, no colors can represent it. Nothing is quiet, nothing at rest; all is activity. It is the whole world, and it can be comprehended only by the mind of man, by the soul of the poet, and be symbolized by the ceaseless flow of language. It is not a theme for the painter or sculptor, but for the poet. Ygdrasil is the tree of experience of the Gothic race. It is the symbol of a great race, sprung originally from the same root but divided into many branches, Norsemen, Englishmen, Americans, etc. It has three roots, and experience has taught the Goths that there are in reality but three kinds of people in the world: some that work energetically for noble and eternal purposes, and their root is in Asaheim; some that work equally energetically, but for evil and temporal ends, and their root is in Jotunheim; and many who distinguished themselves only by sloth and impotence, and their root is in Niflheim with the goddess Hel or death, in Hvergelmer, where the serpent Nidhug, with all his reptile brood, gnaws at their lives. Thus the Gothic race is reflected in Ygdrasil, and if our poets will study it they will find that this grand myth is itself in fact a root in the Urdar-fountain, and from it may spring an Ygdrasil of poetry, extending long branches throughout the poetical world and delighting the nations of the earth.

Beneath that root of Ygdrasil, which shoots down to Jotunheim, there is a fountain called after its watcher *Mimer's Fountain,* in which wisdom and knowledge are concealed. The name Mimer means the *knowing.* The giants, being older than the asas, looked deeper than the latter into the darkness of the past. They had witnessed the birth of the gods and the beginning of the world, and they foresaw their downfall. Concerning both these events, the gods had to go to them for knowledge, an idea which is most forcibly expressed in the Völuspá, the first song in the Elder Edda, where a vala, or prophetess, from Jotunheim is represented as rising up from the deep and unveiling the past and future to gods and men. It is this wisdom that Mimer keeps in his fountain. Odin himself must have it. In the night, when the sun has set behind the borders of the earth, he goes to Jotunheim. Odin penetrates the mysteries of the deep, but he must leave his eye in pawn for the drink which he receives from the fountain of knowledge. But in the glory of morning dawn, when the sun rises again from Jotunheim, Mimer drinks from his golden horn the clear mead which flows over Odin's pawn. Heaven and this lower world mutually impart their wisdom to each other.

The norns watch over man through life. They spin his thread of fate at his birth and mark out with it the limits of his sphere of action in life. Their decrees are inviolable destiny, their dispensations inevitable necessity. The gods themselves must bow before the laws of the norns; they are limited by time; they are born and must die. Urd and Verdande, the Past and Present, are represented as stretching a web from

14

east to west, from the radiant dawn of life to the glowing sunset, and Skuld, the Future, tears it to pieces.
There is a deeply-laid plan in the universe, a close
union between spirit and matter. There is no such
thing as independent life or action. The ends of the
threads wherewith our life is woven lie deeply hid in
the abyss of the beginning. Self-consciousness is merely
an abstraction. The self-conscious individual is merely
a leaf, which imagines itself to be something, but is in
fact only a bud that unfolds itself and falls off from
the tree of the universe. The self-contradiction between
absolute necessity and free will was an unsolved riddle
with our heathen ancestors, and puzzles the minds of
many of our most profound thinkers still. Thus, says
the Elder Edda, the norns came to decide the destiny
of Helge Hundingsbane:

> It was in times of yore,
> When the eagles screamed,
> Holy waters fell
> From the heavenly hills;
> Then to Helge,
> The great of soul,
> Berghild gave birth
> In Braalund.
>
> In the mansion it was night:
> The norns came,
> Who should the prince's
> Life determine;
> They him decreed
> A prince most famed to be,
> And of leaders
> Accounted best.
>
> With all their might they span
> The fatal threads,
> When that he burghs should overthrow
> In Braalund.

They stretched out
The golden cord,
And beneath the middle
Of the moon's mansion fixed it.

East and west
They hid the ends,
Where the prince had
Lands between ;
Toward the north
Nere's sister
Cast a chain,
Which she bade last forever.

Nay, in the Norseman's faith, man and all things about him were sustained by divine power. The norns decreed by rigid fate each man's career, which not even the gods could alter. Man was free to act, but all the consequences of his actions were settled beforehand.

# PART II.

---

## THE LIFE AND EXPLOITS OF THE GODS.

# VERDANDE.

Vatin er Verðandi reyk.

# CHAPTER I.

## ODIN.

### SECTION I. ODIN.

THE first and eldest of the asas is Odin. His name is derived from the verb *vada* (imperfect *ód*), to walk, (compare watan, wuot, wuth, wüthen, wuothan, wodan). He is the all-*pervading* spirit of the world, and produces life and spirit (*önd, aand*). He does not create the world, but arranges and governs it. With Vile and Ve he makes heaven and earth from Ymer's body; with Hœner and Loder he makes the first man and woman, and he gives them spirit. All enterprise in peace and in war proceeds from him. He is the author of war and the inventor of poetry. All knowledge comes from him and he is the inventor of the runes. As the spirit of life he permeates all animate and inanimate matter, the whole universe; he is the infinite wanderer. He governs all things, and although the other deities are powerful they all serve and obey him as children do their father. He confers many favors on gods and men. As it is said in the Elder Edda, in the lay of Hyndla:

### FREYJA.

Wake maid of maids!
Wake, my friend!
Hyndla! Sister,
Who in the cavern dwellest.

(215)

Now there is dark of darks;
We will both to Valhal ride
And to the holy fane.

Let us Odin pray
Into our minds to enter;
He gives and grants
Gold to the deserving.
He gave Hermod
A helm and corselet,
And from him Sigmund
A sword received.

Victory to his sons he gives,
But to some riches;
Eloquence to the great
And to men wit;
Fair wind he gives to traders,
But visions to skalds;
Valor he gives
To many a warrior.

Especially are the heroes constantly the object of his care. He guides and protects the brave hero through his whole life; he watches over his birth and over his whole development; gives him wonderful weapons, teaches him new arts of war; assists him in critical emergencies, accompanies him in war, and takes the impetus out of the enemy's javelins; and when the warrior has at last grown old, he provides that he may not die upon his bed, but fall in honorable combat. Finally, he protects the social organization and influences the human mind. He revenges murder, protects the sanctity of the oath, subdues hatred, and dispels anxieties and sorrows.

## SECTION II.   ODIN'S NAMES.

Odin is called Allfather, because he is the father of all the gods, and Valfather (father of the slain), because he chooses for his sons all who fall in combat. For their abode he has prepared Valhal and Vingolf, where they are called einherjes (heroes). In Asgard, Odin has twelve names, but in the Younger Edda forty-nine names are enumerated, and if to these are added all the names by which the poets have called him, the number will reach nearly two hundred. The reason for his many names, says the Younger Edda, is the great variety of languages. For the various nations were obliged to translate his name into their respective tongues in order that they might supplicate and worship him. Some of his names, however, are owing to adventures that have happened to him on his journeys and which are related in old stories. No one can pass for a wise man who is not able to give an account of these wonderful adventures.

### SECTION III. ODIN'S OUTWARD APPEARANCE.

In appearance, Odin is an old, tall, one-eyed man, with a long beard, a broad-brimmed hat, a striped cloak of many colors, and a spear in his hand. On his arm he wears the gold ring Draupner, two ravens sit on his shoulders, two wolves lie at his feet, and a huge chariot rolls above his head. He sits upon a high throne and looks out upon the world, or he rides on the winds upon his horse Sleipner. There is a deep speculative expression on his countenance. In the Volsung Saga, Odin is revealed as follows: King Volsung had made preparations for an entertainment. Blazing fires burned along the hall, and in the middle of the hall stood a large tree, whose green and fair foliage covered the roof. (This reminds us of Ygdrasil.) King Volsung had placed it there, and it was called Odin's tree. Now as the guests sat around the fire in the evening, a man

entered the hall whose countenance they did not know.
He wore a variegated cloak, was bare-footed, his breeches
were of linen, and a wide-brimmed hat hung down
over his face. He was very tall, looked old, and was
one-eyed. He had a sword in his hand. The man
went to the tree, struck his sword into it with so powerful a blow that it sunk into it even to the hilt. No
one dared greet this man. Then said he: He who
draws this sword out of the trunk of the tree shall
have it as a gift from me, and shall find it true that
he never wielded a better sword. Then went the old
man out of the hall again, and no one knew who he
was or whither he went. Now all tried to draw the
sword out, but it would not move, before Volsung's son,
Sigmund, came; for him it seemed to be quite loose.
Farther on in the Saga Sigmund had become king,
and had already grown old when he waged war with
King Lynge. The norns protected him so that he could
not be wounded. In a battle with Lynge there came a
man to Sigmund, wearing a large hat and blue cloak.
He had but one eye, and had a spear in his hand.
The man swung his spear against Sigmund. Sigmund's
sword broke in two, luck had left him, and he fell. The
same Saga afterwards tells us that Sigmund's son, Sigurd, sailed against the sons of Hunding, on a large
dragon. A storm arose, but Sigurd commanded that
the sails should not be taken down, even though the
wind should split them, but rather be hoisted higher.
As they passed a rocky point, a man cried to the ship
and asked who was the commander of the ships and
men. They answered that it was Sigurd Sigmundson,
the bravest of all young men. The man said, all agree
in praising him; take in the sails and take me on
board! They asked him for his name. He answered:

Hnikar they called me, when I gladdened the raven after the battle; call me now Karl, from the mountain, Fengr or Fjolner, but take me on board! They laid to and took him on board. The storm ceased and they sailed until they came to the sons of Hunding; then Fjolner (Odin) disappeared. In the same Saga he also comes to Sigurd in the garb of an old man with long flowing beard, and teaches him how to dig ditches by which to capture Fafner.

### SECTION IV. ODIN'S ATTRIBUTES.

Odin's hat represents the arched vault of heaven, and his blue or variegated cloak is the blue sky or atmosphere, and both these symbolize protection.

Odin's ravens, Hugin (reflection) and Munin (memory), have been mentioned before. They are perched upon his shoulders and whisper into his ears what they see and hear. He sends them out at daybreak to fly over the world, and they come back at eve toward mealtime. Hence it is that Odin knows so much and is called Rafnagud (raven-god). Most beautifully does Odin express himself about these ravens in Grimner's lay, in the Elder Edda:

> Hugin and Munin
> Fly each day
> Over the spacious earth.
> I fear for Hugin
> That he come not back,
> Yet more anxious am I for Munin.

And in Odin's Raven-song, Hug (Hugin) goes forth to explore the heavens. Odin's mind, then, is the flying raven; he is the spiritual ruler.

Odin has two wolves, Gere and Freke (the greedy one and the voracious one). Odin gives the meat that

is set on his table to these two wolves; for he himself
stands in no need of food. Wine is for him both meat
and drink. Thus the Elder Edda, in Grimner's lay:

> Gere and Freke
> Feeds the war-faring,
> Triumphant father of hosts;
> For 't is with wine only
> That Odin in arms renowned
> Is nourished forever.

To meet a wolf is a good omen. Odin amusing himself with his wolves is an exquisite theme for the sculptor.

Odin had a ring called Draupner. We find its history in the conversations of Brage, the second part of
the Younger Edda. Loke had once out of malice cut
all the hair off Sif, the wife of Thor. But when Thor
found this out he seized Loke and would have crushed
every bone in him if he had not sworn to get the elves
of darkness to make golden hair for Sif, that would grow
like other hair. Then went Loke to the dwarfs, that are
called Ivald's sons, and they made the hair, and Skidbladner (Frey's ship), and the spear that Odin owned and
is called Gungner. Then Loke wagered his head with
the dwarf, whose name is Brok, that his brother, Sindre,
would not be able to make three more treasures as good
as those three just named. The brothers went to the
smithy. Sindre put a pig-skin in the furnace and bade
Brok blow the bellows and not stop before Sindre took
that out of the furnace which he had put into it. A fly
set itself on Brok's hand and stung him, but still he
continued blowing the bellows, and that which Sindre
took out was a boar with golden bristles. Then Sindre
put gold into the furnace. This time the fly set itself
on Brok's neck, and stung him worse, but he continued
blowing the bellows, and that which the smith took out

was the gold ring Draupner (from the verb meaning *to drop*). The third time Sindre put iron in the furnace, and bade his brother be sure to continue blowing or all would be spoiled. Now the fly set itself between his eyes and stung his eye-lids. The blood ran down into his eyes, so that he could not see; then Brok let go of the bellows just for a moment to drive the fly away. That which the smith now took out was a hammer. Sindre gave his brother these treasures and bade him go to Asgard to fetch the wager. As now Loke and Brok came each with his treasures, the asas seated themselves upon their thrones and held consult, and Odin, Thor and Frey were appointed judges who should render a final decision. Then Loke gave Odin the spear, which never would miss its mark; Thor he gave the hair, which immediately grew fast upon Sif's head; and to Frey he gave the ship, which always got fair wind as soon as the sails were hoisted, no matter where its captain was going, and it could also be folded as a napkin and put into the pocket, if this were desirable. Thereupon Brok came forward and gave Odin the ring, and said that every ninth night a ring equally heavy would drop from it. To Frey he gave the boar, and said that it could run in the air and on the sea, night and day, faster than any horse, and the night never was so dark, nor the other worlds so gloomy, but that it would be light where this boar was present, so bright shone its bristles. To Thor he gave the hammer, and said that with it he might strike as large an object as he pleased; it would never fail, and when he threw it he should not be afraid of losing it, for no matter how far it flew it would always return into his hand, and at his wish it would become so small that he might conceal it in his bosom, but it had one fault, and that was that the handle was rather short. According to the decision of the gods, the hammer was the best of all the treasures, and especially as a protection against the frost-giants; they accordingly decided that the dwarf had won the wager. The latter now wanted Loke's head. Loke offered to redeem it in some way, but the dwarf would accept no alternatives. Well take me then, said Loke, and in a moment he was far away, for he had shoes with which he could run through the air and over the sea. Then the dwarf asked Thor to seize him, which was done; but when the dwarf wanted to cut his head off, Loke said: The head is yours, but not the neck.[*] Then took the dwarf thread and knife and wanted to pierce Loke's lips, so as to sew his lips together, but the knife was not sharp enough. Now it were well, if I had my brother's awl, said he, and instantaneously the awl was there, and it was sharp. Then the dwarf sewed Loke's lips together. (The dwarfs are here represented as smiths of the gods.)

The ring Draupner is a symbol of fertility. Odin placed this ring on Balder's funeral pile and it was burnt with Balder (the summer), and when Balder sent this ring back to Odin, his wife, the flower-goddess Nanna, sent Frigg, the wife of Odin, a carpet (of grass), which represents the return of vegetation and fruitfulness. Balder sends the ring back as a memento of the fair time when he and his father (Odin) worked together, and reminds the father of all, that he must continue to bless the earth and make it fruitful. But this is not all; this ring also symbolizes the fertility of the mind, the creative power of the poet, the evolution

---

[*] Compare *Shakespeare* — Shylock and the pound of flesh:

. . . No jot of blood;
The words expressly are "a pound of flesh."

of one thought from the other, the wonderful chain of thought. The rings fell from Draupner as drop falls from drop. Ideas do not cling fast to their parent, but live an independent life when they are born; and the idea or thought, when once awakened, does not slumber, but continues to grow and develop in man after man, in generation after generation, evolving constantly new ideas until it has grown into a unique system of thought. If we, as our fathers undoubtedly did, make this gold ring typify the historical connection between times and events, a ring constantly multiplying and increasing with ring interlinked with ring in time's onward march, what a beautiful golden chain there has been formed from time's morning until now!

Odin had a spear called Gungner. The word means producing a violent shaking or trembling, and it most thoroughly shook whomsoever was hit by it. As has been seen above, it was made by the sons of Ivald (the dwarfs), and was presented to Odin by Loke. Odin speeds forth to the field of battle with golden helmet, resplendent armor, and his spear Gungner. Oath was taken on the point of Gungner. This spear is frequently referred to in the semi-mythological Sagas, where spears are seen flying over the heads of the enemy; they are panic-stricken and defeated. Spears are sometimes seen as meteorical phenomena, showing that war is impending. The spear symbolizes Odin's strength and power. When Odin's spear was thrown over anybody, Odin thereby marked him as his own. Did not Odin wound himself with a spear, and thereby consecrate himself to heaven? (See pp. 254–261.) When Odin puts the spear into the hands of the warrior, it means that he awakens and directs his deeds of valor. When Odin is the god of poetry and eloquence (Anglo-Saxon *wód*), then the

spear Gungner is the keen, stinging satire that can be
expressed in poetry and oratory.

Odin's horse Sleipner (slippery) was the most excellent horse. Runes were carved on his teeth. The following myth gives us an account of his birth: When
the gods were constructing their abodes, and had already
finished Midgard and Valhal, a certain artificer came
and offered to build them, in the space of three half
years, a residence so well fortified that they should be
perfectly safe from the incursions of the frost-giants and
the giants of the mountains, even though they should
have penetrated within Midgard. But he demanded for
his reward the goddess Freyja, together with the sun and
moon. After long deliberation the gods agreed to his
terms, provided he would finish the whole work himself without any one's assistance, and all within the
space of one winter; but if anything remained unfin-
ished on the first day of summer, he should forfeit the
recompense agreed on. On being told these terms, the
artificer stipulated that he should be allowed the use
of his horse, called Svadilfare (slippery-farer), and this
by the advice of Loke was granted to him. He accordingly set to work on the first day of winter, and during
the night let his horse draw stone for the building.
The enormous size of the stones struck the gods with
astonishment, and they saw clearly that the horse did
one half more of the toilsome work than his master.
Their bargain, however, had been concluded in the presence of witnesses and confirmed by solemn oaths, for
without these precautions a giant would not have
thought himself safe among the gods, especially when
Thor returned from an expedition he had then undertaken toward the east against evil demons.

As the winter drew to a close, the building was far

advanced, and the bulwarks were sufficiently high and massive to render this residence impregnable. In short, when it wanted but three days to summer, the only part that remained to be finished was the gateway. Then sat the gods on their seats of justice and entered into consultation, inquiring of one another who among them could have advised to give Freyja away to Jotunheim or to plunge the heavens in darkness by permitting the giant to carry away the sun and the moon. They all agreed that none but Loke Laufeyarson and the author of so many evil deeds could have given such bad counsel, and that he should be put to a cruel death if he did not contrive some way or other to prevent the artificer from completing his task and obtaining the stipulated recompense. They immediately proceeded to lay hands on Loke, who in his fright promised upon oath, that let it cost him what it would he would so manage matters that the man should lose his reward. That very night, when the artificer went with Svadilfare for building-stone, a mare suddenly ran out of a forest and began to neigh. The horse being thus excited, broke loose and ran after the mare into the forest, which obliged the man also to run after his horse, and thus between one and the other the whole night was lost, so that at dawn the work had not made the usual progress. The man, seeing that he had no other means of completing his task, resumed his own gigantic stature, and the gods now clearly perceived that it was in reality a mountain giant who had come amongst them. No longer regarding their oaths, they therefore called on Thor, who immediately ran to their assistance, and lifting up his mallet Mjolner (the crusher) that the dwarfs had made, he paid the workman his wages, not with the sun and moon, and not even by

15

sending him back to Jotunheim, for with the first blow
he shattered the giant's skull to pieces, and hurled him
headlong into Niflheim. But Loke had run such a race
with Svadilfare, that shortly after the mischief-maker
(Loke) bore a gray foal with eight legs. This is the
horse Sleipner, which excels all horses ever possessed by
gods or men. The gods perjured themselves, and in
reference to this says the Elder Edda:

> Then went the rulers there,
> All gods most holy,
> To their seats aloft,
> And counsel together took ;
> Who all the winsome air
> With guile had blended,
> Or to the giant's race
> Oder's maiden given.*

> Then Thor, who was there,
> Arose in wrathful mood,
> For seldom sits he still
> When such things he hears.
> Annulled were now all oaths,
> And words of promise fair,
> And faith not long before
> In council plighted.

This riddle is propounded. Who are the two who
ride to the Thing ? Three eyes have they together, ten
feet and one tail; and thus they travel through the
lands. The answer is Odin, who rides on Sleipner; he
has one eye, the horse two; the horse runs on eight
feet, Odin has two; only the horse has a tail.

Odin's horse, Sleipner, symbolizes the winds of
heaven, that blow from eight quarters. In Skaane and
Bleking, in Sweden, it was customary to leave a sheaf
of grain in the field for Odin's horse, to keep him from

* Freyja, whom the gods had promised the giant, was Oder's wife.

treading down the grain. Wednesday is named after Odin (Odinsday), and on this day his horse was most apt to visit the fields. But in a higher sense Sleipner is a Pegasos. Pegasos flew from the earth to the abodes of the gods; Sleipner comes from heaven, carries the hero unharmed through the dangers of life, and lifts the poet, who believes in the spirit, up to his heavenly home. Grundtvig calls Sleipner the courser of the poet's soul; that is to say, of the Icelandic or Old Norse strophe. in poetry, which consisted of eight verses, or four octometers. The most poetic is the most truthful interpretation of the myths.

### SECTION V. ODIN'S JOURNEYS.

A whole chapter might be written about the wanderings of Odin, his visits to the giants, to men, to battles, etc.; but as these records are very voluminous, and are found to a great extent in the semi-mythological Sagas, in which it is difficult to separate the mythical and historical elements, we will make but a few remarks on this subject. All his wanderings of course describe him as the all-pervading spirit of the universe. They have the same significance as his horse Sleipner, his ravens Hugin and Munin, etc. He descends to the bottom of the sea for wisdom, he descends to earth to try the minds of men. In the Elder Edda journeys of Odin form the subjects of the lays of Vafthrudner, Grimner, Vegtam, etc. (See pp. 120–124.) In the lay of Vafthrudner Odin visits the giant Vafthrudner for the purpose of proving his knowledge. They propose questions relating to the cosmogony of the Norse mythology, on the condition that the baffled party forfeit his head. The giant incurs the penalty. Odin calls himself Gangraad, but by the last question the giant recognizes him and is stricken with

awe and fear. The giant must perish since he has ven-
tured into combat with Odin. The mind subdues physical nature. When the giant recognizes Odin he realizes his own depressed nature and must die. No rogue
can look an honest man in the eye. In Grimnersmál
Odin assumes the name of Grimner, and goes to try the
mind of his foster-son Geirrod. Geirrod tortures him and
places him between two fires. And here begins the lay,
in which Odin glorifies himself and the power of the
gods and pities his fallen foster-son, but finally discloses
himself and declares death to Geirrod for his want of
hospitality. Thus Odin closes his address to Geirrod in
the lay of Grimner:

> Many things I told thee,
> But thou hast few remembered:
> Thy friends mislead thee.
> My friend's sword
> Lying I see
> With blood all dripping.
>
> The fallen by the sword
> Ygg shall now have;
> Thy life is now run out:
> Wrath with thee are the dises,
> Odin thou now shalt see:
> Draw near to me, if thou canst.
>
> Odin I am named,
> Ygg I was called before,
> Before that Thund,
> Vaker and Skilfing,
> Vafud and Hroptatyr;
> With the gods Gaut and Jalk,*
> Ofner and Svafner;
> All which I believe to be
> Names of me alone.

* Jack the Giant-killer.

## SECTION VI. ODIN AND MIMER.

In the lay of Vegtam, Odin goes to Hel, and wakes the prophetess to learn the fate of his son Balder. He also takes counsel from the utmost sources of the ocean, and listens to the voice from the deep. Some myths refer to Odin's pawning his eye with Mimer, others to his talking with Mimer's head.

The Younger Edda, having stated that Mimer's well is situated under that root of the world-ash Ygdrasil that extends to Jotunheim, adds that wisdom and wit lie concealed in it, and that Odin came to Mimer one day and asked for a drink of water from the fountain. He obtained the drink, but was obliged to leave one of his eyes in pawn for it. To this myth refers the following passage from the Völuspá in the Elder Edda:

> Alone she* sat without,
> When came that ancient
> Dreaded prince† of the gods,
> And in his eye she gazed.

The vala to Odin:

> Of what wouldst thou ask me?
> Odin! I know all,
> Where thou thine eye didst sink
> In the pure well of Mimer.
>
> Mimer drinks mead each morn
> From Valfather's pledge.
> Understand ye yet, or what?

This myth was given in connection with Ygdrasil, but it is repeated here to shed a ray of light upon the character of Odin, and in this wise Mimer is brought into a clearer sunlight also.

* The vala, or prophetess.     † Odin.

In regard to Odin's speaking with Mimer's head, we have the following passage in the lay of Sigdrifa:

> On the rock he* stood
> With edged sword,
> A helm on his head he bore.
> *Then spake Mimer's head*
> Its first wise word,
> And true sayings uttered.

And in Völuspá, when Ragnarok is impending:

> Mimer's sons dance,
> But the central tree takes fire
> At the resounding
> Gjallarhorn,
> Loud blows Heimdal,
> His horn is raised;
> *Odin speaks*
> *With Mimer's head.*

Odin's eye is the sun. Mimer's fountain is the utmost sources of the ocean. Into it, Odin's eye, the sun sinks every evening to search the secrets of the deep, and every morning Mimer drinks the gold-brown mead (aurora). When the dawn colors the sea with crimson and scarlet, then Mimer's white fountain is changed to golden mead; it is then Mimer, the watcher of the fountain of knowledge, drinks with his golden horn the clear mead which flows over Odin's pledge. But Mimer means memory† (Anglo-Saxon *meomor*), and as we know that our ancestors paid deep reverence to the memories of the past, and that the fallen heroes, who enjoyed the happiness of Valhal with Odin, reveled in the memory of their deeds done on earth, it is proper to add that Mimer is an impersonation of memory. Our spirit (Odin, *od*, *aand*) sinks down into the depths of the

---

* Odin.       † See Vocabulary under the word *Mimer*.

past (memory, the sea, Odin's fountain), and brings back golden thoughts, which are developed by the knowledge which we obtained from the depths beneath the sea of past history and experience. What a vast ocean is the history and experience of our race!

## SECTION VII. HLIDSKJALF.

Hlidskjalf is Odin's throne. The accounts of it are very meagre. The Younger Edda speaks of a stately mansion belonging to Odin called Valaskjalf, which was built by the gods and roofed with pure silver, and in which is the throne called Hlidskjalf. When Odin is seated on this throne he can see over the whole world. But he not only looks, he also listens.

> Odin listened
> In Hlidskjalf,

it is said in Odin's Raven-song; in Grimner's lay it is stated that Odin and Frigg, his wife, were sitting in Hlidskjalf, looking over all the world; and in the lay of Skirner we read that Frey, son of Njord, had one day seated himself in Hlidskjalf. As Odin every morning sends out his ravens, it seems to be his first business, as a good father, to look out upon the world that he hás made, and see how his children are doing, and whether they need his providential care in any respect. Hlidskjalf and Valhal must not be confounded. Valhal will be explained hereafter. It is situated in Gladsheim, where Odin sat with his chosen heroes and drank wine. But Valaskjalf is a place apart from Gladsheim, and on its highest pinnacle above the highest arches of heaven is Odin's throne, Hlidskjalf.

## SECTION VIII.   THE HISTORICAL ODIN.

We have now presented the mythological Odin as based on the inscrutable phenomena of nature, and have given some hints in regard to the ethical or anthropomorphic element contained in each myth. Our next subject will be Odin's wives, their maid-servants, his sons, etc.; but before we proceed to them we will give a short outline of the historical Odin, as he is presented in the Heimskringla of Snorre Sturleson by Saxo Grammaticus and others. Mr. Mallet, the French writer on Northern Antiquities, has given a synoptical view of all that these writers have said about the wanderings and exploits of this famous person, and we will make an abstract from him.

The Roman Empire had arrived at its highest point of power, and saw all the then known world subject to its laws, when an unforeseen event raised up enemies against it from the very bosom of the forests of Scythia and on the banks of the Tanais. Mithridates by flying had drawn Pompey after him into those deserts. The king of Pontus sought there for refuge and new means of vengeance. He hoped to arm against the ambition of Rome all the barbarous nations, his neighbors, whose liberty she threatened. He succeeded in this at first, but all those peoples, ill united as allies, poorly armed as soldiers, and still worse disciplined, were forced to yield to the genius of Pompey. Odin is said to have been of this number. He was obliged to flee from the vengeance of the Romans and to seek, in countries unknown to his enemies, that safety which he could no longer find in his own.

Odin commanded the Asas, whose country was situated between the Pontus Euxinus and the Caspian Sea.

Their principal city was Asgard. Odin having united under his banners the youth of the neighboring nations, marched toward the west and north of Europe, subduing all the peoples he met on his way and giving them to one or other of his sons for subjects. Many sovereign families of the North are said to be descended from these princes. Thus Hengist and Horsa, the Saxon chiefs who conquered Britain in the fifth century, counted Odin in the number of their ancestors. So did also the other Anglo-Saxon princes, as well as the greater part of the princes of Lower Germany and the North.

After having disposed of so many countries and confirmed and settled his new governments, Odin directed his course toward Scandinavia, passing through Holstein and Jutland. These provinces made him no resistance. Then he passed into Funen (Denmark), which submitted as soon as he appeared. In this island he remained for a long time and built the city of Odense (*Odins-ve*, Odin's sanctuary), which still preserves in its name the memory of its founder. Hence he extended his authority over all the North. He subdued the rest of Denmark and placed his son Skjold upon its throne. The descendants of Skjold continued for many generations to rule Denmark, and were called Skjoldungs.

Odin, who seems to have been better pleased to give crowns to his children than to wear them himself, afterwards passed over into Sweden, where at that time ruled a prince by name Gylfe, who paid him great honors and even worshiped him as a divinity. Odin quickly acquired in Sweden the same authority as he had obtained in Denmark. The Swedes came in crowds to do him homage, and by common consent bestowed the title of king upon his son Yngve and his posterity. Hence sprung the Ynglings, a name by which the kings of Sweden

were for a long time distinguished. Gylfe died and was
forgotten ; Odin acquired lasting fame by his distinguished rule.   He enacted new laws, introduced the
customs of his own country, and established at Sigtuna,
an ancient city in the same province as Stockholm, a
supreme council or tribunal, composed of twelve judges.
Their business was to watch over the public weal, to
distribute justice to the people, to preside over the new
worship, which Odin had brought with him into the
North, and to preserve faithfully the religious and mag-
ical secrets which that prince deposited with them.   He
levied a tax on every man throughout the country, but
engaged on his part to defend the inhabitants against
all their enemies and to defray the expense of the worship rendered to the gods at Sigtuna.

These great acquisitions seem not, however, to have
satisfied his ambition.   The desire of extending further
his religion, his authority, and his glory, caused him to
undertake the conquest of Norway.   His good fortune
followed him thither, and this kingdom quickly obeyed
a son of Odin named Sæming, who became the head of
a family the different branches of which reigned for a
long time in Norway.

After Odin had finished these glorious achievements
he retired into Sweden, where, perceiving his end to
draw near, he would not wait for a lingering disease to
put an end to that life which he had so often and so
valiantly hazarded in the battle-field, but gathering round
him the friends and companions of his fortune, he gave
himself nine wounds in the form of a circle with the
point of a lance, and many other cuts in his skin with
his sword.   As he was dying he declared he was going
back to Asgard to take his seat among the gods at an
eternal banquet, where he would receive with great

honors all who should expose themselves intrepidly in
battle and die bravely with their swords in their hands.
As soon as he had breathed his last they carried his
body to Sigtuna, where, in accordance with a custom
introduced by him into the North, his body was burned
with much pomp and magnificence.

Such was the end of this man, whose death was
as extraordinary as his life. It has been contended by
many learned men that a desire of being revenged on
the Romans was the ruling principle of his whole conduct. Driven by those enemies of universal liberty from
his former home, his resentment was the more violent,
since the Goths considered it a sacred duty to revenge
all injuries, especially those offered to their relations or
country. He had no other view, it is said, in traversing
so many distant kingdoms, and in establishing with so
much zeal his doctrines of valor, but to arouse all
nations against so formidable and odious a nation as
that of Rome. This leaven which Odin left in the
bosoms of the worshipers of the gods, fermented a long
time in secret; but in the fullness of time, the signal
given, they fell upon this unhappy empire, and, after
many repeated shocks, entirely overturned it, thus re-
venging the insult offered so many ages before to their
founder.

The Sagas paint Odin as the most persuasive of men.
Nothing could resist the force of his words. He sometimes enlivened his harangues with verses, which he composed extemporaneously, and he was not only a great
poet, but it was he who taught the art of poetry to the
Norsemen. He was the inventor of the runic characters,
which so long were used in the North. This marking
down the unseen thought that is in man with written
characters is the most wonderful invention ever made;

it is almost as miraculous as speech itself, and well
may it be called a sort of second speech. But what
most contributed to make Odin pass for a god was his
skill in magic. He could run over the world in the
twinkling of an eye; he had the command of the air
and the tempests, he could transform himself into all
sorts of shapes, could raise the dead, could foretell
things to come, could by enchantments deprive his
enemies of health and strength and discover all the
treasures concealed in the earth. He knew how to
sing airs so tender and melodious, that the very plains
and mountains would open and expand with delight;
the ghosts, attracted by the sweetness of his songs,
would leave their infernal caverns and stand motionless
around him.

But while his eloquence, together with his august
and venerable deportment, procured him love and respect in a calm and peaceable assembly, he was no less
dreadful and furious in battle. He inspired his enemies
with such terror that they thought they could not describe it better than by saying he rendered them blind
and deaf. He would appear like a wolf all desperate and
biting his very shield for rage, he would throw himself
amidst the opposing ranks, making around him the
most horrible carnage, without receiving any wound
himself. Such is the historical Odin of the North,
such was, in other words, the great example that the
Norsemen had to imitate in war and in peace.

### SECTION IX. ODIN'S WIVES.

Odin's wives are Jord (Fjorgyn, Hlodyn), Rind and
Frigg. Heaven is married to earth. This we find in
all mythologies (Uranos and Gaia, Zeus and Demeter,
etc.) Among the Norsemen also the ruler of heaven

and earth (Odin) enters into marriage relations with his
own handiwork. This relation is expressed in three
ways: Odin is married to Jord, to Frigg, and to Rind.
Jord is the original, uninhabited earth, or the earth
without reference to man; Frigg is the inhabited, cultivated earth, the abode of man, and Rind is the earth
when it has again become unfruitful, when the white
flakes of winter have covered its crust; it is in this
latter condition that she long resists the loving embraces
of her husband. These three relations are expressed still
more clearly by their children. With Jord Odin begets
Thor, with Frigg Balder, and with Rind Vale. Jord
is the Greek Gaia, Frigg is Demeter, but the fortunate
Greeks had no goddess corresponding to Rind; they
knew not the severe Norse winter.

Jord is sometimes called Fjorgyn and Hlodyn, but
neither of these names occur many times in the Eddas.
There are only found occasional allusions to her, such
as the flesh of Ymer, the daughter of Annar, sister of
Dag, mother of Thor, etc.

Frigg is the daughter of Fjorgyn and the first among
the goddesses, the queen of the asas and asynjes. Odin
is her dearly beloved husband. She sits with him in
Hlidskjalf and looks out upon all the worlds, and for
the death of their son, the light Balder, they mourn together with all nature. Frigg knows the fate of men,
but she never says or prophesies anything about it herself. She possesses a falcon-disguise, which Loke once
borrowed of her. She possesses a magnificent mansion
Fensal, where she sat weeping over Valhal's misfortune
after the death of Balder. It is not certain whether
Friday is named after Frigg or Freyja or after Frey, but
the probabilities are that it is Freyja's day *(dies Veneris)*.
While Frigg and Freyja are by many authors confounded.

they are nevertheless wholly different characters. Frigg
is *asa*queen, Freyja is *vana*dis. Frigg is a *mother's* love;
Freyja is the love of the *youth* or *maiden*. The asas
are land deities, the vans are divinities of the water.
The vana-goddess Freyja represents the surging, billowy,
unsettled love; the asynje Frigg represents love in its
nobler and more constant form.

### SECTION X.   FRIGG'S MAID-SERVANTS.

Fulla, Hlyn, Gnaa, Snotra, Var, Lofn (Sjofn), and
Syn, are enumerated as maid-servants of Frigg.

Fulla goes about with her hair flowing over her
shoulders and her head adorned with a golden ribbon.
She is intrusted with the toilette and slippers of Frigg
and admitted into the most important secrets of that
goddess. The word Fulla means full, fulness, and as
the servant of Frigg she represents the fulness of the
earth, which is beautifully suggested by her waving hair
and golden ribbon (harvest), and when Balder sent the
ring Draupner from Hel, his wife Nanna sent Frigg a
carpet, and Fulla a gold ring.*

Hlyn has the care of those whom Frigg intends to
deliver from peril.

Gnaa is the messenger that Frigg sends into the
various worlds on her errands. She has a horse that
can run through air and water, called Hofvarpner (the
hoof-thrower). Once, as she drove out, certain vans
saw her car in the air, when one of them exclaimed:

> What flies there?
> What goes there?
> In the air aloft what glides?

She answered:

> I fly not, though I go,
> And glide through the air

On Hofvarpner,
Whose sire's Hamskerper *
And dame Gardrofa.†

Gnaa is interpreted to mean the mild breezes, that Frigg sends out to produce good weather.

Var listens to the oaths that men take, and particularly the troth plighted between man and woman, and punishes those who keep not their promises. She is wise and prudent, and so penetrating that nothing remains hidden from her. Her name Var means *wary*, careful.

Lofn (*lofa, loben,* love) is so mild and gracious to those who invoke her, that by a peculiar privilege which either Odin himself or Frigg has given her, she can remove every obstacle that may prevent the union of lovers sincerely attached to each other. Hence her name is applied to denote love, and whatever is beloved by men.

Sjofn delights in turning men's hearts and thoughts to love; hence love is called from her name *sjafni.*

Syn keeps the door in the hall and shuts it against those who ought not to enter. She presides at trials, when anything is to be denied on oath; whence the proverb, Syn (negation) is set against it, when anything is denied.

### SECTION XI.   GEFJUN, EIR.

The norns or destinies have been previously explained (see p. 190); Nanna will be discussed in connection with Balder, and Freyja, the goddess of love, in connection with Njord and Frey; but there are besides these a few other goddesses, who demand our attention here.

* He who hardens the hide.     † Fence-breaker.

Gefjun is a maid, and all those who die maids become her hand-maidens. Of her there is the following anecdote in the Younger Edda. King Gylfe ruled over the land which is now called Sweden. It is related of him that he once gave a wayfaring woman, as a recompense for her having diverted him, as much land in his realm as she could plow with four oxen in a day and a night.* This woman was however of the race of the asas, and was called Gefjun. She took four oxen from the North, out of Jotunheim, (but they were the sons she had had with a giant,) and set them before a plow. Now the plow made such deep furrows that it tore up the land, which the oxen drew westward out to the sea until they came to a sound. There Gefjun fixed the land and called it Seeland. And the place where the land had stood became water, and formed a lake which is now called Logrinn (the sea) in Sweden, and the inlets of this lake correspond exactly with the headlands of Seeland in Denmark. Thus saith the Skald, Brage:

> Gefjun drew from Gylfe,
> Rich in stored up treasure,
> The land she joined to Denmark.
> Four heads and eight eyes bearing,
> While hot sweat trickled down them,
> The oxen dragged the reft mass
> That formed this winsome island.

The etymology of Gefjun is uncertain. Some explain it as being a combination of the Greek γῆ and Norse *fjón*, separation (*terræ separatio*). Grimm compares it with the Old Saxon *geban*, Anglo-Saxon *geofon*, *gifan*, the ocean. Grundtvig derives it from Anglo-Saxon *gefean*, gladness. He says it is the same word as Funen (*Fyn*), and that the meaning of the myth is that

---

* Compare with this myth Dido and the founding of Carthage.

Funen and Jutland with united strength tore Seeland from Sweden. This would then be a historical interpretation.

The derivation from *gefa,* to give, has also been suggested, and there is no doubt that the plowing Gefjun is the goddess of agriculture. She unites herself with the giants (the barren and unfruitful fields or deserts) and subdues them, thus preparing the land for cultivation. In this sense she is Frigg's maid-servant. Gefjun, the plowed land, develops into Frigg, the fruit-bearing earth; hence she is a maid, not a woman. The maid *is not,* but *shall become* fruitful.

Eir is the goddess of the healing art, and this is about all that we know of her; but that is a great deal. A healer for our frail body and for the sick mind! what a beneficent divinity!

## SECTION XII. RIND.

This goddess was mentioned in Section IX. It is the third form of earth in its relation to Odin. Thus the lay of Vegtam, in the Elder Edda:

> Rind a son shall bear
> In the wintry halls,
> He shall slay Odin's son
> When one night old.
> He a hand will not wash,
> Nor his hair comb,
> Ere he to the pile has borne
> Balder's adversary.

Odin's repeated wooing of this maid is expressed in Hávamál, of the Elder Edda, as follows:

> The mind only knows
> What lies near the heart;

16

That alone is conscious of our affections.
No disease is worse
To a sensible man
Than not to be content with himself.

That I experienced
When in the reeds I sat
Awaiting my delight.
Body and soul to me
Was that discreet maiden:
Nevertheless I possess her not.

Billing's lass*
On her couch I found,
Sun-bright, sleeping.
A prince's joy
To me seemed naught,
If not with that form to live.

Yet nearer night, she said,
Must thou, Odin, come,
If thou wilt talk the maiden over;
All will be disastrous
Unless we alone
Are privy to such misdeed.

I returned,
Thinking to love
At her wise desire;
I thought
I should obtain
Her whole heart and love.

When next I came,
The bold warriors were
All awake,
With lights burning,
And bearing torches:
Thus was the way to pleasure closed.

⁓ Rind was daughter of Billing.

But at the approach of morn,
When again I came,
The household all was sleeping ;
The good damsel's dog
Alone I found
Tied to the bed.

Many a fair maiden,
When rightly known,
Toward men is fickle :
That I experienced
When that discreet maiden I
Strove to win :
Contumely of every kind
That wily girl
Heaped upon me ;
Nor of that damsel gained I aught.

This is clearly the same story as is related by Saxo
Grammaticus, as follows :   Odin loves a maiden, whose
name is Rind, and who has a stubborn disposition.
Odin tried to revenge the death of his son Balder.   Then
he was told by Rosthiof that he with Rind, the daughter of the king of the Ruthenians, would beget another
son, who would revenge his brother's death.   Odin put
on his broad-brimmed hat and went into the service of
the king, and won the friendship of the king, for as
commander he put a whole army to flight.   He revealed
his love to the king, but when he asked the maiden
for a kiss, she struck his ear.   The next year he came
as a smith, called himself Rosterus, and offered the
maiden a magnificent bracelet and beautiful rings ; but
she gave his ear another blow.   The third time he came
as a young warrior, but she thrust him away from her
so violently that he fell head first to the ground.
Finally he came as a woman, called himself Vecha, and
said he was a doctress.   As Rind's servant-maid, he

washed her feet in the evening, and when she became sick he promised to cure her, but the remedy was so bitter that she must first be bound. He represented to her father that it, even against her wish, must operate with all its dissolving power, and permeate all her limbs before she could be restored to health. Thus he won the maiden, as some think, with the secret consent of her father. But the gods banished Odin from Byzantium, and accepted in his place a certain Oller, whom they even gave Odin's name. This Oller had a bone, which he had so charmed by incantations that he could traverse the ocean with it as in a ship. Oller was banished again by the gods, and betook himself to Sweden; but Odin returned in his divine dignity and requested his son Bous, whom Rind had borne, and who showed a great proclivity for war, to revenge the death of his brother. Saxo Grammaticus relates this as confidently as if it were the most genuine history, not having the faintest suspicion as to its mythical character.

Saxo's Rosthiof is mentioned in the Elder Edda as Hross-thiofr (horse-thief), of Hrimner's (the frost's rime's) race. Saxo's Vecha is Odin, who in the Elder Edda is called Vak. The latter portion of the myth is not given in Hávamál, and were it not for faithful Saxo we should scarcely understand that portion of the Elder Edda which was quoted above. But with the light that he sheds upon it there is no longer any doubt. Rind is the earth, not generally speaking, but the earth who after the death of Balder is consigned to the power of winter. Does not the English word *rind* remind us of the hard-frozen crust of the earth? Defiantly and long she resists the love of Odin; in vain he proffers her the ornaments of summer; in vain he reminds her of his warlike deeds, the Norseman's most cherished enterprise in the summer-season. By his all-powerful witchcraft he must dissolve and as it were melt her stubborn mind. Finally she gives birth to Vale, the strong warrior.

In the incantation of Groa, in the Elder Edda, this is the first song that the mother sings to her son:

> I will sing to thee first
> One that is thought most useful,
> Which Rind sang to Ran;*
> That from thy shoulders thou shouldst cast
> What to thee seems irksome:
> Let thyself thyself direct. (Be independent!)

What is it that seems so irksome to Rind and Ran, and that both cast from their shoulders in order to become independent? It is the ice. When Rind had thrown it off she requested the sea-goddess Ran to do likewise.

The Greeks have a myth corresponding somewhat to this. The god of the heavens, Zeus, comes down in the rain into Hera's lap; but when she resisted his entreaties Zeus let fall a shower of rain, while she was sitting on the top of a mountain, and he changed himself to a nightingale (a symbol of spring-time). Then Hera compassionately took the wet and dripping bird into her lap. But look at the difference! Hera soon gives way and pities, but our Norse Rind makes a desperate resistance. It repeatedly looks as if Odin had conquered, but the maid reassumes her stubborn disposition. How true this is of the climate in the northern latitudes! Rind is not inapplicable to our Wisconsin winters.

Such is the physical interpretation of Odin's relation to Frigg and Rind. Heaven and earth are wedded together; and upon this marriage earth presents itself in two forms: fruitful and blest, unfruitful and imprisoned

* The goddess of the sea.

in the chains of cold and frost.  As the king of the year
Odin embraces both of them.  But Odin is also the
spiritual (*aand*) king, who unites himself with the human
earthly mind.  He finds it crude and uncultured, but
susceptible of impressions.  Pure thoughts and noble
feelings are developed, which grow into blooming activities.  But then comes back again the unfeeling coldness
and defiant stubbornness which take possession of the
mind, shutting out the influence of truth upon the mind.
It is a sad time when doubt and skepticism and despair
every night lay their leaden weight upon the poor man's
soul.  However to the honest seeker of truth it is only
a transitory state of trial.  A wise Providence takes him
with tender and patient hands again to his bosom.  He
sends down showers of blessings or misfortunes upon
him.  With his mild breath he melts the frozen heart,
and it at once clothes itself with garlands of divinest
hues.  With all his charms he touches the wintry *rind*
that encases us, and the mind stands forth unmanacled
and free.  What to the year is light summer and dark
winter is to us bright and gloomy periods of our existence, that succeed each other in their turn, advancing
or impeding our spiritual development, which must continue forever.  This is also contained in the myth about
Odin and Rind, nay, it is the better half.

### SECTION XIII.  GUNLAD.  THE ORIGIN OF POETRY.

Poetry is represented as an inspiring drink.  He who
partakes of it is *skáld*, poet.  This drink was kept with
the giants, where Gunlad protected it.  Odin goes down
to the giants, conquers all obstacles, wins Gunlad's affection, and gets permission to partake of the drink.  He
brings it to the upper world and gives it to men.  Thus

poetry originated and developed. Thus it is related in the Younger Edda:

Æger having expressed a wish to know how poetry originated, Brage, the god of poetry, informed him that the asas and vans having met to put an end to the war which had long been carried on between them, a treaty of peace was agreed to and ratified by each party spitting into a jar. As a lasting sign of the amity which was thenceforward to subsist between the contending parties, the gods formed out of this spittle a being, to whom they gave the name of Kvaser, and whom they endowed with such a high degree of intelligence that no one could ask him a question that he was unable to answer. Kvaser then traversed the whole world to teach men wisdom, but the dwarfs, Fjalar and Galar, having invited him to a feast, treacherously murdered him. They let his blood run into two cups and a kettle. The name of the kettle is Odrœrer, and the names of the cups are Son and Bodn. By mixing up his blood with honey they composed a drink of such surpassing excellence that whoever partakes of it acquires the gift of song (becomes a poet or man of knowledge, *skáld, eða fræðamaðr*). When the gods inquired what had become of Kvaser, the dwarfs told them that he had been suffocated with his own wisdom, not being able to find anyone who, by proposing to him a sufficient number of learned questions, might relieve him of its superabundance.

The dwarfs invited a giant, by name Gilling, and his wife. They proposed to the giant to take a boat-ride with them out on the sea, but they rowed on to a rock and capsized. Gilling could not swim, and perished, but the dwarfs rowed ashore, and told his wife of his death, which made her burst forth in a flood of tears. Then

Fjalar asked her whether it would not be some consolation to her to look out upon the water, where her husband had perished; and when she consented to this, Fjalar said to his brother Galar that he should get up above the door, and, as she passed out through it, he should let fall a mill-stone upon her head, for he was sick and disgusted with her crying. The brother did so, and thus she perished also. A son of Gilling, a giant by name Suttung, avenged these treacherous deeds. He took the dwarfs out to sea and placed them on a shoal, which was flooded at high water. In this critical position they implored Suttung to spare their lives, and accept the verse-inspiring beverage, which they possessed, as an atonement for their having killed his parents. Suttung, having agreed to these conditions, released the dwarfs, and, carrying the mead home with him, committed it to the care of his daughter Gunlad. Hence poetry is indifferently called Kvaser's blood, Suttung's mead, the dwarfs' ransom, etc.

How did the gods get possession of this valuable mead of Suttung? Odin being fully determined to acquire it, set out for Jotunheim, and after journeying for some time he came to a meadow, in which nine thralls were mowing. Entering into conversation with them, Odin offered to whet their scythes, an offer which they gladly accepted. He took a whetstone from his belt and whetted their scythes, and finding that it had given their scythes an extraordinarily keen edge the thralls asked him whether he was willing to dispose of it; but Odin threw the whetstone up into the air, and as all the thralls attempted to catch it as it fell, each brought his scythe to bear on the neck of one of his comrades, so that they were all killed in the scramble. Odin took up his night's lodging at the house of Suttung's brother

Bauge, who told him he was sadly at a loss for laborers, his nine thralls having slain each other. Odin who here called himself Bolverk (one who can perform the most difficult work), said that for a draught of Suttung's mead he would do the work of nine men for him. Bauge answered that he had no control over it. Suttung wanted it alone, but he would go with Bolverk and try to get it. These terms were agreed on, and Odin worked for Bauge the whole summer, doing the work of nine men; but when winter set in he wanted his reward. Bauge and Odin set out together, and Bauge explained to Suttung the agreement between him and Bolverk, but Suttung was deaf to his brother's entreaties and would not part with a drop of the precious drink, which was carefully preserved in a cavern under his daughter's custody. Into this cavern Odin was resolved to penetrate. We must invent some stratagem, said he to Bauge. He then gave Bauge the augur, which is called Rate, and said to him that he should bore a hole through the rock, if the edge of the augur was sharp enough. Bauge did so, and said that he now had bored through. But Odin, or Bolverk as he is here called, blew into the augurhole and the chips flew into his face. He then perceived that Bauge intended to deceive him and commanded him to bore clear through. Bauge bored again, and, when Bolverk blew a second time, the chips flew the other way. Then Odin transformed himself into a worm, crept through the hole, and resuming his natural shape won the heart of Gunlad. Bauge put the augur down after him, but missed him. After having passed three nights with the fair maiden, he had no great difficulty in inducing her to let him take a draught out of each of the three jars called Odrœrer, Bodn, and Son, in which the mead was kept. But wishing to make the most of his advantage, he drank so deep that not a drop was left in the vessels. Transforming himself into an eagle, he then flew off as fast as his wings could carry him, but Suttung becoming aware of the stratagem, also took upon himself an eagle's guise and flew after him. The gods, on seeing him approach Asgard, set out in the yard all the jars they could lay their hands on, which Odin filled by disgorging through his beak the wonder-working liquor he had drunk. He was however so near being caught by Suttung. that he sent some of the mead after him backwards, and as no care was taken of this it fell to the share of poetasters. It is called the drink of silly poets. But the mead discharged into the jars was kept for the gods and for those men who have sufficient wit to make a right use of it. Hence poetry is called Odin's booty, Odin's gift, the beverage of the gods, etc.

But let us look at this myth in its older and purer form. Thus the Elder Edda, in Hávamál:

> Oblivion's heron 't is called
> That over potations hovers;
> He steals the minds of men.
> With this bird's pinions
> I was fettered
> In Gunlad's dwelling.
>
> Drunk I was,
> I was over-drunk
> At that cunning Fjalar's.
> It's the best drunkenness
> When every one after it
> Regains his reason.

This passage then refers to the effects of the strong drink of poetry, and Odin recommends us to use it with moderation. Would it not be well for some of our poets to heed the advice?

Thus Hávamál again :

> The old giant* I sought ;
> Now I am come back ;
> Little got I there by silence;
> In many words
> I spoke to my advantage
> In Suttung's halls.

> Gunlad gave me,
> On her golden seat,
> A draught of the precious mead ;
> A bad recompense
> I afterwards made her,
> For her whole soul,
> Her fervent love.

> Rate's mouth I caused
> To make a space,
> And to gnaw the rock ;
> Over and under me
> Were the giant's ways :
> Thus I my head did peril.

> Of a well-assumed form
> I made good use :
> Few things fail the wise ;
> For Odrœrer
> Is now come up
> To men's earthly dwellings.

> 'T is to me doubtful
> That I could have come
> From the giant's courts
> Had not Gunlad aided me
> That good damsel
> Over whom I laid my arm.

> On the day following
> Came the frost-giants

---

\* Suttung.

To learn something of the High One.
In the High One's hall:
After Bolverk they inquired
Whether he with the gods were come,
Or Suttung had destroyed him.

Odin, I believe,
A ring-oath gave.
Who in his faith will trust?
Suttung defrauded,
Of his drink bereft,
And Gunlad made to weep.

It is a beautiful idea that Odin creeps into Suttung's hall as a serpent, but when he has drunk the mead of poetry, when he has become inspired, he soars away on eagles' pinions.

Odin's name, Bolverk, may mean the one working evil, which might be said of him in relation to the giants, or the one who accomplishes difficult things, which then would impersonate the difficulty in mastering the art of poetry. Without a severe struggle no one can gain a victory in the art of poetry, and least of all in the Old Norse language. Gunlad (from *gunnr*, struggle, and *laða*, to invite) invites Odin to this struggle. She sits well fortified in the abode of the giant. She is surrounded by stone walls. The cup in which was the mead is called Odrœrer (*od-rœrer*, that which moves the spirit); that is, the cup of inspiration; and the myth is as clear as these names. Kvaser is the fruit of which the juice is pressed and mixed with honey; it produces the inspiring drink. It is also pertinently said that Kvaser perishes in his own wisdom. Does not the fruit burst from its superabundance of juice? But do not take only the outside skin of this myth; press the ethical juice out of it.

It should be noticed here that Kvaser (the spit, the ripe fruit) is produced by a union of asas and vans, an intimate union of the solid and liquid elements.

This myth also illustrates the wide difference between the Elder and the Younger Edda. How much purer and poetic in the former than in the latter! *Ex ipso fonte dulcius bibuntur aquæ.* In the Elder Edda is water in which it is worth our while to fish.

### SECTION XIV. SAGA.

Odin is not only the inventor of poetry, he also favors and protects history, Saga. The Elder Edda:

> Sokvabek hight the fourth dwelling,
> Over it flow the cool-billows;
> Glad drink there Odin and Saga
> Every day from golden cups.

The charming influence of history could not be more beautifully described.

Sokvabek is the brook of the deep. From the deep arise the thoughts and roll as cool refreshing waves through golden words. Saga can tell. Odin can think, about it. Thus they sit together day after day and night after night and refresh their minds from the fountain of history. Saga is the second of the goddesses. She dwells at Sokvabek, a very large and stately abode. The stream of history is large, it is broad and deep. Saga is from the word meaning *to say.* In Greece Klio was one of the muses, but in Norseland Saga is alone, united with Odin. the father of heroic deeds. Her favor is the hope of the youth and the delight of the old man.

SECTION XV.   ODIN AS THE INVENTOR OF RUNES.

The original meaning of the word rune is *secret,* and it was used to signify a mysterious song, mysterious doctrine, mysterious speech, and mysterious writing. Our ancestors had an alphabet called runes, before they learned the so-called Roman characters. The runic stave-row was a futhorc (*f, u, th, o, r, k*), not an alphabet (*A, B*) as in Greek or Latin. But what does it mean mythologically, that Odin is the inventor of the runes? Odin himself says in his famous Rune-song in the Elder Edda:

> I know that I hung
> On a wind-rocked tree*
> Nine whole nights,
> With a spear wounded
> And to Odin offered,
> Myself to myself;
> On that tree
> Of which no one knows
> From what root it springs.
>
> Bread no one gave me
> Nor a horn of drink,
> Downward I peered,
> To runes applied myself
> Wailing learnt them,
> Then fell down thence.
>
> Potent songs nine
> From the famed son I learned
> Of Bolthorn, Bestla's father,
> And a draught obtained
> Of the precious mead,
> Drawn from Odrœrer.
>
> Then I began to bear fruit
> And to know many things,

*Ygdrasil.

To grow and well thrive:
Word by word
I sought out words,
Fact by fact
I sought out facts.

Runes thou wilt find
And explained characters,
Very large characters,
Very potent characters,
Which the great speaker depicted
And the high powers formed
And the powers' prince graved.

Odin among the asas,
But among the elves, Daain;
Odin as inventor of runes
And Dvalin for the dwarfs;
Aasvid for the giants runes risted,
Some I myself risted.

Knowest thou how to rist them?
Knowest thou how to expound them?
Knowest thou how to depict them?
Knowest thou how to prove them?
Knowest thou how to pray?
Knowest thou how to offer?
Knowest thou how to send?
Knowest thou how to consume?

'T is better not to pray
Than too much offer;
A gift ever looks to a return.
'T is better not to send
Than too much consume.
So Thund risted
Before the origin of men,
There he ascended
Where he afterwards came.

Those songs I know
Which the king's wife knows not,

Nor son of man.
*Help* the first is called,
For that will help thee
Against strifes and cares.

For the second I know,
What the sons of men require
Who will as leeches live.

For the third I know,
If I have great need
To restrain my foes,
The weapon's edge I deaden:
Of my adversaries
Nor arms nor wiles harm aught.

For the fourth I know,
If men place
Bonds on my limbs,
I so sing
That I can walk;
The fetter starts from my feet
And the manacle from my hands.

For the fifth I know,
I see a shot from a hostile hand,
A shaft flying amid the host,
So swift it cannot fly,
That I cannot arrest it,
If only I get sight of it.

For the sixth I know,
If one wounds me
With a green tree's root,*
Also if a man
Declares hatred to me,
Harm shall consume *them* sooner than me.

For the seventh I know,
If a lofty house I see

---

* Roots of trees were especially fitted for hurtful trolldom (witchcraft).
They produced mortal wounds.

Blaze o'er its inmates,
So furiously it shall not burn
That I cannot save it ;
That song I can sing.

For the eighth I know,
What to all is
Useful to learn ;
Where hatred grows
Among the sons of men —
That I can quickly assuage.

For the ninth I know,
If I stand in need
My bark on the water to save,
I can the wind
On the waves allay,
And the sea lull.

For the tenth I know,
If I see troll-wives
Sporting in air,
I can so operate
That they will forsake
Their own forms
And their own minds.

For the eleventh I know,
If I have to lead
My ancient friends to battle,
Under their shields I sing,
And with power they go
Safe to the fight,
Safe from the fight ;
Safe on every side they go.

For the twelfth I know,
If on a tree I see
A corpse swinging from a halter,
I can so rist
And in runes depict,
That the man shall walk,
And with me converse.

For the thirteenth I know,
If on a young man
I sprinkle water,*
He shall not fall,
Though he into battle come:
That man shall not sink before swords.

For the fourteenth I know,
If in the society of men
I have to enumerate the gods,
Asas and elves,
I know the distinctions of all.
This few unskilled can do.

For the fifteenth I know,
What the dwarf of Thodrœrer† sang
Before Delling's doors.
Strength he sang to the asas,
And to the elves prosperity,
Wisdom to Hroptatyr (Odin).

For the sixteenth I know,
If a modest maiden's favor and affection
I desire to possess,
The soul I change
Of the white-armed damsel,
And wholly turn her mind.

For the seventeenth I know,
That that young maiden will
Reluctantly avoid me.
These songs, Lodfafner,
Thou wilt long ·have lacked :
Yet it may be good, if thou understandest them,
Profitable if thou learnest them.

For the eighteenth I know,
That which I never teach
To maid or wife of man,

---

* The old heathen Norsemen sprinkled their children with water when
they named them.

† The waker of the people.

(All is better
What *one* only knows:
This is the closing of the songs)
Save her alone
Who clasps me in her arms,
Or is my sister.

Now are sung the
*High One's* songs
In the High One's hall,
To the sons of men all useful,
But useless to the giants' sons.
Hail to him who has sung them!
Hail to him who knows them!
May he profit who has learnt them!
Hail to those who have listened to them!

Odin's sister or wife is, as we have seen, Frigg, the earth, and there is much between heaven and earth of which the wisest men do not even dream, much that the profoundest philosophy is unable to unravel, and this is what Odin never teaches to maid or wife of man.

The runes of Odin were risted on the shield which stands before the shining god, on the ear of Aarvak (the ever-wakeful), and on the hoof of Alsvin; on the wheels that roll under Rogner's chariot, on Sleipner's reins, on the paw of the bear and on the tongue of Brage : on the claws of the wolf, on the beak of the eagle, on bloody wings and on the end of the bridge (the rainbow); on glass, on gold, on wine and on herb; on Vile's heart, on the point of Gungner (Odin's spear), on Grane's breast, on the nails of the norn and on the beak of the owl. All, that were carved, were afterwards scraped off, mixed with the holy mead and sent out into all parts of the world. Some are with the asas, some with the elves, and some are with the sons of men.

All this and even more that is omitted we find in the

Elder Edda. What are Odin's runes? What but a new expression of his being? Odin's runes represent the might and wisdom with which he rules all nature, even its most secret phenomena. Odin, as master of runes, is the spirit that subdues and controls physical nature. He governs inanimate nature, the wind, the sea, the fire, and the mind of man, the hate of the enemy and the love of woman. Everything submits to his mighty sway, and thus the runes were risted on all possible things in heaven and on earth. He is the spirit of the world, that pervades everything, the almighty creator of heaven and earth, or, to use a more mythological expression, the father of gods and men.

Odin hung nine days on the tree (Ygdrasil) and sacrificed himself to himself, and wounded himself with his own spear. This has been interpreted to mean the nine months in which the child is developed in its mother's womb. Turn back and read the first strophes carefully, and it will be found that there is some sense in this interpretation ; but, kind reader, did you ever try to subdue and penetrate into the secrets of matter with your mind? Do you know that knowledge cannot be acquired without labor, without struggle, without sacrifice, without solemn consecration of one's self to an idea? Do you remember that Odin gave his eye in pawn for a drink from Mimer's fountain? The spear with which he now wounds himself shows how solemnly he consecrates himself. For the sake of this struggle to acquire knowledge, the spirit offers itself to itself. It knows what hardships and sufferings must be encountered on the road to knowledge, but it bravely faces these obstacles, it wants to wrestle with them ; that is its greatness, its glory, its power. Nine nights Odin hangs on the tree. Rome was not built in a day. *Tantæ molis erat Romanas condere gentes!* Neither is knowledge acquired in a day. The mind is developed by a slow process. He neither eats nor drinks, he fasts. You must also curb your bodily appetites, and, like Odin, look down into the depths and penetrate the mysteries of nature with your mind. Then will you learn all those wonderful songs that Odin learned crying before he fell from the tree.

Odin is the author of the runic incantations that played so conspicuous a part in the social and religious life of the Norseman. The belief in sorcery (*galdr* and *seiðr*) was universal among the heathen Norsemen, and it had its origin in the mythology, which represents the magic arts as an invention of Odin.

### SECTION XVI. VALHAL.

Thus the Elder Edda, in the lay of Grimner:

> Gladsheim is named the fifth dwelling;
> There the golden-bright
> Valhal stands spacious;
> There Hropt* selects
> Each day those men
> Who die by weapons.

> Easily to be known is,
> By those who to Odin come,
> The mansion by its aspect.
> Its roof with spears is laid,
> Its hall with shields is decked,
> With corselets are its benches strewed.

> Easily to be known is,
> By those who to Odin come,
> The mansion by its aspect.
> A wolf hangs
> Before the western door,
> Over it an eagle hovers.

* Odin.

Odin was preëminently the god of war. He who fell in battle came after death to Odin in Valhal. There he began the battle anew, fell and arose again. Glorious was the life in Valhal.

The hall was called Valhal, that is, the hall of the slain; Odin was called Valfather (father of the slain), and the maids he sent out to choose the fallen heroes on the field of battle were called valkyries. Valhal must not, as before stated, be confused with the silver-roofed valaskjalf.

The heroes who came to Valhal were called einherjes, from *ein* and *herja*, which together mean the excellent warrior, and we find that Odin was also called Herja-father (father of heroes).

Valhal is situated in Gladsheim. It is large and resplendent with gold; spears support its ceiling, it is roofed with shields, and coats of mail adorn its benches. Swords serve the purpose of fire, and of its immense size we can form some idea when we read in the Elder Edda that

> Five hundred doors
> And forty more
> Methinks are in Valhal;
> Eight hundred heroes through each door
> Shall issue forth
> Against the wolf to combat.

Outside of Valhal stands the shining grove Glaser. All its leaves are red gold, whence gold is frequently called Glaser's leaves.

What does Odin give all his guests to eat? If all the men who have fallen in fight since the beginning of the world are gone to Odin in Valhal, there must be a great crowd there. Yes, the crowd there is indeed great, but great though it be, it will still be thought too little when the wolf comes (the end of the world). But however **great** the band of men in Valhal may be, the flesh of the boar Sæhrimner will more than suffice for their sustenance. This boar is cooked every morning, but becomes whole **again** every night. The cook is called Andhrimner and the kettle Eldhrimner. Thus the Elder Edda:

> Andhrimner cooks
> In Eldhrimner
> Sæhrimner;
> 'T is the best of flesh;
> But few know
> What the einherjes eat.

What do the guests of Odin drink? Do you imagine that Allfather would invite kings and jarls and other great men and give them nothing but water to drink? In that case many of those, who had endured the greatest hardships and received deadly wounds in order to obtain access to Valhal, would find that they had paid too great a price for their water drink, and would indeed have reason to complain were they there to meet with no better entertainment. But we shall see that the case is quite otherwise; for the she-goat Heidrun (the clear stream) stands above Valhal and feeds on the leaves of a very famous tree. This tree is called Lerad (affording protection), and from the teats of the she-goat' flows mead in such great abundance that every day a bowl, large enough to hold more than would suffice for all the heroes, is filled with it. And still more wonderful is what is told of the stag, Eikthyrner (the oak-thorned, having knotty horns), which also stands over Valhal and feeds upon the leaves of the same tree, and while he is feeding so many drops fall from his antlers down into Hvergelmer that they furnish sufficient water for the thirty-six rivers that issuing thence flow twelve to the abodes of the gods, twelve to the abodes of men, and twelve to Niflheim.

Ah! our ancestors were uncultivated barbarians, and that is proved by the life in Valhal, where the heroes ate pork and drank mead! But what are we, then, who do the same thing? Let us look a little more carefully at the words they used. Food they called flesh, and drink, mead,—expressions taken from life; but they connected an infinitely higher idea with the heavenly nourishment. Although but few know what the ein-herjes eat, we ought to know it. When we hear the word ambrosia, we think of a very fine nourishment, although we do not know what it was. In the *Iliad* (14, 170), it is used of pure water. The words used in the Norse mythology in reference to the food and drink of the gods are very simple, And-hrimner, Eld-hrimner, and Sæ-hrimner. Hrim, (rime) is the first and most delicate transition from a liquid to a solid; hrimner is the one producing this transition. The food was formed, as the words clearly show, by air (*and, önd, aande,* breath), by fire (*eld*), and by water (*sæ,* sea). We have here the most delicate formation of the most delicate elements. There is nothing earthly in it. The funda-mental element is water boiled by the fire, which is nourished by the air; and the drink is the clear stream, which flows from the highest abodes of heaven, the pure ethereal current, which comes from the distant regions where the winds are silent. Nay, we cannot even call it a drink, but it is the purest and most delicate breath of the air, that fills the lungs of the immortal heroes in Valhal.

A mighty band of men there is in Valhal, and Odin must indeed be a great chieftain to command such a numerous host; but how do the heroes pass their time when they are not drinking? Answer: Every day, as soon as they have dressed themselves, they ride out into the court, and there fight until they cut each other into pieces. This is their pastime. But when meal-time approaches, they remount their steeds and return to drink mead from the skulls of their enemies* in Valhal. Thus the Elder Edda:

> The einherjes all
> On Odin's plain
> Hew daily each other,
> While chosen the slain are.
> From the battle-field they ride
> And sit in peace with each other.

## SECTION XVII. THE VALKYRIES (VALKYRJUR).

As the god of war, Odin sends out his maids to choose the fallen heroes (*kjósa val*). They are called valkyries and valmaids (*valmeyar*). The valkyries serve in Valhal, where they bear in the drink, take care of the drinking-horns, and wait upon the table. Odin sends them to every field of battle, to make choice of those who are to be slain and to sway the victory. The youngest of the norns, Skuld, also rides forth to choose the slain and turn the combat. More than a dozen valkyries are named in the Elder Edda, and all these have reference to the activities of war.

This myth about Odin as the god of war, about Valhal and the valkyries, exercised a great influence upon

---

* If the *North American Review*, or anybody else, thinks this is proof of barbarism. we can refer them to the monks in Trier, who preserved the skull of Saint Theodulf and gave sick people drink from it: and we know several other such instances. Our Norse ancestors were not, then, in this respect any more savage than the Christian bishops and monks. See *North American Review*. January, 1875, p. 195.

the mind and character of our ancestors. The dying
hero knows that the valkyries have been sent after him
to invite him home to Odin's hall, and he receives their
message with joy and gladness. That the brave were
to be taken after death to Valhal was one of the fundamental points, if not the soul, of the Norse religion.*
The Norsemen felt in their hearts that it was absolutely
necessary to be brave. Odin would not care for them,
but despise and thrust them away from him, if they were
not brave. And is there not some truth in this doctrine?
Is it not still a preëminent duty to be brave? Is it not
the first duty of man to subdue fear? What can we
accomplish until we have got rid of fear? A man is
a slave, a coward, his very thoughts are false, until he
has got fear under his feet. Thus we find that the
Odinic doctrine, if we disentangle the real kernel and
essence of it, is true even in our times. A man must
be valiant — he must march forward and acquit himself
like a man. How much of a man he is will be determined in most cases by the completeness of his victory
over fear. Their views of Odin, Valhal and the valkyries made the Norsemen think it a shame and misery
not to die in battle; and if natural death seemed to be
coming on, they would cut wounds in their flesh,
that Odin might receive them as warriors slain. Old
kings, about to die, had their bodies laid in a ship;
the ship was sent forth with sails set, and a slow fire
burning it, so that once out at sea it might blaze up
in flame, and in such manner bury worthily the hero
both in the sky and in the ocean. The Norse viking
fought with an indomitable, rugged energy. He stood
in the prow of his ship, silent, with closed lips, defying
the wild ocean with its monsters, and all men and

* See Thomas Carlyle's *Heroes and Hero-worship.*

things. No Homer sang of these Norse warriors and
sea-kings, but their heroic deeds and wild deaths are
the ever-recurring theme of the skalds.

The death of the Norse viking is beautifully described in the following strophe from Professor Hjalmar
Hjorth Boyesen's poem, entitled *Odin's Ravens:*

> In the prow with head uplifted
> Stood the chief like wrathful Thor;
> Through his locks the snow-flakes drifted
> Bleached their hue from gold to hoar.
> Mid the crash of mast and rafter
> Norsemen leaped through death with laughter
> Up through Valhal's wide-flung door.

Regner Lodbrok thus ends his famous song, the
Krákumál:

> Cease, my strain! I hear a voice
> From realms where martial souls rejoice;
> I hear the maids of slaughter call,
> Who bid me hence to Odin's hall:
> High-seated in their blest abodes
> I soon shall quaff the drink of gods.
> The hours of life have glided by,
> I fall, but smiling shall I die.

And in the death-song of Hakon (*Hákonarmál*) we find
the valkyries Gondul and Skogul in the heat of battle:

> The god Tyr sent
> Gondul and Skogul
> To choose a king
> Of the race of Ingve,
> To dwell with Odin
> In roomy Valhal.

The battle being described, the skald continues:

> When lo! Gondul,
> Pointing with her spear,
> Said to her sister,

Soon shall increase
The band of the gods:
To Odin's feast
Hakon is bidden.

The king beheld
The beautiful maids
Sitting on their horses
In shining armor,
Their shields before them,
Solemnly thoughtful.

The king heard
The words of their lips,
Saw them beckon
With pale hands,
And thus bespake them:
Mighty goddesses,
Were we not worthy
You should choose us
A better doom?

Skogul answered:
Thy foes have fallen,
Thy land is free,
Thy fame is pure;
Now we must ride
To greener worlds,
To tell Odin
That Hakon comes.

An interpretation of the valkyries is not necessary. The god of war sends his thoughts and his will to the carnage of the battle-field in the form of mighty armed women, in the same manner as he sends his ravens over all the earth.

Ethically considered, then, Odin symbolizes the matchless hope of victory that inspired the Norsemen, and from which their daring exploits sprang; and we know that this hope of victory did not leave the hero when he fell bleeding on the field of battle, but followed him borne in valkyrian arms to Valhal, and thence he soared on eagle pinions to Gimle on the everlasting hights. Thus the Elder Edda, in the Vala's Prophecy:

Valkyries she saw
That much had traveled;
Ready they were
To Godthjod * to ride.
Skuld held the child,
Skogul followed
Hild with Gondul
And Geirskogul.
Now have I named
The valkyries all.
Ready were Herjan's † maids
Over the earth to ride.

And in Grimner's Lay:

Hrist and Mist
Shall hand me the norn;
Skeggold and Skogul,
Hild and Thrud,
Hlok and Harfjoter,
Gol and Geironul,
Randgrid and Radgrid,
And Reginleif
Give the einherjes ale.

It should also be remembered that the Norse versions of the Niblung epic represent Brynhild as a valkyrie, who on account of disobedience to Odin had been pricked by a sleep-thorn and condemned to cease being a chooser of the slain on the field of battle, and to wed a mortal man.

* The divine race.    † Odin.

# CHAPTER II.

## HERMOD, TYR, HEIMDAL, BRAGE, AND IDUN.

### SECTION I.  HERMOD.

ODIN'S sons are emanations of his own being. As the god of war, warlike valor is one of his servants, and honor another. He invents the art of poetry, but the execution of it he leaves to his son Brage. He does not meddle with thunder, having left this work of a lower order to his son Thor. He is the father of light and darkness, and he leaves the beneficent light to diffuse itself and struggle with darkness independently (Balder and Hoder). Nor does he himself watch the rainbow, but lets the watchful Heimdal take care of it.

Hermod (the valiant in combat) was the son of Odin and the messenger of the gods. Odin himself gave him helmet and corselet, the means by which to display his warlike character, and he is sent on all dangerous missions. Of his many exploits the most important one is when he was sent on Sleipner to Hel to bring Balder back. It was Hermod and Brage who were sent to bid Hakon, the king, welcome, when he arrived at Valhal.

### SECTION II.  TYR.

Tyr's name is preserved in Tuesday. He is the god of martial honor (compare the German *Zier*). Tyr is the most daring and intrepid of all the gods. It is he who dispenses valor in war; hence warriors do well to invoke him. It has become proverbial to say of a man who surpasses all others in valor, that he is Tyr-strong, or valiant as Tyr. A man noted for his wisdom is also said to be wise as Tyr. He gives a splendid proof of his intrepidity when the gods try to persuade the wolf Fenrer, as we shall see hereafter, to let himself be bound up with the chain Gleipner. The wolf fearing that the gods would never afterwards unloose him, consented to be bound only on the condition that while they were chaining him he should keep Tyr's hand between his jaws. Tyr did not hesitate to put his hand in the monster's mouth, but when the Fenriswolf perceived that the gods had no intention to unchain him, he bit the hand off at that point which has ever since been called the wolf's joint (*úlfliðr**), the wrist. From that time Tyr has but one hand.

Tyr is the son of Odin, and it is through him the latter, as the god of war, awakens wild courage. Thus he is the god of honor, and when the noble gods desire to tame the raging flames he naturally has to arouse all his courage and even sacrifice a part of himself, just as we frequently have to sacrifice some of our comforts to keep clear of rogues and scoundrels.

## SECTION III. HEIMDAL (HEIMDALLR).

Heimdal is the son of Odin, and is called the white god (*hvíti áss*, the pure, innocent god). He is the son of nine virgins, who were sisters, and is a very sacred and powerful deity. Thus he says in the Elder Edda:

> Born was I of mothers nine,
> Son I am of sisters nine.

He also bears the appellation of the gold-toothed, for his teeth were of pure gold, and the appellation Hallinskide

---

* This old etymology is erroneous. The word is properly ðln-liðr. the ell-joint; as in ðln-bogi, the ell-bow — elbow; ðln (*alin*, Lat. *ulna*, ell) being the arm from the elbow to the end of the middle finger.

(*hallinskiði*, the owner of the vaulted arch). His horse
is called Gulltop (*goldtop*), and he dwells in Himminbjorg,
the mountains of heaven, at the end of Bifrost, the rainbow.   He is the warder of the gods, and is therefore
placed on the borders of heaven to prevent the giants
from forcing their way over the bridge.   He requires less
sleep than a bird and sees by night as well as by day a
hundred miles around him.   So acute is his ear that no
sound escapes him, for he can even hear the grass growing on the earth and the wool on a sheep's back.   He
has a horn called Gjallar-horn, which is heard throughout the universe.   Thus the Elder Edda, in the lay of
Grimner:

> 'T is Himminbjorg called
> Where Heimdal they say
> Hath dwelling and rule.
> There the gods' warder drinks
> In peaceful old halls
> Gladsome the good mead.

Heimdal has a sword called Hofud (head); he figures
at the death of Balder and appears in Ragnarok.   Phys-
ically interpreted, Heimdal is the god of the rainbow,
but the brilliant rainbow most beautifully symbolizes
the favoring grace of the gods.   The rainbow itself is
called *ásbrú* (asabridge) or Bifrost (the trembling way),
and he who has seen a perfect rainbow can appreciate
how this resplendent arch among all races has served
as a symbol of peace, the bridge between heaven and
earth, the bridge connecting the races of the earth with
the gods.   Did not God in Genesis set his bow in the
cloud that it should be for a token of a covenant between
him and the earth?   And when our poor laboring
masses get their taste cultivated for poetry, art, and
mythological lore,— when they have learned to appre-

ciate our common inheritance,— they will find that our
Gothic history, folk-lore and mythology together form

> A link
> That binds us to the skies,
> A bridge of *rainbows* thrown across
> The gulf of tears and sighs.*

In Greece we find the goddess Iris as the impersonation of the rainbow; while in the Bible the rainbow
is not personified, and in no mythological system does
the graceful divinity of the rainbow enter so prominently
into the affairs of men as does our Heimdal. In the first
verse of Völuspá, all mankind is called the sons of Heimdal, and this thought is developed in a separate lay in
the Elder Edda, called Rigsmál, the lay of Rig (Heimdal), to which the reader is referred.

## SECTION IV. BRAGE AND IDUN.

Brage is the son of Odin, and Idun is Brage's wife.
Brage is celebrated for his wisdom, but more especially for his eloquence and correct forms of speech. He
is not only eminently skilled in poetry, but the art itself
is from his name called *Brage*, which epithet is also used
to denote a distinguished poet or poetess. Runes are
risted on his tongue. He wears a long flowing beard,
and persons with heavy beard are called after him, beard-
brage (*skeggbragi*). His wife Idun (*Iðunn*) keeps in a
box the apples which the gods, when they feel old age
approaching, have only to taste of to become young again.
It is in this manner they will be kept in renovated youth
until Ragnarok. This is a great treasure committed to
the guardianship and good faith of Idun, and it shall be
related how great a risk the gods once ran.

* Barry Cornwall.

18

At the feast after the death of a king or jarl, it was customary among the Norsemen for the heir to occupy a lower bench in front of the chief seat, until Brage's bowl was brought in. Then he arose, made a pledge, and drank the cup of Brage. After that he was conducted into the seat of his father.

At the sacrificial feasts of the Norsemen, the conductor of the sacrifice consecrated the drinking-horns as well as the sacrificed food. The guests first drank Odin's horn, for the victory and rule of the king; next they drank Njord's and Frey's horns, for prosperous seasons and for peace; and then many were accustomed to drink a horn to Brage, the god of poetry. A characteristic ceremony in connection with this horn was, that when the bowl was raised, the promise of performing some great deed was made, which might furnish material for the songs of the skalds. This makes the character of Brage perfectly clear.

Idun's name is derived from the root *ið*, and expresses a constant activity and renovation, which idea becomes more firmly established by the following myth.

### SECTION V. IDUN AND HER APPLES.

Æger, the god of the sea, who was well skilled in magic, once went to Asgard, where the gods gave him a very good reception. Supper-time having come, the twelve mighty gods, together with the goddesses Frigg, Freyja, Gefjun, Idun, Gerd, Sigun, Fulla, and Nanna, seated themselves on their lofty doom seats, in a hall around which were arranged swords of such surpassing brilliancy that no other light was necessary. While they were emptying their capacious drinking-horns, Æger, who sat next to Brage, requested him to relate something concerning the asas. Brage instantly complied with his request by informing him of what had happened to Idun.

Once, he said, when Odin, Loke and Hœner went on a journey, they came to a valley where a herd of oxen were grazing, and, being sadly in want of provisions, did not scruple to kill one for their supper. Vain, however, were their efforts to boil the flesh; they found it, every time they took the lid off the kettle, as raw as when first put in. While they were endeavoring to account for this singular circumstance a noise was heard above them, and on looking up they beheld an enormous eagle perched on the branch of an oak tree. If you are willing to let me have my share of the flesh, said the eagle, it shall soon be boiled. And on assenting to this proposal it flew down and snatched up a leg and two shoulders of the ox — a proceeding which so incensed Loke that he picked up a large pole and made it fall pretty heavily on the eagle's back. It was, however, not an eagle that Loke struck, but the renowned giant Thjasse, clad in his eagle-plumage. Loke soon found this out to his sorrow, for while one end of the pole stuck fast to the eagle's back, he was unable to let go his hold of the other end, and was consequently trailed by the eagle-clad giant over rocks and forests until he was almost torn to pieces, and he thought his arms would be pulled off at the shoulders. Loke in this predicament began to sue for peace, but Thjasse told him that he should never be released from his hold until he bound himself by a solemn oath to bring Idun and her apples out of Asgard. Loke very willingly gave his oath to bring about this, and went back in a piteous plight to his companions.

On his return to Asgard, Loke told Idun that in a forest not very far from the celestial residence he had found apples growing, which he thought were of a much better quality than her own, and that at all events it was worth while to make a comparison between them. Idun, deceived by his words, took her apples and went with him into the forest, but they had no sooner entered it than Thjasse, clad in his eagle-plumage, flew rapidly toward them, and, catching up Idun, carried her and her treasure off with him to Jotunheim. The gods being thus deprived of their renovating apples, soon became wrinkled and gray, old age was creeping fast upon them when they discovered that Loke had been, as usual, the contriver of all the mischief that had befallen them. Inquiry was made about Idun in the assembly which was called, and the last anybody knew about her was that she had been seen going out of Asgard in company with Loke. They therefore threatened him with torture and death if he did not instantly hit upon some expedient for bringing back Idun and her apples to Asgard. This threat terrified Loke, and he promised to bring her back from Jotunheim if Freyja would lend him her falcon-plumage. He got the falcon-plumage of Freyja, flew in it to Jotunheim, and finding that Thjasse was out at sea fishing, he lost no time in transforming Idun into a nut and flying off with her in his claws. But when Thjasse returned and became aware of what had happened, he put on his eagle-plumage and flew after them. When the gods saw Loke approach, holding Idun changed into a nut between his claws, and Thjasse with his outspread eagle-wings ready to overtake him, they placed on the walls of Asgard bundles of chips, which they set fire to the instant Loke had flown over them; and as Thjasse could not stop his flight, the fire caught his plumage, and he thus fell into the power of the gods, who slew him within the portals of the celestial residence.

When these tidings came to Thjasse's daughter, Skade (*Skaði*, German *Schade*, harm), she put on her armor and went to Asgard, fully determined to avenge her father's death; but the gods having declared their willingness to atone for the deed, an amicable arrangement was entered into. Skade was to choose a husband in Asgard, and the gods were to make her laugh, a feat which she flattered herself it would be impossible for any one to accomplish. Her choice of a husband was to be determined by a mere inspection of the feet of the gods, it being stipulated that the feet should be the only part of their persons visible until she had made known her determination. In inspecting the row of feet placed before her, Skade took a fancy to a pair which from their fine proportions she thought certainly must be those of Balder. I choose these, she said, for on Balder there is nothing unseemly. The feet were however Njord's, and Njord was given her for a husband; and as Loke managed to make her laugh by playing some diverting antics with a goat, the atonement was fully effected. It is even said that Odin did more than had been stipulated, by taking out Thjasse's eyes and placing them to shine as stars in the firmament.

This myth, interpreted by the visible workings of nature, means that Idun (the ever-renovating spring) being in the possession of Thjasse (the desolating winter), all the gods — that is, all nature — languishes until she is delivered from her captivity. On this being effected, her presence again diffuses joy and gladness, and all things revive; while her pursuer, winter, with his icy breath, dissolves in the solar rays indicated by the fires lighted on the walls of Asgard. The wintry blasts rage so fearfully in the flames, that the flesh cannot be boiled, and the wind even carries a burning (Loke) stick with it. The ethical interpretation will suggest itself to every reader, and Idun is to Brage, who sings among the trees and by the musical brooks of spring, what a poetical contemplation of the busy forces of nature in producing blossoms and ripening fruit must always be to every son of Brage.

# CHAPTER III.

## BALDER AND NANNA, HODER, VALE AND FORSETE.

### SECTION I. BALDER.

BALDER is the favorite of all nature, of all the gods and of men. He is son of Odin and Frigg, and it may be truly said of him that he is the best god, and that all mankind are loud in his praise. So fair and dazzling is he in form and features, that rays of light seem to issue from him; and we may form some idea of the beauty of his hair when we know that the *whitest of all plants* is called *Balder's brow.** Balder is the mildest, the wisest and the most eloquent of all the gods, yet such is his nature that the judgment he has pronounced can never be altered. He dwells in the heavenly mansion called Breidablik (the broad-shining splendor), into which nothing unclean can enter. Thus the Elder Edda, in the lay of Grimner:

> Breidablik is the seventh,
> Where Balder has
> Built for himself a hall,
> In that land
> In which I know exists
> The fewest crimes.

* The *anthemis cotula* is generally called *Baldersbraa* in the North.

SECTION II.   THE DEATH OF BALDER THE GOOD.

This was an event which the asas deemed of great importance.   Balder the Good having been tormented by terrible dreams, indicating that his life was in great peril, communicated them to the assembled gods, who, sorrow-stricken, resolved to conjure all things to avert from him the threatened danger.   Then Frigg exacted an oath from fire and water, from iron and all other metals, as well as from stones, earths, diseases, beasts, birds, poisons, and creeping things, that none of them would do any harm to Balder.   Still Odin feared that the prosperity of the gods had vanished.   He saddled his Sleipner and rode down to Niflheim, where the dog from Hel met him; it was bloody on the breast and barked a long time at Odin.   Odin advanced; the earth trembled beneath him, and he came to the high dwelling of Hel.   East of the door he knew the grave of the vala was situated; thither he rode and sang magic songs (*kvað galdra*), until she unwillingly stood up and asked who disturbed her peace, after she had been lying so long covered with snow and wet with dew.   Odin called himself Vegtam, a son of Valtam, and asked for whom the benches were strewn with rings and the couches were swimming in gold. She replied that the mead was brewed for Balder, but all the gods would despair.   When Odin asked further who should be Balder's bane, she answered that Hoder would hurl the famous branch and become the bane of Odin's son; but Rind should give birth to a son who, only one night old, should wield a sword, and would neither wash his hands nor comb his hair before he had avenged his brother.   But recognizing Odin by an enigmatical question, she said: You are not Vegtam, as I believed, but you are Odin, the old ruler.   Odin replied: You are no vala, but the mother of three giants. Then the vala told Odin to ride home and boast of his journey, but assured him that no one should again visit her thus before Loke should be loosed from his chains and the ruin of the gods had come. Thus the lay of Vegtam in the Elder Edda:

Together were the gods
All in council,
And the goddesses
All in conference;
And they consulted
The mighty gods,
Why Balder had
Oppressive dreams.

To that god his slumber
Was most afflicting;
His auspicious dreams
Seemed departed.
They the giants questioned,
Wise seers of the future,
Whether this might not
Forebode calamity.

The responses said
That to death destined was
Uller's kinsman,
Of all the dearest:
That caused grief
To Frigg and Svafner,
And to the other powers,—
On a course they resolved:

That they would send
To every being,
Assurance to solicit,
Balder not to harm.
All species swore
Oaths to spare him:
Frigg received all
Their vows and compacts.

Valfather fears
Something defective;
He thinks the haminjes*
May have departed;
The gods he convenes,
Their counsel craves:
At the deliberation
Much is devised.

Up stood Odin,
Lord of men,
And on Sleipner he
The saddle laid;
Rode he thence down
To Niflheim.
A dog he met,
From Hel coming.

It was blood-stained
On its breast,
On its slaughter-craving throat,
And nether jaw.
It barked
And widely gaped
At the father of magic song:
Long it howled.

Forth rode Odin —
The ground thundered —
Till to Hel's lofty
House he came;
Then rode Ygg (Odin)
To the eastern gate,
Where he knew there was
A vala's grave.

To the prophetess he began
A magic song to chant,
Toward the north looked,
Potent runes applied,

* Guardian spirits.

A spell pronounced,
An answer demanded,
Until compelled she rose
And with death-like voice she said:

#### THE VALA:

What man is this,
To me unknown,
Who has for me increased
An irksome course?
I have with snow been decked,
By rain beaten,
And with dew moistened,—
Long have I been dead.

#### VEGTAM:

Vegtam is my name,
I am Valtam's son.
Tell thou me of Hel;
From earth I call on thee.
For whom are these benches
Strewed o'er with rings,—
Those costly couches
O'erlaid with gold?

#### THE VALA:

Here stands mead
For Balder brewed,
Over the bright drink
A shield is laid;
But the race of gods
Is in despair.
By compulsion I have spoken,
Now will I be silent.

#### VEGTAM:

Be not silent, vala!
I will question thee
Until all I know:
I will yet know
Who will Balder's
Slayer be.

And Odin's son
Of life bereave.

### THE VALA:

Hoder will hither
His glorious brother send;
He of Balder will
The slayer be,
And Odin's son
Of life bereave.
By compulsion I have spoken,
Now will I be silent.

### VEGTAM:

Be not silent, vala!
I will question thee
Until all I know:
I will yet know
Who on Hoder vengeance
Will inflict,
Or Balder's slayer
Raise on the pile.

### THE VALA:

Rind a son shall bear          .
In the wintry halls;
He shall slay Odin's son,
When one night old.
He a hand will not wash,
Nor his hair comb,
Ere to the pile he has borne
Balder's adversary.
By compulsion I have spoken,
Now will I be silent.

### VEGTAM:

Be not silent, vala!
I will question thee
Until all I know:
I will yet know
Who are the maids
That weep at will

And heavenward cast
Their neck-veils.
Tell me that;
Till then thou sleepest not.

THE VALA :
Not Vegtam art thou,
As I before believed ;
Rather art thou Odin,
Lord of men.

ODIN.
Thou art no vala,
Nor wise woman ;
Rather art thou the mother
Of three thurses (giants).

THE VALA :
Home ride thou, Odin !
And exult.
Thus shall never more
Man again visit me
Until Loke free
From his bonds escapes,
And Ragnarok
All-destroying comes.

When it had been made known that nothing in the
world would harm Balder, it became a favorite pastime
of the gods, at their meetings, to get Balder to stand up
and serve them as a mark, some hurling darts at him,
some stones, while others hewed at him with their swords
and battle-axes; for whatever they did none of them
could harm him, and this was regarded by all as a great
honor shown to Balder.  But when Loke Laufeyarson
beheld the scene he was sorely vexed that Balder was
not hurt.  Assuming, therefore, the guise of a woman
he went to Fensal, the mansion of Frigg.  That goddess,
seeing the pretended woman, inquired of her whether
she knew what the gods were doing at their meetings.

The woman (Loke) replied that they were throwing darts and stones at Balder, without being able to hurt him.

Ay, said Frigg, neither metal nor wood can hurt Balder, for I have exacted an oath from all of them.

What! exclaimed the woman, have all things sworn to spare Balder?

All things, replied Frigg, except one little shrub that grows on the eastern side of Valhal, and is called mistletoe, and which I thought too young and feeble to crave an oath from.

As soon as Loke heard this he went away, and, resuming his natural form, pulled up the mistletoe and repaired to the place where the gods were assembled. There he found Hoder standing far to one side without engaging in the sport, on account of his blindness. Loke going up to him said: Why do not you also throw something at Balder?

Because I am blind, answered Hoder, and cannot see where Balder is, and besides I have nothing to throw with.

Come then, said Loke, do like the rest, and show honor to Balder by throwing this twig at him, and I will direct your arm toward the place where he stands.

Hoder then took the mistletoe, and under the guidance of Loke darted it at Balder, who, pierced through and through, fell down lifeless. Surely never was there witnessed, either among gods or men, a more atrocious deed than this! When Balder fell the gods were struck speechless with horror, and then they looked at each other; and all were of one mind to lay hands on him who had done the deed, but they were obliged to delay their vengeance out of respect for the sacred place (place of peace) where they were assembled. They at length

gave vent to their grief by such loud lamentations that
they were not able to express their grief to one another.
Odin, however, felt this misfortune most severely, because
he knew best how great was the mischief and the loss
which the gods had sustained by the death of Balder.
When the gods were a little composed, Frigg asked who
among them wished to gain all her love and favor by
riding to the lower world to try and find Balder, and
offer a ransom to Hel if she will permit Balder to return
to Asgard; whereupon Hermod, surnamed the Nimble,
offered to undertake the journey. Odin's horse, Sleipner,
was then led forth and prepared for the journey; Hermod
mounted him and galloped hastily away.

The gods then took the dead body of Balder and
carried it to the sea, where lay Balder's ship, Ringhorn,
which was the largest of all ships. But when they
wanted to launch this ship, in order to make Balder's
funeral pile on it, they were unable to move it from the
place. In this predicament they sent a messenger to
Jotunheim for a certain giantess named Hyrroken (the
smoking fire), who came riding on a wolf and had
twisted serpents for her reins. As soon as she alighted
Odin ordered four berserks to hold her steed, but they
were obliged to throw the animal down on the ground
before they could manage it. Hyrroken then went to
the prow of the ship, and with a single push set it
afloat; but the motion was so violent that fire sparkled
from the underlaid rollers and the whole earth shook.
Thor, enraged at the sight, grasped his mallet and would
have broken the woman's skull, had not the gods inter-
ceded for her. Balder's body was then carried to the
funeral pile on board the ship, and this ceremony had
such an effect upon Balder's wife, Nanna, daughter of

Nep, that her heart broke with grief, and her body was
laid upon the same pile and burned with that of her
husband. Thor stood beside the pile and consecrated it
with his hammer Mjolner. Before his feet sprang up a
dwarf called Lit. Thor kicked him with his foot into
the fire, so that he also was burned. There was a vast
concourse of various kinds of people at Balder's funeral
procession. First of all came Odin, accompanied by
Frigg, the valkyries, and his ravens. Then came Frey
in his chariot, drawn by the boar Gullinburste (gold-
brush), or Slidrugtanne (the sharp-toothed). Heimdal
rode his horse Goldtop, and Freyja drove in her chariot
drawn by cats. There were also a great number of
frost-giants and mountain-giants present. Odin cast
upon the funeral pile the famous ring Draupner, which
had been made for him by the dwarfs, and possessed the
property of producing every ninth night eight rings of
equal weight. Balder's horse, fully caparisoned, was
also laid upon the pile, and consumed in the same flames
with the body of his master.

Meanwhile Hermod was proceeding on his mission.
Of him it is to be related that he rode nine days and as
many nights through dark and deep valleys, so dark
that he could not discern anything, until he came to the
river Gjol and passed over the Gjallar bridge (bridge
over the river Gjol), which is covered with glittering
gold. Modgud, the maiden who kept the bridge, asked
him his name and parentage, and added that the day
before five fylkes (kingdoms, bands) of dead men had
ridden over the bridge; but, she said, it did not shake
as much beneath all of them together as it does under
you alone, and you have not the complexion of the dead;
why then do you ride here on your way to Hel? I ride
to Hel, answered Hermod, to seek for Balder; have you

perchance seen him pass this way? She replied that
Balder had ridden over the Gjallar bridge, and that the
road to the abodes of death (to Hel) lay downward and
toward the north.

Hermod then continued his journey until he came
to the barred gates of Hel. Then he alighted from his
horse, drew the girths tighter, remounted him and
clapped both spurs into him. The horse cleared the gate
with a tremendous leap without touching it. Hermod
then rode forward to the palace, alighted and went in,
where he found his brother Balder occupying the most
distinguished seat in the hall, and spent the night in his
company. The next morning he entreated Hel (death)
to let Balder ride home with him, representing to her
the sorrow which prevailed among the gods. Hel replied
that it should now be tried whether Balder was so
universally beloved as he was said to be; if therefore,
she added, all things in the world, the living as well as
the lifeless, will weep for him, then he shall return to
the gods, but if anything speak against him or refuse
to weep, then Hel will keep him.

After this Hermod rose up, Balder went with him
out of the hall and gave him the ring Draupner, to
present as a keepsake to Odin. Nanna sent Frigg a
carpet together with several other gifts, and to Fulla
she sent a gold finger-ring. Hermod then rode back to
Asgard and related everything that he had heard and
witnessed.

The gods upon this dispatched messengers throughout all the world to beseech everything to weep, in
order that Balder might be delivered from the power of
Hel. All things very willingly complied with the request.— men, animals, the earth. stones, trees, and all
metals, just as we see things weep when they come out

19

of the frost into the warm air. When the messengers were returning, with the conviction that their mission had been quite successful, they found on their way home a giantess (ogress, Icel. *gýgr*), who called herself Thok. They bade her also weep Balder out of the dominion of Hel. But she answered:

Thok will weep
With dry tears *
For Balder's death ;
Neither in life nor in death
Gave he me gladness.
Let Hel keep what she has.

It is supposed that this giantess (*gýgr*) was no other than Loke Laufeyarson himself, who had caused the gods so many other troubles. Thus the Elder Edda refers to the death of Balder in Völuspá:

I saw the concealed
Fate of Balder,
The blood-stained god,
The son of Odin.
In the fields
There stood grown up,
Slender and passing fair,
The mistletoe.

From that shrub was made,
As to me it seemed,
A deadly noxious dart ;
Hoder shot it forth ;
But Frigg bewailed
In Fensal
Valhal's calamity.
Understand ye yet, or what?

To conquer Vafthrudner, and to reveal himself, Odin asks him to solve this last problem:

* The sparks of fire are dry tears.

What said Odin
In his son's ear,
Ere he on the pile was laid?

This is the question that Vafthrudner was unable to answer, and hence he had to forfeit his head. N. M. Petersen thinks that Odin whispered into Balder's ear the name of the supreme god.

This myth about the death of Balder finds an apt explanation in the seasons of the year, in the change from light to darkness, in Norseland. Balder represents the bright and clear summer, when twilight and daybreak kiss each other and go hand in hand in these northern latitudes. His death by Hoder is the victory of darkness over light, the darkness of winter over the light of summer. and the revenge by Vale is the breaking forth of new light after the wintry darkness.

In this connection it is also worthy of notice that there used to be a custom, which is now nearly forgotten, of celebrating the banishment of death or darkness, the strife between winter and summer, together with the arrival of the May-king and election of the May-queen. Forgotten! yes. well may we ask how it could come to pass that we through long centuries have worried and tortured ourselves with every scrap of Greek and Latin we could find, without caring the least for our own beautiful and profound memories of the past. Death was carried out in the image of a tree and thrown in the water or burned. In the spring two men represent summer and winter, the one clad in wintergreen or leaves, the other in straw. They have a large company of attendants with them, armed with staves. and they fight with each other until winter (or death) is subdued. They prick his eyes out or throw him into the water. These customs, which prevailed throughout the middle ages, had their root and origin in the ancient myth given above.

No myth can be clearer than this one of Balder. The Younger Edda says distinctly that he is so fair and dazzling in form and features that rays of light seem to issue from him. Balder, then, is the god of light, the light of the world. Light is the best thing we have in the world; it is white and pure; it cannot be wounded; no shock can disturb it; nothing in the world can kill it excepting its own negative, darkness (Hoder). Loke (fire) is jealous of it; the pure light of heaven and the blaze of fire are each other's eternal enemies. Balder does not fight, the mythology gives no exploits by him; he only shines and dazzles, conferring blessings upon all, and this he continues to do steadfast and unchangeable, until darkness steals upon him, darkness that does not itself know what harm it is doing; and when Balder is dead, cries of lamentation are heard throughout all nature. All nature seeks light. Does not the eye of the child seek the light of the morning, and does not the child weep when light vanishes, when night sets in? Does not this myth of Balder repeat itself in the old man, who like Gœthe, when death darkened his eyes, cried out: *mehr licht* (more light)? Does not the eagle from the loftiest pinnacle of the mountain seek light? The lark soars on his lofty pinions and greets in warbling notes the king of day welcome back into his kingdom. The tree firmly rooted in the ground strains toward the light, spreading upward in search of it. The bird of passage on his free wing flies after and follows the light. Is it not the longing after light that draws the bird southward in the fall when the days shorten in the north, and draws the little wanderer back again as soon as the long northern days set in with all their luminous and long-drawn hours? As Runeberg epigrammatically has it:

> The bird of passage is of noble birth;
> He bears a motto, and his motto is,
> *Lux mea dux*, Light is my leader.

Nay all living things, even the shells in the sea, every leaf of the oak and every blade of grass, seeks light, and the blind poet sings:

> Hail, holy light! offspring of heaven first born!
> He that hath light within his own clear breast
> May sit in the center and enjoy bright day;
> But he that hides a dark soul and foul thoughts
> Benighted walks under the midday sun.*

And another bard:

> Light down from heaven descends,
> Ether pure in flowing bowls;
> Light up to heaven ascends,
> A mediator for our souls.

Ay, it would be resting satisfied with the shell to interpret Balder as the mere impersonation of the natural light of heaven. He represents and symbolizes in the profoundest sense the heavenly light of the soul and of the mind, purity, innocence, piety. There can be no doubt that our ancestors combined the ethical with the physical in this myth. All light comes from heaven. The natural light shines into and illuminates the eye, the spiritual shines into and illuminates the heart. Innocence cannot be wounded. Arrogance and jealousy throw their pointed arrows of slander at it, but they fall harmless to the ground. But there is one inclination, one unguarded spot among our other strong guarded passions. The mischief-maker knows how to find this and innocence is pierced. When Balder dies, a dark veil

* Milton.

enshrouds all nature, and thus history clothes herself in
mourning, not because the hero dies, but because the
innocent Lincoln is pierced by the bullet of the foul
assassin, who turns to the night and flees. Every time
light is slain by darkness it is the beautiful and good
that is stricken down, but it is never stricken down
except to return and shine with increased splendor.
Balder dies in nature when the woods are stripped of
their foliage, when the flowers fade and the storms of
winter howl. Balder dies in the spiritual world when
the good are led away from the paths of virtue, when the
soul becomes dark and gloomy, forgetting its heavenly
origin. Balder returns in nature when the gentle winds
of spring stir the air, when the nightingale's high note
is heard in the heavens, and the flowers are unlocked to
paint the laughing soil, when light takes the place of
gloom and darkness: Balder returns in the spiritual
world when the lost soul finds itself again, throws off
the mantle of darkness, and like a shining spirit soars
on wings of light to heaven, to God, who gave it.

The flower which is sacred to Balder, the Balder's
brow, is the *anthemis cotula*. It is a complete flower
with a yellow disc and white rays, a symbol of the sun
with its beaming light, a sunflower. What a poetical
thought! The light pouring down upon the earth from
beneath Balder's eye-brows, and the hairs of his eye-lids
are the beams. What a theme for a Correggio, who
succeeded so well in painting the innocence of woman
beaming from her half-closed eyes!

Balder's wife is Nanna. She dies broken-hearted at
his death. She is the floral goddess who always turns
her smiling face toward the sun. Her father was Nep
(*nepr*, a bud), son of Odin. Nanna's and Balder's sending the ring Draupner to Odin, a carpet to Frigg, and

a ring to Fulla, has been explained heretofore, and how beautifully it symbolizes the return of earth's flowery carpet, with fruitfulness and abundance, will be evident to every thoughtful reader.

The sorrow of all nature we easily understand when we know that Loke represents fire and Balder is gone to Hel. All things weep, become damp, when brought from the cold to the warm air, excepting fire, and we remember that Thok, that is, Loke in disguise, wept dry tears (sparks); but all genuine tears are caused by a change of the heart from coldness to warmth. It is a common expression in Iceland yet to say that the stones, when covered with dew, weep for Balder (*gráta Baldr*). Balder's ship, Ringhorn, is rightly called the largest of all ships. Ringhorn is the whole world, and the whole earth is Balder's funeral pile. The tops of the mountains are the masts of this ship, which is round (ring) as the whirling world.

It is time we ceased talking about our barbarous ancestors, for, if we rightly comprehend this myth of Balder, we know that they appreciated, nay, profoundly and poetically appreciated, the light that fills the eye and blesses the heart, and were sensitive to the pain that cuts through the bosom of man even into its finest and most delicate fibers. In this myth of Balder is interwoven the most delicate feelings with the sublimest sentiments. Read it and comprehend it. Let the ear and heart and soul be open to the voiceless music that breathes through it. And when you have thus read this myth, in connection with the other myths and in connection with the best Sagas, then do not say another word about the North not having any literature! Thanks be to the norns, that the monks and priests, whose most zealous work it was to root out the memories of the

past and reduce the gods of our fathers to common-
place demons, did not succeed in their devastating mission in faithful Iceland! Thanks be to Shakespeare, that
he did not forget the stern, majestic, impartial and
beautiful norns, even though he did change them into
the wrinkled witches that figure in Macbeth! Nay, that
this our ancient mythology, in spite of the wintry blasts
that have swept over it, in spite of the piercing cold
to which it has been exposed at the hand of those who
thought they came with healing for the nations, in
spite of all the persecution it has suffered from monks
and bishops, professors and kings; that it, in spite of all
these, has been able to bud and blossom in our Teutonic
folk-lore, our May-queens, and popular life, is proof of
the strong vital force it contained, and proof, too, of the
vigorous thought of our forefathers who preserved it.
And nowhere is this more evident than in Norway.
These stories which have their root in the Norse mythology have been handed down by word of mouth from
generation to generation with remarkable fidelity. Look
at those long and narrow and deep valleys of Norway!
Those great clefts are deep furrows plowed in the mountain mass in order that it might yield a bountiful crop
of folk-lore, the seed of which is the Edda mythology.
Let us give our children a share in the harvest!

### SECTION III.    FORSETE.

Forsete is the son of Balder and Nanna. He possesses
the heavenly mansion called Glitner, and all disputants
at law who bring their cases before him go away perfectly
reconciled. His tribunal is the best that is to be found
among gods and men. Thus the Elder Edda, in the
lay of Grimner:

Glitner is the tenth mansion ;
It is on gold sustained,
And also with silver decked.
There Forsete dwells
Throughout all time,
And every strife allays.

Forsete means simply *president*. The island Helgoland was formerly called Forseteland. Justice was dealt out in Norseland during the bright season of the year, and only while the sun was up, in the open air, in the flowering lap of nature. The sanctity of the assembly and purity of justice is expressed by the golden columns and the silver roof of Glitner. The splendor of Balder shone upon his son.

# CHAPTER IV.

## THOR, HIS WIFE SIF AND SON ULLER.

### SECTION I. GENERAL SYNOPSIS.

THOR (þórr, þunarr, Anglo-Saxon þunor, German donner, thunder), after whom Thursday is named (Thor's-day), is the chief god next after Odin. He is a spring god, subduing the frost-giants.

Thor wears a red beard, his nature is fire, he is girded with the belt of strength, swings a hammer in his hand, rides in a chariot drawn by two goats, from whose hoofs and teeth sparks of fire flash, and the scarlet cloud reflects his fiery eyes, over his head he wears a crown of stars, under his feet rests the earth, and it shows the footprints of his mighty steps. He is called Asathor and also Akethor (from *aka*, to ride*), and is the strongest of gods and men. He is enormously strong and terrible when angry, but, as is so frequently the case with very strong men, his great strength is coupled with a thoroughly inoffensive good-nature. His realm is named Thrudvang and his mansion Bilskirner, in which are five hundred and forty halls. It is the largest house ever built. Thus the Elder Edda, in the lay of Grimner:

> Five hundred halls
> And forty more
> Methinks has
> Bowed Bilskirner;

* This is the usual explanation based on the Younger Edda. More recent investigations show that he was called Öku-thor, a corruption of Ukko-Thor. Ukko is of Finnish origin, and is the name of the thunder-god of the Tshudic tribes. See *Kalevala*, the Finnish epic. (298)

> Of houses roofed
> There is none I know
> My son's* surpassing.

Thor's chariot is drawn by two goats, called Tanngn-jost and Tanngrisner. It is from his driving about in this chariot he is called Akethor (charioteer-Thor). He possesses three very precious articles. The first is a mallet called Mjolner, which both the frost and mountain giants know to their cost, when they see it hurled against them in the air; and no wonder, for it has split many a skull of their fathers and kindred. The second rare thing he possesses is called the belt of strength or prowess (Megingjarder). When he girds it about him his divine strength is redoubled. The third precious article which he possesses is his iron gauntlet, which he is obliged to put on whenever he lays hold on the handle of his mallet. No one is so wise as to be able to relate all Thor's marvelous exploits.

Now the reader will easily comprehend the following beautiful strophes from the pen of Longfellow,† who has so ingeniously sprinkled his literature with dews from Ygdrasil:

> I am the god Thor,
> I am the war god,
> I am the Thunderer!
> Here in my Northland,
> My fastness and fortress,
> Reign I forever!
>
> Here amid icebergs
> Rule I the nations;
> This is my hammer,
> Mjolner, the mighty
> Giants and sorcerers
> Cannot withstand it!

---

* Thor's.      † From *Tales of a Wayside Inn.*

These are the gauntlets
Wherewith I wield it
And hurl it afar off;
This is my girdle,
Whenever I brace it
Strength is redoubled!

The light thou beholdest
Stream through the heavens,
In flashes of crimson,
Is but my red beard
Blown by the night-wind,
Affrighting the nations.

Jove is my brother;
Mine eyes are the lightning;
The wheels of my chariot
Roll in the thunder,
The blows of my hammer
Ring in the earthquake!

Force rules the world still,
Has ruled it, shall rule it;
Meekness is weakness,
Strength is triumphant;
Over the whole earth
Still is Thor's-day!

Thor is the father of Magne, whose mother is Jarn-saxa, and of Mode. He is the husband of Sif and step-father of Uller; he is the protector of Asgard and Mid-gard, and is frequently called Midgardsveor; his servants are Thjalfe, and the sister of the latter, Roskva. Among Thor's several names the most common ones are Ving-thor, Vingner, and Hlorride. All this of course has ref-erence to him as the god of thunder. Thor, as has been observed, is *punarr*, thunder. Thrudvang, his realm, is the heavy compact cloud, where he reigns; his man-sion, Bilskirner (*bil-skirnir*), are the flashes of light-ning that for a moment (*bil**) light up the heavens;

_____

* *Bil* is a common word in Norseland, meaning *moment*.

his goats, Tanngnjost (teeth-gnasher) and Tanngrisner (fire-flashing teeth), symbolize the flashes of lightning, and so does also his red beard. Mjolner, his hammer, is the crusher (compare the English word *mill* *); his belt, Megingjarder, is the girdle of strength; his sons, Magne and Mode, symbolize strength and courage. Vingthor is the flying thunderstorm and Hlorride is he who rides in the flaming chariot. His servant Thjalfe is the busy one, and Roskva is the rapid or nimble one. That Thor is the god of thunder is also most clearly shown in the Younger Edda, where it is related that Thor goes on foot and is obliged every day to wade the rivers Kormt and Ormt, and two others called Kerlaung, when he goes to sit in judgment with the other gods at the Urdar-fount, and cannot ride, as do the other gods. If he did not walk as he goes to the doomstead under the ash Ygdrasil, the Asabridge would be in flames and the holy waters would become boiling hot, that is, if Thor should drive over Bifrost in his thunder-chariot.

Thor's wife, Sif, is another symbol of the earth. She is called the fair-haired. Gold is called Sif's hair on account of the myth already related, according to which Loke cuts off her hair and gets dwarfs to forge for her golden locks. The interpreters of mythology are not willing to give to Sif the field waving with ripe grain, which belongs to the god Frey, being symbolized by his boar Goldenbristle, but say that Sif is the mountain clad with grass, in contradistinction to Jarnsaxa, who reigns in the barren deserts. Hrungner, that is, the naked rock, tried to win the favor of Sif, but did not succeed.

Uller is the son of Sif and the step-son of Thor. He is so well skilled in the use of the bow, and can go

* But see also Vocabulary, under the word *Mjolner.*

so fast on his snow-skates (*skees*), that in these arts no
one can contend with him. He is also very handsome
in his person and possesses every quality of a warrior;
wherefore it is proper to invoke him in single combats.
Uller's mansion is Ydaler (valleys of rain). From his
running on skees we judge that he is a personification
of winter, and if the artist chooses him for his theme,
he must represent him standing on snow-shoes, clad in
a winter-suit, with bow and arrow in his hands. We
are now prepared to give some of Thor's adventures.

### SECTION II.  THOR AND HRUNGNER.

Thor had once gone eastward to crush trolls, but
Odin rode on his horse, Sleipner, to Jotunheim, and
came to a giant by name Hrungner. Then asked
Hrungner what man that was, who with a helmet of
gold rode through the air and over the sea, and added
that it was an extraordinarily good horse he had. Odin
replied that he would wager his head that so good a
horse could not be found in Jotunheim. Hrungner
said that it was indeed a very excellent horse, but he
had one, by name Goldfax (gold-mane), that could take
much longer paces, and he immediately sprang upon
his horse and galloped away after Odin. Odin constantly kept ahead, but Hrungner's giant nature had
become so excited that before he was himself aware of
it he had come within the gates of Asgard. When he
came to the door of the hall the gods invited him to
drink, which as soon as he had entered he demanded.
Then the gods set before him the bowls out of which
Thor was accustomed to drink, and them he emptied
each in one draught. And when he had become drunk,
he gave the freest vent to his loud boastings. He was
going to take Valhal, he said, and carry it off to Jotun-

heim; he would demolish Asgard and kill the gods, except Freyja and Sif, whom he would take home with him; and while Freyja was pouring the celestial beverage into the bowls for him he remarked that he was going to drink up all the ale of the gods. When the gods at length grew tired of his arrogance, they named Thor, who immediately came, and swung his hammer and was very much enraged, and asked who was to blame that dogwise giants should be permitted to drink there, or who had given safety to Hrungner in Valhal, and why Freyja should pour ale for him as she did at the feasts of the gods. Hrungner, looking at Thor with anything but a friendly eye, answered that Odin had invited him and that he was under his protection. Thor said that Hrungner should come to rue that invitation before he came out; but the giant answered that it would be but little honor to Asathor to kill him, unarmed as he was; it would be a better proof of his valor if he dared contend with him at the boundaries of his territory, at Grjottungard (*Grjöttunagarðar*). Foolish was it also of me, continued Hrungner, to leave my shield and my flint-stone at home; had I my weapons here we would now try a holmgang;* but I declare you to be a coward if you kill me unarmed. Thor would not excuse himself from a duel when he was challenged out on a holm; this was something that no one had ever offered him before. Hrungner now went his way and hastened home. This journey of Hrungner was much talked of by the giants, and especially did his challenge of Thor awaken

---

* Holmgang (literally *isle-gang*) is a duel taking place on a small island. Each combatant was attended by a second, who had to protect him with a shield. The person challenged had the right to strike the first blow. When the opponent was wounded, so that his blood stained the ground, the seconds might interfere and put an end to the combat. He that was the first wounded had to pay the holmgang fine.

their interest, and it was of great importance to them
which of the two should come out from the combat
victorious. For if Hrungner, who was the most powerful among the giants, should be conquered, they
might look for nothing but evil from Thor. They
therefore made at Grjottungard a man of clay, nine
rasts (miles?) high and three rasts broad between the
shoulders; they could not find a heart corresponding
to his size, and therefore took one out of a mare; but
this fluttered and trembled when Thor came. Hrungner had a heart of hard stone, sharp and three-cor-
nered; his head was also of stone, and likewise his
shield, which was broad and thick, and this shield he
held before himself when he stood at Grjottungard
waiting for Thor. His weapon was a flint-stone, which
he swung over his shoulders, so that it was no trifle to
join in combat with him. By his side stood the clay-
giant, that is called Mokkerkalfe (*Mökkrkálfi*), and was
so extremely terrified that the sweat poured from off
him. Thor went to the holmgang together with Thjalfe,
a servant, whom he had got from a peasant by the sea.
Thjalfe ran to the place where Hrungner was standing,
and said to him: You stand unguarded, giant; you
hold the shield before you, but Thor has seen you; he
comes with violence from beneath the earth and attacks
you. Then Hrungner hastily put the shield beneath his
feet and stood on it, but he seized his flint-stone with
both hands. Presently he saw flashes of lightning and
heard loud crashings, and then he saw Thor in his asa-
might, rushing forward with impetuous speed, swinging
his hammer and throwing it from the distance against
Hrungner. The latter lifted the flint-stone with both
his hands and threw it with all his might against the
hammer; the two met in the air and the flint-stone

broke into two pieces, one piece of which fell on the ground (and hence the flint mountains), while the other fell with such force against the head of Thor that he fell forward to the ground; but the hammer Mjolner hit Hrungner right in the head and crushed his skull into small pieces, he himself falling over Thor, so that his foot lay across Thor's neck. Thjalfe contended with Mokkerkalfe, who fell with little honor. Then Thjalfe went over to Thor, and was going to take Hrungner's foot away, but he was not able to do it. Thereupon came all the gods to Grjottungard, when they had learned that Thor had fallen, but neither was any one of them able to remove the foot of the giant. Then came Magne (*magni*, strength), the son of Thor and Jarnsaxa; he was only three nights old and he threw Hrungner's foot off from Thor saying: It was a great mishap, father, that I came so late; this giant. I think, I could have slain with my fist. Thor stood up and lovingly greeted his son, adding that he would give him the giant's horse Goldfax; but Odin remarked that this was wrongfully done of Thor to give the son of a hag (*gýgjar syni*, son of Jarnsaxa) and not his father so excellent a horse.

Thor returned home to Thrudvang, and the flint-stone sat fast in his head. Then came a sorceress, whose name was Groa, wife of Orvandel the Wise; she sang her magic songs over Thor until the flint-stone became loose. But when Thor perceived this, and was just expecting that the stone would disappear, he desired to reward Groa for her cure, and gladden her heart. He accordingly related to her how he had waded from the north over the rivers Elivagar and had borne Orvandel on his back in a basket from Jotunheim; and in evidence he told her that one toe of Orvandel had

· 20

protruded from the basket and had frozen, wherefore he
had broken it off and thrown it up into the sky and
made of it the star which is called Orvandel's toe.
Finally he added that it would not be long before Orvandel would come home again. But Groa became so
delighted with this news that she forgot all her magic
songs and the flint-stone became no looser than it was,
and it sticks fast in Thor's head yet. Therefore no one
must throw a flint-stone across the floor, for then the
stone in Thor's head is moved. Thus sings the Skald,
Thjodolf of Hvin :

> We have ample evidence
> Of the terrible giant's journey
> To Grjottungard,
> With berg-folks' consuming fire
> The blood boiled in Meile's brother,*
> The moon-land trembled,
> When earth's son went
> To the steel-gloved contest.

> In bright flame stood
> All the realms of the sky
> For Uller's step-father,
> And the earth rocked ;
> To pieces flew Svolner's widow
> When the span of goats
> Drew the sublime chariot
> And its divine master
> To the meeting with Hrungner.

The most prominent feature of this myth is the
lightning which strikes down among the rocks and
splits them. Hrungner (from *hruga*, to wrinkle, to heap
up) is the naked, wrinkled mountains with their peaks.
Everything is made of stone. Hrungner's heart and
head and shield and weapon were all of stone; beside

*A name for Thor.

him stands the clayey mountain (Mokkerkalfe) clad in mist (*mökkr*), and the contest is at Grjottungard, on the boundary of the stone-covered field. Thor crushes the mountain to make way for agriculture. Thjalfe is the untiring labor, which prepares the rock for cultivation. He advises Hrungner to protect himself from below with his shield. The cultivation of the mountain must begin at the foot of it; there labors the industrious farmer. When he looks up the mountain lifts its rocky head like a huge giant of stone, but the clouds gather around the giant's head, the lightnings flash and split it. Thjalfe may also be regarded as a concomitant of the thunderstorm, and would then represent the pouring rain, as Thor had got him from a peasant by the sea, and he contends with the mountain of clay, from which the water pours down. Thor's forehead may also represent the face of the earth, from which he rises as the son of earth, and we know that Minerva sprang forth full-grown and equipped from the brain of Zeus. Orvandel* and Groa (to grow) refer to the seed sprouting (Orvandel) and growing. Thor carries the seed in his basket over the ice-cold streams (Elivagar), that is, he preserves plant-life through the winter; the sprout ventures out too early in the spring and a toe freezes off; and it is a beautiful idea that the gods make shining stars of everything in the realm of giants that has become useless on earth, and what more charming theme can the painter ask for than Thor carrying on his divine shoulders the reckless Orvandel wading through the ice streams of winter?

Before proceeding to the next myth, we will pause here for a moment and take a cursory look at history, to see whether a few outlines of it do not find their com-

---

* Orvandel, from *aur*, earth, and *vendill*, the sprout (*vöndr*), ruler = the seed.

pletest reflection in this stone-hearted myth about
Hrungner and Thor.

Hrungner on his horse *Goldfax*, racing with Odin and
Sleipner, in the most perfect manner represents the
Roman *poetastry* reveling in the *wealth* robbed from the
nations of the earth, in rivalry with the genuine Greek
*poetry* and philosophy; for Sleipner is Pegasos; and
when the Roman poetasters are in the hight of their
glory Hrungner is entertained at Asgard, drunk and
crazy, bragging and swearing that he will put all the gods
to death excepting Sif (Fortuna) and Freyja (Venus),
destroy Asgard and move Valhal to Jotunheim; or, in
other words, Venus and Fortuna are the only divinities
that shall be worshiped; all religion (Asgard) shall be
rooted out and history (Valhal) shall only serve to glorify
Rome.

But in the course of time the North begins to take
part in determining the destinies of the world; Thor
comes home, and shortly afterwards a duel is fought
between the Goth and Roman (Vandal) in which Rome is
worsted, which could not be expressed more fitly than by
the fortunate blow of Mjolner, which crushes the stone-
hearted and stone-headed Giant (Roman Vandalism).

But the Goth becomes Romanized, he becomes a slave
of Roman thought and Roman civilization, and thus
Hrungner falls upon Thor, with his foot upon Thor's
neck, until his son Magne comes and takes it away.
Magne is the Anglo-Saxon who created a Gothic Christianity and a Gothic book-speech; and well might the
Anglo-Saxon be called Magne, son of Asathor and the
hag Jarnsaxa, for Magne is the mythical representation
of the mechanical arts, which have received their most
perfect development in England and America (the Anglo-
Saxons). And we need only to look at the literature of

England and America to observe with what pleasure Magne (the Anglo-Saxon) is a great child, who rides the horse Goldfax (the Latin language), at which Odin (the Goth) may well complain that it was wrongfully done, although the spirit of the North (Odin) might rather envy the horse (Romanism) its rider than the rider (the Anglo-Saxon) his horse.

In regard to the piece of flint-stone that remained in Thor's forehead, and sticks there yet, we know, alas! that it is too true that the schools and the literature of all the Teutonic races suffer more or less from the curse of Romanism; and this they suffer in spite of the German sorceress Groa (Luther), who in the sixteenth century loosened the ugly Roman popery in Thor's forehead, without his getting rid of it; for he began boasting too soon, and Groa (the Lutheran Reformation) became so glad on account of her husband with his frozen toe (German scholasticism and soulless philosophy elevated to the skies), that she forgot not her Latin but her magic Teutonic songs; and hence we look in vain for a complete system of German mythology and old German poetry.

Who the Mokkerkalfe who assisted Hrungner is, in this picture, it is difficult to say, unless it be the Arab, and he may well be called a brother of the Roman (Hrungner) against Thor. The Mokkerkalfe had a mare's heart in him, and we know that love of horses has forever been a characteristic of the Arabs; and the Frank, who defeated the Arab on the historical arena, must then be Thjalfe, who was a servant of Thor.

Thus this myth is disposed of and its application in a prophetic sense has been pointed out. It is not claimed that the ancient Norsemen had in their minds Arabs and Greeks and Romans and Franks and Anglo-Saxons. but that they had in their minds a profound comprehension of the relations of things, the supreme law of the universe; and history is but the reflection of the sublimest riddles in nature.

### SECTION III.    THOR AND GEIRROD.*

It is worth relating how Thor made a journey to Geirrodsgard without his hammer Mjolner, or belt Megingjarder, or his iron gloves; and that was Loke's fault. For when Loke once, in Frigg's falcon-guise, flew out to amuse himself, curiosity led him to Geirrodsgard, where he saw a large hall. He sat down and looked in through an opening in the wall, but Geirrod observed him and ordered one of his servants to seize the bird and bring it to him. But the wall was so high that it was difficult to climb up, and it amused Loke that it gave the servant so much trouble, and he thought it was time enough to fly away when the servant had got over the worst. As the latter now caught at him, he spread his wings and made efforts (stritted) with his feet, but the feet were fast, so that he was seized and brought to the giant. When the latter saw his eyes he mistrusted that it was no bird; and when Loke was silent and refused to answer the questions put to him, Geirrod locked him down in a chest and let him hunger for three months. Thus Loke finally had to confess who he was, and to save his life he had to make an oath to Geirrod that he should get Thor to Geirrodsgard without his hammer or his belt of strength.

On the way Thor visited the hag Grid, mother of Vidar the Silent. She informed him, in regard to Geirrod, that he was a dogwise and dangerous giant, and she lent him her belt of strength, her iron gloves and her staff. which is called Gridarvold. Thor then went to

* This Geirrod must not be confounded with Odin's foster-son Geirrod, son of Hraudung (see p. 228).

the river Vimer, which is exceedingly large; then he buckled the belt around him and stemmed the wild torrent with his staff, but Loke and Thjalfe held themselves fast in the belt. When he had come into the middle of the river it grew so much that the waves washed over his shoulders. Then quoth Thor:

> Wax not, Vimer,
> Since to wade I desire
> To the realms of giants!
> Know, if thou waxest
> Then waxes my asamight
> As high as the heavens!

Up in a cleft he saw Geirrod's daughter, Gjalp, who stood on both sides of the stream and caused its growth; then took he a large stone and threw after her. At its source the stream must be stemmed, and he always hit what he aimed at. At the same time he reached the land and got hold of a shrub, and so he escaped out of the river; hence comes the adage that a shrub saved Thor. When Thor with his companions had now come to Geirrod, lodgings were given them in a house, but there was only one chair in it, and on this Thor sat down. Then he noticed that the chair was raised under him toward the roof. He then put Grid's staff against the beams and pressed himself down against the chair; then a noise was heard, upon which followed a great screaming, for Geirrod's daughters, Gjalp and Greip, had been sitting under the chair and he had broken the backs of both of them. Then quoth Thor:

> Once I employed
> My asamight
> In the realm of giants,
> When Gjalp and Greip,
> Geirrod's daughters,
> Wanted to lift me to heaven.

Then Geirrod invited Thor into the hall to see games. Large fires burned along the hall, and when Thor had come opposite to Geirrod the latter took with a pair of tongs a red-hot iron wedge and threw it after Thor; he seized it with the iron gloves and lifted it up into the air, but Geirrod ran behind an iron post to defend himself. Thor threw the wedge, which struck through the post and through Geirrod and through the wall, so that it went outside and into the ground.

Geirrod is the intense heat which produces violent thunderstorms, and hence his daughter the violent torrent. Of course Loke (fire) is locked up and starved through the hottest part of the summer; but this myth needs no explanation, and we proceed to the next.

### SECTION IV. THOR AND SKRYMER.

One day the god Thor, accompanied by Loke, set out on a journey in his car drawn by his goats. Night coming on, they put up at a peasant's cottage, when Thor killed his goats, and, after flaying them, put them in a kettle. When the flesh was boiled he sat down with his fellow-traveler to supper, and invited the peasant and his wife and their children to partake of the repast. The peasant's son was named Thjalfe, and his daughter Roskva. Thor bade them throw all the bones into the goats' skins, which were spread out near the fireplace, but young Thjalfe broke one of the shank-bones to come at the marrow. Thor having passed the night in the cottage, rose at the dawn of day, and when he had dressed himself he took his hammer, Mjolner, and, lifting it up, consecrated the goats' skins, which he had no sooner done than the two goats reassumed their wonted form, with the exception that one of them now limped on one of its hind legs. Thor, perceiving this,

said that the peasant or one of his family had handled
the shank-bone of this goat too roughly, for he saw
clearly that it was broken. It may readily be imagined
how frightened the peasant was, when he saw Thor
knit his brows and seize the handle of his hammer with
such force that the knuckles of his fingers grew white
with the exertion. But the peasant, as we might expect,
and his whole family, screamed aloud, sued for peace,
and offered all they possessed as an atonement for the
offense committed. But when Thor saw their fright he
desisted from his wrath and became appeased, and he
contented himself by requiring their children, Thjalfe and
Roskva, who thus became his servants and have accompanied him ever since. Thor let his goats remain there,
and proceeded eastward on the way to Jotunheim clear
to the sea. Then he went across the deep ocean, and
when he came to the other shore he landed with Loke,
Thjalfe and Roskva. They had traveled but a short distance when they came to a large forest, through which
they wandered until night set in. Thjalfe was exceedingly
fleet-footed; he carried Thor's provision-sack, but the
forest was a bad place for finding anything eatable to
stow into it. When it had become dark they looked
around for lodgings for the night and found a house.
It was very large, with a door that took up the whole
breadth of one of the ends of the building; here they
chose them a place to sleep in. At midnight they were
alarmed by a great earthquake. The earth trembled
beneath them and the whole house shook. Then Thor
stood up and called his companions to seek with him a
place of safety. On the right they found an adjoining
chamber, into which they entered; but while the others,
trembling with fear, crept into the farthest corner of this
retreat, Thor remained in the doorway, with his hammer

in his hand, prepared to defend himself whatever might happen. Then they heard a rumbling and roaring. When the morning began to dawn, Thor went out and saw a man lying a short distance from the house in the woods. The giant was large, lay sleeping, and snored loudly. Then Thor could understand whence the noise had come in the night. He girded himself with his belt of strength, and his divine strength grew; at the same time the man awoke and arose hastily. But it is related that Thor on this occasion became so amazed that he forgot to make use of his mallet; he asked the man for his name, however. The latter answered that his name was Skrymer; but your name I do not need to ask about, said he; I know you are Asathor; but what have you done with my mitten? Thereupon Skrymer stretched out his hand and picked up his mitten, which Thor then perceived was what they had taken over night for a house, the chamber where they had taken refuge being the thumb. Skrymer asked whether Thor wanted him for a traveling companion, and when Thor consented to this, Skrymer untied his provision-sack and began to eat his breakfast. Thor and his companions did the same in another place. Then Skrymer proposed that they should put their provisions together, and when Thor gave his consent to this, Skrymer put all the food into one sack and slung it on his back. He went before them all day with tremendous strides, but toward evening he sought out for them a place where they might pass the night, beneath a large oak. Then said Skrymer to Thor that he was going to lie down to sleep; the others might in the meantime take the provision-sack and prepare their supper. Then Skrymer fell asleep, and snored tremendously, and Thor took the provision-sack to untie it; but, incredible though it may appear, not a single knot could he untie, nor render a single string looser than it was before. Seeing that his labor was in vain, Thor became angry, seized the hammer Mjolner with both hands, went over to Skrymer and struck him on the head. But Skrymer awoke and asked whether there had fallen a leaf down upon his head, and whether they had eaten their supper and were ready to go to sleep? Thor answered that they were just going to sleep, and went to lie down under another oak, but also here it was dangerous to sleep. At midnight Thor again heard how fast Skrymer slept and snored, so outrageously that a thundering noise was heard through the whole woods. Arising he went over to the giant, swung his hammer with all his might, and struck him right in the skull, and the hammer entered the head clear to the handle. Skrymer, suddenly awakening, said: What is the matter now? Did an acorn fall down upon my head? How is it with you, Thor? Thor went hastily away and said that he had just waked up; it was midnight, he said, and time to sleep. Then thought he that if he could get an opportunity to give the giant a third blow he should never see the light of day any more, and he now lay watching to see whether Skrymer was fast asleep again. Shortly before day-break he heard that the giant was sleeping again. He got up, hastened over to him, swung his hammer with all his might, and gave him such a blow on the temples that the head of the hammer was buried in the giant's head. Skrymer arose, stroked his chin and said: Do there sit birds above me in the tree? It seemed to me as I awoke that some moss fell down upon me out of the boughs; but are you awake, Thor? It seems to me that it is time to arise and dress, and you have not now a long journey to the castle which is called Utgard. I have

heard you have whispered among yourselves that I am
not small of stature, but you shall find larger men when
you come to Utgard. I am going to give you good
advice: do not brag too much. Utgard-Loke's courtiers
will not brook the boasting of such insignificant little
fellows as you are. If you will not heed this advice
you had better turn back, and that is in fact the best
thing for you to do. But if you are determined to
go further then hold to the east; my way lies northward to those mountains that you see yonder. Skrymer then taking the provision-sack, slung it on his
back and disappeared in the woods, and it has never
been learned whether the asas wished to meet him again
or not.

Thor now went on with his companions till it was
noon, when their eyes beheld a castle standing on a
great plain, and it was so high that they had to bend
their necks quite back in order to be able to look over
it. They advanced to the castle; there was a gate to
the entrance, which was locked. Thor tried to open it,
but could not, and being anxious to get within the
castle they crept between the bars of the gate. They
saw the palace before them, the door was open, and
they entered, where they saw a multitude of men, of
whom the greater number were immensely large, sitting
on two benches. Then they came into the presence of
the king, Utgard-Loke, and saluted him; but it took
some time before he would deign to look at them, and
he smiled scornfully, so that one could see his teeth,
saying: It is tedious to ask for tidings of a long journey, but if I am not mistaken this little stripling must
be Asathor; perhaps, however, you are really bigger
than you look. Well, what are the feats that you and
your companions are skilled in? No one is tolerated

among us here unless he distinguishes himself by some
art or accomplishment. Then said Loke: I understand
an art, of which I am prepared to give proof, and that
is, that there is none here who can eat his food as fast
as I can. To this Utgard-Loke made reply: Truly that
is an art, if you can achieve it, which we shall now see.
He called to the men, who sat on one end of the bench,
that he, whose name was Loge (flame), should come
out on the floor and contend with Loke. A trough
was brought in full of meat. Loke seated himself at
one end and Loge at the other; both ate as fast as they
could and met in the middle of the trough. Loke had
picked the meat from the bones, but Loge had consumed meat, bones and trough all together; and now
all agreed that Loke was beaten. Then asked Utgard-
Loke, what that young man could do. It was Thjalfe.
He answered, that he would run a race with any one
that Utgard-Loke would appoint. Utgard-Loke replied
that this was a splendid feat, but added that he must
be very swift if he expected to win, but they should
see, for it would soon be decided. Utgard-Loke arose
and went out; there was a very good race-course on
the level field. Then he called a little fellow, by name
Huge (thought) and bade him race with Thjalfe. The
first time they ran Huge was so much in advance that
at the turning back in the course he met Thjalfe. You
must ply your legs better, Thjalfe, said Utgard-Loke, if
you expect to win, though I must confess that there
never came a man here swifter of foot than you are.
They ran a second time, but when Huge came to the
end and turned around, Thjalfe was a full bow-shot
from the goal. Well run, both of you, said Utgard-Loke, but I think Thjalfe will hardly win, but the
third race shall decide it. They accordingly ran a

third time, but Huge had already reached the goal
before Thjalfe had got half-way. Then all who were
present cried out that there had been sufficient trial of
skill in this art. Utgard-Loke then asked Thor in what
arts he would choose to give proof of his skill for
which he was so famous. Thor answered that he preferred to contend in drinking with any one that wished.
Utgard-Loke consented, and entering the palace he called
his cup-bearer, and bade him bring the large horn which
his courtiers were obliged to drink out of when they
had trespassed in any way against established usage.
The cup-bearer brought the horn, gave it to Thor, and
Utgard-Loke said: Whoever is a good drinker will empty
that horn at a single draught, though some men make
two of it; but there is no so wretched drinker that he
cannot exhaust it at the third draught. Thor looked
at the horn and thought it was not large, though tolerably long; however, as he was very thirsty he set it
to his lips, and without drawing breath drank as long
and as deep as he could, in order that he might not be
obliged to make a second draught of it. But when his
breath gave way and he set the horn down, he saw to
his astonishment that there was little less of the liquor
in it than before. Utgard-Loke said: That is well
drunk, but not much to boast of; I should never have
believed but that Asathor could have drunk more; however, of this I am confident, you will empty it at the
second draught. Thor made no reply, but put the horn
to his mouth and drank as long as he had breath, but
the point of the horn did not rise as he expected; and
when he withdrew the horn from his mouth it seemed
to him that its contents had sunk less this time than
the first; still the horn could now be carried without
spilling. Utgard-Loke said: How now, Thor, have you

not saved for the third draught more than you can make
away with ? You must not spare yourself more in performing a feat than befits your skill, but if you mean
to drain the horn at the third draught you must drink
deeply. You will not be considered so great a man
here as you are thought to be among the asas if you
do not show greater skill in other games than you appear to have shown in this. Then Thor became angry,
put the horn to his mouth, and drank with all his
might, so as to empty it entirely; but on looking into
the horn he found that its contents had lessened but
little, upon which he resolved to make no further attempt, but gave back the horn to the cup-bearer. Then
said Utgard-Loke: It is now plain that your strength
is not so great as we thought it to be. Will you try
some other games, for we see that you cannot succeed
in this? Yes, said Thor, I will try something else, but
I am sure that such draughts as I have been drinking
would not have been counted small among the asas, but
what new trial have you to propose? Utgard-Loke
answered: We have a very trifling game here, in which
we exercise none but children. Young men think it
nothing but play to lift my cat from the ground, and I
should never have proposed this to Asathor if I had not
already observed that you are by no means what we
took you for. Thereupon a large gray cat ran out upon
the floor. Thor advancing put his hand under the cat's
body and did his utmost to raise it from the floor, but
the cat, bending its back in the same degree as Thor
lifted, had notwithstanding all Thor's efforts only one
of its feet lifted up, seeing which Thor made no further effort. Then said Utgard-Loke: The game has
terminated just as I expected; the cat is large, but
Thor is small and little compared with our men. Then

said Thor: Little as you call me I challenge any one to
wrestle with me, for now I am angry.  I see no one here,
replied Utgard-Loke, looking around on the benches,
who would not think it beneath him to wrestle with
you; but let somebody call hither that old woman, my
nurse, Elle (old age), and let Thor prove his strength
with her, if he will.  She has thrown to the ground
many a man not less strong and mighty than Thor is.
A toothless old woman then entered the hall and she
was told by Utgard-Loke to wrestle with Thor.  To cut
the story short, the more Thor tightened his hold the
firmer she stood.  Finally, after a violent struggle, Thor
began to lose his footing, and it was not long before
he was brought down on one knee.  Then Utgard-Loke
stepped forward and told them to stop, adding that Thor
had now no occasion to ask anyone else in the hall to
wrestle with him, and it was also getting late.  He
therefore showed Thor and his companions to their
seats, and they passed the night there enjoying the best
of hospitality.

The next morning, at break of day, Thor and his
companions arose, dressed themselves and prepared for
their departure.  Utgard-Loke then came and ordered a
table to be set for them, on which there wanted no good
provisions, either meat or drink.  When they had break-
fasted they set out on their way.  Utgard-Loke accompanied them out of the castle, and on parting he asked
Thor how he thought his journey had turned out, and
whether he had found any man more mighty than himself.  Thor answered that he could not deny that he
had brought great dishonor upon himself; and what
mortifies me the most, he added, is that you will consider me a man of little importance.  Then said Utgard-
Loke: Now I will tell you the truth, since you are out

of my castle, where as long as I live and reign you shall never re-enter, and you may rest assured that had I known before what might you possessed, and how near you came plunging us into great trouble, I would not have permitted you to enter this time. Know then that I have all along deceived you by my illusions; first, in the forest, where I arrived before you, and there you were unable to untie the provision-sack, because I had bound it with tough iron wire in such a manner that you could not discover how the knot ought to be loosened. After this you gave me three blows with your hammer; the first one, though it was the least, would have ended my days had it fallen on me, but I brought a rocky mountain before me, which you did not perceive; but you saw near my castle a mountain in which were three square glens, the one deeper than the other, and those were the marks of your hammer. I have made use of similar illusions in the contests you have had with my courtiers. In the first, Loke was hungry and devoured all that was set before him, but Loge was in reality nothing else but wild-fire, and therefore consumed not only the meat, but the trough which contained it. Huge, with whom Thjalfe contended in running, was my thought, and it was impossible for Thjalfe to keep pace with it. When you tried to empty the horn you performed indeed an exploit so marvelous that had I not seen it myself I should never have believed it. The one end of the horn stood in the sea, which you did not perceive, and when you come to the shore you will see how much the ocean has diminished by what you drank. This is now called the ebb. You performed a feat no less wonderful when you lifted the cat, and, to tell the truth, when we saw that one of his paws was off the floor we were all of us terror-stricken,

21

for what you took for a cat was in reality the great Midgard-serpent, that encompasses the whole earth, and he was then barely long enough to inclose it between his head and tail, so high had your hand raised him up toward heaven. Your wrestling with Elle was also a most astonishing feat, for there never yet was, nor will there ever be, a man for whom Old Age (for such in fact was Elle) will not sooner or later lay low, if he abides her coming. But now, as we are going to part, let me tell you that it will be better for both of us if you never come near me again, for should you do so I shall again defend myself with other illusions, so that you will never prevail against me. On hearing these words Thor grasped his hammer, and lifted it into the air, but as he was about to strike Utgard-Loke was nowhere, and when he turned back to the castle to destroy it, he saw only beautiful verdant plains around him and no castle. He therefore retraced his steps without stopping till he came to Thrudvang. But he had already resolved to make that attack on the Midgard-serpent, which afterwards took place.

It is said in the Younger Edda that no one can tell anything more *true* of this journey of Thor's, but if the reader wants to see the most beautiful thing that has been said about this journey, he must learn Danish and read Œlenschlæger's poem entitled *Thor's Journey to Jotunheim.** We have only to add that as the asas had their Loke, so the giants had their *Utgard-Loke*.

SECTION V.   THOR AND THE MIDGARD-SERPENT.

The gods were having a feast at Æger's, and could not get enough to eat and drink. The reason was that

_____
* The next best thing is William Edward Frye's translation of Œlenschlæger's work entitled *The Gods of the North*. London, 1845.

Æger was in want of a kettle for brewing ale. He asked Thor to go and fetch it, but neither the asas nor the vans knew where it could be found, before Tyr said to Thor: East of the rivers Elivagar, near the borders of heaven, dwells the dogwise Hymer, and this my father has a kettle which is strong and one rast (mile) deep. Do you think we can get it? said Thor. Yes, by stratagem it may be gotten, answered Tyr. Tyr, and Thor under the semblance of a young man, now started out and traveled until they came to Egil. With him they left the goats and proceeded further to Hymer's hall, and we shall presently see how Thor made amends for his journey to Utgard-Loke. At Hymer's hall Tyr found his grandmother, an ugly giantess with nine hundred heads, but his mother, a beautiful woman, brought him a drink. She advised her guests to conceal themselves under the kettles in the hall, for her husband was sometimes cruel toward strangers. Hymer came home from his fishing late in the evening; the jokuls resounded as he entered the hall, and his beard was full of frost. I greet you welcome home, Hymer, said the woman; our son, whom we have been so long expecting, has now come home to your halls, and in company with him is the enemy of the giants and the friend of man, Veor (*i.e.* Asgardsveor, the protector of Asgard). See how they have concealed themselves at the gable end of the hall, behind the post yonder. Hymer threw a glance in the direction pointed out by his wife, and the post instantly flew into shivers at the look of the giant, the beam broke, and eight kettles fell down; one was so hard and strong that it did not break in falling. The gods came forth, and straight the old giant gazed at his enemy. It was no pleasant sight to see Thor before him, but still he ordered three

steers to be killed and served on the table. Thor alone
ate two. This meal seemed to the friend of Hrungner
somewhat extravagant, and he remarked that the next
evening they would have to live on fish. The following
morning, at break of day, when Thor perceived that
Hymer was making his boat ready for fishing, he arose
and dressed himself, and begged the giant to let him row
out to sea with him. Hymer answered that such a puny
stripling as he was could be of no use to him; besides, he
said, you will catch your death of cold if I go so far out
and remain as long as I am accustomed to do. Thor said
that for all that he would row as far from the land as
Hymer had a mind, and was not sure which of them
would be the first who might wish to row back again.
At the same time he was so enraged that he was much
inclined to let his hammer ring at the giant's skull
without further delay, but intending to try his strength
elsewhere he subdued his wrath, and asked Hymer what
he meant to bait with. Hymer told him to look out for
a bait himself. Thor instantly went up to a herd of
oxen that belonged to the giant, and seizing the largest
bull, that bore the name Himinbrjoter (heaven-breaker),
wrung off his head, and returning with it to the boat,
put out to sea with Hymer. Thor rowed aft with two
oars, and with such force that Hymer, who rowed at the
prow, saw with surprise how swiftly the boat was driven
forward. He then observed that they were come to the
place where he was wont to angle for flat-fish, but Thor
assured him that they had better go on a good way further. They accordingly continued to ply their oars, until
Hymer cried out that if they did not stop they would be
in danger from the great Midgard-serpent. Notwithstanding this, Thor persisted in rowing further, and in
spite of Hymer's remonstrances it was a long time before

he would lay down his oars.  When they finally stopped,
Hymer soon drew up two whales at once with his bait.
Then Thor took out a fishing-line, extremely strong,
made with wonderful art and furnished with an equally
strong hook, on which he fixed the bull's head and cast
his line into the sea.  The bait soon reached the bottom,
and it may be truly said that Thor then deceived the
Midgard-serpent not a whit less than Utgard-Loke had
deceived Thor when he obliged him to lift up the serpent in his hand; for the monster greedily caught at
the bait and the hook stuck fast in his palate.  Stung
with the pain, the serpent tugged at the hook so violently
that Thor was obliged to hold fast with both hands in
the pegs that bear against the oars.  But his wrath now
waxed high, and assuming all his divine power he pulled
so hard at the line that his feet forced their way through
the boat and went down to the bottom of the sea, while
with his hands he drew up the serpent to the side of the
vessel.  It is impossible to express by words the scene
that now took place.  Thor on the one hand darting
looks of wrath at the serpent, while the monster on the
other hand, rearing his head, spouted out floods of venom
upon him.  When the giant Hymer beheld the serpent
he turned pale and trembled with fright, and seeing
moreover that the water was entering his boat on all
sides, he took out his knife, just as Thor raised his
hammer aloft, and cut the line, on which the serpent
sank again under water.  According to another version
the valiant Thor hauled the venom-spotted serpent up
to the edge of the boat, his hands struck against the
side of the boat and with both his feet he stepped
through, so that he stood on the bottom of the sea.
With his hammer he struck the serpent in the forehead;
the mountains thundered, the caves howled, and the

whole old earth shrank together; but the serpent sank to
the bottom, for at the sight of it the giant became so
terrified that he cut the line. Then, according to both
versions, Thor struck Hymer such a blow on the ear
with his fist that the giant fell headlong into the water.
The giant was not glad when they rowed back. While
he carried his two whales, Thor took the boat, with
oars and all, and carried it to the house of the giant.
Then the giant challenged Thor to show another evidence
of his strength and requested him to break his goblet.
Thor, sitting, threw it through some large posts, but
it was brought whole to the giant. But Thor's fair
friend gave him friendly advice: Throw it against the
forehead of Hymer, said she, it is harder than any
goblet. Then Thor assumed his asastrength. The
giant's forehead remained whole, but the round wine-
goblet was broken. The giant had lost a great treasure;
that drink, said he, was too hot; but there yet remained
for Thor one trial of his strength, and that was to bring
the kettle out of his hall. Twice Tyr tried to lift it, but
it was immovable. Then Thor himself took hold of it
at the edge with so great force that he stepped through
the floor of the hall; the kettle he lifted onto his head,
and its rings rung at his heels. They had gone a long
distance before Odin's son looked back and saw a many-
headed multitude rushing impetuously from the caves
with Hymer. Then he lifted the kettle from his shoulders, swung the murderous Mjolner and slew all the
mountain-giants. After that he proceeded to Egil, where
he had left his goats; and he had not gone far thence
before one of the goats dropped down half dead. It was
lame, and we remember from a previous myth that a
peasant near the sea had to give Thor his son Thjalfe and
daughter Roskva as bond-servants for laming one of his

goats. Thor finally came to the feast of the gods and had the kettle with him, and there was nothing now to hinder Æger from furnishing ale enough at the feast, that he prepared for the gods at every harvest time.

This myth forms the subject of the lay of Hymer in the Elder Edda. The whole myth of course represents the thunderstorm in conflict with the raging sea; but a historical counterpart of this struggle of Thor with Hymer and the Midgard-serpent is so forcibly suggested that we cannot omit it. It is Luther's struggle with the pope and Romanism. Luther, the heroic Thor, saw his enemy, but did not strike just in the right time and in the right way, and the golden opportunity was lost after Hymer (the pope) had severed the fishing-line; that is, after the old memories were destroyed, when the golden line connecting the Germans with their poetic dawn had been divided, and Romanism, with blood-stained breast, with close embrace first twined around the whole school system of Germany and north Europe, and horribly mangled their grand mission with its fangs, and then seized the Teutonic Laocoon and his sons and bound their unsophisticated Teutonic hearts in its mighty folds. Ay, this *Roman* Midgard-serpent, with its licentiousness, arrogance, despotism, unbridled ambition, unbounded egotism, dry reasoning and soulless philosophy, has grasped the *Goth* twice, yes thrice, about the middle, and winding its scaly back thrice around his neck, has overtopped him. In vain he has striven to tear asunder its knotted and gory spires. He can but shriek to heaven for help, and may Thor hear his cry and come to his rescue! May Thor next time embark well armed with his gloves and belt and hammer; but he had better leave the giant slain on shore. Yet Luther did a

noble work.   Although his first intention was to leave
the giant unmolested, and only take his kettle from
him, still, when he found a determined opposition threatening, he turned around, set down his kettle, and slew
both the giant and the many-headed multitude (pope,
cardinals, bishops, etc.) that followed him.   But Luther
erred in not establishing a thoroughly Teutonic in place
of a Romanic school system.   Thus he left his great
work only half finished.   If he had made good use of
his hammer at the time, much valuable knowledge about
our Teutonic ancestors might have been collected and
preserved which now is lost forever.

### SECTION VI.   THOR AND THRYM.

This is a very beautiful myth, and we will give it
complete as it is found in the Elder Edda, in the lay
of Thrym.   We give our own translation:

> Wrathful was Vingthor
> As he awaked
> And his hammer
> Did miss;
> His beard shook,
> His hair trembled,
> The son of earth
> Looked around him.
>
> Thus first of all
> He spoke:
> Mark now Loke
> What I say!
> What no one knows
> Either on earth
> Or in high heaven,—
> The hammer is stolen.
>
> Went they to Freyja's
> Fair dwelling;

There in these words
Thor first spoke:
Wilt thou, Freyja, lend
Me thy feather-guise,
That I my hammer
Mjolner may fetch?

I gave it thee gladly
Though it were of gold;
I would instantly give it
Though it were of silver.

Flew then Loke —
The feather-guise whizzed;
Out he flew
From home of asas,
In he flew
To home of giants.

On the hill sat Thrym;
The king of giants
Twisted gold-bands
For his dogs,
Smoothed at leisure
The manes of his horses.

THRYM:

How fare the asas?
How fare the elves?
Why comest thou alone
    To Jotunheim?

LOKE:

Ill fare the asas,
Ill fare the elves.
Hast thou concealed
The hammer of Thor?

THRYM:

I have concealed
The hammer of Thor
Eight rasts
Beneath the ground;

No man
Brings it back
Unless he gives me
Freyja as my bride.

Flew then Loke —
The feather-guise whizzed;
Out he flew
From home of giants,
In he flew
To home of asas.
Met him Thor
First of all
And thus addressed him:

Hast thou succeeded
In doing thine errand?
Then tell before perching
Long messages;
What one says sitting
Is often of little value,
And falsehood speaks he
Who reclines.

LOKE:

Well have I succeeded
In doing my errand;
Thrym has thy hammer,
The king of the giants.
No man
Brings it back
Unless he gives him
Freyja as bride.

Went they then the fair
Freyja to find,
First then Thor
Thus addressed her:
Dress thyself, Freyja,
In bridal robes,
Together we will ride
To Jotunheim.

Angry grew Freyja,
And she raged
So the hall of the asas
Must shake.
Her heavy necklace,
Brisingamen, broke:
Then would I be
A lovesick maid
If with thee I would ride
To Jotunheim.

Then all the asas
Went to the *Thing*,
To the *Thing* went
All the asynjes,
The powerful divinities,
And held consult,
How they should get
The hammer back.

Then spake Heimdal
The whitest god —
Foreknowing was he,
As the vans are all:
Dress we Thor
In bridal robes,
Brisingamen
Must he wear.

Let jingle keys
About his waist;
Let a woman's dress
Cover his knees;
On his bosom we put
Broad broaches,
And artfully we
His hair braid.

Spoke then Thor,
The mighty god:
Mock me all
The asas would,

If in bridal robes
I should be dressed.

Spoke then Loke
Laufeyarson:
Be silent Thor;
Stop such talk.
Soon will giants
Build in Asgard
If thou thy hammer
Bring not back.

Dressed they then Thor
In bridal-robes;
Brisengamen
He had to wear;
Keys let they jingle
About his waist,
And a woman's dress
Fell over his knees;
On his bosom they placed
Broad broaches,
And artfully they
His hair did braid.

Spoke then Loke
Laufeyarson:
For thee must I
Be servant-maid;
Ride we both
To Jotunheim.

Home were driven
Then the g ats,
And hitched to the car;
Hasten they must —
The mountains crashed,
The earth stood in flames,
Odin's son
Rode to Jotunheim.

Spoke then Thrym,
The king of giants:

Giants! arise
And spread my benches!
Bring to me
Freyja as bride,
Njord's daughter,
From Noatun.

Cows with golden horns
Go in the yard,
Black oxen
To please the giant;
Much wealth have I,
Many gifts have I;
Freyja, methinks,
Is all I lack.

Early in the evening
Came they all;
Ale was brought
Up for the giant.
One ox Thor ate,
Eight salmon
And all the delicacies
For the women intended;
Sif's husband besides
Drank three barrels of mead.

Spoke then Thrym,
The king of giants:
Where hast thou seen
Such a hungry bride?
I ne'er saw a bride
Eat so much,
And never a maid
Drink more mead.

Sat there the shrewd
Maid-servant near;*
Thus she replied
To the words of Thrym:
Nothing ate Freyja
In eight nights,

* Loke.

So much did she long
For Jotunheim.

Behind the veil
Thrym sought a kiss,
But back he sprang
The length of the hall:
Why are Freyja's
Eyes so sharp?
From her eyes it seems
That fire doth burn.

Sat there the shrewd
Maid-servant near,
And thus she spake,
Answering the giant:
Slept has not Freyja
For eight nights,
So much did she long
For Jotunheim.

In came the poor
Sister of Thrym;
For bridal gift
She dared to ask:
Give from thy hand
The golden rings,
If thou desirest
Friendship of me,
Friendship of me —
And love.

Spoke then Thrym,
The king of giants:
Bring me the hammer
My bride to hallow:
Place the hammer
In the lap of the maid;
Wed us together
In the name of Var.*

* The goddess who presides over marriages.

Laughed then Thor's
Heart in his breast;
Severe in mind
He knew his hammer.
First slew he Thrym,
The king of giants,
Crushed then all
That race of giants;

Slew the old
Sister of Thrym,
She who asked
For a bridal gift;
Slap she got
For shining gold,
Hammer blows
For heaps of rings;
Thus came Odin's son
Again by his hammer.

Thrym (from *pruma*) is the noisy, thundering imitator of Thor. While the thunder sleeps, the giant forces of nature howl and rage in the storms and winds, they have stolen the hammer from Thor. Thor goes and brings his hammer back and the storms are made to cease. It has been suggested that Thor is the impersonation of truth, and the Younger Edda speaks of him as one *never having yet uttered an* UNTRUTH. It has also been claimed that the name of his realm *Thrud*-vang contains the same root as our English word *truth*, but this we leave for the reader to examine for himself. Before the Norsemen learned to make the sign of the cross, they made the sign of the hammer upon themselves and upon other things that they thereby wished to secure against evil influences.

Now let us glance at the last appearance of Thor on the stage of this world. The Norse king, Olaf the saint, was eagerly pursuing his work of Christian reform in Norway, and we find him sailing with fit escort along the western shore of that country from haven to haven, dispensing justice or doing other royal work. On leaving a certain haven, it is found that a stranger of grave eyes and aspect, with red beard and of a robust and stately figure, has stepped in. The courtiers address him; his answers surprise by their pertinency and depth. At length he is brought to the king. The stranger's conversation here is not less remarkable, as they sail along the beautiful shore; but after awhile he addresses King Olaf thus: Yes, King Olaf, it is all beautiful, with the sun shining on it there; green, fruitful, a right fair home for you; and many a sore day had Thor, many a wild fight with the mountain giants, before he could make it so. And now you seem minded to put away Thor. King Olaf, have a care! said the stranger, knitting his brows; and when they looked again he was nowhere to be found. This is the last myth of Thor, a protest against the advance of Christianity, no doubt reproachfully set forth by some conservative pagan.*

* Thomas Carlyle, *Heroes and Hero-worship.*

# CHAPTER V.

## VIDAR.

ON the way to Geirrod (see p. 310) we noticed that Thor visited the hag Grid, and she lent him three things, counterparts of Thor's own treasures, her belt of strength, iron gloves and staff. Grid belongs to the race of giants; she dwells in the wild, unsubdued nature, but is not hostile toward the gods. Her belt, gloves and staff, her name, the place where she dwells between Asgard and Jotunheim, her ability to give Thor information about Geirrod, all give evidence of her wild and powerful character.

She is the mother of Vidar, who is a son of Odin. Hence we have here, as in the case of Tyr, a connecting link between the giants and asas. Through Tyr the gods are related to the raging sea, through Vidar to the wild desert and the forests. Vidar is surnamed the Silent. He is almost as strong as Thor himself, and the gods place great reliance on him in all critical conjunctures. He is the brother of the gods. He has an iron shoe; it is a thick shoe, of which it is said that material has been gathered for it through all ages. It is made of the scraps of leather that have been cut off from the toes and heels in cutting patterns for shoes. These pieces must therefore be thrown away by the shoemaker who desires to render assistance to the gods. He is present at Æger's feast, where Odin says to him:

Stand up, Vidar!
And let the wolf's father *
Be guest at the feast,
That Loke may not
Bring reproach on us
Here in Æger's hall.

His realm is thus described in the Elder Edda:

Grown over with shrubs
And with high grass
Is Vidar's wide land.
There sits Odin's
Son on the horse's back;
He will avenge his father.

He avenges his father in the final catastrophe, in Ragnarok; for when the Fenris-wolf has swallowed Odin, Vidar advances, and setting his foot on the monster's lower jaw he seizes the other with his hand, and thus tears and rends him till he dies. It is now his shoe does him such excellent service. After the universe has been regenerated

There dwell Vidar and Vale
In the gods' holy seats,
When the fire of Surt is slaked.

Vidar's name (from *viðr*, a forest) indicates that he is the god of the primeval, impenetrable forest, where neither the sound of the ax nor the voice of man was ever heard; and hence he is also most fittingly surnamed the Silent God. Vidar is, then, imperishable and incorruptible nature represented as an immense indestructible forest, with the iron trunks of the trees rearing their dense and lofty tops toward the clouds. Who has ever entered a thick and pathless forest, wandered about in its huge shadows and lost himself in its

* Loke.

solemn darkness, without feeling deeply sensible to the loftiness of the idea that underlies Vidar's character. Vidar is the Greek Pan, the representative of incorruptible nature. He is not the ruler of the peaceful grove near the abode of the gods, where Idun dwells, but of the great and wild primeval forest, that man never yet entered. The idea of Vidar's woods is imperishableness, while that of Idun's grove is the constant renovation and rejuvenation of the life of the gods. The gods and all the work of their hands shall perish, and it is nowhere stated that Idun survives Ragnarok. Odin himself perishes, and with him all his labor and care for man; but nature does not perish. If that should be entirely destroyed, then it could not be *regenerated.* If matter should perish, where would then the spirit take its dwelling? If Vidar did not exist, where would Vale be? The glory of the world, the development that has taken place, and the spirit revealed in it, perish; but not Vidar, for he is the imperishable, wild, original nature, the eternal matter, which reveals its force to, but is not comprehended by, man; a force which man sees and reveres, without venturing an explanation; but when all the works of man are destroyed by consuming flames, this force of eternal matter will be revealed with increased splendor.

Thus we find the power and strength of the gods expressed in two myths, in Thor and in Vidar, both sons of Odin, who is, as the reader knows, the father of all the gods. Thor is the thundering, noisy, crushing, but withal beneficent, god; Vidar is silent, dwells far away from, and exercises no influence upon, the works of man, except as he inspires a profound awe and reverence. Thor is the visible, in their manifestations wonderful, constantly returning and all-preserv-

ing, workings of nature; Vidar is the quiet, secretly
working, hidden and self-supporting imperishableness.
Popularity, fame, position, influence, wealth,— all that
makes so much stir and bustle in the world — shall
perish; but the quiet working of the soul, the honest
pursuit of knowledge, the careful secret development
of the powers of the human mind, shall live forever.
And Vidar and Vale (mind and knowledge) shall together inhabit the sacred dwellings of the gods, when
the waves of time have ceased to roll: Vidar as the god
of imperishable matter, Vale as the god of eternal light
(spirit) that shines upon it.

# CHAPTER VI.

## THE VANS.

TWO opposite elements in nature are united in order to produce life. The opposite elements are expressed in the mythology by the terms asas and vans. In our language and mode of expression that would mean the solid and the liquid, the masculine and the feminine. Water, the *par excellence* representative of liquids, may symbolize various ideas. It may typify sorrow; it then manifests itself in tears, and sorrow is as fleeting as the flowing tears. Water may symbolize gladness, happiness, and blessings, that flow in gushing streams along the pathway of life; and it may also be used as the symbol of innocence, purity, and wealth. These ideas may be regarded as a general interpretation of the *vans,*\* and we find them reflected in the triune vana-deity: Njord with his children Frey and Freyja, who rise from the sea and unite themselves with the asa-divinity in heaven and on earth.

Njord is called Vanagod, and he dwells in the heavenly region called Noatun. He rules over the winds and checks the fury of the sea and of fire, and is therefore invoked by seafarers and fishermen. He is so wealthy that he can give possessions and treasures to those who call on him for them. Yet Njord is not of the lineage of the asas, for he was born and bred in Vanaheim.

\* Compare Vainamoinen, the son of Ukko, in the Finnish epic *Kalevala*.

But the vans gave him as hostage to the asas, receiving from them in his stead Hœner. By this means peace was reëstablished between the asas and vans. (See Part II, Chap. 1, Sec. 13.)

Njord took to wife Skade, the daughter of the giant Thjasse.* She preferred dwelling in the abode formerly belonging to her father, which is situated among rocky mountains in the region called Thrymheim, but Njord loved to reside near the sea. They at last agreed that they should pass together nine nights in Thrymheim and then three in Noatun. But one day, when Njord came back from the mountains to Noatun. he thus sang:

> Am weary of the mountains,
> Not long was I there,
> Only nine nights;
> The howl of the wolves
> Methought sounded ill
> To the song of the swans.

To which Skade sang in reply:

> Sleep could I not
> On my sea-strand couch
> For screams of the sea-fowl.
> *There* wakes me
> When from the wave he comes
> Every morn the mew (gull).

Skade then returned to the rocky mountains and dwelt in Thrymheim. There fastening on her skees and taking her bow she passes her time in the chase of wild beasts. and is called Andre-dis (Skee-goddess). Thus it is said:

> Thrymheim it's called
> Where Thjasse dwelled,

---

* How Skade came to choose Njord when she was permitted to choose a husband among the gods, seeing only their feet, was related on page 277.

That stream-mighty giant;
But Skade now dwells,
Pure bride of the gods,
In her father's old mansion.

Njord is the god of the sea; that is to say, of that part of the sea which is immediately connected with the earth, that part of the sea which is made serviceable to man, where fishing and commerce is carried on. His dwelling is Noatun, which means land of ships (*nór*, ship; *tún*, yard, place). Njord's realm is bounded on the one side by the earth, the land, and on the other by the raging ocean, where Æger with his daughters reigns. Njord's wife is Skade (harm). the wild mountain stream, which plunges down from the high rocks, where she prefers to dwell, and pours herself into the sea. Her dwelling is Thrymheim, the *roaring home*, at the thundering waterfall. Taken as a whole, the myth is very clear and simple.

The compromise between Njord and Skade, to dwell nine nights in Thrymheim (home of uproar, storms) and three nights in Noatun, of course has reference to the severe northern latitudes, where rough weather and wintry storms prevail during the greater part of the year.

## SECTION II.  ÆGER AND RAN.

These do not belong to the vana-divinities, but are given here in order to have the divinities of the sea in one place. As Njord is the mild, beneficent sea near the shore, so Æger is the wild, turbulent. raging sea, far from the land, where fishing and navigation cannot well be carried on; the great ocean, and yet bordering on the confines of the asas. Hence Æger's twofold nature; he is a giant, but still has intercourse with

the gods. Thus in Mimer, Æger and Njord, we have
the whole ocean represented, from its origin, Mimer, to
its last stage of development, to Njord, in whom, as a
beneficent divinity, it unites itself with the gods; that
is to say, blesses and serves the enterprises of men.

Æger visits the gods, and the latter visit him in
return; and it was once when the gods visited him
that his brewing-kettle was found too small, so that
Thor had to go to the giant Hymer and borrow a
larger one. In Æger's hall the bright gold was used
instead of fire, and there the ale passed around spontaneously. Ran is his wife. She has a net, in which
she catches those who venture out upon the sea. Æger
and Ran have nine daughters, the waves. Loke once
borrowed Ran's net, to catch the dwarf Andvare, who
in the guise of a fish dwelt in a waterfall. With her
hand she is able to hold the ships fast. It was a
prevailing opinion among the ancient Norsemen that
they who perished at sea came to Ran; for Fridthjof,
who with his companions was in danger of being
wrecked, talks about his having to rest on Ran's couch
instead of Ingeborg's, and as it was not good to come
empty-handed to the halls of Ran and Æger, he divided
a ring of gold between himself and his men.

Thus Tegner has it in *Fridthjof at Sea:*

> Whirling cold and fast
> Snow-wreaths fill the sail;
> Over deck and mast
> Patters heavy hail.
>
> The very stem they see no more,
> So thick is darkness spread,
> As gloom and horror hover o'er
> The chamber of the dead.

Still to sink the sailor dashes
Implacable each angry wave ;
Gray, as if bestrewn with ashes,
Yawns the endless, awful grave.

Then says Fridthjof:

For us in bed of ocean
Azure pillows *Ran* prepares,
On thy pillow, Ingeborg,
Thou thinkest upon me.
Higher ply, my comrades,
Ellida's sturdy oars ;
Good ship, heaven-fashioned,
Bear us on an hour.

The storm continues:

O'er the side apace
Now a sea hath leapt ;
In an instant's space
Clear the deck is swept.

From his arm now Fridthjof hastens
To draw his ring, three marks in weight;
Like the morning sun it glistens,
The golden gift of Bele great.
With his sword in pieces cutting
The famous work of pigmied art,
Shares he quickly, none forgetting,
Unto every man a part.

Then says Fridthjof again :

Gold is good possession
When one goes a-wooing ;
Let none go empty-handed
Down to azure *Ran.*
Icy are her kisses,
Fickle her embraces ;
But we'll charm the sea-bride
With our ruddy gold.

How eager Ran is to capture those who venture out upon her domain is also illustrated in another part of Fridthjof's Saga, where King Ring and his queen Ingeborg ride over the ice on the lake to a banquet. Fridthjof went along on skates. Thus Tegner again:

> They speed as storms over ocean speed;
> The queen's prayers little King Ring doth heed.

> Their steel-shod comrade standeth not still,
> He flieth past them as swift as he will.

> Many a rune on the ice cutteth he;
> Fair Ingeborg's name discovereth she.

> So on their glittering course they go,
> But *Ran*, the traitress, lurketh below.

> A hole in her silver roof she hath reft,
> Down sinketh the sleigh in the yawning cleft.*

But, fortunately, Fridthjof was not far away. He came to their rescue, and

> With a single tug he setteth amain
> Both steed and sleigh on the ice again.

Of Æger's and Ran's daughters, the waves, it is said that they congregate in large numbers according to the will of their father. They have pale locks and white veils; they are seldom mild in their disposition toward men; they are called billows or surges, and are always awake when the wind blows. They lash the sounding shores, and angrily rage and break around the holms;† they have a hard bed (stones and rocks), and seldom play in calm weather. The names of the daughters of Æger and Ran represent the waves in their various magnitudes and appearances. Thus Himinglœfa, the

---

* See *Viking Tales of the North*, Cantos X and XVIII.    † Rocky islands.

sky-clear; Duva, the diver; Blodughadda, the bloody-
or purple-haired; Hefring, the swelling ; Bylgja, billow;
Kolga, raging sea, etc.

These myths are very simple and need no extended
explanations. Æger is the Anglo-Saxon *eagor*, the sea.
He is also called Hler, the shelterer (*hlé*, Anglo-Saxon
*hleo*, Danish *Læ*, English *lee*), and Gymer, the conceal-
ing (*geyma*, Anglo-Saxon *gyman*, Norse *gjemme*, to conceal, to keep). These names express the sea in its uproar, in its calmness, and as the covering of the deep.
The name of his wife, Ran (robbery or the robbing;
*ræna*, to plunder), denotes the sea as craving its sacrifice of human life and of treasures. It is a common
expression in Norseland that the sea brews and seethes,
and this at once suggests Æger's kettles. The foaming
ale needs no butler but passes itself around, and there
is plenty of it. That Æger, when visited by the gods,
illuminated his hall with shining gold, refers of course
to the phosphorescent light of the sea (Icelandic
*marelldr*, Norse *morild*). Those who are familiar with
the sea cannot fail to have seen the sparks of fire that
apparently fly from it when its surface is disturbed in
the dark. Thus the servants of Æger, Elde and Funfeng (both words meaning fire), are properly called excellent firemen. The relation between Njord and Æger
seems to be the same as between Okeanos, the great
water encircling the earth, and Pontus, the Mediterranean, within the confines of the earth.

Some of the old Norse heroes are represented as pos-
sessing a terrifying helmet, Æger's helmet (*ægishjálmr*):
and thus, as Odin's golden helmet is the beaming sky, and
as the dwarfs cover themselves with a helmet of fog, so
Æger wears on his brow a helmet made of dense darkness and heaven-reaching, terrifying breakers.

Æger and his family, it is certain, did not belong among the asas, yet they were regarded, like them, as mighty beings, whose friendship was sought by the gods themselves; and England, that proud mistress of the sea, is the reflection of the myth of Æger, showing what grand results are achieved historically, when human enterprise and heroism enter into friendly relations with the sea, making it serve the advancement of civilization,— when the gods go to Æger's hall to banquet.

### SECTION III. FREY.

Njord had two children — a son Frey and a daughter Freyja, both fair and mighty. Frey is one of the most celebrated of the gods.* He presides over rain and sunshine and all the fruits of the earth, and should be invoked to obtain good harvests, and also for peace. He moreover dispenses wealth among men. He is called van and vanagod, yeargod and goods-giver (*fégjafi*). He owns the ship Skidbladner and also Goldenbristle (*gullinbursti*) or Slidrugtanne (the sharp-toothed), a boar with golden bristles, with which he rides as folk-ruler to Odin's hall. In time's morning, when he was yet a child, the gods gave him Alfheim (home of elves) as a present.

Of Frey's ship Skidbladner, we have before seen (see p. 220) how it was made by the dwarfs, sons of Ivald, and presented to Frey. It was so large that all the gods with their weapons and war stores could find room on board it. As soon as the sails are set a favorable breeze arises and carries it to its place of destination, and it is made of so many pieces, and with so much skill, that when it is not wanted for a voyage Frey may fold it together like a piece of cloth and put it into his pocket.

* Generally speaking, both asas and vans are included in the term gods, both being propitious.

Njord had the consolation, when he was sent as hostage to the gods, that he begat a son whom no one hates, but who is the best among the gods. Thus the Elder Edda, in Æger's banquet to the gods, where Loke also was present:

NJORD:

It is my consolation —
For I was from a far-off place
Sent as a hostage to the gods —
That I begat that son*
Whom no one hates,
And who is regarded
Chief among the gods.

To which LOKE makes reply:

Hold thy tongue, Njord!
Subdue thy arrogance;
I will conceal it no longer
That with thy sister
A son thou didst beget
Scarcely worse than thyself.

But TYR defends Frey:

Frey is the best
Of all the chiefs
Among the gods.
He causes not tears
To maids or mothers:
His desire is to loosen the fetters
Of those enchained.

LOKE:

Hold thy tongue, Tyr!
Never thou couldst
Use both hands,†
Since thy right one,

* Frey.          † See p. 271.

As I now remember,
The wolf Fenrer took from you.

TYR:

I lack a hand,
Thou lackest good reputation,—
Sad it is to lack such a thing;
Nor does the wolf fare well,—
In chains he pines
Till the end of the world.

LOKE:

Hold thy tongue, Tyr!
Thy wife and I
Had a son together,
But thou, poor fellow,
Received not a farthing
In fine from me.

FREY:

The wolf I see lie
At the mouth of the river
Until the powers perish.
Mischief-maker!
If thou dost not hold thy tongue
*Thou* also shalt be bound.

LOKE:

For gold thou bought'st
Gymer's daughter,
And sold thy sword
At the same time;
But when the sons of Muspel
Come riding from the dark woods,
What hast thou, poor fellow,
To rely upon?

Frey has a servant by name BYGVER, who responds
to Loke:

Know that, were I born
Of so noble a race

> As Ingun's Frey,
> And had I
> So glorious a hall,
> I would crush the evil crow,
> Break his bones to the marrow!

LOKE then turns upon Bygver, and calls him a little impertinent thing, that always hangs about Frey's ears and cries under the millstone (can the reader help thinking at this moment of Robert Burns' famous poem, *John Barleycorn?*); a good-for-nothing fellow, who never would divide good with men, and when the heroes fought they could not find him, for he was concealed in the straw of the bed.

Frey's maid-servant is Beyla, Bygver's wife, whom Loke calls the ugliest and filthiest hag that can be found among the offspring of the gods. Of course Loke exaggerates and uses abusive language, but it was in truth a sorry thing for Frey that he traded his sword away, for it is to this fact he owes his defeat when he encounters Surt in Ragnarok.

Frey's wife was Gerd, a daughter of Gymer, and their son was Fjolner. Frey was worshiped throughout the northern countries. In the common formula of the oath his name was put first: HJÁLPI MÉR SVÁ FREYR OK NJÖRÐR OK HINN ALMÁTTKI ÁS! that is, So help me Frey and Njord and the almighty Asa (Odin). On Jul-eve (Christmas eve) it was customary to lead out a boar, which was consecrated to Frey, and which was called the atonement boar. On this the persons present laid their hands and made solemn vows; and at the feast, where the flesh of the sacrificed animal was eaten by the assembled guests, there was drunk, among other horns, a horn to Njord and Frey for prosperous seasons and for peace.

Everything about Frey goes to show that he is the god of the earth's fruitfulness. The sea, Njord, rises as vapor and descends in rain upon the land, making it fruitful. There has been much dispute about the etymological meaning of the word Frey. Finn Magnússon derives it from *fræ*, Norse *frö*, meaning seed. Grimm, on the other hand, thinks the fundamental idea is mildness, gladness (compare German *froh*, Norse *fryd*). A derived meaning of the word is man, masculine of Freyja (German *frau*), meaning woman.

### SECTION IV.  FREY AND GERD.

Frey had one day placed himself in Hlidskjalf, and looked out upon all the worlds. He also saw Jotunheim, and perceived a large and stately mansion which a maid was going to enter, and as she raised the latch of the door so great a radiancy was thrown from her hand, that the air and waters and all worlds were illuminated by it. It was Gerd, a daughter of the giant Gymer and Aurboda, relatives of Thjasse. At this sight Frey, as a just punishment for his audacity in mounting on that sacred throne, was struck with sudden sadness, so that on his return home he could neither speak nor sleep nor drink, nor did any one dare to inquire the cause of his affliction. Frey's messenger was named Skirner. Njord sent for him and requested of him, as did also Skade, that he should ask Frey why he thus refused to speak to any one.

Thus the Elder Edda, in the lay of Skirner:*

SKADE:

Skirner, arise, and swiftly run
Where lonely sits our pensive son;

* Herbert's translation.

Bid him to parley, and inquire
'Gainst whom he teems with sullen ire.

SKIRNER:

Ill words I fear my lot will prove,
If I your son attempt to move;
If I bid parley, and inquire
Why teems his soul with savage ire.

Reluctantly Skirner then proceeded to Frey, and
thus addressed him:

SKIRNER:

Prince of the gods, and first in fight!
Speak, honored Frey, and tell me right:
Why spends my lord the tedious day
In his lone hall, to grief a prey?

FREY:

Oh, how shall I, fond youth, disclose
To you my bosom's heavy woes?
The ruddy god* shines every day,
But dull to me his cheerful ray.

SKIRNER:

Your sorrows deem not I so great
That you the tale should not relate:
Together sported we in youth,
And well may trust each other's truth.

FREY:

In Gymer's court I saw her move,
The maid who fires my breast with love;
Her snow-white arms and bosom fair
Shone lovely, kindling sea and air.
Dear is she to my wishes, more
Than e'er was maid to youth before;
But gods and elves, I wot it well,
Forbid that we together dwell.

* The sun.

23

SKIRNER:

Give me that horse of wondrous breed
To cross the nightly flame with speed;
And that self-brandished sword to smite
The giant race with strange affright.

FREY:

To you I give this wondrous steed
To pass the watchful fire with speed;
And this, which borne by valiant wight,
Self-brandished will his foemen smite.

Frey, having thus given away his sword, found himself without arms when he on another occasion fought with Bele, and hence it was that he slew him with a stag's antlers. This combat was, however, a trifling affair, for Frey could have killed him with a blow of his fist, had he felt inclined; but the time will come when the sons of Muspel will sally forth to the fight in Ragnarok, and then indeed will Frey truly regret having parted with his falchion. Having obtained the horse and sword, Skirner set out on his journey, and thus he addressed his horse:

Dark night is spread; 't is time, I trow,
To climb the mountains hoar with snow;
Both shall return, or both remain
In durance, by the giant ta'en.

Skirner rode into Jotunheim, to the court of Gymer. Furious dogs were tied there before the gate of the wooden inclosure which surrounded Gerd's bower. He rode toward a shepherd, who was sitting on a mound, and thus addressed him:

Shepherd, you, that sit on the mound,
And turn your watchful eyes around,
How may I lull these bloodhounds? say;
How speak unharmed with Gymer's may?*

* *May*, maid.

### THE SHEPHERD:

Whence and what are you? doomed to die?
Or, dead, revisit you the sky?
For ride by night or ride by day,
You ne'er shall come to Gymer's may.

### SKIRNER:

I grieve not, I, a better part
Fits him who boasts a ready heart:
At hour of birth our lives were shaped;
The doom of fate can ne'er be 'scaped.

But Gerd inside hears the stranger, and thus speaks
to her maid-servant:

What sounds unknown my ears invade,
Frightening this mansion's peaceful shade;
The earth's foundation rocks withal,
And trembling shakes all Gymer's hall.

### THE MAID-SERVANT:

Dismounted stands a warrior sheen;
His courser crops the herbage green.

### GERD:

Haste! bid him to my bower with speed,
To quaff unmixed the pleasant mead;
And good betide us; for I fear
My brother's murderer is near.

Skirner having entered, Gerd thus addresses him:

What are you, elf or asas' son?
Or from the wiser vanas sprung?
Alone to visit our abode,
O'er bickering flames, why have you rode?

### SKIRNER:

Nor elf am I, nor asas' son;
Nor from the wiser vanas sprung:
Yet o'er the bickering flames I rode
Alone to visit your abode.

Eleven apples here I hold,
Gerd, for you, of purest gold;
Let this fair gift your bosom move
To grant young Frey your precious love.

GERD:

Eleven apples take not I
From man as price of chastity:
While life remains, no tongue shall tell
That Frey and I together dwell.

SKIRNER:

Gerd, for you this wondrous ring,
Burnt on young Balder's pile, I bring,
On each ninth night shall other eight
Drop from it, all of equal weight.

GERD:

I take not, I, that wondrous ring,
Though it from Balder's pile you bring:
Gold lack not I, in Gymer's bower;
Enough for me my father's dower.

SKIRNER:

Behold this bright and slender wand,
Unsheathed and glittering in my hand!
Refuse not, maiden! lest your head
Be severed by the trenchant blade.

GERD:

Gerd will ne'er by force be led
To grace a conqueror's hateful bed;
But this I trow, with main and might
Gymer shall meet your boast in fight.

SKIRNER:

Behold this bright and slender wand,
Unsheathed and glittering in my hand!
Slain by its edge your sire shall lie,
That giant old is doomed to die.

As this has no effect upon Gerd's mind, Skirner heaps
blows upon her with a magic wand, and at the same
time he begins his incantations, scoring runic characters
as he sings:

E'en as I list, the magic wand
Shall tame you! Lo, with charmed hand
I touch you, maid! There shall you go
Where never man shall learn your woe.
On some high, pointed rock, forlorn
Like eagle, shall you sit at morn;
Turn from the world's all-cheering light,
And seek the deep abyss of night.
Food shall to you more loathly show
Than slimy serpent creeping slow,
When forth you come, a hideous sight,
Each wondering eye shall stare with fright;
By all observed, yet sad and lone;
'Mongst shivering giants wider known
Than him\* who sits unmoved on high,
The guard of heaven with sleepless eye.
'Mid charms and chains and restless woe,
Your tears with double grief shall flow.
Now sit down, maid, while I declare
Your tide of sorrow and despair.
Your bower shall be some giant's cell,
Where phantoms pale shall with you dwell;
Each day to the frosty giant's hall,
Comfortless, wretched, shall you crawl;
Instead of joy, and pleasure gay,
Sorrow and tears and sad dismay;
With some three-headed giant wed,
Or pine upon a lonely bed;
From morn to morn love's secret fire
Shall gnaw your heart with vain desire;
Like barren root of thistle pent
In some high ruined battlement.
O'er shady hill, through greenwood round,
I sought this wand; the wand I found.

\* Heimdal, the god of the rainbow.

Odin is wroth, and mighty Thor;
E'en Frey shall now your name abhor.
But ere o'er your ill-fated head
The last dread curse of heaven be spread,
Giants and Thurses far and near,
Suttung's sons, and ye asas, hear
How I forbid with fatal ban
This maid the joys, the fruit of man.
Cold Grimner is that giant hight
Who you shall hold in realms of night;
Where slaves in cups of twisted roots
Shall bring foul beverage from the goats;
Nor sweeter draught, nor blither fare
Shall you, sad virgin, ever share.
    'Tis done! I wind the mystic charm;
Thus, thus I trace the giant form;
And three fell characters below,
Fury and Lust and restless Woe.
E'en as I wound, I straight unwind
This fatal spell, if you are kind.

### GERD:

Now hail, now hail, you warrior bold!
Take, take this cup of crystal cold,
And quaff the pure metheglin old.
Yet deemed I ne'er that love could bind
To vana-youth my hostile mind.

### SKIRNER:

I turn not home to bower or hall
Till I have learnt mine errand all;
Where you will yield the night of joy
To brave Njord's, the gallant boy.

### GERD:

Bar-isle is hight, the seat of love;
Nine nights elapsed, in that known grove
Shall brave Njord's, the gallant boy,
From Gerd take the kiss of joy.

Then Skirner rode home. Frey stood forth and
hailed him and asked what tidings.

FREY:

Speak, Skirner, speak and tell with speed!
Take not the harness from your steed,
Nor stir your foot, till you have said,
How fares my love with Gymer's maid!

SKIRNER:

Bar-isle is hight, the seat of love;
Nine nights elapsed, in that known grove
To brave Njord's, the gallant boy,
Will Gerd yield the kiss of joy.

FREY:

Long is one night, and longer twain;
But how for three endure my pain?
A month of rapture sooner flies
Than half one night of wishful sighs.

This poem illustrates how beautifully a myth can be elaborated. Gerd is the seed; Skirner is the air that comes with the sunshine. Thus the myth is easily explained: The earth, in which the seed is sown, resists the embrace of Frey; his messenger Skirner, who brings the seed out into the light, in vain promises her the golden ears of harvest and the ring, the symbol of abundance. She has her giant nature, which has not yet been touched by the divine spirit; she realizes not the glory which she can attain to by Frey's love. Skirner must conjure her, he must use incantations, he must show her how she, if not embraced by Frey, must forever be the bride of the cold frost, and never experience the joys of wedded life. She finally surrenders herself to Frey, and they embrace each other, when the buds burst forth in the grove. This myth then corresponds to Persephone, the goddess of the grain planted in the ground. Demeter's sorrow on account of the naked, forsaken field, from which the sprout shall shoot forth from the hidden reed, is Frey's impatient longing; and Skirner is Mercurius, who brings Proserpina up from the lower world.

But the myth has also a deeper ethical signification. Our forefathers were not satisfied with the mere shell; and Frey's love to Gerd, which is described so vividly in the Elder Edda, is taken from the nature of love, with all its longings and hopes, and is not only a symbol of what takes place in visible nature. As the warmth of the sun develops the seed, thus love develops the heart; love is the ray of light (Skirner) sent from heaven, which animates and ennobles the clump of earth. Gerd is the maid, who is engaged in earthly affairs and does not yet realize anything nobler than her every-day cares. Then love calls her; in her breast awakens a new life; wonderful dreams like gentle breezes embrace her, and when the dreams grow into consciousness her eyes are opened to a higher sphere of existence. This myth is most perfectly reflected in the love-story of Fridthjof's Saga, an old Norse romance moulded into a most fascinating Epic Poem by Tegner. A good English translation of this poem appeared a few years ago in London, and was republished in this country under the auspices of Bayard Taylor. It is also translated into almost every other European language, and is justly considered one of the finest poetical productions of this century.

### SECTION V. WORSHIP OF FREY.

The Sagas tell us, as has already been stated, that Frey was worshiped extensively throughout the northern countries.

In Throndhjem there was during the reign of Olaf Tryggvesson a temple in which Frey was zealously worshiped. When the king, having overthrown the statue of the god, blamed the bondes* for their stupid idolatry, and asked them wherein Frey had evinced his power, they answered: Frey often talked with us, foretold us the future, and granted us good seasons and peace.

The Norse chieftain Ingemund Thorstenson, who in the days of the tyrant Harald Hairfair emigrated from Norway and settled in Vatnsdal, Iceland, built near his homestead a temple, which appears to have been specially dedicated to Frey, who had in a manner pointed out a dwelling-place to him; for in digging a place for his pillars of the high-seat (*öndvegis-súlur*, something similar to the Greek Hermes and Roman Penates), Ingemund found in the earth an image of Frey, which he had lost in Norway.

The Icelander Thorgrim of Seabol was a zealous worshiper of Frey, and conducted sacrificial festivals in his honor during the winter nights. He was killed in his bed by Gisle, and a famous funeral service was given him; but one thing, says the Saga of Gisle Surson, also happened, which seemed remarkable. Snow never settled on Thorgrim's how (grave-mound) on the south side, nor did it freeze; it was thought that Frey loved him so much, because he had sacrificed to him, that he did not want it to grow cold between them.

In the vicinity of the estate Tver-aa, in Eyjafjord in Iceland, there was a temple dedicated to Frey, and the place became so holy that no guilty person dared to tarry there, for Frey did not allow it. When the chieftain Thorkel the Tall was banished from Tver-aa by Glum Eyjolfson, who is universally known as Vigaglum, he led a full-grown ox to Frey's temple before he left, and thus addressed the god: Long have you been to me a faithful friend, O Frey! Many gifts have you

* Farmers, peasants.

received from me and rewarded me well for them. Now I give you this ox, in order that Glum may some day have to leave Tver-aa no less reluctantly than I do. And now give to me a sign to show whether you accept this offering or not. At that moment the ox bellowed loudly and fell dead upon the ground. Thorkel considered this a good omen, and moved away with a lighter heart. Afterwards (it is related in Vigaglum's Saga) Glum in his old days became involved in a dangerous suit for manslaughter, which ended in his having to relinquish Tver-aa to Ketil, son of Thorvald Krok, whom he confessed having killed. On the night before he rode to the *thing* (assembly, court), where his case was to be decided, he dreamed that there had congregated a number of men at Tver-aa to meet Frey; he saw many down by the river (*á* is river in Icelandic), and there sat Frey on a bench. Glum asked who they were, and they answered: We are your departed relatives, and have come to pray Frey that you may not be driven from Tver-aa; but it avails us nothing. Frey answers us short and angrily and now remembers the ox which Thorkel the Tall gave to him. Glum awoke, and from that time he said that he was on unfriendly terms with Frey.

In the temple at Upsala, in Sweden, Frey, together with Odin and Thor, was especially worshiped; and by the story of the Norseman Gunnar Helming, who in Sweden gave himself out as Frey, it is attested that the people in some provinces of Sweden put their highest trust in this god, and even believed him sometimes to appear in human form.

The horse, it appears, was regarded as a favorite animal of Frey. At his temple in Throndhjem it is said there were horses belonging to him. It is related of the

Icelander Rafnkel that he loved Frey above all other gods, and bestowed upon him an equal share in all his best possessions. He had a brown horse called Frey-fax (compare Col-fax, Fair-fax,* etc.), which he loved so highly that he made a solemn vow to kill the man who should ride this horse against his will, a vow which he also fulfilled. Another Icelander, Brand, also had a horse called Frey-fax, which he made so much of that he was said to believe in it as in a divinity.

Frey's boar, Gullinburste, has been referred to in connection with the Jul or Christmas festivities, and there are found many examples of swine-sacrifice in the old Norse writings. King Hedrek made solemn vows on the atonement-boar on Jul-eve, and in one of the prose supplements to the ancient Eddaic poem of Helge Hjorvardson we find that the atonement-boar is mentioned as being led out on Jul-eve, in order that they might lay hands upon it and make solemn vows.

A highly valued wooden statue or image of Frey was found in a temple at Throndhjem, which king Olaf Tryggvesson hewed in pieces in the presence of the people. Kjotve the Rich, king of Agder in Norway, one of the chiefs who fought against Harald Fairhair, had a weight upon which the god Frey was sculptured in silver. This treasure, which he held in great veneration, fell after the battle into the hands of King Harald, and he presented it to his friend, the chieftain Ingemund Thorstenson, who afterwards carried the image in a purse and held it in very high esteem. This last-mentioned image was probably borne as an amulet, as was often the case, no doubt, with the gold bracteates which are found in the grave-hows and in the earth. having upon them the images of men and animals, and which are furnished with a clasp for fastening to a necklace.

* Fax means *hair*.

## SECTION VI.  FREYJA.

The goddess of love is Freyja, also called Vanadis or
Vanabride.  She is the daughter of Njord and the sister
of Frey.  She ranks next to Frigg.  She is very fond
of love ditties, and all lovers would do well to invoke
her.  It is from her name that women of birth and
fortune are called in the Icelandic language *hús freyjur*
(compare Norse *fru* and German *frau*).  Her abode in
heaven is called Folkvang, where she disposes of the
hall-seats.  To whatever field of battle she rides she
asserts her right to one half the slain, the other half
belonging to Odin.  Thus the Elder Edda, in Grimner's lay:

> Folkvang 't is called
> Where Freyja has right
> To dispose of the hall-seats.
> Every day of the slain
> She chooses the half
> And leaves half to Odin.

Her mansion, Sessrymner (having many or large
seats), is large and magnificent; thence she rides out
in a car drawn by two cats.  She lends a favorable ear
to those who sue for her assistance.  She possesses a
necklace called Brisingamen, or Brising.  She married
a person called Oder, and their daughter, named Hnos,
is so very handsome that whatever is beautiful and
precious is called by her name *hnossir* (that means,
nice things).  It is also said that she had two daughters,
Hnos and Gerseme, the latter name meaning precious.
But Oder left his wife in order to travel into very
remote countries.  Since that time Freyja continually
weeps, and her tears are drops of pure gold; hence she
is also called the fair-weeping goddess (*it grátfagra goð*).
In poetry, gold is called Freyja's tears, the rain of

Freyja's brows or cheeks. She has a great variety of names, for, having gone over many countries in search of her husband, each people gave her a different name. She is thus called Mardal, Horn, Gefn, Syr, Skjalf and Thrung. It will also be remembered, from the chapter about Thor, that Freyja had a falcon-guise, and how the giant Thrym longed to possess her. In the lay of Hyndla, in the Elder Edda, Freyja comes to her friend and sister, the giantess Hyndla, and requests her to ride to Valhal, to ask for success for her favorite Ottar; promising the giantess to appease Odin and Thor, who of course were enemies to the giants. Hyndla is inclined to doubt Freyja's remarks, especially as she comes to her with Ottar in the night. Who this Ottar was we do not know, excepting that he was a son of the Norse hero, Instein, and hence probably a Norseman. He was heir to an estate, but his right to it was disputed by Angantyr. It was therefore necessary to make his title good, and to enumerate his ancestors, but for this he was too ignorant. Meanwhile he had always been a devout worshiper of the asynjes (goddesses), and had especially worshiped Freyja by making sacrifices, images, and erecting altars to her. Hence it is that she wishes to help him in this important case, but finds that she is not able, and it was for this reason she saddled her golden boar and went to the wise giantess Hyndla, who was so well posted in regard to the pedigrees, origin and fates of gods, giants and men. Hyndla consents to giving the information asked for, and so she enumerates first the immediate ancestors of Ottar on his father's and mother's side, then speaks of the king so famous in olden times, Halfdan Gamle, the original progenitor of the Skjolds and several other noble families of the North. And as these royal families were said to be descended from the gods and the latter again from the giants, Hyndla gives some of their genealogies also. Thus she gets an opportunity to speak of Heimdal and his giant mothers, then of Loke and of the monsters descended from him, which shall play so conspicuous a part in Ragnarok, then of the mighty god of thunder, and finally of a god yet more mighty, whom she ventures not to name, and here she ends her tale. She will not prophesy further than to where Odin is swallowed by the Fenris-wolf and the world by the yawning abyss. Freyja after this asks her for a drink of remembrance to give to Ottar, her guest and favorite, in order that he might be able to remember the whole talk and the pedigree two days afterwards, when the case between him and Angantyr should be decided by proofs of this kind. Hyndla refuses to do this, and upbraids her with abusive language. By this Freyja is excited to wrath and threatens to kindle a fire around the giantess, from which she would not be able to escape, if she did not comply with her request. When the threat begins to be carried out (at the breaking forth of the flaming aurora in the morning) Hyndla gives the requested drink, but at the same time curses it. Freyja is not terrified by this, but removes the curse by her blessing and earnest prayers to all divinities for the success of her beloved Ottar.

We should like to give the lay in full, as it is found in the Elder Edda, but having quoted several strophes from it before, and it being quite long, we reluctantly omit it. We advise our readers, however, by all means to read the ELDER EDDA. There is more profound thought in it than in any other human work, not even Shakespeare excepted. What a pity that it is so little known !

Women came after death to Freyja. When Egil Skallagrimson had lost his young son, and was despairing unto death on this account, his daughter Thorgerd, who was married to Olaf in Lax-aa-dal, comes to console him; and when she hears that he will neither eat nor drink, then she also says that she has not and will not eat or drink before she comes to Freyja. With *her*, lovers who have been faithful unto death are gathered; therefore Hagbard sings: Love is renewed in Freyja's halls.

Freyja is the goddess of love between man and woman. Hence we find in her nature, beauty, grace, modesty, the longings, joys, and tears of love, and we find also that burning love in the heart which breaks out in wild flames. She rules in *Folk*vang, in the human dwellings, where there are seats enough for all. No one escapes her influence. Odin shares the slain equally with her, for the hero has *two* grand objects in view — to conquer his enemy and to win the heart of the maiden.

Thus the Norse mythology teaches us that the sturdy Norseman was not insusceptible to impressions from beauty nor unmoved by love. The most beautiful flowers were named after Freyja's hair and eye-dew, and even animate objects, which, like the flowers, were remarkable for their beauty, were named after this goddess, as for instance the butterfly (Icel. *Freyjuhœna* — Freyja's hen).

There is a semi-mythological Saga called Orvarodd's Saga. Orvarodd signifies Arrow-odd; and as this same Arrow-odd is implicated in a large number of love exploits, it has been suggested that he may be Freyja's husband, whose name the reader remembers was Oder, the stem of which is *od*, and hence we have in the North also not only a *goddess* of love, but also a god of love (Cupid), with his arrows!

Freyja's cats symbolize sly fondling and sensual enjoyment. The name of her husband, Oder, means sense, understanding, but also wild desire. The various names bestowed upon Freyja when she travels among the different nations denote the various modes by which love reveals itself in human life. The goddesses Sjofn, Lofn, and Var, heretofore mentioned, were regarded as messengers and attendants of Freyja. Friday (*dies Veneris*) is named after her. (See page 237.)

### SECTION VII.   A BRIEF REVIEW.

The lives and exploits of the propitious divinities have now been presented; and in presenting the myths we have not only given the forces and phenomena of nature symbolized by the myths, but we have also tried to bring the mythology down from heaven to the earth, and exhibit the value it had in the minds of our ancestors. We have tried, as Socrates did with his philosophy, to show what influence the myths have had upon the life of our forefathers; in other words, we have tried to put a kernel into the shell. We have tried to present the mythology, not as the science and laws by which the universe is governed, but as something — call it science or what you will — by which to illustrate how the contemplation of the forces and phenomena of nature have influenced human thought and action. Language is in its origin nothing but impressions from nature, which having been revolved for a time in the human mind find their expression in words. Poetry is in its origin nothing else but expressions of human thought and feeling called forth by the contemplation of the wonderful works of God. And this is also true of mythology.

We have found the propitious divinities divided into three classes, those of heaven, those of earth, and those of the sea. The union or marriage between heaven and earth has been presented in various myths. The king of heaven is but *one*, but he embraces the earth in various forms, and the earth is, in a new form, wedded to the god of thunder; nay, the vans, or divinities of the sea, arise and fill the land with blessings in various ways. The manner in which the gods are combined and interlinked with each other in one grand system is a feature peculiar to the Norse mythology. There is not, as in the Greek, a series of separate groups and separate dwellings, but the gods come in frequent contact with each other. Odin rules in the heavens, Thor in the clouds, Heimdal in the rainbow, Balder in the realms of light, Frey with his elves of light in the earth, but the sun affects them all: it is Odin's eye, it is Balder's countenance, Heimdal needs it for his rainbow, and Frey governs its rays; and still the sun itself rides as a beaming maid with her horses from morning until evening. The earth has its various forms, and the seed planted in the earth has its own god (Frey), surrounded by the spirits of the groves, the forests and the fountains. And the king of heaven unites man with nature; he not only provides for his animal life, but also breathes into him a living soul and inspires him with enthusiasm. He sits with Saga at the fountain of history; he sends out his son Brage, the god of poetry and eloquence, and unites him with Idun, the rejuvenating goddess, whose carefully protected rivers meander through the grove full of fruit trees bearing golden apples; and he lets his other son, Balder, the ruler of light, marry the industrious flower-goddess, Nanna, who with her maids spreads a fragrant carpet over the earth. And as the god of thunder rule*

24

but to protect heaven and earth, so the naked desert and the impenetrable forest exist only to remind us of the incorruptible vital force of nature, safe against all attacks. The imperishableness of nature appears more strikingly in the stupendous mountains and gigantic forests than in the fertile, cultivated and protected parts of the earth. Now let us again ask: Is there nothing here for the poet or artist? Has the Norse mythology nothing that can be elaborated and clothed with beauful forms and colors? Does this mythology not contain germs that art can develop into fragrant leaves, swelling buds and radiant blossoms? Does not this our Gothic inheritance deserve a place with the handmaids of literature? Will not our poets, public speakers, lecturers, essayists, and writers of elegant literature generally, who make so many quaint allusions to, and borrow so many elegant and suggestive illustrations from, Greek mythology; will they not, we say, do their own ancestors the honor to dip their pen occasionally into the mythology of the Gothic race? It is bad practice to borrow when we can get along without it, besides the products of the south thrive not well in our northern Gothic soil and climate. Ygdrasil grows better here, and that is a tree large enough and fruitful enough to sustain the Gothic race with enthusiasm and inspiration for centuries yet to come, and to supply a whole race of future bards and poets and artists with a precious and animating elixir. Our next generation will comprehend this.

# CHAPTER VII.

## THE DEVELOPMENT OF EVIL. LOKE AND HIS OFFSPRING.

### SECTION I. LOKE.

WE have now made an acquaintance with the lives and exploits of the good and propitious divinities, with the asas and vans. But what of the evil? Whence come they, and how have they been developed? Many a philosopher has puzzled his brain with this vexed question, and the wisest minds are still engaged in deep meditations in regard to it. It is and will remain an unsolved problem. But what did the old Goths, and particularly our Norse forefathers, think about the development of evil? What forms did it assume among them? How did it spring forth in nature, and how did it impress the minds and hearts of the people? These are questions now to be answered.

There are in the Norse mythology two individuals by the name of Loke. The one is *Utgard*-Loke, hideous in his whole being, and his character was sketched in the myth about Thor and Skrymer (see pp. 312–322); he represents physical and moral evil in all its naked loathsomeness. The other is *Asa*-Loke, of whom there also have been accounts given at various times in connection with the propitious gods; and it is of him solely we are now to speak, as the former belongs wholly to the race of giants. Asa-Loke, whom we shall hereafter call by his

(371)

common name, Loke, is the same evil principle in all its
various manifestations; but as he makes his appearance
among the gods, he represents evil in the seductive and
seemingly beautiful form in which it glides about through
the world. We find him flowing in the veins of the
human race and call him sin, or passion. In nature he
is the corrupting element in air, fire and water. In the
bowels of the earth he is the volcanic flame, in the sea
he appears as a fierce serpent, and in the lower world
we recognize him as pale death. Thus, like Odin, Loke
pervades all nature. And in no divinity is it more clear
than in this, that the idea proceeding from the visible
workings of nature entered the human heart and mind
and there found its moral or ethical reflection. Loke
symbolizes sin, shrewdness, deceitfulness, treachery, malice, etc. Loke is indeed in his development one of the
profoundest myths. In the beginning he was intimately
connected with Odin, then he became united with the air,
and finally he impersonates the destructive fire. And in
these changes he keeps growing worse and worse.

In the banquet of Æger he reminds Odin that they
in the beginning of time had their blood mixed. Thus
the Elder Edda:

LOKE:

Do thou mind, Odin,
That we in time's morning
Mixed blood together!
Then thou pretendedst
That thou never wouldst ask a drink
Unless it was offered to both of us.

Sameness of blood symbolizes sameness of mind, and
Loke is in the Younger Edda called Odin's brother, the
uncle of the gods. Under the name of Loder, or Lopter,
Loke took part in the creation of man; he gave the
senses, the sources of evil desires, the passions, the fire

of the veins. Thus he is like the fire, which is beneficent and necessary for development, but also dangerous
and destructive. With the giantess Angerboda (producing sorrow) he begat the wolf Fenrer, but the most
disgusting monster is the woman Hel, who is a daughter
of Loke. *Odin* unites himself with the gigantic force
in nature, but he does this to develop, ennoble and
elevate it. *Loke* unites himself with crude matter, but
by this union he only still further develops the evil
principle, which then expresses itself in all kinds of
terrible phenomena: the sea tosses its waves against
heaven itself, and rushes out upon the land; the air
trembles; then comes snow and howling winds; the rain
splashes down upon the earth, etc. Such is also his
influence upon the human mind. He is the sly, treacherous father of lies. In appearance he is beautiful and
fair, but in his mind he is evil, and in his inclinations
he is inconstant. Notwithstanding his being ranked
among the gods, he is the slanderer of the gods, the
grand contriver of deceit and fraud, the reproach of
gods and men. Nobody renders him divine honors.
He surpasses all mortals in the arts of perfidy and
craft.

There is some dispute about the real meaning of
Loke's name. Some derive it from the Icelandic *lúka*,
to end, thus arguing that Loke is the end and consummation of divinity. Another definition is given, taken
from the Icelandic *logi* (Anglo-Saxon *líg*), according to
which the primary meaning would be fire, flame. He
is also called Loder, or Lopter (the aërial; compare
Norse *luft*, Anglo-Saxon *lyft*, air); and this would seem
to corroborate the definition of Loke as fire. Loder
(*lodern*, to blaze) would then designate him in the character of the blazing earthly fire, and Lopter as the

heated and unsteady air. He is son of the giant Far-baute, that is, the one who strikes the ships, the wind. His mother is Laufey, or Nal, the former meaning leaf-isle, and the latter needle. Oak trees produce leaves and pines produce needles; both Laufey and Nal are there-fore combustibles. His brothers are Byleist (dwelling destroyer, raging flame), and Helblinde, the latter being another name for Odin.

In the previous chapters it has frequently been seen how Loke time and again accompanied the gods, they making use of his strength and cunning; but it has also been shown how he acted in concert with the jotuns and exposed the gods to very great perils and then extricated them again by his artifices. By Loke's advice the gods engage the artificer to build a dwelling so well fortified that they should be perfectly safe from the incursions of the frost-giants. For this the artificer is to receive Freyja, providing he completes his work within a stipulated time; but Loke prevented him from completing his task by the birth of Sleipner. When the dwarfs forge the precious things for the gods, it is he who brings about that the work lacks perfection, and even the handle of Thor's mallet, Mjolner, becomes too short; for evil is everywhere present and makes the best things defective. He cuts the hair of the goddess Sif, and by this he makes way for the forging of the precious arti-cles; thus evil often in spite of itself produces good results. Examples of this abound in the history of the world. Loke gives Thjasse an opportunity to rob Idun, but brings her back again and thus causes Thjasse's death. He hungers at Geirrod's, and causes Thor to undertake his dangerous journey; but he also looks after Thor's hammer, and accompanies him as maid-servant to get it back. He steals Freyja's Brisingamen, and quarrels with Heimdal about it. But his worst deed is Balder's death. For these reasons Loke is in Old Norse poetry called: son of Farbaute, son of Laufey, son of Nal, brother of Byleist, brother of Helblinde, father of the Fenris-wolf, father of the Midgard-serpent, father of Hel, uncle of Odin, visitor and chest-goods of Geirrod, thief of Brisingamen and of Idun's apples, defender of Sigyn (his wife), Sif's hair destroyer, adviser of Balder's bane, etc.

Odin, Hœner and Loke are often together. It is related that they once set out to explore the whole world. They came to a stream, and followed it until they came to a force (cascade) where there sat an otter near the force. It had caught a salmon in the force and sat half sleeping eating it. Then Loke picked up a stone and threw it at the otter, struck it in the head and then boasted of his deed, for he had killed or captured both the otter and salmon with one stone. They then took the salmon and otter with them and came to a gard (farm), where they entered the house. The bonde,* who lived there, hight Hreidmar, an able fellow well skilled in necromancy. The gods asked for night lodgings, but added that they were supplied with provisions; whereupon they showed what they had caught. But when Hreidmar saw the otter he called to him his sons Fafner and Regin, and told them that their brother Odder (otter) had been slain, and who had done it. Father and sons then attack the gods, overpower and bind them, and then inform them that the otter was Hreidmar's son. The gods offered a ransom for their lives, as large as Hreidmar himself would determine it; they made a treaty accordingly, confirming it with oaths. When the otter then had been flayed, Hreidmar took the skin and demanded that they should fill it with shining gold and then perfectly cover it with the same.

* Peasant, farmer.

These were the terms of agreement. Then Odin sent
Loke to the home of the swarthy elves (Svartalf-heim),
where he met the dwarf Andvare (wary, cautious spirit),
who lived as a fish, in the water. Loke borrowed Ran's
net and caught him, and demanded of him, as a ransom for his life, all the gold he had in the rock, where
he dwelt. And when they came into the rock the dwarf
produced all the gold which he possessed, which was a
considerable amount; but Loke observed that the dwarf
concealed under his arm a gold ring, and ordered him
to give it up. The dwarf prayed Loke by all means to
let him keep it; for when he kept this ring, he said,
he could produce for himself more of the metal from
it. But Loke said that he should not keep so much as
a penny, and took the ring from him, and went out.
Then said the dwarf, that that ring should be the
bane of the person who possessed it. Loke had no
objection to this, and said that, in order that this purpose should be kept, he should bring these words to the
knowledge of him who should possess it. Then Loke
returned to Hreidmar, and showed Odin the gold; but
when the latter saw the ring he thought it was pretty;
he therefore, taking it, gave Hreidmar the rest of the
gold. Hreidmar then filled the otter-skin as well as he
could, and set it down when it was full. Then Odin went
to cover the bag with gold, and afterwards bade Hreidmar see whether the bag was perfectly covered; but
Hreidmar examined, and looked carefully in every place,
and found an uncovered hair near the mouth, which
Odin would have to cover, or the agreement would be
broken. Then Odin produced the ring and covered the
hair with it, and said that they now had paid the otter-
ransom. But when Odin had taken his spear, and Loke
his shoes, so that they had nothing more to fear, Loke

said that the curse of the dwarf Andvare should be fulfilled, and that this gold and this ring should be the bane of him who possessed it. From this myth it is that gold is poetically called otter-ransom.

And the curse was fulfilled. This curse of ill-gotten gold became the root of a series of mortal calamities, which are related in the latter part of the Elder Edda, in the songs about Sigurd Fafner's bane, or the Slayer of Fafner; about Brynhild, about Gudrun's sorrow, Gudrun's revenge, in the song about Atle, etc. The curse on the gold, pronounced upon it by Andvare, the dwarf, is the grand moral in these wonderful songs, and never was moral worked out more terribly. Even Shakespeare has no tragedy equal to it. When Odin and Loke had gone away, Fafner and Regin demanded from their father, Hreidmar, a share of the ransom in the name of their brother Odder; but Hreidmar refused, so Fafner pierced his father with a sword while he slept. Thus Hreidmar died, but Fafner took all the gold. Then Regin demanded his paternal inheritance, but Fafner refused to give it, and disappeared. Another prominent character in the Edda is Sigurd, who frequently visited Regin and told him that Fafner, having assumed the shape of a monstrous dragon, lay on Gnita Heath, and had Æger's helmet, the helmet of terror, before which all living trembled. Regin made a sword for Sigurd, which was called Gram; it was so sharp that when it stood in the river and a tuft of wool floated on the current, the sword would cut the wool as easily as the water. With this sword Sigurd cut Regin's anvil in twain. Regin excites Sigurd to kill Fafner, and accordingly Sigurd and Regin proceeded on their way to Gnita Heath, and discovered Fafner's path, whereupon the latter (Fafner) crept into the water. In the way Sigurd dug a large grave and went down into it. When Fafner now crept away from the gold he spit poison, but this flew over Sigurd's head, and as Fafner passed over the grave Sigurd pierced him with his sword to the heart. Fafner trembled convulsively, and fiercely shook his head and tail. Sigurd sprang out of the grave when they saw each other. Then a conversation takes place between them, in which Fafner heaps curses upon Sigurd until the former expires. Regin had gone away while Sigurd killed Fafner, but came back while Sigurd was wiping the blood off the sword.

REGIN:

Hail to thee now, Sigurd!
Now thou hast victory won
And Fafner slain.
Among all men who tread the earth
Most fearless
I proclaim thee to be born.

SIGURD:

Uncertain it is to know,
When we all come together,
Sons of victorious gods,
Who was born most fearless;
Many a man is brave
Who still does not thrust the blade
Into another man's breast.

REGIN:

Glad art thou now, Sigurd,
Glad of thy victory,
As thou wipest Gram on the grass.
Thou hast my
Brother wounded,
Let myself have some share therein.

SIGURD:

It was thou who caused
That I should ride

Hither over frosty mountains;
His wealth and life
Would the spotted snake still possess,
Hadst thou not excited me to fight.

Then went Regin to Fafner and cut the heart out
of him with the sword called Ridel, and afterwards
drank the blood from the wound. He said:

Sit down now, Sigurd!
I will go to sleep:
Hold Fafner's heart by the fire.
Such a repast
Will I partake of
After this drink of blood.

SIGURD:

Thou didst absent thyself
When I in Fafner's blood
My sharp blade stained.
I set my strength
Against the power of the dragon
While thou didst lie in the heath.

REGIN:

Long wouldst thou
Have let the old
Troll lie in the heath,
Hadst thou not used
The sword which I made,
Thy sharpened blade.

SIGURD:

Courage is better
Than sword-strength
Where angry men must fight;
For the brave man
I always see win
Victory with a dull blade.
It is better for the brave man
Than for the coward
To join in the battle,
It is better for the glad

> Than for the sorrowing
> In all circumstances.

Sigurd took Fafner's heart, put it on a spit and roasted it; but when he thought it must be roasted enough, and when the juice oozed out of the heart, he felt of it with his fingers to see whether it was well done. He burned himself, and put his finger into his mouth, but when the blood of Fafner's heart touched his tongue he understood the song of birds. He heard birds singing in the bushes, and seven birds sang a strophe each, talking about how Regin might avenge his brother, kill Sigurd, and possess the treasure alone, when Sigurd finally says:

> Not so violent
> Will fate be, that Regin
> Shall announce my death;
> For soon shall both
> Brothers go
> Hence to Hel.

And he cut the head off Regin, ate afterwards Fafner's heart, and drank both his and Regin's blood. Then Sigurd heard the birds sing:

> Sigurd! gather
> Golden rings;
> It is not royal
> To be smothered by fear.
> I know a maid
> Fairer than all
> Endowed with gold,
> If thou couldst but get her.
> To Gjuke lie
> Green paths,
> Fortune beckons
> The wanderers forward;
> There a famous king
> Has fostered a daughter,—
> Her thou, Sigurd, must win.

Sigurd followed the track of the dragon to his nest and found it open. Its doors and door-frames, and all the beams and posts of the place, were of iron, but the treasure was buried in the ground. There Sigurd found a large heap of gold, with which he filled two chests. Then he took the helmet of terror (Æger's helmet), a gold cuirass, the sword Hrotte, and many treasures, which he put on the back of the horse Grane, but the horse would not proceed before Sigurd mounted it also.

This is but the beginning of this terrible tragedy, but our space does not allow us here to enter upon all the fatal results of the curse of Andvare. In the fate, first of Sigurd and Brynhild, and afterwards of Sigurd and Gudrun, is depicted passion, tenderness and sorrow with a vivid power which nowhere has a superior. The men are princely warriors and the women are not only fair, but godlike, in their beauty and vigor. The noblest sentiments and most heroic actions are crossed by the foulest crimes and the most terrific tragedies. In this train of events, produced by the curse of Andvare alone, there is material for a score of dramas of the most absorbing character. In the story of Sigurd and Brynhild, as we find it in the latter part of the Elder Edda, there are themes for tragic and heroic composition that would become as immortal as Dante's *Inferno* or Shakespeare's *Macbeth*, for they are based on our profoundest sympathies, and appeal most forcibly to our ideas of the beautiful and the true.

The ring Andvarenaut (Andvare's gift), as it is called, here as elsewhere, symbolizes wealth, which increases in the hands of the wary, careful Andvare (*and-vari*, wary). But for avarice, that never gets enough, it becomes a destructive curse. It is perfectly in harmony with Loke's

character to be satisfied and pleased with the curse
attached to the ring.*

### SECTION II.  LOKE'S CHILDREN.  THE FENRIS-WOLF.

Loke's wife was Sigyn; their son was Nare or Narfe,
and a brother of him was Ale (Ole) or Vale.

With the hag, Angerboda, Loke had three children.
Angerbode was a giantess of Jotunheim, and her name
means anguish-boding.  The children's names are Fenrer
or Fenris-wolf, the Midgard-serpent called Jormungander,
and Hel.  The gods were not long ignorant that these
monsters continued to be bred up in Jotunheim, and,
having had recourse to divination, became aware of all
the evils they would have to suffer from them; that they
were sprung from such a bad mother was a bad omen,
and from such a father, one still worse.  Allfather (Odin)
therefore deemed it advisable to send the gods to bring
them to him.  When they came, he threw the serpent
into that deep ocean by which the earth is encircled.  But
the monster has grown to such an enormous size, that
holding his tail in his mouth he engirdles the whole
earth.  Hel he cast headlong into Niflheim, and gave her
power over nine worlds (regions), into which she dis-
tributes those who are sent to her,— that is to say, all who
die through sickness or old age.  Here she possesses a
habitation protected by exceedingly high walls and
strongly-barred gates.  Her hall is called Elvidner (place
of storm); hunger is her table; starvation, her knife;
delay, her man-servant; slowness, her maid-servant;
precipice, her threshold; care, her bed; and burning
anguish forms the hangings of her apartments.  The

* To anyone who wishes to read this great epic of the North, we would
recommend the *Völsunga Saga* translated by Eiríkr Magnússon and William
Morris.  London, 1872.  See p 14.

one half of her body is livid, the other half the color of human flesh. She may therefore easily be recognized; the more so as she has a dreadfully stern and grim countenance.

The wolf Fenrer was bred up among the gods, but Tyr alone had courage enough to go and feed him. Nevertheless, when the gods perceived that he every day increased prodigiously in size, and that the oracles warned them that he would one day become fatal to them, they determined to make a very strong iron chain for him, which they called Leding. Taking this fetter to the wolf, they requested him to try his strength on it. Fenrer, perceiving that the enterprise would not be very difficult for him, let them do what they pleased, permitted himself to be bound, and then by great muscular exertion burst the chain and set himself at liberty. The gods having seen this, made another chain, twice as strong as the former, and this they called Drome. They prevailed on the wolf to put it on, assuring him that, by breaking this, he would give an incontestible proof of his strength; it would be a great honor to him if so great a chain could not hold him.

The wolf saw well enough that it would not be so easy to break this fetter, but finding at the same time that his strength had increased since he broke Leding, and thinking that he could never become famous without running some risk, he voluntarily submitted to be chained. When the gods told him that they had finished their task, Fenrer shook himself violently, stretched his limbs, rolled on the ground, and at last burst his chains, which flew in pieces all around him. He thus freed himself from Drome. From that time we have the proverbs, to get loose out of Leding, or to dash out of

Drome, when anything is to be accomplished by powerful efforts.

After this the gods despaired of ever being able to bind the wolf; wherefore Odin sent Skirner, the messenger of Frey, down to the abode of the dark elves (Svartalf-heim), to engage certain dwarfs to make the chain called Gleipner. It was made out of six things, namely, the noise made by the footstep of a cat, the beard of a woman, the roots of the mountains, the sinews of the bear, the breath of the fish, and the spittle of birds (the enumeration of these things produces alliteration in Icelandic). And although you, says he who relates this in the Younger Edda, may not have heard of these things before, you may easily convince yourself that I have not been telling you lies. You may have observed that woman has no beard, that cats make no noise when they run, and that there are no roots under the mountains; but it is nevertheless none the less true what I have related, although there may be some things that you are not able to furnish proof of.

How was this chain smithied? It was perfectly smooth and soft like a silken string, and yet, as we shall presently see, very firm and strong. When this fetter was brought to the gods, they were profuse in their thanks to Skirner for the trouble he had given himself and for having done his errand so well, and taking the wolf with them they proceeded to a lake called Amsvartner, to a holm (rocky island) which is called Lyngve. They showed the string to the wolf, and expressed their wish that he would try to break it, at the same time assuring him that it was somewhat stronger than its thinness would warrant a person in supposing it to be. They took it themselves one after another in their hands, and, after attempting in vain to break it, said: You alone, Fenrer are able to accomplish such a feat. Methinks, replied the wolf, that I shall acquire no fame by breaking such a slender thread, but if any deceit or artifice has been employed in making it, slender though it seems, it shall never come on my feet.

The gods assured him that he would easily break a limber silken cord, since he had already burst asunder iron fetters of the most solid construction; but if you should not succeed in breaking it, they added, you will show that you are too weak to cause the gods any fear, and we will not hesitate to set you at liberty without delay. I fear much, replied the wolf, that if you once bind me so fast that I shall be unable to free myself by my own efforts, you will be in no haste to loose me. Loath am I therefore to have this cord wound around me, but in order that you may not doubt my courage, I will consent, provided one of you put his hand into my mouth, as a pledge that you intend me no deceit. The gods looked wistfully at one another, and thought the conditions severe, finding that they had only the choice of two evils, and no one would sacrifice his hand, until Tyr, as has formerly been related, stepped forward and intrepidly put his hand between the monster's jaws. Thereupon the gods having tied up the wolf, he violently stretched himself as he had formerly done, and used all his might to disengage himself, but the more efforts he made the tighter became the cord. Then all the gods burst out in laughter at the sight, excepting Tyr, who lost his hand.

When the gods saw that the wolf was effectually bound, they took the chain called Gelgja, which was attached to the cord, and drew it through the middle of a large rock called Gjol, which they sank deep into

25

the earth ; afterwards, to make it still more secure, they fastened the end of the cord to another massive stone called Thvite, which they sank still deeper. The wolf made in vain the most violent efforts to break loose, and, opening his tremendous jaws, and turning in every possible direction, endeavored to bite the gods. They, seeing this, thrust a sword into his mouth within his outstretched jaws, so that the hilt stood in his lower jaw and the point in the roof of the mouth; and this is called his palate-spar (*gómsparri*). He howls horribly, and the foam flows continually from his mouth in such abundance that it forms the river called Von; from which the wolf is also sometimes called Vonargander. There he will remain until Ragnarok, the Twilight of the gods. But why did not the gods slay the wolf, when they have so much evil to fear from him? Because they had so much respect for the sanctity of their peace-steads that they would not stain them with the blood of the wolf, although prophecies foretold to them that he must one day become the bane of Odin.

The Fenris-wolf is the earthly fire chained by man, exceedingly ferocious when let loose, as has been terribly illustrated by our recent fires in Chicago and her sister city Boston; as a devouring wolf it attacks and licks up the dwellings of men, as it is said in the lay of Haakon:

> Fearfully fares
> The Fenris-wolf
> Over the fields of men
> When he is loosed.

Once it shall, with its upper jaw reaching to the heavens and with the lower jaw on the earth, advance with terror and destruction, and destroy the fire and flame of heaven, Odin (the sun). At present it is fettered on the island, where a grave is dug and a furnace is built of stone, with the draft (mouth) partially barred, so that the fire is surrounded by things which prevent its spreading. It is managed and controlled by men for their advantage, and it is so useful that no one would think of entirely destroying it (killing it).

SECTION III. JORMUNDGANDER, OR THE MIDGARD-SERPENT.

The Midgard- or world-serpent we have already become tolerably well acquainted with, and recognize in him the wild tumultuous sea. Thor contended with him; he got him on his hook, but did not succeed in killing him. We also remember how Thor tried to lift him in the form of a cat. The North abounds in stories about the sea-serpent, which are nothing but variations of the original myth of the Eddas. Odin cast him into the sea, where he shall remain until he is conquered by Thor in Ragnarok.

SECTION IV. HEL.

The goddess, or giantess (it is difficult to decide what to call her), Hel, is painted with vivid colors. She rules over nine worlds in Niflheim, where she dwells under one of the roots of Ygdrasil. Her home is called Helheim. The way thither, Hel-way, is long. Hermod traveled it in nine days and nine nights. Its course is always downward and northward. Her dwelling is surrounded by a fence or inclosure with one or more large gates. Gloomy rivers flow through her world. One of these streams is called Slid, which rises in the east and flows westward through valleys of venom, and is full of mud and swords. A dog stands outside of a cave (Gnipahellir). With blood-stained breast and loud howling

this dog came from Hel to meet Odin, when the latter
rode down to wake the vala, who lay buried in her
grave-mound east of the Hel-gate, and to inquire about
the fate of Balder. Horrible is the coming of Hel, for
she binds the dying man with strong chains that cannot
be broken. Anguish gnaws his heart, and every evening
Hel's maids come and invite him. These maids are also
represented as dead women, who come in the night and
invite him who is dying to their benches. And to the
vision of the dying man opens a horrible, gloomy world
of fog; he sees the sun, the genuine star of day, sink
and disappear, while he, on the other hand, hears the
gate of Hel harshly grate on its hinges, opening to
receive him. Hel receives all that die of sickness or old
age. But it also seems that others, both good and evil,
come there; for Balder we know came to Hel, after he
had been slain by Hoder. And Sigurd, who we remember slew Fafner, was afterwards assassinated by Gunnar
and went to Hel; and thither went also Brynhild, in
her beautiful car, after she had been burned on her
funeral pile. Hel's company is large, but she has dwellings enough for all; for her regions extend widely, and
her palaces are terribly high and have large gates. Of
course it is all shadows, but it has the appearance of
reality.

For Balder,

> The decorated seats
> Were strewn with rings;
> The lordly couch
> Was radiant with gold,
> And the pure mead
> Was brewed for him.

But there seems to have been a place set aside far
down in the deepest abyss of Hel for the wicked; for
it is said that the evil went to Hel, and thence to

Niflhel, that is, down into the ninth world. And it is here, in this most infernal pit, that the palace is named Anguish; the table, Famine; the waiters, Slowness and Delay; the threshold, Precipice, and the bed, Care. It is here Hel is so livid and ghastly pale that her very looks inspire horror.

Hel's horse has three feet. Hel-shoes were tied on to the feet of the dead, even though they went to Valhal.

Our English word *hell* is connected with the goddess Hel,\* and to kill is in Norse *at slaa ihel* (i-Hel). The faith in this goddess is not yet perfectly eradicated from the minds of the people. Her dog is yet heard barking outside of houses as a warning that death is near. She wanders about from place to place as a messenger of death. In the story of Olaf Geirstada-alf it is a large ox, that goes from farm to farm, and at his breath people sink down dead. In the popular mind in Norway this messenger of death is sometimes thought to be a three-footed goat, and at other times a white three-footed horse. To see it is a sure sign of death. When a person has recovered from a dangerous illness, it is said that he has given Death a bushel of oats, for her wants must be supplied, and Hel wandering about in the guise of a goat, ox or horse, may accept oats as a compromise.

It may also be noticed here, that the so-called Black Plague, or Black Death, that ravaged Norway as well as many other European countries about the middle of the fourteenth century, assumed in the minds of the Norsemen the form of an old hag (Thok, Hel, Loke), going through the realm from parish to parish with a rake and a broom. In some parishes she used the rake, and there a few were spared; in other parishes she used the

* They are both derived from the Anglo-Saxon *hêlan* or *helian*, to cover, to conceal; compare the English *to hill*.

broom, and there all perished, and the parishes were swept clean.

### SECTION V. THE NORSEMEN'S IDEA OF DEATH.*

The Norse mythology shows that our ancestors had a deeply-rooted belief in the immortality of the soul. They believed in a state of retribution beyond the grave. The dissolution of the body was typified by Balder's death, and like the latter it was a result of Loke's malignity, just as the devil brought death upon Adam and Eve, and through them upon all mankind.

But while we find the belief in the imperishableness of the soul firmly established, the ideas regarding the state of existence after death were somewhat unsettled. We are soon to present the Eddaic doctrines of future life, but in connection with Hel it seems proper to give some further explanation of the ideas that our fore-fathers entertained of death. Hel's gate is open, or ajar, said the old Goths, when the shades of death went out through the darkness of night and terrified all; but it is also open to receive the child with rosy cheeks as well as the man with hoary locks and trembling gait.

The future state was regarded as a continuation of our earthly existence. This is proved by the custom so prevalent among the Norsemen of supplying the dead with the best part of their property and the first necessi-ties of life. A coin was put under the dead man's tongue, that he might be able to defray his first expenses with it on his way to his final abode. Of course the dead went either to Odin or to Hel, but the relation between Valhal and Helheim presented difficulties which the

* For a more complete discussion of this subject the reader is referred to Keyser's *Religion of the Northmen* translated by Barclay Pennock. New York, 1854.

Norsemen strove in various ways to solve. It was said that they who are slain in battle go to Odin in Valhal, while those who die of sickness or old age go to Hel in Helheim. But according to this it would be the kind of death alone which decided the soul's future state; only those who fell by weapons would ascend to the glad abodes of heaven, while all who die of sickness would have to wander away to the dark world of the abyss, and there were people in whose eyes nothing except warlike deeds was praiseworthy. But the Odinic mythology, taken as a whole, presents a different view, although it must be admitted, as has before repeatedly been stated, that bravery was a cardinal virtue among our Norse ancestors.

We remember, from a previous chapter in this book, that the spirit or soul of man was a gift of Odin, while the body, blood and external beauty were a gift of Loder, who afterwards separated from the trinity of Odin, Hœner and Loder and became the mischievous Loke. Thus the soul belonged to the spirit-world, or Heaven, and the body to the material world, to the Deep. The two, soul and body, were joined together in this earthly life, but at its close they were separated, and each returned to its original source. The soul, with its more refined bodily form in which it was thought to be enveloped, went to the home of the gods, while the body, with the grosser material life, which was conceived to be inseparable from it, went to the abodes of Hel to become the prey of Loke's daughter. Thus man's being was divided between Odin and Hel. Odin, whose chief characteristic was *god of war*, seems to have claimed his share chiefly from those who fell in battle; and this probably may suggest to us some reason why Balder went to Hel. Balder is not a fighting god, he only shines, conferring numberless blessings on mankind, and death finally steals upon him. Odin seems not to have much need of his like. Thus death by arms came to be considered a happy lot, by the zealous followers of the asa-faith, for it was a proof of Odin's favor smiling upon them. He who fell by arms was called by Odin to himself, before Hel laid claim to her share of his being; he was Odin's chosen son, who with longing was awaited in Valhal, that he, in the ranks of the einherjes, might assist and sustain the gods in their last battle, in Ragnarok. In accordance with this theory we find in the ancient song of praise to the fallen king Erik Blood-ax, that Sigmund asks Odin this question:

> Why snatch him then, father,
> From fortune and glory?
> Why not leave him rather
> To fill up his story
> On victory's road?

> ODIN:

> Because no man knows
> When gray wolf* so gory
> His grisly maw shows
> In Asgard's abode;
> Therefore Odin calls
> And Erik fain falls
> To follow his liege lord
> And fight for his god.

By this Odin means to say, we do not know when the Fenris-wolf may come, and therefore we may need Erik's assistance. In the same sense the valkyrie is made by Eyvind Skaldespiller, in Hákonarmál, to say:

> Now *are strengthened the host of the gods,*
> Since they have Haakon
> And his valiant army
> Home to themselves brought.

> * The Fenris-wolf.

But because the dead who were slain by arms were thought to be called to Valhal, to unite themselves with the hosts of the einherjes, it was not supposed that Hel did not get her share in their being; nor was it supposed, on the other hand, that the soul of every one who died a natural death was shut out from heaven and forced to follow the body down into the abodes of Hel. That it was virtue, on the whole, and not bravery alone, which was to be rewarded in another life, and that it was wickedness and vice that were to be punished, is distinctly shown in the first poem of the Elder Edda, where it says of Gimle:

> The virtuous there
> Shall always dwell,
> And evermore
> Delights enjoy;

while perjurers, murderers and adulterers shall wade through thick venom-streams in Naastrand. But it must be remembered that Gimle and Naastrand had reference to the state of things after Ragnarok, the Twilight of the gods; while Valhal and Hel have reference to the state of things between death and Ragnarok,—a time of existence corresponding somewhat to what is called *purgatory* by the Catholic church. It may however be fairly assumed that the ideas which our ancestors had of reward and punishment concerning the preceding middle state (purgatory) of the dead, were similar to those which they had concerning the state after Ragnarok.

It was certainly believed that the soul of the virtuous, even though death by arms had not released it from the body and raised it up to the rank of the real einherjes, still found an abode in heaven, either in Valhal or in Vingolf or in Folkvang. The skald, Thjodolf of Hvin, makes King Vanlande go to Odin, although Hel tortured him;

and Egil Skallagrimson, lamenting the death of his drowned son, knows that the son has come to the home of the gods (Gudheimr), while of himself he says that he fearlessly awaits the coming of Hel.

Of Nanna we read that she went with her husband, Balder, to Hel; but the souls of noble women were believed to go to heaven after death.   There they found an abode with Freyja, and the spirits of maidens with Gefjun.   When it is said that Freyja shares the slain with Odin, it may be supposed to mean that the slain, who in life had loved wives, were united to them again with Freyja.

On the other hand, it was as certainly believed that blasphemy and baseness might shut out even the bravest from Valhal.   In the Saga of Burnt Njal, Hakon Jarl says of the bold but wicked Hrap, who had seduced his benefactor's daughter and burned a temple: The man who did this shall be banished from Valhal and never come thither.

The reader may think that the statements here presented show some inconsistency in the theory and plan of salvation according to the doctrines of the Norse mythology.   We admit that there *seems* to be some inconsistency, but let us ask, is not this charge also frequently made against the Scriptures?   Is not the church, on this very question of the plan of salvation, divided into two great parties, the one insisting on faith and the other on works?   The one party quoting and requoting Paul, in his epistle to the Romans (iii, 28), where he says, that man is justified by *faith* without the deeds of the law; and the other appealing to James' epistle (ii, 24), where he says, that by works a man is justified, and not by faith only.   And as the most eminent divines have found harmony in the principles of the Mosaic-Christian religion

as laid down in the Scriptures, so we venture to assert
that a profound study of the Odinic mythology will
enable the student to elicit a sublime harmony in its
doctrines and principles.

The strict construction of the asa-doctrine appears
to be this, that although man in the intermediate state,
between death and Ragnarok, was divided between Odin
and Hel, yet each one's share of his being, after death,
was greater or less according to the life he had lived.
The spirit of the virtuous and the brave had the power
to bear up to heaven with it after death the better part
of its corporeal being, and Hel obtained only the dust.
But he whose spirit, by wickedness and base, sensual lust
was drawn away from heaven, became in all his being
the prey of Hel. His soul was not strong enough to
mount freely up to the celestial abodes of the gods, but
was drawn down into the abyss by the dust with which
it had ever been clogged. Perhaps the representation of
Hel as being half white and half pale-blue had its origin
in this thought, that to the good, death appeared as a
bright (white) goddess of deliverance, but to the wicked,
as a dark and punishing deity.

When the drowned came to the halls of Ran, the
sea-goddess took the part of Hel: that is, Ran claimed
the body as her part, while the spirit ascended to heaven.

Bondsmen came to Thor after death. This seems to
express the idea, that their spirits had not the power to
mount up with free-born heroes to the higher celestial
abodes, but were obliged to linger midway, as it were,
among the low floating clouds under the stern dominion
of Thor; — a thought painful to the feelings of human-
ity, but nevertheless not inconsistent with the views of
our ancestors in ancient times. But when the bondsmen, as was the custom in the most ancient Gothic

times, followed their master on the funeral pile, the
motive must have been that they would continue to
serve him in the future life, or their throwing themselves on their master's funeral pile could have no
meaning whatever.

The old Norsemen had many beautiful ideas in connection with death. Thus in the lay of Atle it is said
of him who dies that he goes to the other light. That
the dead in the mounds were in a state of consciousness is illustrated by the following passages from Frid-
thiof's Saga:

> Now, children, lay us in two lofty graves
> Down by the sea-shore, near the deep-blue waves:
> Their sounds shall to our souls be music sweet,
> Singing our dirge as on the strand they beat.
>
> When round the hills the pale moonlight is thrown
> And midnight dews fall on the Bauta-stone,
> We'll sit, O Thorsten, in our rounded graves
> And speak together o'er the gentle waves.

Finally, it is a beautiful thought that there was a
sympathetic union between the dead and the living.
As the Persians believed that the rivers of the lower
world grew by the tears of the living and interfered
with the happiness of the departed, so the Norse peasant still believes that when a daughter weeps for the
death of her father she must take care that no tear
falls on his corpse, for thereby the peace of the deceased
would be disturbed. We find this same thought expressed in the Elder Edda, where Helge says to Sigrun:

> Thou alone causest, Sigrun
> From Sevafjeld,
> That Helge is bathed
> In sorrow's dew.

Thou weepest, gold-adorned,
Sunbright woman!
Cruel tears,
Before thou goest to sleep.
Every bloody tear
Fell on the king's breast,
Ice-cold and swelling
    With sorrow.

Thus also in the old song of Aage and Else:

Whenever thou grievest,
My coffin is within
As livid blood:
Whenever thou rejoicest,
My coffin is within
Filled with fragrant roses.

## SECTION VI. LOKE'S PUNISHMENT.

Loke and Balder struggled for the government of the world. Loke gradually grew victorious in his terrible children, while Balder, defenseless and innocent, had nothing but his shining purity with which to oppose Loke's baseness. Loke's wickedness reached its culminating point in the death of Balder and in the hag Thok, who with arid tears would wail Balder from Hel.

According to the Younger Edda it would seem that Loke was punished immediately after the death of Balder, but according to the Elder Edda the banquet of Æger seems to have taken place after the death of Balder, and there Loke was present to pour out in words his enmity to the defeated gods. When Æger had received the large kettle, that Thor had brought him from the giant Hymer, he brewed ale for the gods and invited them to a banquet. The gods and elves were gathered there, but Thor was not present. Æger's servants were praised for their attentiveness and agility. This Loke could not bear to hear,

and he killed one of them by name Funfeng. The
gods drove him into the woods, but when they had
seated themselves at the table and had begun to drink
he came back again, and asked Elder, the other servant
of Æger, what the gods talked about at the banquet.
They talk about their weapons and about their bravery,
replied Elder, but neither the gods nor the elves speak
well of you. Then, said Loke, I must go into Æger's
hall, to look at the banquet: scolding and evil words
bring I to the sons of the gods and mix evil in their ale.
Then Loke went into the hall; but when they who were
there saw who had entered, they were all silent. Then
said Loke to the gods:

> Thirsty I hither
> To the hall came —
> Long way I journeyed —
> The gods to ask
> Whether one would grant me
> A drink of the precious mead.
>
> Why are ye silent, gods!
> And sit so stubborn?
> Have ye lost your tongues?
> Give me a seat
> And place at the banquet,
> Or turn me away.
>
> BRAGE:
> The gods will never
> Give you a seat
> And place at the banquet;
> Well know the gods
> To whom they will give
> Pleasure at the banquet.

Then Loke begins to abuse the gods, and reminds
Odin how they once mixed blood together,—and Vidar
must yield him his seat. But before Loke drank he

greeted all the gods and goddesses excepting Brage, who occupied the innermost bench. And now Loke pours out his abuse upon all the gods and goddesses, much of which has been given heretofore. His last quarrel is with Sif, the wife of Thor. But then Beyla hears the mountains quake and tremble. It is Thor that is coming; and when he enters the hall he threatens to crush every bone in Loke's body; and to him Loke finally yields, for he knows that Thor carries out his threats. On going out he heaps curses upon Æger, and hopes that he (Æger) may never more make banquets for the gods, but that flames may play upon his realm and burn him too.

Loke now fled and hid himself in the mountains. There he built him a dwelling with four doors, so that he could see everything that passed around him. Often in the daytime he assumed the likeness of a salmon and concealed himself under the waters of a cascade called Fraananger Force, where he employed himself in divining and circumventing whatever stratagems the gods might have recourse to in order to catch him. One day as he sat in his dwelling he took flax and yarn and worked them into meshes, in the manner that nets have since been made by fishermen. Odin had however, sitting in Hlidskjalf, discovered Loke's retreat; and the latter, becoming aware that the gods were approaching, threw his net into the fire and ran to conceal himself in the river. When the gods entered Loke's house, Kvaser, who was the most distinguished among them all for his quickness and penetration, traced out in the hot embers the vestiges of the net which had been burnt, and told Odin that it must be an invention to catch fish. Whereupon they set to work and wove a net after the model they saw imprinted in the ashes. This net, when finished, they

threw into the river in which Loke had hid himself.
Thor held one end of the net and all the other gods laid
hold of the other end, thus jointly drawing it along the
stream. Notwithstanding all their precautions the net
passed over Loke, who had crept between two stones,
and the gods only perceived that some living thing had
touched the meshes. They therefore cast their net a
second time, hanging so great a weight to it that it everywhere raked the bed of the river. But Loke, perceiving
that he had but a short distance to the sea, swam onward
and leapt over the net into the force. The gods instantly
followed him and divided themselves into two bands.
Thor, wading along in mid-stream, followed the net,
whilst the others dragged it along toward the sea. Loke
then perceived that he had only two chances of escape,—
either to swim out to the sea, or to leap again over the
net. He chose the latter, but as he took a tremendous
leap Thor caught him in his hand. Being however
extremely slippery, he would have escaped had not Thor
held him fast by the tail; and this is the reason why
salmon have had their tails ever since so fine and slim.

The gods having thus captured Loke, they dragged
him without commiseration into a cavern, wherein they
placed three sharp-pointed rocks, boring a hole through
each of them. Having also seized Loke's children, Vale
and Nare, or Narfe, they changed the former into a wolf,
and in this likeness he tore his brother to pieces and
devoured him. The gods then made cords of his intestines, with which they bound Loke on the points of the
rocks, one cord passing under his shoulders, another
under his loins, and a third under his hams, and afterwards transformed these cords to fetters of iron. Then
the giantess Skade took a serpent and suspended it over
him in such a manner that the venom should fall into

his face, drop by drop. But Sigyn, Loke's wife, stands by him and receives the drops, as they fall, in a cup, which she empties as often as it is filled. But while she is doing this, venom falls upon Loke, which makes him shriek with horror and twist his body about so violently that the whole earth shakes; and this produces what men call earthquakes. There will Loke lie until Ragnarok.

Here we have Loke in the form of a salmon. Slippery as a salmon, is as common an adage in Norseland as our American: slippery as an eel. Loke himself makes the net by which he is caught and ruined. This is very proper; sin and crime always bring about their own ruin. The chaining of Loke is one of the grandest myths in the whole mythology. That Loke represents fire in its various forms, becomes clearer with every new fact, every new event in his life. Skade is the cold mountain stream, that pours its venom upon Loke. Sigyn takes much of it away, but some of it will, in spite of her, come in contact with the subterranean fire, and the earth quakes and the geysers spout their scalding water. But who cannot see human life represented in this grand picture? All great convulsions in the history of man are brought about in the same manner, and beside the great forces of revolution stand the pious, gentle and womanly minds who with the cup of religion or with the eloquence of the pure spirit prevent the most violent outbreaks of storm among the nations, and pour their quieting oils upon the disturbed waters. And who does not remember cases at the shrine of the family, where the inevitable consequences of man's folly and crime produce convulsive crises, misfortunes and misery, which the wife shares, prevents and moderates with her soft hand, gentle tears, and soothing words,— always cheerful and never growing weary. It is wo-

26

man's divine work in life, in a quiet manner to bring consolation and comfort, and never to despair.

As the earth and sea in their various manifestations are represented by various divinities, so the fire also presents various forms. It is celestial, united with Odin; it is earthly in the Fenris-wolf, and it is subterranean in the chained Loke. That Loke symbolizes fire, is also illustrated by the fact that the common people in Norway, when they hear the fire crackling, say that Loke is whipping his children. In a wider sense Loke is in one word the evil one, the devil. The common people also know Loke as a divinity of the atmosphere. When the sun draws water, they say that Loke is drinking water. When vapors arise from the earth and float about in the atmosphere, this phenomenon is also ascribed to Loke. When he sows his oats among the grain, he produces a peculiar aërial phenomenon, of which the novelist Blicher speaks in one of his romances, saying that this trembling motion of the air, which the people call Loke's oats, confuses and blinds the eyes. Nay, truly it confuses and blinds, for we need not take this only in a literal sense. It is that motion which shocks the nerves of man when the soul conceives evil thoughts; it is that nervous concussion which shocks the whole system of the criminal when he goes to commit his foul misdeed.

Having now given a description of Loke,—having painted with words the character of this wily, mischievous, sly and deceitful divinity,—we ask, with Petersen, where is the painter who will present him in living colors on canvas? We want a personal representation of him. We want his limbs, his body and his head. Where is the painter who can give his chin the proper form, his mouth the right shape, paint his dimples with those

deep and fine wrinkles when he smiles, and do justice to
his nose and upper lip? Who will paint those delicate
elevations and depressions of his cheeks, that terrible
brilliancy of his eyes. his subtle and crafty forehead, and
his hair at once stiff and wavy? Who will paint this
immortal youth who yet everywhere reveals his old age,
or this old man whose face mocks at everything like a
reckless youth? Here is a theme without a model, a
theme for a master of the art.

### SECTION VII. THE IRON POST.

The following story from the south of Germany
illustrates how stories can be remodeled and changed as
to their external adornment and still preserve their fundamental feature. The reader will not fail to discover
Loke in the following tradition, entitled *Der Stock im
Eisen*, a story which in its most original form must
date back to the time when Loke was known in Germany.

Opposite St. Stephen's Tower in Vienna there is
found, it is said, one of the old landmarks of this city,
the so-called *Stock im Eisen* (the iron post). It is a
post that has in the course of time become blackened
and charred, and into which nail after nail has been
driven so close together that there is not room for a
single one more, and the post is literally inclosed in an
iron casing. This covering of iron keeps the. dry post
in an upright position, and near the ground it is fastened
by an iron ring with an unusually wonderful lock. In
olden times this post was a landmark, for to it extended
the great Wienerwald. In connection with it the following tale is told by H. Meinert:

A young good-looking locksmith apprentice, by name Reinbert,
had secretly won the heart and become engaged to his master's
daughter Dorothea ; but there was not much hope that she

would ever become his wife.  One evening the two lovers agreed
to meet outside the city; they forget themselves in their conversation, in their doubts and their hopes, and hear not the clock
that strikes the hour when the gate of the city is to be closed;
and the lover has forgotten to take money along to get it opened.
But what a misfortune if they should be shut out, what a disgrace
to his beloved, if it should become known that she has spent the
night outside the city, outside of her father's house, in company
with a man!  Suddenly there arises as it were from the ground
a pale man, with the contour of his face sharply marked, with
wonderful flashing eyes, wearing a black cloak and black hat,
and in the latter waves a cock-feather.  Reinbert involuntarily
shudders as he sees him, but still he does not forget his misfortune in being shut out of the city; he therefore explains his
distress to the stranger, and asks him to lend him enough to pay
the gate-watch.  Like for like!  whispers the stranger into Reinbert's ear; if I am to help you and your beloved out of your
distress, then you must promise me upon the salvation of your
soul never on any Sunday to neglect the holy mass.  Reinbert
hesitates; but it is in fact a pious promise, and necessity knows
no laws.  He promises, and the gate opens as it were spontaneously.

Four weeks later, when Reinbert sat in his workshop, the
door opens and that strange man enters.  Reinbert shudders at
the sight of him; but when the stranger does not even care to
look at him, and only asks for his master, he regains his peace
of mind.  When the apprentices had called the master, the visitor
ordered an iron fastening, with lock and bolt, and the master is
willing to undertake the work.  But now began the stranger (cunning as Loke) with a wonderful knowledge of details to mention
all the different parts of the lock, explained with great eloquence
the whole plan of it, and took special pains to describe the manner
in which the springs must necessarily be bent and united; and although both the master and the apprentices had to admit that such
a lock was not without the range of possibilities,—nay, that it
would indeed be a masterpiece,—still their heads began to swim
when they tried to think of its wonderful construction and arrange
the plan in their minds, and they had to admit that they did not
trust themselves to do the work.  Then the stranger's mouth
assumed a deeply-furrowed, indescribably scornful smile; and

he said with contempt: Call yourselves master and apprentices, when you do not know how to undertake a work that the youngest one among you can do in less than an hour! The youngest one among us, murmured the apprentices; do you think that Reinbert would be able to do it,— he is the youngest one among us? O yes, said the stranger, he there can do it, or his look must deceive me much. With these words he called out the astounded Reinbert, explained to him once more the plan of the lock, and added: If you do not save the honor of the smiths, the whole world shall know their disgrace; but if you can get the lock ready within two hours, no master will refuse you his daughter, after you have saved his reputation. Yes indeed, said the master, if you can perform such an impossibility, Dorothea shall be yours. While the stranger described the nature of the lock, Reinbert had sunk into deep reflections; to his soul the narrow workshop widened into a large plain; he saw a beautiful, happy future blooming before him; by strange and wonderful voices he heard himself styled the master of masters; and his beloved he saw approaching him with the bridal wreath entwined in her locks; and just at that moment he heard his master's words: If you can perform such an impossibility, Dorothea shall be yours. He immediately· began his work; it seemed as if he were working with a hundred arms; each blow of the hammer gave form to a part of the work; by a peculiar resounding the hammer-blows seemed to multiply, as if more invisible hands hammered with him, while the stranger in the red glare of the flame looked like a pillar of fire (Loke). After the lapse of an hour the work was finished. Apprentices and master looked at it and examined it, shaking their heads, and with mouths wide open; but there was no doubt that Reinbert had accomplished a masterpiece never seen before, and the master ascribed it to his enthusiasm awakened by his love. The stranger took the lock and went ahead; the master with Reinbert and all his apprentices and the members of his family followed, and all proceeded to the place where the iron post (Stock im Eisen) now stands. Here the stranger placed an iron chain around the post and fastened it with Reinbert's lock. When they returned, the stranger had disappeared, and with him the key to the marvelous lock.

We omit a part of the story, taking only that part which has reference to Loke.

On account of slander, Reinbert had to travel far and wide before he finally got his beloved Dorothea. A few days after he had returned, the government issued a proclamation to the effect that whatever smith could make a key that would open that lock should thereby get his diploma of mastership. Reinbert announced himself as a candidate, and repaired to his workshop to make the key. But for the first time his work did not seem to succeed. The iron was stubborn and would not assume the form required; and it seemed astonishing to him, when he at last had succeeded in giving the key the proper form, and put it into the furnace to temper it, it was turned and twisted when he took it out again. His impatience grew into wrath. But when he at length, after many unsuccessful attempts, had got the key ready and put it into the furnace and carefully scrutinized to see what it was that thus always ruined his work, he saw in the midst of the fire a claw seize after the key, and terror-stricken he discovered that disagreeable stranger's twisted face (Loke) staring at him out of the burning furnace. He quickly snatched the key away, turned it, seized it with the tongs at the other end, and put it into the fire again; and lo and behold! when he took it out the handle was somewhat twisted, but the head preserved its right shape. (We remember that it was Loke's fault that the handle of Thor's hammer became rather short.)

Reinbert now announced to the government that the key was ready; and the day after the government officials and the citizens marched in procession to the iron post, and Reinbert's key opened the lock. In his enthusiasm at his success he threw the key high up in the air, but to everybody's surprise it did not come down again. It was sought for everywhere, but could nowhere be found, and Reinbert had to promise to make a new one some time. To commemorate the fact that it had been possible to open the lock he drove a nail into the wooden post, and since that time every smith has done the same when he left Vienna; thus this post was formed with its numberless nails.

Reinbert became a master and married his beloved. Up to this time he had kept his promise and had attended upon the holy mass every Sunday; he began to drink and gamble, but he conscientiously continued to keep his promise. Finally it happens that he once stayed a little too long at the gambling-house, and hastens terrified in order not to come too late to church. But the door of St. Stephen's church is closed. Outside sits an old woman (Loke assumed the guise of a woman* after Balder's death), who, in answer to his question, informs him that mass is out. Filled with deadly anguish he rushes back to his comrades, who laughed at him and insisted that, as mass began at half-past eleven o'clock, and as it was only three-quarters past eleven, the mass could not yet be over. He hastens back again; the church-door is now open, but at the very moment he enters, the priest leaves the altar — the mass is over. The old woman rises, seizes him by the arms, and his soul departs from him.

Thus the myth develops into traditionary story, and one story begets another; they wander about from the south to the north and from the north to the south, and change with the times, reminding us of the various manifestations of life; reminding us how human things circulate and develop, each inextricably interwoven with all, and always reminding us, too, that there is a heaven above the earth and an existence beyond what is allotted to us mortals on earth.

SECTION VIII. A BRIEF REVIEW.

We have now completed the second part of our work, and witnessed the life and exploits of the gods. It remains now to sum up briefly the main features of, and the principal lessons taught in, this portion of the mythology.

We cannot fail to have observed that the life of the gods is, in the first place, a reflection of the workings of visible nature, and, in the second place, a reflection and foreshadowing of the life of man, particularly of life in its various manifestations in the history of the Gothic race. We have also witnessed how wonderfully the interests and works of the gods — nay, how abso-

* Thok.

lutely the gods themselves — are interlinked with each
other,— that centralizing thought which, as has been
said before, forms one of the most prominent characteristics of Norse or Gothic mythology, thought and
history.

We have seen how the divinities and demons, after
having been created, enter upon various activities, contend with each other and are reconciled, and how new
beings are developed in this struggle, all destined to
fight on one side or the other in the final conflict.

The myth reflects nature and society, the one inextricably in communion with the other; and in the development of nature and society we find three relations:
the relation of the asas to the giants, the relation of the
asas to the vans, and the relation of Loke to Odin. The
asas and giants try to unite, but meet with poor success,
their natures are too opposite. The union of the asas
and vans is accomplished with but little difficulty; while
between Odin and Loke there is a tendency to separate
more and more. The beginning of warfare between the
gods and the giants is the beginning of nature's development; the giants storm the heavens and are repulsed;
this struggle lasts through life, and in it Sleipner is
produced. Later, begins the war between the asas and
vans, which ends in peace, and with this peace begins
the development of society; the asas and vans together
forming a series of beautiful myths, that have reference
to war, to the cultivation of the earth, to the civilizing
influences of the water, to the greater development of
the mind and heart,— that is, to knowledge, love, hu-
manity and peace,— the object of which is reconcilia-
tion, reached by labor and struggles. But enmity soon
arises among the gods themselves. Odin's union with
Loke is dissolved. In the midst of the good there is

evil. The evil proceeds from the good by separation. by taking a wrong course. The unity of the spirit is destroyed when anything tears itself loose from it and assumes an independent position in opposition to it. Loke separates himself from Odin and develops himself independently. He acts like Odin: he permeates all nature and the soul of man; but he does it independently, and the result is that the powers of evil spread over the earth in the form of Loke's children. Everything becomes wild and tumultuous. Fire rages in its frantic fury in the character of the Fenris-wolf. The Midgard-serpent represents the furious convulsions of the sea; cowardice seizes the heart and begets the pale Hel, death without conflict, life as a mere shadow. Thus it goes on. Knowledge rightly used is a blessing, but unconstrained by prudence it degenerates into cunning and deceitfulness; killing is honorable, but unconstrained by justice and valor it becomes foul murder; to break a promise that can no longer be kept is proper, but when done recklessly it is perjury. We find, throughout the life of the gods, light and darkness well defined and distinctly separated. Loke fluctuates between the two: he gradually leaves light and unites himself to darkness. The darkness of night supplants the light of day: the gloomy winter overcomes the shining summer. The gods learn that they are subject to the infirmities of old age: the rejuvenating Idun sinks into the abyss. From the depths below, Odin receives warnings that the light of life may be extinguished. Loke begins his conflict with Balder: finally his stratagem and cunning gain a victory, and all the sorrowing of nature is in vain. Loke is chained, but Balder does not return from Hel. Vale has avenged his brother's death, but the end of life is at hand. And now we are prepared for RAGNAROK, followed by the REGENERATION OF THE EARTH.

# PART III.

---

## RAGNAROK AND REGENERATION.

# SKULD.

Lítið sjáum aptr,
En ekki fram:
Skyggir Skuld fyrir sjón.

# CHAPTER I.

## RAGNAROK.

THE final destruction of the world, and regeneration of gods and men, is called Ragnarok; that is, the Twilight of the gods (*Ragna,* from *regin,* gods, and *rökr,* darkness).

The journey through life has been a long one, and yet we have not reached the end, for the end is also the beginning. Death is the center, where the present and future existence meet. When life ends, there is a change, there comes a new day and a sun without a shadow.

In comparing the Greek mythology with the Norse, it was stated, that the Norse has a theoktonic myth, while the Greek lacks the final act of the grand drama. The Greeks knew of no death of the gods; their gods were immortal. And yet, what were they but an ideal conception of the forms of life? And this life with all its vanity, pomp and glory, the Greek loved so dearly, that he thought it must last forever. He imagined an everlasting series of changes. But what will then the final result be? Shall the thundering Zeus forever continue to thunder? Shall the faithless Aphrodite forever be unfaithful? Shall Typhon forever go on with his desolations? Shall the sinner continue to sin forever, and shall the world continue without end to foster and nourish evil? These are questions that find no satisfactory answer in the Greek mythology.

(413)

Among the Norsemen, on the other hand, we find
in their most ancient records a clearly expressed faith
in the perishableness of all things; and we find this
faith at every step that the Norsemen has taken. The
origin of this faith we seek in vain; it conceals itself
beneath the waters of the primeval fountains of their
thoughts and aspirations. They regarded death as but
the middle of a long life. They considered it cowardice
to spare a life that is to return; they thought it folly to
care for a world that must necessarily perish; while
they knew that their spirits would be clothed with
increased vigor in the other world. Happy were they
who lived beneath the polar star, for the greatest fear
that man knows, the fear of death, disturbed them not.
They rushed cheerfully upon the sword; they entered
the battle boldly, for, like their gods, who every moment
looked forward to the inevitable Ragnarok, they knew
that life could be purchased by a heroic death.

The very fact that the gods in the creation proceeded
from the *giant* Ymer foreshadowed their destruction.
The germ of death was in their nature from the beginning, and this germ would gradually develop as their
strength gradually became wasted and consumed. That
which is born must die, but that which is not born
cannot grow old.

The gradual growth of this germ of death, and corresponding waste of the strength of the gods, is profoundly sketched throughout the mythology. The gods
cannot be conquered, unless they make themselves weak;
but such is the very nature of things, that they must do
this. To win the charming Gerd, Frey must give away
his sword, but when the great final conflict comes he
has no weapon. In order that the Fenris-wolf may be
chained, Tyr must risk his right hand, and he loses it.

How shall he then fight in Ragnarok? Balder could not have died, had not the gods been blind and presumptuous; their thoughtlessness put weapons into the hands of their enemy. Hoder would never have thrown the fatal mistletoe, had not their own appointed game been an inducement to him to honor his brother. When Loke became separated from Odin, the death of the gods was a foregone conclusion.

The imperfection of nature is also vividly depicted in the Eddas. The sun was so scorching hot that the gods had to place a shield before it; the fire was so destructive that the gods had to chain it, in order that it might not bring ruin upon the whole world. Life, after the natural death, was not continued only in the shining halls of Valhal, but also in the subterranean regions among the shades of Hel.

Our old Gothic fathers, in the poetic dawn of our race, investigated the origin and beginning of nature and time. The divine poetic and imaginative spark in them lifted them up to the Eternal, to that wonderful secret fountain which is the source of all things. They looked about them in profound meditation to find the image and reflection of that glorious harmony which their soul in its heavenly flight had found, but in all earthly things they discovered strife and warfare. When the storms bent the pine trees on the mountain tops, and when the foaming waves rolled in gigantic fury against the rocky cliffs, the Norseman saw strife. When the growl of the bear and the howl of the wolf blended with the moaning of the winds and the roaring of the waters, he heard strife. In unceasing conflict with the earth, with the beasts and with each other, he saw men stand, conquer, and fall. If he lifted his weary eye toward the skies, he saw the light struggling with darkness and with itself. When light arose out of darkness, it was greeted with enthusiasm; when it sank again into darkness, its rays were broken and it dissolved in glimmering colors; and if he looked down into the heart of man, into his own breast, he found that all this conflict of opposing elements in the outward world did but faintly symbolize that terrible warfare pervading and shattering his whole being. Well might he long for peace, and can we wonder that this deep longing for rest and peace, which filled his heart in the midst of all his struggles,— can we wonder, we say, that his longing for peace found a grand expression in a final conflict through which imperishableness and harmony were attained?

This final conflict, this dissolution of nature's and life's disharmony, the Edda presents to us in the death of the gods, which is usually, as stated, called Ragnarok.

There is nothing more sublime in poetry than the description, in the Eddas, of Ragnarok. It is preceded by ages of crime and terror. The vala looks down into Niflheim, and

> There saw she wade
> In the heavy streams
> Men — foul murderers,
> And perjurers,
> And them who other's wives
> Seduce to sin.

The growing depravity and strife in the world proclaim the approach of this great event. First there is a winter called Fimbul-winter, during which snow will fall from the four corners of the world; the frosts will be very severe, the winds piercing, the weather tempestuous, and the sun will impart no gladness. Three such winters shall pass away without being tempered

by a single summer. Three other similar winters follow,
during which war and discord will spread over the whole
earth. Brothers for the sake of mere gain shall kill
each other, and no one shall spare either his parents
or his children. Thus the Elder Edda:

> Brothers slay brothers;
> Sisters' children
> Shed each other's blood.
> Hard is the world;
> Sensual sin grows huge.
> There are sword-ages, ax-ages;
> Shields are cleft in twain;
> Storm-ages, murder-ages;
> Till the world falls dead,
> And men no longer spare
> Or pity one another.

Then shall happen such things as may truly be
regarded as great miracles. The Fenris-wolf shall devour
the sun, and a severe loss will that be to mankind.
The other wolf * will take the moon, and this, too, will
cause great mischief. Then the stars shall be hurled
from the heavens, and the earth shall be shaken so
violently that trees will be torn up by the roots, the
tottering mountains will tumble headlong from their
foundations, and all bonds and fetters will be shivered
to pieces. The Fenris-wolf then breaks loose and the
sea rushes over the earth on account of the Midgard-
serpent writhing in giant rage and gaining the land.
On the waters floats the ship Naglfar (nail-ship), which
is constructed of the nails of dead men. For this reason
great care should be taken to die with pared nails, for
he who dies with his nails unpared supplies materials
for the building of this ship, which both gods and men
wish may be finished as late as possible. But in this

---

* Moongarm. See Vocabulary.

flood shall Naglfar float, and the giant Hrym be its
steersman.

The Fenris-wolf advances and opens his enormous
mouth; the lower jaw reaches to the earth and the
upper one to heaven, and he would open it still wider
had he room to do so. Fire flashes from his eyes and
nostrils. The Midgard-serpent, placing himself by the
side of the Fenris-wolf, vomits forth floods of poison,
which fill the air and the waters. Amidst this devasta-
tion the heavens are rent in twain, and the sons of
Muspel come riding through the opening in brilliant
array. Surt rides first, and before and behind him
flames burning fire. His sword outshines the sun itself.
Bifrost (the rainbow), as they ride over it, breaks to
pieces. Then they direct their course to the battle-field
called Vigrid. Thither repair also the Fenris-wolf and
the Midgard-serpent, and Loke with all the followers of
Hel, and Hrym with all the frost-giants. But the sons
of Muspel keep their effulgent bands apart on the battle-
field, which is one hundred miles (rasts) on each side.

Meanwhile Heimdal arises, and with all his strength
he blows the Gjallar-horn to arouse the gods, who assemble without delay. Odin then rides to Mimer's fountain
and consults Mimer how he and his warriors are to enter
into action. The ash Ygdrasil begins to quiver, nor is
there anything in heaven or on earth that does not fear
and tremble in that terrible hour. The gods and all the
einherjes of Valhal arm themselves with speed and sally
forth to the field, led on by Odin with his golden helmet,
resplendent cuirass, and spear called Gungner. Odin
places himself against the Fenris-wolf. Thor stands by
his side, but can render him no assistance, having himself to combat the Midgard-serpent. Frey encounters
Surt, and terrible blows are exchanged ere Frey falls;

and he owes his defeat to his not having that trusty sword which he gave to Skirner. That day the dog Garm, that had been chained in the Gnipa-cave, breaks loose. He is the most fearful monster of all, and attacks Tyr, and they kill each other. Thor gains great renown for killing the Midgard-serpent, but at the same time, retreating nine paces, he falls dead upon the spot, suffocated with the floods of venom which the dying serpent vomits forth upon him. The wolf swallows Odin, but at that instant Vidar advances, and setting his foot upon the monster's lower jaw he seizes the other with his hand, and thus tears and rends him till he dies. Vidar is able to do this because he wears those shoes which have before been mentioned, and for which stuff has been gathered in all ages, namely, the shreds of leather which are cut off to form the toes and heels of shoes; and it is on this account that those who desire to render service to the gods should take care to throw such shreds away. Loke and Heimdal fight and kill each other. Then Surt flings fire and flame over the world. Smoke wreathes up around the all-nourishing tree (Ygdrasil), the high flames play against the heavens, and earth consumed sinks down beneath the sea.

All this is vividly and sublimely presented in the Elder Edda, thus:

> East of Midgard in the Ironwood
> The old hag* sat,
> Fenrer's terrible
> Race she fostered.
> One† of them
> Shall at last
> In the guise of a troll
> Devour the moon.

---

* Angerboda. See p. 179.     † Moongarm. See p. 180.

It feeds on the bodies
Of men, when they die:
The seats of the gods
It stains with red blood:
The sunshine blackens
In the summers thereafter
And the weather grows bad —
Know ye now more or not?

The hag's watcher,
The glad Edger,
Sat on the hill-top
And played his harp;
Near him crowed
In the bird-wood
A fair-red cock
Which Fjalar hight.

Among the gods crowed
The gold-combed cock,
He who wakes in Valhal
The hosts of heroes;
Beneath the earth
Crows another,
The root-red cock,
In the halls of Hel.

Loud barks Garm
At Gnipa-cave;
The fetters are severed,
The wolf is set free,—
Vala knows the future.
More does she see
Of the victorious gods
Terrible fall.

The wolf referred to in the first strophe is Maanegarm (the moon-devourer), of whom we have made
notice before. The hag in the Ironwood is Angerboda
(anguish-boding), with whom Loke begat children. Evil
is being developed. The gods become through Loke

united with the giants. The wood is of iron, hard and barren ; the children are ravenous wolves. On the hill-top sits Egder (an eagle), a storm-eagle, the howling wind that rushes through the wood, and howling wind is the music produced upon his harp. The cock is a symbol of fire, and it is even to this day a common expression among the Norsemen, when a fire breaks out, that *the red cock is crowing over the roof of the house.* There are three cocks, one in the bird-wood, one in heaven, and one in the lower regions with Hel. The idea then is, that the cock as a symbol of fire announces the coming of Ragnarok in all the regions of the world. The vala continues:

> Mimer's sons play ;
> To battle the gods are called
> By the ancient
> Gjallar-horn.
> Loud blows Heimdal,
> His sound is in the air ;
> Odin talks
> With the head of Mimer.
>
> Quivers then Ygdrasil,
> The strong-rooted ash ;
> Rustles the old tree
> When the giant gives way.
> All things tremble
> In the realms of Hel,
> Till Surt's son
> Swallows up Odin.
>
> How fare the gods?
> How fare the elves ?
> Jotunheim shrieks.
> The gods hold Thing ;
> The dwarfs shudder
> Before their cleft caverns,
> Where behind rocky walls they dwell.
> Know ye now more or not ?

Loud barks Garm*
At Gnipa-cave;
The fetters are severed,
The wolf is set free,—
Vala knows the future.
More does she see
Of the victorious gods'
Terrible fall.

From the east drives Hrym,
Bears his child before him;
Jormungander welters
In giant fierceness;
The waves thunder;
The eagle screams,
Rends the corpses with pale beak,
And Naglfar is launched.

A ship from the east nears,
The hosts of Muspel
Come o'er the main,
But Loke is pilot.
All grim and gaunt monsters
Conjoin with the wolf,
And before them all goes
The brother of Byleist.†

From the south wends Surt
With seething fire;
The sun of the war-god
Shines in his sword;
Mountains together dash,
And frighten the giant-maids;
Heroes tread the paths to Hel,
And heaven in twain is rent.

Over Hlin‡ then shall come
Another woe,
When Odin goes forth
The wolf to combat,

---

* Hel's dog.       † Loke.       ‡ One of Frigg's maid-servants.

And he * who Bele slew
'Gainst Surt rides;
Then will Frigg's
Beloved husband † fall.

Loud barks Garm
At Gnipa-cave;
The fetters are severed,
The wolf is set free,—
Vala knows the future.
More does she see
Of the victorious gods'
Terrible fall.

Then Vidar, the great son
Of Victory's father,
Goes forth to fight
With the ferocious beast;
With firm grasp his sword
In the giant-born monster's heart
Deep he plants,
And avenges his father.

Then the famous son ‡
Of Hlodyn § comes;
Odin's son comes
To fight with the serpent;
Midgard's ward ‖
In wrath slays the serpent.
Nine paces away
Goes the son of Fjorgyn;
He totters, wounded
By the fierce serpent.
All men
Abandon the earth.

The sun darkens,
The earth sinks into the ocean;
The lucid stars
From heaven vanish;

* Frey.　† Odin.　‡ Thor.　§ Another name for Frigg.　‖ Defender.

Fire and vapor
Rage toward heaven;
High flames
Involve the skies.

Loud barks Garm
At Gnipa-cave;
The fetters are severed,
The wolf is set free,—
Vala knows the future.
More does she see
Of the victorious gods'
Terrible fall.

These strophes are taken from Völuspá (the prophecy
of the vala); and besides these we also have a few
strophes of the lay of Vafthrudner, in the Elder Edda,
referring to the final conflict:

VAFTHRUDNER:

Tell me, Gagnraad,*
Since on the floor thou wilt
Prove thy proficiency,
How that plain is called,
Where in fight shall meet
Surt and the gentle gods?

GAGNRAAD (ODIN):

Vigrid the plain is called,
Where in fight shall meet
Surt and the gentle gods;
A hundred rasts it is
On every side.
That plain is to them decreed.

And in the second part of this same poem, in which
Odin asks and Vafthrudner answers:

* Odin.

GAGNRAAD (ODIN):

What of Odin will
The end of life be,
When the powers perish?

VAFTHRUDNER:

The wolf will
The father of men devour;
Him Vidar will avenge:
He his cold jaws
Will cleave
In conflict with the wolf.

The terrible dog mentioned several times is Hel's bloody-breasted and murderous hound. Like the Fenris-wolf and Loke, this dog had been bound at Gnipa-cave, although the Eddas tell us nothing about when or how this was done.

When it is said that another woe comes over Hlin, the maid-servant is placed for Frigg herself; and the former woe implied is the death of Balder, *the other woe* meaning the approaching death of Odin.

It is worthy of notice, that as this final conflict is inevitable, the gods proceed to it, not with despair and trembling, but joyfully and fearlessly as to a game, for it is the last. Odin rides to the battle adorned; he knows that he must die, and for this very reason he decorates himself as does a bride for the wedding, and the gods follow him; even those who are defenseless voluntarily expose themselves on the plain of Vigrid. They are determined to die.

Which are the powers that now oppose each other? On the one side we have those who have ruled and blessed heaven and earth; and fighting against them we find their eternal enemies, those powers which had sprung into being before heaven and earth were created, and those which had developed in the earth and in the sea, and which no asa-might can conquer. From Muspelheim come the sons of Muspel in shining armor; from Muspel's world came originally the sun, moon and stars. It is a fundamental law in nature that all things destroy themselves, all things contain an inherent force that finally brings ruin; that is the meaning of perishableness or corruption. A second host consists of the frost-giants. From the body of the old giant Ymer was formed the earth, the sea, the mountains, the trees, etc.; the giants must therefore assist in the destruction of their own work. The third host is Loke and his children, born in time and the offspring of that which was created. They are the destructive elements in that which was created; the ocean becoming a fierce serpent, and the fire a devouring wolf. Loke himself is the volcanic fire which the earth has produced within its bowels; and then there is all that is cowardly represented by the pale Hel with her bloodless shadows, the life which has turned into shadowy death. All these forces oppose each other. Those who fought in life mutually conquer each other in death. Odin, whose heaven is the source of all life, is slain by the Fenriswolf, the earthly fire, which has brought all kinds of activities into the life of man; but the wolf, after he has conquered, falls again at the hands of Vidar, the imperishable, incorruptible force of nature. In this duel heaven and earth are engaged. The god of the clouds, Thor, contends with the Midgard-serpent,—many a struggle they have had together; now the clouds and ocean mutually destroy each other. Since the death of Balder, Frey is the most pure and shining divinity. His pure and noble purpose and longing are still within him, but his sword, his power, is gone. Hence he is stricken down by Surt, the warder of Muspelheim. Heimdal stretched his brilliant rainbow over the earth, Loke his variegated stream of fire within the earth; the one proclaiming mercies and blessings, the other destruction; both perish in Ragnarok. Hel and her pale host also betake themselves to the final contest, but the Eddas say nothing about their taking part in the fight. How can they? They are nothing but emptiness, the mere vanity of the heart, in which there is no substance; they are but the darkness which enwraps the earth, and are not capable of deeds.

Thus is Ragnarok! The great antagonism pervading the world is removed in a final struggle, in which the contending powers mutually destroy each other. Ragnarok is an outbreak of all the chaotic powers, a conflict between them and the established order of creation. Fire, water, darkness and death work together to destroy the world. The gods and their enemies meet in a universal, world-embracing wrestle and duel, and mutually destroy each other. The flames of Surt, the supreme fire-god, complete the overthrow, and the last remnant of the consumed earth sinks into the ocean.

# CHAPTER II.

## REGENERATION.

BUT when the heavens and the earth and the whole world have been consumed in flames, when the gods and all the einherjes and all mankind have perished,— what then? Is not man immortal? Are not all men to live in some world or other forever? The vala looks again, and

> She sees arise
> The second time,
> From the sea, the earth
> Completely green:
> Cascades do fall,
> The eagle soars,
> From lofty mounts
> Pursues its prey.
>
> The gods convene
> On Ida's plains,
> And talk of the powerful
> Midgard-serpent;
> They call to mind
> The Fenris-wolf
> And the ancient runes
> Of the mighty Odin.
>
> Then again
> The wonderful
> Golden tablets
> Are found in the grass:

(428)

In time's morning
The leader of the gods
And Odin's race
Possessed them.

The fields unsown
Yield their growth;
All ills cease;
Balder comes.
Hoder and Balder,
Those heavenly gods,
Dwell together in Hropt's* halls.
Conceive ye this or not?

Vidar and Vale survive; neither the flood nor Surt's flame has harmed them, and they dwell on the plain of Ida, where Asgard formerly stood. Thither come the sons of Thor, Mode and Magne, bringing with them their father's hammer, Mjolner. Hœner is there also, and comprehends the future. Balder and Hoder sit and converse together; they call to mind their former knowledge and the perils they underwent, and the fight with the wolf Fenrer, and with the Midgard-serpent. The sons of Hoder and Balder inhabit the wide Wind-home. The sun brings forth a daughter more lovely than herself, before she is swallowed by Fenrer; and when the gods have perished, the daughter rides in her mother's heavenly course.

During the conflagration caused by Surt's fire, a woman by name Lif (life) and a man named Lifthraser lie concealed in Hodmimer's forest. The dew of the dawn serves them for food, and so great a race shall spring from them that their descendants shall soon spread over the whole earth.

Then the vala

* Odin's.

> Sees a hall called Gimle;
> It outshines the sun,
> Of gold its roof;
> It stands in heaven:
> The virtuous there
> Shall always dwell,
> And evermore
> Delights enjoy.

Toward the north on the Nida-mountains stands a large hall of shining gold, which the race of Sindre, that is the dwarfs, occupy. There is also another hall called Brimer, which is also in heaven, in the region Okolner, and there all who delight in quaffing good drink will find plenty in store for them. Good and virtuous beings inhabit all these halls.

But there is also a place of punishment. It is called Naastrand (strand of dead bodies). In Naastrand there is a vast and terrible structure, with doors that face to the north. It is built entirely of the backs of serpents, wattled together like wicker-work. But all the serpents' heads are turned toward the inside of the hall, and continually vomit forth floods of venom, in which wade all those who have committed murder, perjury, or adultery. The vala, in the Elder Edda,

> Saw a hall
> Far from the sun,
> On the strand of dead bodies,
> With doors toward the north.
> Venom drops
> Through the loopholes;
> Formed is that hall
> Of wreathed serpents
>
> There saw she wade
> Through heavy streams,
> Perjurers
> And murderers

And adulterers;
There Nidhug sucked
The bodies of the dead
And the wolf tore them to pieces.
Conceive ye this or not?

Then comes the mighty one*
To the great judgment;
From heaven he comes,
He who guides all things:
Judgments he utters;
Strifes he appeases,
Laws he ordains
To flourish forever.

Or as it is stated in Hyndla's lay, after she has described Heimdal, the sublime protector of the perishable world:

Then comes another
Yet more mighty,
But him dare I not
Venture to name;
Few look further forward
Than to the time
When Odin goes
To meet the wolf.

And when the vala in Völuspá, beginning with the primeval time, has unveiled, in the most profound sentences, the whole history of the universe,—when she has gone through every period of its development down through Ragnarok and the Regeneration, the following is her last vision:

*There* comes the dark
Dragon† flying,
The shining serpent
From the Nida-mountains
In the deep.

* The Supreme God.        † Nidhug.

> Over the plain it flies;
> Dead bodies Nidhug
> Drags in his whizzing plumage,-
> Now must Nidhug sink.

Thus ends the vala's prophecy (*völuspá*.) She has revealed the decrees of the Father of Nature; she has described the conflagration and renovation of the world, and now proclaims the fate of the good and of the evil.

The world and the things in it perish, but not the forces. Some of the gods reappear in the regenerated earth, while some do not. They who reappear are mentioned in pairs, excepting Hœner, who is alone. Balder and Hoder are together; likewise Vidar and Vale, and Mode and Magne. Neither Odin nor Thor nor the vans appear. They perished with the world, for they represented the developing forces of this world; they were divinities representing that which came into being and had existence in it. On the other hand, Balder and Hoder came back from Hel. They represent light and darkness; but they are alike in this respect, that they are nothing substantial, nothing real, they are only the condition for something to be, or we might say they are the space, the firmament, in which something may exist. They are the two brothers whose sons shall inhabit the wide Wind-home. Thus when heaven and earth have passed away there is nothing remaining but the wide expanse of space with light and darkness, who not only rule together in perfect harmony, but also permeate each other and neutralize each other.

Hœner comes back. He was originally one of the trinity with Odin and Loder (Loke); but the gods received Njord as a hostage from the vans, and gave to the vans in return Hœner, as a security of friendship between them. This union between the asas and vans is now dissolved. Hœner has nothing more to do among the vans. Their works all perished with the old earth. He is the developing, creative force that is needed now in the new world as it was in the old.

Vidar is the imperishable force in original nature, that is, in crude nature, but at the same time united with the gods. He is the connecting link between gods and giants. His mother was Grid, a giantess, and his father was Odin. The strong Vale begotten of Odin and Rind (the slumbering earth) is the imperishable force of nature which constantly renews itself in the earth as a habitation of man. Both Vidar and Vale are avenging gods. Vale avenges the death of Balder, and Vidar the death of Odin, and thus we have in Vidar and Vale representatives of the imperishable force of nature in two forms, the one without and the other within the domain of man, both purified and renewed in the regenerated earth.

In the atmosphere and in the dense clouds reigned Thor, with his flashing fire and clattering thunder. Thunder and lightning have passed away, but the forces that produced them, courage and strength, are preserved in Thor's sons, Mode (courage) and Magne (strength). They have their father's hammer, Mjolner, and with it they can strike to the right and to the left, permeating the new heaven and the new earth. What a well of profound thought are the Eddas!

The parents of the new race of men are called Lif and Lifthraser. Life cannot perish. It lies concealed in Hodmimer's forest, which the flame of Surt was not able to destroy. The new race of mankind seem to possess a far nobler nature than the former, for they subsist on the morning dew.

Do Mimer and Surt live? They are the fundamental

28

elements of fire and water. The Eddas are not clear on this point, but an affirmative answer seems to be suggested in the fact that the better part of every being is preserved.

The good among men find their reward in Gimle; for he that made man gave him a soul, which shall live and never perish, though the body shall have mouldered away or have been burnt to ashes; and all that are righteous shall dwell with him in the place called Gimle, says the Younger Edda. The dwarfs have their Sindre, and their golden hall on the Nida-mountains; and the giant has his shining drinking hall, Brimer, but it is situated in Okolner (not cool), where there is no more frost.

The Elder Edda seems to point out two places of punishment for men. Giants and dwarfs are not punished, for they act blindly, they have no free will. But the wicked of mankind go to Naastrand and wade in streams of serpent-venom, and thence they appear to be washed down into Hvergelmer, that horrible old kettle, where their bodies are torn by Nidhug, the dragon of the uttermost darkness.

There is a day of judgment. The good and bad are separated. The god, whom the Edda dare not name, is the judge. The Younger Edda once calls him Allfather, for he is to the new world what Odin was to the old. He was before the beginning of time, and at the end of time he enters upon his eternal reign.

The reward is eternal. Is the punishment also eternal? When light and darkness (Balder and Hoder) can live peaceably together,— when darkness can resolve itself into light,— cannot then the evil be dissolved in the good; cannot the eternal streams of goodness wash away the evil? We think so, and the Edda seems to justify us in this thought; at least the Elder Edda seems to take this view of the subject. Listen again to the last vision of the vala:

> *There* comes the dark
> Dragon flying,
> The shining serpent
> From the Nida-mountains
> In the deep.
> Over the plain it flies;
> Dead bodies Nidhug
> Drags in his whizzing plumage,—.
> *Now must Nidhug sink.**

When there is an intermediate state, a transition, a purification, a purgatory, then this purification must sooner or later be accomplished; and that is the day of the great judgment, *when Nidhug must sink,* and nevermore lift his wings loaded with dead bodies. This idea is beautifully elaborated in *Zendavista.* The Edda has it in a single line, but the majority of its interpreters have not comprehended it. We who are permeated by the true Christian spirit, we know how great joy there is in heaven over a sinner who is converted; we know the God of mercy, who does not desire the ruin of a single sinner, and the God of omnipotence, who with his hand is able to press the tears of repentance from the heart, though it be hard as steel; we comprehend why he lets Nidhug sink down. All darkness shall be cleared up and be gilded by the shining light of heaven.

---

* We present this view of the subject from N. M. Petersen, who suggests that the common reading of this passage *hon* ought to be *hann,*—that is *he,* not *she.* In our translation we have supplied the noun *Nidhug,* while if we had followed the other authorities we would have used the noun *vala.* Petersen remarks that the word sink (*sökkvask*) is a natural expression when applied to the dragon, who sinks into the abyss, but forced and unnatural when applied to the vala. He also quotes another passage (the last line in Brynhild's Helride, where Brynhild says to the hag: Sink thou (*sökkstu!*) of giantkind!) from the Elder Edda which corroborates his view. As the reader will observe, we have adopted Petersen's view entirely.

Such was the origin, the development, the destruction and regeneration of the world. And now, says the Younger Edda, as it closes the deluding of King Gylfe, if you have any further questions to ask, I know not who can answer you; for I never heard tell of anyone who could relate what will happen in the other ages of the world. Make therefore the best use you can of what has been imparted to you.

Upon this Ganglere heard a terrible noise all around him. He looked, but could see neither palace nor city anywhere, nor anything save a vast plain. He therefore set out on his return to his kingdom, where he related all that he had seen and heard; and ever since that time these tidings have been handed down from man to man by oral tradition, and we add, may the stream of story never cease to flow! May the youth, the vigorous man, and the grandfather with his silvery locks, forever continue to refresh their minds by looking into and drinking from the fountain that reflects the ancient history of the great Gothic race!

In closing, we would present this question: Shall we have northern art? We have southern art (Hercules and Hebe), we have oriental art (Adam and Eve), and now will some one complete the trilogy by adding Loke and Sigyn? Ay, let us have another Thorvaldsen, and let him devote himself to *northern art*. Here is a new and untrodden field for the artist. Ye Gothic poets and painters and sculptors! why stand ye here idle?

# VOCABULARY

OF THE

## PRINCIPAL PROPER NAMES

OCCURRING IN THE

# NORSE MYTHOLOGY,

WITH

A BRIEF SYNOPSIS OF THE CHARACTER AND EXPLOITS OF
THE GODS, EXPLANATIONS, ETYMOLOGICAL
DEFINITIONS, ETC.,

GIVING

## THE ORIGINAL ICELANDIC FORM OF THE WORD IN THE VOCABULARY,

AND ADDING, AFTER THE SYNOPSIS,

THE ANGLICIZED FORM USED BY THE AUTHOR
THROUGHOUT THE WORK.

ARRANGED BY THE AUTHOR FROM THE BEST SOURCES.

●

# VOCABULARY.

## A

ÆGIR [Anglo-Sax. *eagor*, the sea]. The god presiding over the stormy sea. He entertains the gods every harvest, and brews ale for them. It still survives in provincial English for the sea-wave on rivers. Have a care, there is the *eager* coming!—(Carlyle's Heroes and Hero-worship.) *Æger.*

AGNAR. A son of King Hraudung and foster-son of Frigg. *Agnar.*

AGNAR. A son of King Geirrod. He gives a drink to Grimner (Odin). *Agnar*

ÁLFR [Anglo-Sax. *ælf, munt-ælfen, sæ-elfen, wudu-elfen*, etc.; Eng. *elf, elves;* Germ. *alb* and *elfen, Erl-* in *Erl*könig (Goethe) is, according to Grimm, a corrupt form from the Danish *Elle*konge like *Elver*konge; in the west of Iceland the word is also pronounced *álbr*]. An elf, fairy; a class of beings like the dwarfs, between gods and men. They were of two kinds: elves of light (*Ljósálfar*) and elves of darkness (*Dökkálfar*). The abode of the elves is *Álfheimr*, fairy-land, and their king is the god Frey *Elf.*

ALFÖÐR or ALFAÐIR [Father of all]. The name of Odin as the supreme god. It also refers to the supreme and unknown god. *Allfather.*

ÁLFHEIMR [*álf*, elf, and *heimr*, home]. Elf-land, fairy-land. Frey's dwelling, given him as a tooth-gift. *Alfheim.*

ALSVIÐR [*sviðr* (*svinnr*), rapid, wise]. All-wise. One of the horses of the sun. *Alsvid.*

ALVÍSS [All-wise]. The dwarf who answers Thor's questions in the lay of Alvis. *Alvis.*

AMSVARTNIR. [The etymology is doubtful; perhaps from *ama*, to vex, annoy, and *svartnir* (*svartr*), black.] The name of the sea, in which the island was situated where the wolf Fenrer was chained. *Amsvartner.*

ÁNNARR or ÓNARR. Husband of night and father of Jord (*jörð* earth). *Annar.*

ANDHRÍMNIR [*önd*, soul, spirit, breath, and *hrímnir*, *hrím.* Anglo-Sax. *hrím ;* Eng. *rime*, hoar-frost ; *hrímnir*, the one producing the hoar-frost]. The cook in Valhal. *Andhrimner.*

ANDVARI. The name of a gurnard-shaped dwarf ; the owner of the fatal ring called *Andvaranautr. Andvare.*

ANDVARAFORS. The force or waterfall in which the dwarf Andvare kept himself in the form of a gurnard (pike). *Andvare-Force.*

ANDVARANAUTR [*önd*, spirit ; *varr*, cautious ; *nautr*, Germ. ge-*nosse* (from Icel. *njota*), a donor]. The fatal ring given by Andvare (the wary spirit). *Andvarenaut.*

ANGANTYR. He has a legal dispute with Ottar Heimske, who is favored by Freyja. *Angantyr.*

ANGEYJA. One of Heimdal's nine mothers. Says the Elder Edda in the Lay of Hyndla : Nine giant maids gave birth to the gracious god, at the world's margin. These are . Gjalp, Greip, Eistla, Angeyja, Ulfrun, Eyrgjafa, Imd, Atla, and Jarnsaxa. *Angeyja.*

ANGRBOÐA [Anguish-boding]. A giantess ; mother of the Fenris-wolf by Loke. *Angerboda.*

ÁRVAKR [Early awake]. The name of one of the horses of the sun. *Aarvak.*

ÁSS or ÁS ; plural ÆSIR. The *asas*, gods. The word appears in such English names as *Os*born, *Os*wald, etc. With an *n* it is found in the Germ. *Ans*gar (Anglo-Sax. *Os*car). It is also found in many Scandinavian proper names, as *As*björn, *As*trid, etc. The term *æsir* is used to distinguish Odin, Thor, etc., from the *vanir* (vans). *Asa.*

ÁSA-LOKI. Loke, so called to distinguish him from Utgard-Loke, who is a giant. *Asa-Loke.*

ÁSA-ÞÓRR. A common name for Thor. *Asa-Thor.*

ÁSGARÐR. The residence of the gods (*asas*). *Asgard.*

ASKR [Anglo-Sax. *äsc*, an ash]. The name of the first man created by Odin, Hœner and Loder. *Ask.*

ÁSYNJA ; plural ÁSYNJUR. A goddess ; feminine of *Áss. Asynje.*

ATLA. One of Heimdal's nine mothers. *Atla.*

AUÐHUMLA ; also written AUÐHUMBLA. [The etymology of this word is uncertain. Finn Magnússon derives it from *auðr*, void, and *hum*, darkness, and expresses the name by *aër nocturnus*.] The cow formed from the frozen vapors resolved into drops. She nourished the giant Ymer. *Audhumbla*.

AURBOÐA [*aurr*, wet clay or loam; *boða*, to announce]. Gymer's wife and Gerd's mother. *Aurboda*.

AURGELMIR [*aurr*, wet clay or loam]. A giant; grandfather of Bergelmer; called also Ymer. *Aurgelmer*.

AUSTRI. A dwarf presiding over the east region. *Austre. East.*

# B

BALDR [Anglo-Sax. *baldor*, princeps, the best, foremost]. The god of the summer-sunlight. He was son of Odin and Frigg; slain by Hoder, who was instigated by Loke. He returns after Ragnarok. His dwelling is Breidablik. *Balder*.

BARREY [Needle-isle]. A cool grove in which Gerd agreed with Skirner to meet Frey. *Barey*.

BAUGI. A brother of Suttung, for whom (Baugi) Odin worked one summer in order to get his help in obtaining Suttung's mead of poetry. *Bauge*.

BELI. A giant, brother of Gerd, slain by Frey. *Bele*.

BERGELMIR [*berg*, rock]. A giant; son of Thrudgelmer and grandson of Aurgelmer. *Bergelmer*.

BESTLA. Wife of Bur and mother of Odin. *Bestla*.

BEYLA. Frey's attendant; wife of Bygver. *Beyla*.

BIFRÖST [*bifast*, to tremble, *röst* (compare Eng. *rest*), a space, a way; the trembling way, *via tremula*]. The rainbow. *Bifrost*.

BILSKIRNIR [*bil*, a moment; *skir*, serene, shining]. The heavenly abode of Thor, from the flashing of light in the lightning. *Bilskirner*.

BÖLÞORN [Evil thorn]. A giant; father of Bestla, Odin's mother. *Bolthorn*.

BÖLVERKR [Working terrible things]. An assumed name of Odin, when he went to get Suttung's mead. *Bolverk*.

BOÐN. [Compare Anglo-Sax. *byden*, dolium.] One of the three vessels in which the poetical mead was kept. Hence poetry is called the wave of the *boðn*. *Bodn*.

BÖRR [*burr*, a son; compare Eng. *born*, Scotch *bairn*, Norse *barn*, a child]. A son of Bure and father of Odin, Vile and Ve. *Bor*.

BRAGI. [Compare Anglo-Sax. *brego*, princeps.] The god of poetry. A son of Odin. He is the best of skalds. *Brage.*

BREIÐABLIK [Literally broad-blink, from *breiðr*, broad, and *blika* (Germ. *blicken;* Eng. to *blink*), to gleam, twinkle]. Balder's dwelling. *Breidablik.*

BRÍSINGAMEN. Freyja's necklace or ornament. *Brisingamen.*

BURI. [This word is generally explained as meaning *the bearing, i. e.* father; but we think that it is the same as the Anglo-Saxon *býre*, son, descendant, offspring. We do not see how it can be conceived as an active participle of the verb *bera*, to bring forth. See p. 195, where we have followed Keyser.] The father of Bor. He was produced by the cow's licking the stones covered with rime. *Bure.*

BYGGVIR. Frey's attendant; Beyla's husband. *Bygver.*

BYLEIPTR [The flame of the dwelling]. The brother of Loke. *Byleipt.*

# D

DAGR [Day]. Son of Delling. *Dag.*

DÁINN. A hart that gnaws the branches of Ygdrasil. *Daain.*

DELLINGR [*deglinger (dagr*, day), dayspring]. The father of Day. *Delling.*

DÍS; plural DÍSIR. Attendant spirit or guardian angel. Any female mythic being may be called Dís. *Dis.*

DRAUPNIR [*drjúpa;* Eng. *drip;* Germ. *traufen;* Dan. *dryppe*]. Odin's ring. It was put on Balder's funeral-pile. Skirner offered it to Gerd. *Draupner.*

DRÓMI. One of the fetters by which the Fenris-wolf was fettered. *Drome.*

DUNEYRR, ⎫ Harts that gnaw the branches of Ygdrasil. *Duneyr; Durathror.*
DURAPRÓR. ⎭

DURINN. The dwarf, second in degree. *Durin.*

DVALINN. A dwarf. *Dvalin.*

DVERGR [Anglo-Sax. *dweorg;* Eng. *dwarf;* Germ. *zwerg;* Swed. *dwerg*]. A dwarf. In modern Icelandic lore dwarfs disappear, but remain in local names, as Dverga-steinn (compare the Dwarfie Stone in Scott's *Pirate*), and in several words and phrases. From the belief that dwarfs lived in rocks an echo is called *dwerg-mál* (dwarf-talk), and *dwerg-móla* means to echo. The dwarfs were skilled in metal-working.

# E

EDDA. The word means a great-grandmother. The name is usually applied to the mythological collection of poems dis- covered by Brynjolf Sveinsson in the year 1643. He, led by a fanciful and erroneous suggestion, gave to the book which he found the name Sæmundar Edda, Edda of Sæmund. This is the so-called *Elder Edda*. Then there is the *Younger Edda*, a name applied to a work written by Snorre Sturle- son, and containing old mythological lore and the old arti- ficial rules for verse-making. The ancients applied the name *Edda* only to this work of Snorre. The *Elder Edda* was never so called. And it is also uncertain whether Snorre himself knew his work by the name of Edda. In the Rigs- mál (Lay of Rig) Edda is the progenitrix of the race of thralls.

EGÐIR. An eagle that appears at Ragnarok. *Egder.*

EGILL. The father of Thjalfe; a giant dwelling near the sea. Thor left his goats with him on his way to the giant Hymer. *Egil.*

EIKÞYRNIR [*eik*, oak, and *þyrnir*, a thorn]. A hart that stands over Odin's hall (Valhal). From his antlers drops into the abyss water from which rivers flow. *Eikthyrner.*

EINHERI; plural EINHERJAR. The only (*ein*) or great champions; the heroes who have fallen in battle and been admitted into Valhal. *Einherje.*

EIR. [The word means *peace, clemency.*] An attendant of Menglod, and the best of all in the healing art. *Eir.*

EISTLA. One of Heimdal's nine mothers. *Eistla.*

ELDHRÍMNIR [*eld*, fire, and *hrímnir*, the one producing rime]. The kettle in which the boar Sæhrimner is cooked in Val- hal. *Eldhrimner.*

ELDIR. The fire-producer; a servant of Æger. *Elder.*

ÉLIVÁGAR. The ice-waves; poisonous cold streams that flow out of Niflheim. *Elivagar.*

EMBLA. The first woman. The gods found two lifeless trees, the *ask* (ash) and the *embla;* of the ash they made *man*, of the embla, *woman.* It is a question what kind of tree the embla was; some suggest a metathesis, viz. *emla*, from *almr* (elm). but the compound *emblu-askr*, in one of Egil's poems, seems

to show that the *embla* was in some way related to the ash.
*Embla.*

EYRGJAFA.  One of Heimdal's nine mothers.  *Eyrgjafa.*

# F

FÁFNIR.  Son of Hreidmar.  He kills his father to get possession of the Andvarenaut.  He afterwards changes himself into a dragon and guards the treasure on Gnita-heath.  He is slain by Sigurd, and his heart is roasted and eaten.  *Fafner.*

FALHÓFNIR [Barrel-hoof, hollow-hoof].  One of the horses of the gods.  *Falhofner.*

FARBAUTI [Ship-beater, ship-destroyer].  The father of Loke. *Farbaute.*

FENRIR or FENRISÚLFR.  The monster-wolf.  He is the son of Loke.  He bites the hand of Tyr.  The gods put him in chains, where he remains until Ragnarok.  In Ragnarok he gets loose, swallows the sun and conquers Odin, but is killed by Vidar.  *Fenrer or Fenris-wolf.*

FENSALIR.  The abode of Frigg.  *Fensal.*

FJALAR.  A misnomer for Skrymer, in whose glove Thor took shelter.  *Fjalar.*

FJALAR.  A dwarf, who slew Kvaser, and composed from his blood the poetic mead.  *Fjalar.*

FJALAR.  A cock that crows at Ragnarok.  *Fjalar.*

FIMAFENGR [*fimr*, quick, nimble].  The nimble servant of Æger. He was slain by the jealous Loke.  *Fimafeng.*

FIMBUL.  [Compare Germ. *fimmel*, an iron wedge; Bohem. *fimol;* Swed. *fimmel-stång*, the handle of a sledge-hammer; in Icel. obsolete, and only used in four or five compounds in old poetry.]  It means *mighty great.*  In the mythology we have:

FIMBULFAMBI.  A mighty fool.  *Fimbulfambe.*

FIMBULTÝR.  The mighty god, great helper (Odin).  *Fimbultyr.*

FIMBULVETR [*vetr*, winter].  The great and awful winter of three years' duration preceding the end of the world.  *Fimbul-winter.*

FIMBULÞUL.  A heavenly river (*þul*, roaring.)  *Fimbulthul.*

FIMBULÞULR.  The great wise man (Odin's High-song, 143).  *Fimbulthuler.*

FJÖLNIR.  A name of Odin.  *Fjolner.*

FJÖRGYN. A personification of the earth; mother of Thor. *Fjorgyn.*

FÓLKVANGR [Anglo-Sax. *folc;* Germ. *volk;* Eng. *folk,* people, and *vangr* (Ulfilas, *waggs*), paradise; Anglo-Sax. *wang;* Dan. *vang,* a field]. The folk-field. Freyja's dwelling. *Folkvang.*

FORNJÓTR. The ancient giant. He was father of Æger or Hler, the god of the ocean; of Loge, flame or fire, and of Kaare, wind. His wife was Ran. These divinities are generally regarded as belonging to an earlier mythology, probably that of the Fins or Celts, and we omitted them in our work. *Fornjot.*

FORSETI [The fore-sitter, president, chairman]. Son of Balder and Nanna. His dwelling is Glitner, and his office is peace-maker. *Forsete.*

FRÁNANGRS-FORS. The force or waterfall into which Loke, in the likeness of a salmon, cast himself, and where the gods caught him and bound him. *Fraananger-Force.*

FREKI. One of Odin's wolves. *Freke.*

FREYJA [Feminine of Freyr]. The daughter of Njord and sister of Frey. She dwells in Folkvang. Half the fallen in battle belong to her. She lends her feather disguise to Loke. She is the goddess of love. Her husband is Oder. Her neck-lace is Brisingamen. She has a boar with golden bristles. *Freyja.*

FREYR [Goth. *frauja;* Gr. κύριος; Anglo-Sax. *freá;* Heliand *fró,* a lord]. He is son of Njord, husband of Skade, slayer of Bele, and falls in conflict with Surt in Ragnarok. Alfheim was given him as a tooth-gift. The ship Skidbladner was built for him. He falls in love with Gerd, Gymer's fair daughter. He gives his trusty sword to Skirner. *Frey.*

FRIGG. [Compare Anglo-Sax. *frigu,* love]. She is the wife of Odin, and mother of Balder and of other gods. She is the queen of the gods. She sits with Odin in Hlidskjalf. She exacts an oath from all things that they shall not harm Balder. She mourns Balder's death. *Frigg.*

FULLA [Fullness]. Frigg's attendant. She takes care of Frigg's toilette, clothes and slippers. Nanna sent her a finger-ring from Helheim. She wears her hair flowing over her shoul-ders. *Fulla.*

# G

GALAR. One of the dwarfs who killed Kvaser. Fjalar was the other. *Galar.*

GAGNRÁÐE. A name assumed by Odin when he went to visit Vafthrudner. *Gagnraad.*

GANGLERI. One of Odin's names in Grimner's Lay. *Ganglere.*

GANGLERI. A name assumed by King Gylfe when he came to Asgard. *Ganglere.*

GARÐROFA [Fence-breaker]. The goddess Gnaa has a horse by name Hofvarpner. The sire of this horse is Hamskerper, and its mother is Garðrofa. *Gardrofa.*

GARMR. A dog that barks at Ragnarok. He is called the largest and best among dogs. *Garm.*

GEFJUN or GEFJON. A goddess. She is a maid, and all those who die maids become her maid-servants. She is present at Æger's feast. Odin says she knows men's destinies as well as he does himself. *Gefjun.*

GEIRRÖÐR. A son of King Hraudung and foster-son of Odin; he becomes king and is visited by Odin, who calls himself Grimner. He is killed by his own sword. There is also a giant by name Geirrod, who was once visited by Thor. *Geirrod.*

GEIRSKÖGUL. A valkyrie. *Geirskogul.*

GEIRVIMUL. A heavenly river. *Geirvimul.*

GERÐR. Daughter of Gymer, a beautiful young giantess; beloved by Frey. *Gerd.*

GERI [*gerr*, greedy]. One of Odin's wolves. *Gere.*

GERSEMI [Anglo-Sax. *gersuma*, a costly thing.] One of Freyja's daughters. *Gerseme.*

GJALLARBRÚ [*gjalla*, to yell, to resound; Anglo-Sax. *giellan*]. The bridge across the river Gjol, near Helheim. The bridge between the land of the living and the dead. *Gjallar-bridge.*

GJALLARHORN. Heimdal's horn, which he will blow at Ragnarok. *Gjallar horn.*

GILLING. Father of Suttung, who possessed the poetic mead. He was slain by Fjalar and Galar. *Gilling.*

GIMLI [*gimill, himill, himin*, heaven]. The abode of the righteous after Ragnarok. *Gimle.*

**GJÁLP.** One of Heimdal's nine mothers. *Gjalp.*

**GINNUNGA-GAP.** [Compare Anglo-Sax. *gin* or *ginn*, vast, wide. (The *unga* may be the adverbial ending added to *ginn*, as in *eall-unga*, adv. from *all*, all.)] The great yawning gap, the premundane abyss, the chaos or formless void, in which dwelt the supreme powers before the creation. In the eleventh century the sea between Greenland and Vinland (America) was called Ginnunga-gap. *Ginungagap.*

**GJÖLL.** The one of the rivers Elivagar that flowed nearest the gate of Hel's abode. *Gjol.*

**GÍSL** [Sunbeam]. One of the horses of the gods. *Gisl.*

**GLAÐR** [Clear, bright]. One of the horses of the gods. *Glad.*

**GLAÐSHEIMR** [Home of brightness or gladness]. Odin's dwelling. *Gladsheim.*

**GLASIR.** A grove in Asgard. *Glaser.*

**GLEIPNIR.** The last fetter with which the wolf Fenrer was bound. *Gleipner.*

**GLER** [The glassy]. One of the horses of the gods. *Gler.*

**GLITNIR** [The glittering]. Forsete's golden hall. *Glitner.*

**GNÁ.** She is the messenger that Frigg sends into the various worlds on her errands. She has a horse called Hofvarpner, that can run through air and water. *Gnaa.*

**GNÍPAHELLIR.** The cave before which the dog Garm barks. *The Gnipa-cave.*

**GNÍTAHEIÐR.** Fafner's abode, where he kept the treasure called Andvarenaut. *Gnita-heath.*

**GÓINN.** A serpent under Ygdrasil. *Goin.*

**GÖLL.** A valkyrie. *Gol.*

**GÖMUL.** A heavenly river. *Gomul.*

**GÖNDUL.** A valkyrie. *Gondul.*

**GÖPUL.** A heavenly river. *Gopul.*

**GRÁBAKR** [Gray-back]. One of the serpents under Ygdrasil. *Graabak.*

**GRÁÐ.** A heavenly river. *Graad.*

**GRAFVITNIR,** } Serpents under Ygdrasil. *Grafvitner; Graf-*
**GRAFVÖLLUÐR.** } *vollud.*

**GREIP** [Anglo-Sax. *gráp;* Eng. *grip*]. One of Heimdal's nine giant mothers. *Greip.*

**GRÍMNIR** [Icel. *grima;* Anglo-Sax. *gríma;* Dan. *grime*, a horse-halter]. A kind of hood or cowl covering the upper part of the face. Grimner is a name of Odin from his traveling in disguise. *Grimner.*

GRÓA [Icel. *gróa;* Anglo Sax. *growan;* Eng. *grow;* Lat. *crescere, crev-*i]. The giantess mother of Orvandel. Thor went to her to have her charm the flint-stone out of his forehead. *Groa.*

GULLFAXI [Gold-mane]. The giant Hrungner's horse. *Goldfax.*

GULLINKAMBI [Gold-comb]. A cock that crows at Ragnarok. *Gullinkambe* or *Goldcomb*

GULLTOPPR [Gold-top]. Heimdal's horse. *Goldtop.*

GULLVEIG [Gold-drink, gold-thirst]. A personification of gold. She is pierced and thrice burnt, and yet lives. *Gulveig.*

GULLINBURSTI [Golden bristles]. The name of Frey's hog. *Gullinburste.*

GUNGNIR [Dan. *gungre,* to tremble violently]. Odin's spear. *Gungner.*

GUNNLÖÐ; genitive GUNNLAÐAR [Icel. *gunnr,* war, battle; Anglo-Sax. *gûð;* Old High Germ. *gundia;* and Icel. *löð* (*laða,* to invite), invitation; Anglo-Sax. *gelaðian,* to invite]. One who invites war. She was daughter of the giant Suttung, and had charge of the poetic mead. Odin got it from her. *Gunlad.*

GYLFI. A king of Svithod, who visited Asgard under the name of Ganglere. The first part of the Younger Edda is called Gylfaginning, which means the Delusion of Gylfe. *Gylfe.*

GYLLIR [Golden]. One of the horses of the gods. *Gyller.*

GÝMIR. A giant; the father of Gerd, the beloved of Frey. *Gymer.*

GÝMIR. Another name of the ocean divinity Æger. *Gymer.*

# H

HALLINSKÍÐI. Another name of the god Heimdal. The possessor of the leaning (*halla*) way (*skeið*). *Hallinskid.*

HAMSKERPIR [Hide-hardener]. A horse: the sire of Hofvarpner, which was Gnaa's horse. *Hamskerper.*

HÁR [Anglo-Sax. *heáh;* Eng. *high;* Ulfilas *hauhs*]. The High One, applied to Odin. *Haar.*

HÁRBARÐR. The name assumed by Odin in the Lay of Harbard. *Harbard.*

HEIÐRUNR [Bright-running]. A goat that stands over Valhal. *Heidrun.*

HEIMDALR. The etymology has not been made out. He was the heavenly watchman in the old mythology, answering to St. Peter in the medieval. According to the Lay of Rig (Heimdal), he was the father and founder of the different classes of men, nobles, churls and thralls. He has a horn called Gjallar-horn, which he blows at Ragnarok. His dwelling is Himinbjorg. He is the keeper of Bifrost (the rainbow). Nine giantesses are his mothers. *Heimdal.*

HEL [Ulfilas *halja*, ᾅδης; Anglo-Sax. and Eng. *hell;* Heliand and Old High Germ. *hellia;* Germ. *Hölle;* Dan. at slaa, i-*hjel*, to kill]. The goddess of death, born of Loke and Angerboda. She corresponds to Proserpina. Her habitation is Helheim, under one of the roots of Ygdrasil. *Hel.*

HELBLINDI. A name of Odin. *Helblinde.*

HELGRINDR. The gates of Hel. *Helgrind* or *Helgate.*

HELHEIM. The abode of Hel. *Helheim.*

HERFÖÐR, } [The father of hosts]. A name of Odin. *Her*
HERJAFÖÐR } *father.*

HERMOÐR [Courage of hosts]. Son of Odin, who gives him helmet and corselet. He went on Sleipner to Hel to bring Balder back. *Hermod.*

HILDISVINI [*hildr* (Anglo-Sax. *hild*) means war]. Freyja's hog. *Hilde-svine.*

HIMINBJÖRG [*himinn*, heaven, and *björg*, help, defense; hence heaven defender]. Heimdal's dwelling. *Himinbjorg.*

HIMINBRJÓTR [Heaven-breaker]. One of the giant Hymer's oxen. *Himinbrjoter.*

HLÉSEY. The abode of Æger. *Hlesey.*

HLIÐSKJÁLF [from *hliÐ*, gate, and *skjálf*, shelf, bench]. The seat of Odin, whence he looked out over all the worlds. *Hlidskjalf.*

HLÍN. One of the attendants of Frigg; but Frigg herself is sometimes called by this name. *Hlin.*

HLÓÐYN. A goddess; a name of the earth; Thor's mother. *Hlodyn.*

HLÓRIDI [from *hlóa;* Anglo-Sax. *hlowan;* Eng. *low*, to bellow, roar, and *reiÐ*, thunder]. One of the names of Thor; the bellowing thunderer. *Hloride.*

HNIKARR, } Names of Odin, Hnikar and Hnikuder.
HNIKUÐR. }

29

Hnoss [Anglo-Sax. *hnossian*, to hammer]. A costly thing; the name of one of Freyja's daughters. *Hnos.*

Hoddmímisholt. Hodmimer's holt or grove, where the two human beings Lif and Lifthraser were preserved during Ragnarok. *Hodmimer's forest.*

Höðr. The slayer of Balder. He is blind, returns to life in the regenerated world. The Cain of the Norse mythology. *Hoder.*

Hœnir. One of the three creating gods. With Odin and Loder Hœner creates Ask and Embla, the first human pair. *Hœner.*

Hófvarpnir [Hoof-thrower]. Gnaa's horse. His father is Hamskerper and mother Gardrofa. *Hofvarpner.*

Hræsvelgr [Corpse-swallower]. A giant in an eagle's plumage, who produces the wind. *Hræsvelger.*

Hrauðungr. Geirrod's father. *Hraudung.*

Hreiðmarr. Father of Regin and Fafner. He exacts the bloodfine from the gods for slaying Otter. He is slain by Fafner. *Hreidmar.*

Hrímfaxi [Rime-mane]. The horse of Night. *Rimefax.*

Hrímþursar [Anglo-Sax. *hrím;* Eng. *rime*, hoar-frost]. Rimegiants or frost-giants, who dwell under one of Ygdrasil's roots. *Giants.*

Hroðvitnir. A wolf; father of the wolf Hate. *Hrodvitner.*

Hroptr. One of Odin's names. *Hropt.*

Hrungnir. A giant; friend of Hymer. Thor fought with him and slew him. *Hrungner.*

Hringhorni. The ship upon which Balder's body was burned. *Hringhorn.*

Hrossþjófr [Horse-thief]. A giant. *Hrosthjof.*

Huginn [Mind]. One of Odin's ravens. *Hugin.*

Hvergelmir [The old kettle]. The spring in the middle of Niflheim, whence flowed the rivers Elivagar. The Northern Tartaros. *Hvergelmer.*

Hýmir. A giant with whom Thor went fishing when he caught the Midgard-serpent. His wife was the mother of Tyr. Tyr and Thor went to him to procure a kettle for Æger. *Hymer.*

Hyndla. A vala visited by Freyja, who comes to her to learn the genealogy of her favorite Ottar. *Hyndla.*

# I

**IÐAVÖLLR.** A plain where the gods first assemble, where they establish their heavenly abodes, and where they assemble again after Ragnarok. The plains of Ida. *Idavold.*

**IÐUNN.** Daughter of the dwarf Ivald; she was wife of Brage, and the goddess of early spring. She possesses rejuvenating apples of which the gods partake. *Idun.*

**IFING.** A river which divides the giants from the gods. *Ifing.*

**IMÐ.** One of Heimdal's nine giant mothers. *Imd.*

**ÍMR.** A son of the giant Vafthrudner. *Im.*

**INGUNAR-FREYR.** One of the names of Frey. *Ingun's Frey.*

**INNSTEINN.** The father of Ottar Heimske; the favorite of Freyja. *Instein.*

**ÍVALDI.** A dwarf. His sons construct the ship Skidbladner. *Ivald.*

# J

**JAFNHÁR** [Equally high]. A name of Odin. *Evenhigh. Jafnhaar.*

**JÁLKR.** A name of Odin (Jack the Giant-killer?). *Jalk.*

**JÁRNSAXA** [Iron-chopper]. One of Heimdal's nine giant mothers. *Jarnsaxa.*

**JÁRNVIÐR** [Iron-wood]. A wood east of Midgard, peopled by giantesses called Jarnvids. This wood had iron leaves. *Jarnvid.*

**JÁRNVIÐIUR.** The giantesses in the Iron-wood. *Jarnvids.*

**JÖRD.** Wife of Odin and mother of Thor. Earth. *Jord.*

**JÖTUNN** [Anglo-Sax. *eoten*]. A giant. The giants were the earliest created beings. The gods question them in regard to Balder. Thor frequently contends with them. Famous giants are: Ymer, Hymer, Hrungner, Orvandel, Gymer, Skrymer, Vafthrudner and Thjasse. *Giant.*

**JÖTUNHEIMAR** (plural). The Utgaard; the home of the giants in the outermost parts of the earth. *Jotunheim.*

# K

**KERLAUGAR** (plural). Two rivers which Thor every day must cross. *Kerlaug.*

**KÖRMT.** Another river which Thor every day must pass. *Kormt.*

**KVÁSIR.** The hostage given by the vans to the asas. His blood, when slain, was the poetical mead kept by Suttung. *Kvaser.*

# L

LÆÐINGR. One of the fetters with which the Fenris-wolf was bound. *Læding.*

LÆRAÐR [Furnishing protection]. A tree near Valhal. *Lærad.*

LANDVÍÐI. [A mountain range overgrown with trees is *viði.*] Vidar's abode. The primeval forests. *Landvide.*

LAUFEY [Leafy island]. Loke's mother. *Laufey.*

LEIFÞRASIR, } The two persons preserved in Hodmimer's grove
LÍF.         }   during Surt's conflagration in Ragnarok; the last beings in the old and the first in the new world. *Lif* and *Lifthraser.*

LÉTTFETI [Light-foot]. One of the horses of the gods. *Lightfoot.*

LITR. A dwarf that Thor kicked into Balder's funeral pile. *Liter.*

LODDFÁFNIR. A protégé of Odin. *Lodfafner.*

LOÐURR [Compare Germ. *lodern,* to flame]. One of the three gods (Odin, Hæner and Loder) who create Ask and Embla, the first man and woman. He is identical with Loke. *Loder.*

LOKI [Icel. *lúka,* to end, finish; Loke is the end and consummation of divinity]. The evil giant-god of the Norse mythology. He steers the ship Naglfar in Ragnarok. He borrows Freyja's feather-garb and accompanies Thor to the giant Thrym, who has stolen Thor's hammer. He is the father of Sleipner; but also of the Midgaard serpent, of the Fenris-wolf and of Hel. He causes Balder's death, abuses the gods in Æger's feast, but is captured in Fraanangerforce and is bound by the gods. *Loke.*

LOPTR [The aërial]. Another name of Loke. *Lopter.*

# M

MAGNI [*megin,* might, strength]. A son of Thor. *Magne.*

MÁNI [Ulfilas *mêna ;* Anglo-Sax. *môna ;* Eng. *moon*]. Brother of Sol (the sun, feminine), and both were children of the giant Mundilfare. *Moon* or *Maane.*

MARDÖLL or MARÞOLL. One of the names of Freyja. *Mardallar grátr* (the tears of Mardal), gold. *Mardal.*

MÁNAGARMR [Moon-swallower]. A wolf of Loke's offspring. He devours the moon. *Maanegarm* or *Moongarm.*

MANNHEIMAR (plural) [Homes of man]. Our earth. *Manheim.*

MEILI. A son of Odin. *Meile.*

**MIÐGARÐR.** [In Cumberland, England, are three farms: *High-garth, Middle-garth, Low-garth*.] The mid-yard, middle-town, that is, the earth, is a mythological word common to all the ancient Teutonic languages. Ulfilas renders the Gr. οἰχουμένη by *midjungards;* Heliand calls the earth *middil-gard;* the Anglo-Saxon homilies, instead of earth, say *middan-geard* (*meddlert*, Jamieson), and use the word as an appellative; but the Icelandic Edda alone has preserved the true mythical bearing of this old Teutonic word. The earth (Midgard), the abode of men, is seated in the middle of the universe, bordered by mountains and surrounded by the great sea (*úthaf*); on the other side of this sea is the Utgard (out-yard), the abode of the giants; the Midgard is defended by the yard or burgh Asgard (the burgh of the gods) lying in the middle (the heaven being conceived as rising above the earth). Thus the earth and mankind are represented as a stronghold besieged by the powers of evil from without, defended by the gods from above and from within. *Midgard.*

**MIÐGARÐSORMR** [The serpent of Midgaard]. The world-serpent hidden in the ocean, whose coils gird around the whole Midgard. Thor once fishes for him, and gets him on his hook. In Ragnarok Thor slays him, but falls himself poisoned by his breath. *Midgard-serpent.*

**MÍMAMEIÐR.** A mythic tree; no doubt the same as Ygdrasil. It derives its name from Mimer, and means Mimer's tree. *Mimameider.*

**MÍMIR.** The name of the wise giant keeper of the holy well Mímis-brunnr, the burn (bourn, brun) of Mimer, the well of wisdom, in which Odin pawned his eye for wisdom; a myth which is explained as symbolical of the heavenly vault with its single eye, the sun, setting in the sea. Is the likeness of the word to the Latin *memor* only accidental? The true etymology of Mímir is not known. *Mimer.*

**MJÖLNIR.** [The derivation from *mala* or *mola* (to crush) is, though probable, not certain. The word may be akin to Goth. *milhma*, cloud; Swed. *moln;* Dan. *mulm;* Norse *molnas* (Ivar Aasen), to grow dark from bands of clouds arising.] Thor's formidable hammer. After Ragnarok, it is possessed by his sons Mode and Magne. *Mjolner.*

MISTILTEINN [Old High Germ. *mistil;* Germ. *mistel;* Anglo-Sax. *mistel* or *mistel-tâ;* Eng. *mistletoe*]. The mistletoe or mistle-twig, the fatal twig by which Balder, the white sun-god, was slain. After the death of Balder, Ragnarok set in. Balder's death was also symbolical of the victory of darkness over light, which comes every year at midwinter. The mistletoe in English households at Christmas time is no doubt a relic of a rite lost in the remotest heathendom, for the fight of light and darkness at midwinter was a foreshadowing of the final overthrow in Ragnarok. The legend and the word are common to all Teutonic peoples of all ages. *Mistletoe.*

MÓÐI [Courage]. A son of Thor. *Mode.*

MÓÐSOGNIR. The dwarf highest in degree or rank. *Modsogner.*

MÓINN. A serpent under Ygdrasil. *Moin.*

MUNDILFARI. Father of the sun and moon. *Mundilfare.*

MUNINN [Memory]. One of Odin's ravens. *Munin.*

MÚSPELL. The name of an abode of fire. It is peopled by *Múspells lýðir* (the men of Muspel), a host of fiends, who are to appear at Ragnarok and destroy the world by fire. *Muspel.* (See next word.)

MÚSPELLSHEIMR. The abode of Muspel. This interesting word (*Múspell*) was not confined to the Norse mythology, but appears twice in the old Saxon poem Heliand, thus: (1) *mutspelli cumit on thiustra naht, also thiof ferit* (*mutspelli* comes in dusky night, as a thief fares,—that is, But the day of the Lord will come as a thief in the night), and (2) *mutspellis megin obar man ferit* (the main of *mutspelli* fares over men). A third instance is an Old High German poem on the Last Day, thus: *dâr ni mac denne mac andremo helfan vora demo muspille* (there no man can help another against the *muspel-doom*). In these instances *muspel* stands for the *day of judgment, the last day,* and answers to Ragnarok of the Norse mythology. The etymology is doubtful, for *spell* may be the *weird, doom,* Lat. *fatum;* or it may be *spoil, destruction.* The former part, *mús* or *muod,* is more difficult to explain. The Icelandic *mús* is an assimilated form. *Muspelheim.*

MÖKKURKÁLFI [*mökkr* means a dense cloud]. A clay giant in the myth of Thor and Hrungner. *Mokkerkalfe.*

# N

NAGLFAR [Nail-ship]. A mythical ship made of nail-parings. It appears in Ragnarok. *Naglfar. Nailship.*

NÁL [Needle]. Mother of Loke. *Naal.*

NANNA. Daughter of Nep (bud); mother of Forsete and wife of Balder. She dies of grief at the death of Balder. *Nanna.*

NARI or NARFI. Son of Loke. Loke was bound by the intestines of Nare. *Nare* or *Narfe.*

NÁSTRÖND [The shore of corpses]. A place of punishment for the wicked after Ragnarok. *Naastrand.*

NIÐAFJÖLL. The Nida-mountains toward the north, where there is after Ragnarok a golden hall for the race of Sindre (the dwarfs). *Nidafell.*

NIÐHÖGGR. A serpent of the nether world, that tears the carcases of the dead. He also lacerates Ygdrasil. *Nidhug.*

NIFLHEIMR [*nifl;* Old High Germ. *nibul;* Germ. *nebel;* Lat. *nebula;* Gr. νεφέλη, mist, fog.] The world of fog or mist; the nethermost of the rime worlds. The place of punishment (Hades). It was visited by Odin when he went to inquire after the fate of Balder. *Niflheim.*

NJÖRÐR. A van, vanagod. He was husband of Skade, and father of Frey and Freyja. He dwells in Noatun. *Njord.*

NÓATÚN [Place of ships]. Njord's dwelling; Njord being a divinity of the water or sea. *Noatun.*

NORÐRI [North]. A dwarf presiding over the northern regions. *Nordre* or *North.*

NÓTT. Night; daughter of Norve. *Night.*

NORN; plural NORNIR. The weird sisters; the three heavenly norns (*parcæ*, fates) Urd, Verdande, and Skuld (Past, Present, and Future); they dwelt at the fountain of Urd, and ruled the fate of the world. Three norns were also present at the birth of every man and cast the weird of his life. *Norn.*

# O

ÓÐINN [Anglo-Sax. *Wodan;* Old High Germ. *Wodan*]. Son of Bor and Bestla. He is the chief of the gods. With Vile and Ve he parcels out Ymer. With Hœner and Loder he creates Ask and Embla. He is the fountain-head of wisdom, the founder of culture, writing and poetry, the progenitor of kings, the lord of battle and victory. He quaffs with Saga in Sokvabek. He has two ravens, two wolves and a spear. His throne is Hlidskjalf, from where he looks out over all the worlds. In Ragnarok he is devoured by the Fenris-wolf. *Odin.*

Óðr. Freyja's husband. *Oder.*

Óðrœrir [The spirit-mover]. One of the vessels in which the blood of Kvaser, that is, the poetic mead, was kept. The inspiring nectar. *Odrœrer.*

Ofnir. A serpent under Ygdrasil. *Ofner.*

Ókólnir [Not cool]. After Ragnarok the giants have a hall (ale-*hall*) called Brimer, at Okolner.

Öku-þórr. So called from the Finnish thunder-god Ukko. Incorrectly confounded with *aka*, to ride. See p. 298. *Akethor.*

Óski [Wish]. A name of Odin. *Oske. Wish.*

Otr [Otter]. A son of Hreidmar ; in the form of an otter killed by Loke. *Oter.*

Óttarr or Óttarr Heimski [Stupid]. A son of Instein, a protégé of Freyja. He has a contest with Angantyr. Hyndla gives him a cup of remembrance. *Ottar.*

# R

Ragnarök [*ragna*, from *regin*, god ; *rök* may be Old High Germ. *rahha*, sentence, judgment, akin to *rekja; rök*, from *rekja*, is the whole development from creation to dissolution, and would, in this word, denote the dissolution, doomsday, of the gods; or it may be from *rökr* (*reykkr*, smoke), twilight, and then the word means the twilight of the gods.] The last day ; the dissolution of the gods and the world. *Ragnarok.*

Rán [Rob]. The goddess of the sea; wife of Æger. *Ran.*

Ratatoskr. A squirrel that runs up and down the branches of Ygdrasil. *Ratatosk.*

Rati. An auger used by Odin in obtaining the poetic mead. *Rate.*

Reginn. Son of Hreidmar ; brother of Fafner and Otter. *Regin.*

Rindr [Eng. *rind*, crust]. A personification of the hard frozen earth. Mother of Vale. The loves of Odin and Rind resemble those of Zeus and Europa in Greek legends. *Rind.*

Röskva. The name of the maiden follower of Thor. She symbolizes the ripe fields of harvest. *Roskva.*

# S

SÆHRÍMNIR [*sær*, sea; *hrímnir*, rime-producer]. The name of the boar on which the gods and heroes in Valhal constantly feed. *Sæhrimner.*

SAGA [History]. The goddess of history. She dwells in Sokvabek. *Saga.*

SESSRÚMNIR [Seat-roomy]. Freyja's large-seated palace. *Sesrumner.*

SÍÐHÖTTR [Long-hood]. One of Odin's names, from his traveling in disguise with a large hat on his head hanging down over his face. *Sidhat.*

SÍÐSKEGGR [Long-beard]. One of Brage's names. It is also a name of Odin in the lay of Grimner. *Sidskeg.*

SIF. The wife of Thor and mother of Uller. [Ulfilas *sibja*; Anglo-Sax. *sib*; Eng. gos-*sip*, god-*sib*; Heliand *sibbia*; Old High Germ. *sibba*; Germ. *sippe*. The word denotes affinity.] Sif, the golden-haired goddess, wife of Thor, betokens mother earth with her bright green grass. She was the goddess of the sanctity of the family and wedlock, and hence her name. *Sif.*

SIGFAÐIR [Father of victory]. A name of Odin. *Sigfather.*

SIGYN. Loke's wife. She holds a basin to prevent the venom from dropping into Loke's face. *Sigyn.*

SILFRINTOPPR [Silver-tuft]. One of the horses of the gods. *Silvertop.*

SINDRI. One of the most famous dwarfs. *Sindre.*

SINIR [Sinew]. One of the horses of the gods. *Siner.*

SJÖFN. One of the goddesses. She delights in turning men's hearts to love. *Sjofn.*

SKAÐI [*scathe*, harm, damage]. A giantess; daughter of Thjasse and the wife of Njord. She dwells in Thrymheim. Hangs a venom serpent over Loke's face. *Skade.*

SKEIÐBRÍMIR [Race-runner]. One of the horses of the gods. *Skeidbrimer.*

SKÍÐBLAÐNIR. The name of the famous ship of the god Frey. *Skidbladner.*

SKINFAXI [Shining-mane]. The horse of Day. *Skinfax.*

SKÍRNIR [The bright one]. Frey's messenger. *Skirner.*

SKRÝMIR. The name of a giant; the name assumed by Utgard-Loke. *Skrymer.*

SKULD [Shall]. The norn of the future. *Skuld.*

SKÖGUL. A valkyrie. *Skogul.*

SLEIPNIR [The slipper]. The name of Odin's eight-footed steed. He is begotten by Loke with Svadilfare. *Sleipner.*

SNOTRA [Neat]. The name of one of the goddesses. *Snotra.*

SÖKKMÍMIR [Mimer of the deep]. A giant slain by Odin. *Sokmimer.*

SÖKKVABEKKR. A mansion where Odin and Saga quaff from golden beakers. *Sokvabek.*

SÓL [Sun]. Daughter of Mundilfare. She drives the horses that draw the car of the sun. *Sol.*

SONR. One of the vessels containing the poetic mead. *Son.*

SUDRI [South]. A dwarf presiding over the south region. *Sudre. South.*

SURTR. A fire-giant in Ragnarok; contends with the gods on the plain of Vigrid; guards Muspelheim. *Surt.*

SUTTUNGR. The giant possessor of the poetic mead. *Suttung.*

SVAÐILFARI. A horse; the sire of Sleipner. *Svadilfare.*

SVAFNIR. A serpent under Ygdrasil. *Svafner.*

SVALINN [Cooler]. The shield placed before the sun. *Svalin.*

SVÁSUÐR [Delightful]. The name of a giant; the father of the sun. *Svasud.*

SÝN. A minor goddess. *Syn.*

## T

TÝR; genitive TÝS, dative and accusative TÝ. [Compare Icel. *tivi*, god; *Twisco* (*Tivisco*) in Tacitus' *Germania*. For the identity of this word with Sanscrit *dyaus, dívas*, heaven; Gr. $Z\varepsilon\acute{\upsilon}\varsigma$ ($\Delta\iota\acute{\upsilon}\varsigma$); Lat. *divus*, see Max Müller's *Lectures on the Science of Language*, 2d series, p. 425.] Properly the generic name of the highest divinity, and remains in many compounds. In the mythology he is the one-armed god of war. The Fenris-wolf bit one hand off him. He goes with Thor to Hymer to borrow a kettle for Æger. He is son of Odin by a giantess. *Tyr.*

## Þ (TH).

ÞJÁLFI. The name of the servant and follower of Thor. The word properly means a delver, digger (Germ. *delber, delben*, to dig). The names Thjalfe and Roskva indicate that Thor was the friend of the farmers and the god of agriculture. *Thjalfe.*

ÞJAZI [ÞJASSI]. A giant; the father of Njord's wife, Skade. His dwelling was Thrymheim; he was slain by Thor. *Thjasse.*

ÞÓRR. [Anglo-Sax. *þunor;* Eng. *thunder;* North Eng. *thunner;* Dutch *donder;* Old High Germ. *donar;* Germ. *donner;* Heliand *thunar;* Danish *tor,* in *tor-*den (compare Lat. *tonu* and *tonitrus.*) The word *þórr* is therefore formed by absorption of the middle *n,* and contraction of an old dissyllabic *þonor* into one syllable, and is a purely Scandinavian form; hence in Anglo-Saxon charters or diplomas it is a sure sign of forgery when names compounded with *þur-* appear in deeds pretending to be of a time earlier than the Danish invasion in the ninth century; although in later times they abound. The English *Thursday* is a later form, in which the phonetic rule of the Scandinavian tongue has been followed; but perhaps it is a North English form]. The god of thunder, keeper of the hammer, the ever-fighting slayer of trolls and destroyer of evil spirits, the friend of mankind, the defender of the earth, the heavens and the gods; for without Thor and his hammer the earth would become the helpless prey of the giants. He was the consecrator, the hammer being the cross or holy sign of the ancient heathen, hence the expressive phrase on a heathen Danish runic stone: *þurr vigi þassi runar* (Thor consecrate these runes!) Thor was the son of Odin and Fjorgyn (mother earth); he was blunt, hot-tempered, without fraud or guile, of few words and ready stroke — such was Thor, the favorite deity of our forefathers. The finest legends of the Younger Edda and the best lays of the Elder Edda refer to Thor. His hall is Bilskirner. He slays Thjasse, Thrym, Hrungner, and other giants. In Ragnarok he slays the Midgard-serpent, but falls after retreating nine paces, poisoned by the serpent's breath. *Thor.*

ÞRIÐI [Third]. A name of Odin in Gylfaginning. *Thride.*

ÞRÚÐGELMIR. The giant father of Bergelmer. *Thrudgelmer.*

ÞRÚÐHEIMR or } Thor's abode. *Thrudheim; Thrudvang.*
ÞRÚÐVANGR. }

ÞRÚÐR. The name of a goddess; the daughter of Thor and Sif. *Thrud.*

ÞRYMHEIMR. Thjasse's and Skade's dwelling. *Thrymheim.*

ÞRYMR. The giant who stole Thor's hammer and demanded Freyja for it. *Thrym*.

ÞÖKK. The name of a giantess (supposed to have been Loke in disguise) in the myth of Balder. She would not weep for his death. *Thok*.

# U

ÚLFRÚN. One of Heimdal's nine giant mothers. *Ulfrun*.

ULLR. The son of Sif and stepson of Thor. His father is not named. He dwells in Ydaler. *Uller*.

URÐARBRUNNR. The fountain of the norn Urd. The Urdar-fountain. The weird spring.

URÐR [Anglo-Sax. *wyrd;* Eng. *weird;* Heliand *wurth*]. One of the three norns. The norn of the past, that which has been. *Urd*.

ÚTGARÐAR [The out-yard]. The abode of the giant Utgard-Loke. *Utgard*.

ÚTGARÐA-LOKI. The giant of Utgard visited by Thor. He calls himself Skrymer. *Utgard-Loke*.

# V

VAFÞRÚÐNIR. A giant visited by Odin. They try each other in questions and answers. The giant is defeated and forfeits his life. *Vafthrudner*.

VALASKJÁLF. One of Odin's dwellings. *Valaskjalf*.

VALFÖÐR [Father of the slain]. A name of Odin. *Valfather.*

VALGRIND. A gate of Valhal. *Valgrind*.

VALHÖLL [The hall of the slain. Icel. *valr;* Anglo-Sax. *wœl*, the slain]. The hall to which Odin invited those slain in battle. *Valhal*.

VALKYRJA [The chooser of the slain]. A troop of goddesses, handmaidens of Odin. They serve in Valhal, and are sent on Odin's errands. *Valkyrie*.

VALI. Brother of Balder. Slays Hoder when only one night old. Rules with Vidar after Ragnarok. *Vale*.

VALI. A son of Loke. *Vale*.

VALTAMR. A fictitious name of Odin's father. *Valtam*.

VÉ. A brother of Odin (Odin, Vile and Ve). *Ve.*

VEGTAMR. A name assumed by Odin. *Vegtam*.

VANAHEIMAR. The abode of the vans. *Vanaheim*.

VANR; plural VANIR. Those deities whose abode was in Vana-heim, in contradistinction to the asas, who dwell in Asgard: Njord, Frey and Freyja. The vans waged war with the asas, but were afterwards, by virtue of a treaty, combined and made one with them. The vans were deities of the sea. *Van.*

VÉORR [Defender]. A name of Thor. *Veor.*

VERÐANDI [from *verða*, to become; Germ. *werden*]. The norn of the present, of that which is.

VESTRI. The dwarf presiding over the west region. *Vestre. West.*

VIÐARR. Son of Odin and the giantess Grid. He dwells in Landvide. He slays the Fenris-wolf in Ragnarok. Rules with Vale after Ragnarok. *Vidar.*

VÍGRIÐR [Icel. *víg;* Ulfilas *wiahjo,* μάχη, a fight, a battle]. The field of battle where the gods and the sons of Surt meet in Ragnarok. *Vigrid.*

VÍLI. Brother of Odin and Ve. These three sons of Bor and Bestla construct the world out of Ymer's body. *Vile.*

VIMUR. A river that Thor crosses. *Vimer.*

VINDSVALR [Wind-cool]. The father of winter. *Vindsval.*

VINDHEIMR [Wind-home]. The place that the sons of Balder and Hoder are to inhabit after Ragnarok. *Vindheim. Wind-home.*

VIN GÓLF [The mansion of bliss]. The palace of the asynjes. *Vingolf.*

VINGÞÓRR. A name of Thor. *Vingthor.*

VÓR. The goddess of betrothals and marriages. *Vor.*

# Y

ÝDALIR. Uller's dwelling. *Ydaler.*

YGGR. A name of Odin. *Ygg.*

YGGDRASILL [The bearer of Ygg (Odin)]. The world-embracing ash tree. The whole world is symbolized by this tree. *Yg-drasil.*

ÝMIR. The huge giant in the cosmogony, out of whose body Odin, Vile and Ve created the world. The progenitor of the giants. He was formed out of frost and fire in Ginungagap. *Ymer.*

# INDEX.